healthy
cooking

a commonsense guide

healthy
cooking

a commonsense guide

MURDOCH
B O O K S

CONTENTS

Sweet potato strudel, page 265

Thai beef salad, page 154

Stuffed squid, page 274

Chocolate ice cream sandwich, page 295

THE BENEFITS OF HEALTHY EATING

The food we eat does more than simply fill an empty stomach. Our physical and mental health is directly affected by each and every morsel that passes our lips.

If you want to improve your health, both now and in the future, and the way you look and feel, a healthy lifestyle that includes regular exercise and a balanced diet is the key to achieving this goal. Your dietary habits have a direct affect on your physical and mental health. This isn't surprising when you consider that the foods and drinks you consume actually become part of your body—they are broken down by your digestive system and

then absorbed into your cells to provide you with energy or materials for growth, repair and vital bodily processes. So it's true—you are what you eat. And if you don't feed your body all the elements it needs, you won't feel or perform as well as you could.

It's estimated that more than 50 per cent of people in industrialised countries die from nutrition-related diseases (heart disease, stroke, some cancers, diabetes) and many people are also overweight, which can further increase the risk of developing some diseases. This is a sad state of affairs when many of these early deaths could have been prevented by a healthy lifestyle.

Disease isn't only due to bad luck or genetics, it also depends on how well you treat your body. Lifestyle factors play an important role in determining your state of health, which means you can actually play an active role in protecting yourself.

Many people complain of a lack of energy and vitality, and often feel tired and run-down. This is often due to poor dietary habits, which make it more difficult to cope with life's demands, and a stressful environment. By choosing the best foods for your body and by keeping active, you will feel more energetic and protect yourself against disease at the same time.

Some benefits of a healthy lifestyle
- Better mental and physical performance
- A better-looking body
- A better self-image
- Higher energy levels
- A well-functioning immune system
- Lower blood cholesterol levels
- A reduced risk of many diseases
- Attaining a healthy weight without strict dieting

Another good reason to look after your health as you grow older is that people in western societies have never had such a long life-expectancy and good quality of life to look forward to after they retire. Since the start of the 1900s, the average life-expectancy for men and women has increased by more than 20 years. From a relatively young age, we're encouraged to start saving for our retirement, but you should also be investing in your health. Like your income, your health also needs protection as you age, so that when you retire you'll be able to enjoy all the things you missed during full-time employment or parenthood. If you don't have a healthy lifestyle when you're young, you may have to spend more of your hard-earned retirement money on medication, doctors' fees and higher insurance premiums. Unlike investing in the stock market, there's no risk involved in looking after your health.

Although many people regularly take vitamin and mineral supplements, there's little evidence that they give you the same or as many health benefits as a balanced diet. Spend your money on a wide variety of good-quality fresh foods so that you don't need to take supplements, and make time to prepare some of the great-tasting recipes in this book. You'll soon see how easy  it is to prepare healthy meals, and you'll wonder why anyone thinks healthy eating isn't enjoyable.

Often healthy, low-fat dishes use more flavoursome ingredients than their high-fat counterparts. Far from being boring or bland, healthy food really does taste great

WHY ALL THE CONFUSION ABOUT HEALTHY EATING?

Many people are confused about healthy eating because there is so much contradictory information published in newspapers, magazines, books and on the Internet. This information can be written by qualified health professionals and nutrition scientists, or by journalists and business people—who may not have the relevant qualifications.

Although food manufacturers are subject to strict laws preventing them from printing any misleading health claims on their products, other sources of nutrition information are not subject to the same laws, which is a constant source of

frustration for health professionals. It is difficult for officials to regulate all the information that is published because there's simply too much information and advertising from so many different sources.

Some people also have a vested interest in telling you that particular diets or supplements produce certain effects because they are trying to sell you these products. Others simply don't know that they haven't researched their information thoroughly enough to be able to give you the whole story.

You need considerable training and background knowledge to be able to interpret the results from scientific studies, and also to decide whether or not the studies have used appropriate methods. Nutrition science is a young and dynamic science. As more research tools are being developed, we are learning more about the active chemicals in foods and how they affect our health. There are still many exciting new discoveries to be made.

But here's the good news—official science-based recommendations for healthy eating have changed very little over the last 20 years, despite all of the new research findings. For decades the recipe for health has been a diet based on low-fat grain products, legumes, fruits and vegetables, with moderate amounts of lean meat and dairy products. And there's no indication that this message will change.

ABOUT THIS BOOK

The information in this book is based on current dietary recommendations from health authorities, which have been developed after careful consideration of the results from valid scientific studies.

This book is about healthy eating and the benefits you can expect from a healthy lifestyle. It is designed to provide you with accurate information about how nutrients and different foods can affect your health so you can make informed food choices that will last a lifetime. Good nutrition doesn't mean giving up all the foods you like—it means making smarter choices to help you select a diet that promotes health and provides enjoyment. If you're active and eat well most of the time, there's still room to enjoy your favourite indulgences in moderation. Better still, select a healthier version of your favourite treats. There are plenty of recipes in this book that show you how.

This book also contains practical tips for general healthy eating and cooking, as well as for weight loss and some medical conditions. If you have a medical condition, you should consult your doctor before making any changes to your diet or exercise habits, in case they interfere with your condition or any medication you're taking. Your doctor can also refer you to a dietitian who can design a healthy diet plan that suits you. Pregnant women should also consult their doctor before making any dietary changes.

The healthy eating guidelines in this book are suitable for teenagers and children, in terms of the types of foods they should be eating most often.

 However, children and teenagers may need different quantities of certain foods to adults. In addition, low-fat diets are not suitable for children under five years of age, because they need more fat than adults while their bodies and brains are still developing. For more advice about the types and amounts of foods that are suitable for you and other family members, consult a qualified dietitian.

The recipes

This book also contains a complete set of tested recipes that will provide you with a large range of delicious and nutritious soups, salads, main meals, desserts and snacks—plenty of ideas for everyday meals as well as special events. The recipes have been designed with three things in mind: they're easy to follow, they're healthy, and, most importantly, they're delicious. You'll find plenty of options that will suit everyone's tastes.

All of the recipes comply with the guidelines for a healthy diet, so it will be easy for you to make healthy eating part of your lifestyle. The nutrient content of an average portion is listed underneath each recipe so you can compare different foods and keep a check on your daily energy and fat intakes. There are low-fat alternatives for many popular dishes that are traditionally high in fat, as well as some totally new recipes. In many cases, the ingredients that have been used to lower the fat content of the dish have improved its nutritional quality, which means that you'll get less fat but more nutrients per mouthful. You'll also be able to taste the flavours of the low-fat ingredients and seasonings used in the recipes, rather than the overriding creaminess of fat, and it's almost impossible to distinguish between reduced-fat and full-fat dairy ingredients in many of the recipes.

Fat is often used in cooking to add texture or crispness to foods, so extra ingredients have been added in place of fat in some of the recipes to maintain these qualities. This means that not all of the recipes are low in calories. Make sure that you eat normal-sized portions, so that you benefit from their low fat content.

We hope that this collection of recipes gives you the inspiration and tools for you and your family to enjoy a healthy diet and explore the wide variety of health foods readily available. Food is one of life's greatest pleasures and is an important part of our culture. Sharing a meal with family or friends is an enjoyable way of nurturing important relationships. Taking the time to prepare healthy meals is a great way to care for your family.

DID YOU KNOW?

It's never too late to change your eating habits and start repairing any damage you have done to your body. The body has an amazing capacity to heal itself, especially when fed a nutritious diet. You can reduce your risk of some diseases even after only two weeks of healthy eating. Simple changes to your diet, such as eating less fat, eating fish two to three times a week, and eating fresh fruit and vegetables daily, can quickly reduce your risk of diabetes, heart attack and stroke. Health benefits are even greater if you also exercise regularly and you don't smoke. Even small changes can result in big improvements in your health and quality of life.

NUTRIENTS

Nutrients are the substances in foods that are used by the body to perform its essential functions. There are seven main types of nutrients, none of which your body can live without.

WHAT ARE NUTRIENTS?

Nutrients are the substances in foods needed by the body for life, growth and repair. There are seven main types of nutrients needed by the human body, which must all be obtained from food and drink: carbohydrate, protein, fat, fibre, vitamins, minerals and water. An inadequate intake of just one type of nutrient can result in health problems either in the short or long term.

Carbohydrate, protein, fat, fibre and water are called macronutrients, because relatively large quantities of these nutrients are found in foods and they are needed in large amounts by the body. Vitamins and minerals are called micronutrients, because only small quantities of them are found in foods and they are needed in very small amounts by the body.

Scientists are still discovering more compounds in foods that have beneficial health effects, such as phytochemicals in soya beans and other plant foods, but more research is needed to determine how these nutrients work, how much we need to eat for health, and how many others exist that we don't yet know about. These unknown compounds aren't included in supplements, so a balanced diet is more likely to give you all the elements you need for good health.

WHAT DO NUTRIENTS DO?

Carbohydrate, protein and fat provide the body with the energy or fuel that it needs for life and activity.

Water, protein, fat and minerals are required to maintain the structure of cells and tissues, which form cell membranes, muscles, bones and teeth.

Water, protein, vitamins and minerals have important regulatory roles in the body. Water regulates the body's temperature. Protein is needed to make hormones and enzymes that regulate many biochemical processes. Vitamins and minerals are needed for the reactions that release the energy in carbohydrate, fat and protein; for the muscles, organs and brain to function; for bones to grow; and in the immune system to protect the body from disease.

WHAT IS ENERGY?

Most people measure their energy level by the way they feel, but nutritionists think of energy as the fuel that we obtain from the nutrients in food and drink. With the help of vitamins and minerals, the body can convert the carbohydrate, protein or fat in the food we eat into the energy that is needed to power bodily functions, such as breathing, pumping blood around the body, moving muscles and thinking.

The energy used by the body and the energy in foods is measured in kilojoules (kJ), the metric unit, or kilocalories (Cal),

usually known as Calories, the empirical unit. Kilojoules and kilocalories are simply two different units for measuring energy. One Calorie is equal to approximately 4.2 kilojoules.

The energy value of a food depends on the amount of carbohydrate, protein, fat, fibre and alcohol it contains. Because these nutrients have different chemical structures, they provide different amounts of energy.

NUTRIENT	KILOJOULES PER GRAM	KILOCALORIES PER GRAM
Protein	17	4
Carbohydrate	16	4
Fat	37	9
Alcohol	29	7
Water	0	0

EXAMPLE: A 250 ml glass of full-cream milk contains 8 grams of protein, 12 grams of carbohydrate and 10 grams of fat. Energy content: (8 x 17) + (12 x 16) + (10 x 37) = 698 kJ (166 Cal).

HOW MUCH ENERGY?

The amount of energy you need each day depends on your size, age, gender and level of physical activity. If your weight is below or above the healthy range for your height (see page 35), you're consuming too little or too much energy.

If you consume less energy than you need, your body will use its own stores of

carbohydrate, protein and fat for energy, resulting in weight loss. If you consume more energy than you need, it will be mainly stored as extra body fat, resulting in weight gain. A steady weight over a month or more is a good sign that you're balancing your food intake with your body's energy needs.

DAILY ENERGY REQUIREMENTS

Follow the three steps below to estimate your daily energy needs based on your age, gender and height, and how active you are.

Step 1: Find your approximate basic metabolic rate (the amount of energy your body needs for its basic functions) from the table below, according to your age and gender.

	FEMALES (HEIGHT = 162 CM)		MALES (HEIGHT = 172 CM)	
	KJ	CAL	KJ	CAL
Age				
15–22	7900	1900	10900	2600
23–50	7500	1800	9600	2300
51–65	7100	1700	8400	2000

Step 2: For every 4 cm you are above the average height listed above, add 420 kJ (100 Cal) to the result of step 1.
For every 4 cm you are below the average height listed above, subtract 420 kJ (100 Cal) from the result of step 1.

Step 3: If you're inactive, subtract 840 kJ (200 Cal) from the result of step 2.
If you're active, add 2100 kJ (500 Cal) to the result of step 2.
If you're exceptionally active, add 4200 kJ (1000 Cal) to the result of step 2.

Source: The 12345 + Food and Nutrition Plan. A simple guide to healthy eating and weight control. CSIRO Division of Human Nutrition, Adelaide, Australia and the Anti-cancer Foundation of South Australia, 1992

EXAMPLE: A 40-year-old, 166 cm tall female is an inactive office worker. Approximate daily energy required: (7500 + 420) – 840 = 7080 kJ (1700 Cal).

CARBOHYDRATE

Carbohydrate-rich foods are dietary staples in countries all over the world. Whether they are eaten as rice, flour, potatoes or bread, carbohydrates supply most of our energy.

Carbohydrate is the body's main fuel source, and can supply energy at a fast rate to the brain and muscles. There are three types of carbohydrates found in foods:
■ sugars—in fruit, milk and added to foods
■ starches—in grains, legumes and vegetables
■ dietary fibre.

SUGARS

Sugars are the smallest or simplest form of carbohydrate, and starches and fibre are larger molecules made up of many sugars joined together in chains. The bonds that hold the sugar units together in sugars and starches can be broken by digestive enzymes.

When you eat foods containing sugars or starches, they are digested in your stomach and mostly broken down into

glucose, a single-unit sugar. The glucose is then absorbed into the bloodstream, carried around the body and absorbed by cells that need it. Once it is inside a cell, glucose can be used immediately for energy or it can be stored in muscle or liver cells as glycogen, for later use.

STARCHES

Until recently, it was thought that starches were digested at a much slower rate than sugars, but we now know that this isn't always true. Some processed foods that contain starch but little intact fibre, like regular white or wholemeal bread, are digested at a much faster rate than table sugar because the flour has been ground so finely that digestive enzymes can break it down very fast. These rapidly digested starchy foods produce a faster and higher rise in your blood sugar level than some sugary foods. For these reasons, carbohydrate is no longer classified as being simple or complex, but rather slowly digested (low glycaemic index foods) or rapidly digested (high glycaemic index foods).

DIETARY FIBRE

Dietary fibre is found only in plant foods. Just as there are different vitamins and minerals, there are different types of fibre with different effects in the body. However, there are two main types of fibre: soluble and insoluble.

Soluble fibre either absorbs water or dissolves in water, and can form a gel-like substance in the gut, which slows down the rate of food digestion. Consuming lots of foods that contain soluble fibre, such as

human gut can ferment some of the fibre that reaches the colon, producing certain fatty acids that may help protect you from bowel disease and colon cancer.

HOW MUCH CARBOHYDRATE?

For generally active people (over two years of age), carbohydrate intake should account for at least 55 per cent of the total day's energy intake and should come from a variety of foods. People who have very active lives, and athletes and people participating in endurance sports, need to eat more carbohydrate in order to ensure that their muscles have a sufficient supply of energy.

oats, oat bran, beans, barley and apples, can help control high blood sugar (glucose) and cholesterol levels, and may also help reduce hunger between meals by slowing down the rate of food digestion.

Insoluble fibre is found in wholegrain products, such as grain bread, brown rice and wheat bran, and in nuts and some vegetables. Insoluble fibre does not dissolve in water, but it can bind water, which increases the bulk of the food matter in the digestive tract. This extra bulk helps move the food through your system, keeping your digestive system regular, removing waste and preventing constipation. This is one reason why a high fibre intake can help protect you against colon cancer. In addition, the bacteria that are naturally present in the

GOOD SOURCES OF CARBOHYDRATE

- **Starches**—bread, foccacia, low-fat muffins, crumpets, pikelets, breakfast cereals, oats, rice, pasta, grains, legumes, corn, pumpkin, potatoes, bananas, plain biscuits and crackers
- **Sugars**—table sugar, honey, golden syrup, fresh fruit, canned fruit, dried fruit, jam, dairy products
- **Fibre**—wholegrain bread, muesli, bran, bran cereals, dried fruit, beans, lentils, nuts, seeds, Brussels sprouts, broccoli, passionfruit, strawberries

DAILY CARBOHYDRATE REQUIREMENTS

Use the guide below to estimate your daily carbohydrate needs based on your body weight and activity level.

ACTIVITY LEVEL	CONTINUOUS EXERCISE	GRAMS OF CARBOHYDRATE PER KILOGRAM OF BODY WEIGHT PER DAY
Light	less than 1 hour/day	4.0–4.5
Light–moderate	1 hour/day	4.5–5.5
Moderate	1–2 hours/day	5.5–6.5
Moderate–heavy	2–4 hours/day	6.5–7.5
Heavy	4–5 hours/day	7.5–8.5

Source: Sports Nutrition Basics, H. O'Connor & D. Hay, J.B. Fairfax Press, Sydney, Australia, 1998

EXAMPLE: A 30-year-old, 60 kg female does 1 hour of continuous light exercise each day. Approximate daily carbohydrate required: (4.5 x 60) to (5.5 x 60) = 270–330 g.

PROTEIN

While protein is often associated with strength and stamina, too much protein can be unhealthy, especially if it results in a high fat intake.

Protein is part of every body cell and is needed for growth and repair; the maintenance of body structures (muscles, bones, blood vessels, teeth); the production of enzymes and hormones that regulate the body's processes; and the production of antibodies that protect the body from infection and illness. Protein may also be used as an energy source for the body if not enough carbohydrate or fat is available.

All proteins are made up of chains of smaller units called amino acids. Each different protein has its own unique number and order of amino acids. There are about 20 different amino acids commonly found in proteins. Nine of these amino acids cannot be made in adult human bodies and must be obtained from foods (essential amino acids). The other 11 amino acids can be made in the body or obtained from foods (non-essential amino acids).

If you don't eat enough essential amino acids, your body will obtain them by breaking down other proteins in your body that contain them, compromising the health of your muscles.

SOURCES OF PROTEIN

Animal foods are the best source of 'complete' proteins, which contain all nine of the essential amino acids.

Plant foods usually contain 'incomplete' proteins, which lack some of the essential amino acids. However, it's possible for vegetarians to get all the essential amino acids they need by eating a variety of plant foods each day, such as grains, nuts, seeds and legumes, especially if they combine them with dairy products and eggs. In fact, many people who live in less-developed countries don't eat much meat and rely on plant foods, such as grains, legumes and vegetables, to meet their protein needs.

Many simple meals containing different protein foods have a complete set of essential amino acids, such as muesli and milk, a peanut butter sandwich, rice and lentil dhal, and baked beans on toast with cheese.

Vegans, who don't eat eggs or dairy products, need to make sure that they consume a good variety of grains, seeds, nuts and legumes each day, in order to obtain sufficient essential amino acids. This is particularly important for vegan women who are pregnant or who are trying to conceive.

HOW MUCH PROTEIN?

Although protein has many vital functions, relatively little protein is needed each day to meet the body's amino acid needs because, unlike carbohydrate, large amounts of protein are not burnt for fuel.

The amount of protein you need depends on your body weight and growth status, but this generally corresponds to 10 to 15 per cent of your daily energy intake. Generally, people in western countries eat more than enough protein.

■ **Healthy adults** who include meat and dairy products or a variety of vegetarian foods in their diet generally need only 0.75 grams of protein per kilogram of body weight each day (53 g of protein for an average 70 kg male).

■ **Children** from 4 years and teenagers up until the age of 18 years need slightly more protein because they are still growing, usually 1 gram of protein per kilogram of body weight each day.

■ **Pregnant women** need more protein for their developing baby—0.75 grams of protein per kilogram of normal body weight plus an extra 6 grams of protein each day.

■ **Breast-feeding women** need even more protein to produce breast milk and to help their body recover from childbirth— 0.75 grams of protein per kilogram of normal body weight plus an extra 12 to 16 grams of protein each day.

■ **Some athletes** and very active people undergoing regular, strenuous training, and people suffering from burns or injuries may also need more protein for tissue repair (more than 1 gram of protein per kilogram of body weight per day).

GOOD SOURCES OF PROTEIN

■ **Animal sources**—meat, poultry, fish, seafood, eggs and dairy products
■ **Plant sources**—legumes (beans, lentils, chickpeas), nuts, seeds, grains, grain products, soy milk, tofu, tempeh

DAILY PROTEIN REQUIREMENTS

Use the guide below to estimate your daily protein needs based on your body weight and growth and repair needs.

CATEGORY	GRAMS OF PROTEIN PER KILOGRAM OF BODY WEIGHT PER DAY	
	MALE	FEMALE
SEDENTARY, INACTIVE PEOPLE		
Children and teenagers (4–18 years)	1.0	1.0
Adults	0.75	0.75
ENDURANCE ATHLETES		
Elite	1.6	1.2
Moderate intensity	1.2	0.9
Recreational	0.85	0.84
WEIGHT TRAINING		
Untrained, beginning of program	1.7	1.3
Trained	1.2	0.9
AVERAGE DAILY CONSUMPTION OF PROTEIN		
Children and teenagers	1–2	1–2
Adults	1–1.5	1–1.5
Athletes	1.5–4	1.5–2.8

Source: Sports Nutrition Basics, H. O'Connor & D. Hay, J.B. Fairfax Press, Sydney, Australia, 1998

EXAMPLES: A 30-year-old, 60 kg female does 1 hour of continuous light exercise each day. Approximate daily protein required: 0.75 x 60 = 45 g.
A 25-year-old, 68 kg male begins a heavy weight training program. Approximate daily protein required: 1.7 x 68 = 116 g.

FAT

We all need some fat in our diet, but it is clear that a high intake of dietary fat, particularly saturated fat, increases the risk of serious diseases such as heart disease, stroke and some cancers.

Although many people think that all fat is 'bad', we all need a certain amount of fat to remain in good health. Dietary fat is the most concentrated source of energy in the diet (37 kilojoules per gram) and is a particularly important energy source for babies and young children. Infants start life drinking breast or formula milk, of which fat provides 50 per cent of the calories. This fat helps fuel the rapid growth and development of the brain and body that takes place during the first few years of life. Consequently, low-fat diets are not suitable for children under five years of age. The need for fat gradually decreases as we age.

Dietary fat is a source of essential fatty acids, which cannot be made in the body in sufficient amounts and are especially important for development in children. Fat is also needed for healthy skin and nerves and is a precursor of prostaglandins, hormone-like substances that regulate many vital bodily processes.

The fat-soluble vitamins A, D, E and K are provided by dietary fat, which also helps the body absorb these vitamins. Any extra fat that is eaten is stored in the fatty tissues of the body, so that the body has a supply of energy on hand in case its food supply becomes limited. Body fat deposits not only store energy, but also keep us warm and protect our internal organs.

The fat in foods is a mixture of three main types: saturated, monounsaturated and polyunsaturated. These fats vary in their structures and effects on blood cholesterol levels and the risk of heart disease. Foods usually contain a mixture of the three main types of fat, although one is often present in a larger amount (see page 30).

CHOLESTEROL

Cholesterol is a type of fat that is made in the body, but it can also be consumed in the diet from animal products. Most of

the cholesterol in the body is found in cell membranes. It is also found in the coating around nerve cells that is needed for them to function properly. The body also needs cholesterol to make vitamin D, bile acids (for proper digestion), and hormones such as testosterone and oestrogen, needed for growth and reproduction.

If your body makes more cholesterol than it needs, the level of cholesterol in your blood rises and fatty deposits can build up in your arteries, leading to heart disease. The amount and type of fat in your diet influences the amount of cholesterol in your blood to a greater extent than the amount of cholesterol you eat.

Although there is one type of cholesterol travelling around the bloodstream, it can be attached to different carrier proteins, called lipoproteins. When determining your risk of heart disease, health professionals are concerned about the level of two types of these cholesterol-carriers: low-density lipoprotein (LDL, referred to as 'bad' cholesterol) and high-density lipoprotein (HDL, referred to as 'good' cholesterol). High levels of LDL-cholesterol are a risk factor for heart disease.

HIGH FAT SOURCES

In order to control your fat intake, you need to be aware of hidden and visible fats in foods. Read the nutrient content panel on food labels to help you choose foods that contain less fat.

Visible fats

- All oils, dripping, vegetable shortening and solid frying fat (100% fat)
- Butter (80% fat); reduced-fat butter (41% fat)
- Margarine (80% fat); reduced-fat margarine (40–50% fat)
- Cream (36% fat); reduced-fat cream (27% fat)
- Cheddar cheese (28–35% fat); reduced-fat Cheddar (24% fat); Brie (29% fat)

Hidden fats

- Peanut butter (52% fat)
- Milk chocolate (27% fat); chocolate-coated biscuits (24% fat); chocolate cake (18% fat)
- Croissant (24% fat)
- Cheesecake (22% fat)
- Doughnut (21% fat)
- Sausages (20% fat)
- Devon (18% fat)
- Toasted muesli (17% fat)
- Meat pie (15% fat)
- Pizza (14% fat)
- Muesli bar (13% fat)

HOW MUCH FAT?

To reduce the risk of heart disease and other health problems, dietary fat should provide no more than 20 to 30 per cent of your daily energy intake, with saturated fat providing no more than 7 per cent of the total fat intake, monounsaturated fat 13 per cent and polyunsaturated fat 10 per cent. This amounts to a total of 50 to 80 grams of fat each day for adult males and 40 to 60 grams for females.

DAILY FAT REQUIREMENTS

Use the guide below to estimate your daily fat needs based on your age, gender and activity level.

CATEGORY	APPROXIMATE GRAMS OF FAT PER DAY (BASED ON AVERAGE BODY WEIGHTS)
Weight loss	25–40
Children and inactive women	30–50
Inactive men	40–60
Active female adults and teenagers	40–70
Active male adults and teenagers	50–80

To calculate what 30% of your daily energy intake amounts to in grams of fat, multiply your daily energy intake in kilojoules by 0.3 and then divide by 37 (1 gram of fat contains 37 kJ).

Source: Sports Nutrition Basics, H. O'Connor & D. Hay, J.B. Fairfax Press, Sydney, Australia, 1998

The traditional diets of rural societies around the world have typically been very healthy until recent times, when industrial development has resulted in large changes in physical activity levels and eating habits. Since the 1960s, scientists have been examining the dietary habits of communities around the world that have relatively low rates of heart disease and cancer, in order to discover which aspects of their lifestyle or genetic make-up protect them from diseases that are common in western countries. As no genetic differences have been found, it's clear that the active lifestyle and healthy eating habits of these communities protect them against disease.

The healthy diet pyramid (see page 27) is designed to show people how to eat in a way similar to traditional diets based on plant foods with moderate amounts of lean protein and healthy fats.

People living in modern urban centres have access to a wide variety of healthy foods from all over the world, such as fresh Asian greens and soy foods, European breads and pasta, so they can pick and choose the best produce and tastiest healthy meals the world has to offer.

THE MEDITERRANEAN DIET

In the 1960s, a group of scientists began a study of the dietary habits and health status of more than 12,000 men aged between 40 and 59 years living in seven different countries. After 20 years, they found that the men of the Greek island of Crete in the Mediterranean had much lower rates of sickness and death due to heart disease or cancer than men living in other parts of the world—Finland, Holland, Italy, Yugoslavia, Japan and USA.

The active rural lifestyle and traditional diet of the population of Crete were found to be the main factors responsible for the men's excellent health. These people grew and gathered a lot of their food and their diet was quite simple by modern standards. They ate mostly fresh fruit and vegetables, legumes, coarsely ground wholemeal breads, nuts and seeds. Red meat tended to be eaten infrequently (a few times a month), so fresh fish, seafood, legumes and eggs provided most of their protein. Olive oil was the main source of fat, and butter, cakes and sweets were eaten rarely.

Although the diet contained an average of 35 per cent fat, it was mostly monounsaturated fat from olive oil and omega-3 essential fatty acids from fish and certain vegetables. Garlic, onion and vinegar were used to season many foods, and red wine was consumed in moderation.

By modern standards, the people of Crete were very active—they walked everywhere and spent a lot of time fishing and doing manual tasks.

The high olive oil content has often been claimed to be the main factor responsible for the health benefits of the Mediterranean diet, but the diet also contains high levels of vitamins, minerals, antioxidants, phytochemicals, fibre and omega-3 fatty acids. All of these elements, not just the olive oil, account for the protective effects of the diet.

Compared to living in modern cities, life in Crete was less stressful, which would also help keep blood pressure levels down and protect the heart.

TRADITIONAL ASIAN DIETS

Some modern Asian dishes that have been developed to suit western taste preferences are high in fat and not a good example of healthy traditional Asian cuisine. Like the Mediterranean lifestyle, traditional rural Asian lifestyles have relatively high levels of physical activity and low-fat diets based largely on plant foods, which offer protection against heart disease, obesity and some cancers. In most cases, boiled or steamed rice is the main source of carbohydrate and the staple food.

Asian dishes typically contain a mix of vegetables, seasoned with herbs, spices, vinegar, chilli, or fermented sauces—

providing vitamins, minerals, antioxidants and phytochemicals.

Unlike most western diets, traditional Asian diets generally don't contain dairy products, and lactose intolerance is prevalent among Asian people. However, there are plenty of sources of calcium in Asian cuisines—dark-green leafy vegetables, soy products, small dried fish eaten with their bones, seafood, nuts, seeds, seaweed and spices. People living in traditional rural communities also have very active lifestyles, which helps keep their bones strong, and the isoflavones found in soya beans appear to prevent bone density loss.

Compared to western diets, meat and chicken tend to be eaten in smaller quantities in Asian countries, due to the influence of Buddhism or the high price of meat. However, fish and seafood are important sources of protein in many countries with access to the sea.

In countries like Thailand and Laos, the cuisine highlights an inventive and exotic mix of herbs and spices. Thai curries are usually flavoured with coconut milk, aromatic herbs and spices and served with fragrant jasmine rice. You can lower the fat content by using low-fat coconut milk. The regular use of chilli also has health benefits, as it appears to protect people from respiratory tract infections, and may assist in weight control by slightly increasing the metabolic rate. Many herbs and spices also seem to have medicinal properties.

The use of the wok to cook foods quickly and with a minimum of fat is widespread throughout Asia, and it's likely that crisp wok-seared vegetables will contain more vitamins and minerals than boiled varieties commonly eaten in western households.

VITAMINS AND MINERALS

No supplement can compare with the vitamins and minerals your body will obtain from a healthy diet based on plenty of fresh fruits, vegetables and wholegrain products.

VITAMINS

Vitamins are nutrients that are only needed in small amounts, but they have very powerful effects. They are required for the normal functioning of every organ in the body and for many important processes, such as growth, reproduction and tissue repair. Although vitamins are not a source of energy, they are needed to release the energy from dietary carbohydrate, fat, protein and alcohol. Your body can't make most vitamins, so you need to get them from your diet.

There are two classes of vitamins: fat-soluble and water-soluble vitamins.

The fat-soluble vitamins (A, D, E and K) can be stored in the body, so consuming too much of them can be toxic and adversely affect your health. Fat-soluble vitamins are fairly stable during cooking and processing, but can be destroyed with exposure to air or light.

The water-soluble vitamins (vitamin C and eight B-group vitamins) dissolve in water, so excessive amounts of most of them are removed from the body in urine. However, very high doses of B vitamins, particularly vitamin B6, can cause toxicity problems. Water-soluble vitamins can be lost by soaking or boiling foods in water and may be destroyed by heat, light or air.

MINERALS

Minerals are nutrients in foods also needed in small amounts for important bodily processes, including the maintenance of the body's fluid balance, the structure of certain compounds, such as hormones, bones and teeth, the regulation of blood pressure, wound healing, and the activity of muscles and nerves. Your body can't make any of the minerals, so you need to get all of them from your diet.

There are two classes of minerals: major minerals and trace elements. The seven major minerals—calcium, sodium, potassium, magnesium, phosphorous, chloride and sulphur—are needed by the body in greater amounts than the trace elements, but both classes are equally important for health.

Nine trace elements have specific deficiency disorders and are therefore considered to be essential dietary factors—iron, copper, zinc, manganese, selenium, iodine, chromium, fluoride and molybdenum.

Minerals are more stable than vitamins, but they can be affected by food processing and preparation methods. The body's absorption of minerals from foods can be reduced or enhanced by other nutrients and components in a meal. For example, dietary fibre can reduce mineral absorption, whereas lactose sugar in milk can enhance calcium absorption. The absorption and functions of many minerals are interrelated, so a deficient or excessive intake of one mineral can affect the absorption and function of others. For example, a high iron intake can reduce zinc absorption. For this reason, high-dose mineral supplements should only be taken under medical supervision.

HOW MUCH OF EACH VITAMIN AND MINERAL?

The amount of vitamins and minerals you need each day depends on your age, gender, body size, physical activity, physiological status, medication use and lifestyle factors (pollution, smoking, stress, alcohol and fat intake). Healthy people should be able to get all the vitamins and minerals they need from a balanced and varied diet.

In many countries, committees of health experts have reviewed all of the scientific evidence regarding the amounts of vitamins and minerals needed to prevent deficiency and promote good health. Using this data, the experts have been able to calculate recommended dietary intake (RDI) values for some nutrients, which are the amounts needed daily to prevent deficiency in practically all healthy people.

NUTRIENTS IN SUPPLEMENTS

At the moment, the perfect supplement doesn't exist, but it's clear that a balanced diet offers many health benefits.

Whole foods are a complex package of nutrients and other beneficial factors that are not found in supplements. For example, an orange contains vitamin C with carotene, folate, calcium and fibre, but you won't get these other essential elements in a vitamin C pill. Similarly, a glass of milk contains calcium with protein, vitamin D, phosphorous and magnesium—all of the nutrients needed for healthy bones, which aren't always in calcium supplements. Plant foods contain phytochemicals, which have antioxidant properties and may help protect you against cancer, heart disease and diabetes.

Many scientific studies have found that people who regularly eat plenty of fruits and vegetables have a relatively lower risk of some cancers and heart disease, but there is no good evidence to show that supplements can give you the same protection. The benefits of eating a varied, balanced diet are that fresh foods taste great and they contain an effective mixture of nutrients that work in combination to enhance your health and wellbeing.

WHEN YOU MAY NEED A SUPPLEMENT

A lack of energy is a common complaint, which many people feel is due to an inadequate intake of vitamins. However, this could be due to a lack of sleep or exercise, or too many fatty foods, since vitamin deficiencies are rare. Nonetheless, dietary surveys indicate that many people regularly fail to consume RDI amounts of iron, zinc, calcium or magnesium. While  these people may not be strictly deficient in these minerals, low body reserves of these nutrients can increase the risk of developing iron deficiency or osteoporosis over time. On the other hand, some groups of people are at risk of certain vitamin and/or mineral deficiencies simply because they absorb less or eat less than they need.

Some people don't get all the nutrients they need from their diet because they don't eat a balanced diet or they have greater nutrient requirements due to pregnancy, illness or high activity levels. Many people don't eat fruit or vegetables on a daily basis and some people remove a whole food group from their diet, such as meat or dairy products.

Skipping meals, dieting and eating lots of 'junk' foods also contributes to poor nutrition. High intakes of fat and alcohol and certain medications can increase the body's use of certain vitamins and minerals, and some illnesses and medications prevent them from being absorbed. If you need prescription medication for a period of time, ask your doctor whether it is likely to affect your vitamin or mineral needs. Check with your doctor or a dietitian as to whether a supplement could improve your health or prevent a deficiency from developing, but you should also try to improve your diet at the same time.

Even if you don't have a clinical nutrient deficiency, your doctor or dietitian may recommend a supplement if:
- you have been following a vegan diet (eat no animal products) for an extended period of time, as you may be lacking in vitamin B12 and iron
- you are elderly and don't eat much or are housebound
- you are allergic to certain foods, such as dairy products
- you are pregnant or trying to fall pregnant, as you need more folate before conception and also more iron during the first trimester of pregnancy
- you have a high alcohol intake, as this increases the risk of B group vitamin deficiencies
- you are a heavy smoker, as you need more antioxidants
- you take certain medications, such as antacids, anticonvulsants, and cholesterol-lowering drugs, which increase the need for certain micronutrients
- you are an endurance athlete or are very active, as you may need more iron and protein
- you have an eating disorder or low energy intake, as you may have low iron and calcium intakes
- you have a digestive tract disease or have had surgery.

VITAMINS AND MINERALS IN PROCESSED FOODS

Some people think that modern foods are depleted of vitamins and minerals, but supermarkets are full of nutritious foods—fresh, frozen, canned and processed. Vitamins and minerals are even added to some processed foods to replace those that are lost during manufacturing, such as in breakfast cereals and breads, or to increase the food's nutrient content, such as in some milks and drink powders.

However, heat, light and air inactivate some nutrients, and soaking foods in water can wash away some vitamins. The vitamin content of foods also decreases the longer you store them. For this reason, canned and frozen foods, which are usually processed soon after harvesting, contain equal or greater amounts of some nutrients than fresh produce, which may have been stored for a period of time before reaching the supermarket or greengrocer.

During the canning process, food is washed, prepared, sealed into the can and then pressure-cooked to sterilise the food. The absence of light, air and bacteria ensures that the natural flavours, colours and many nutrients are retained. Some minerals can leach out of food into the liquid in the can, such as brine, gravy, sauce, juice or syrup, but often the liquid is consumed with the food so most of these nutrients will be consumed.

Canned fish is a better source of calcium than fresh fish, because the canning process softens the bones so they can be eaten with the fish.

Over the last ten years, the salt content of many canned foods has been gradually reduced to help people consume less sodium, and many salt-free varieties are now available.

TIPS FOR RETAINING VITAMINS DURING COOKING

■ Store all food at a cool temperature out of direct sunlight.
■ Purchase fresh fruit and vegetables several times a week.
■ Store fruit and vegetables in the fridge or a cool place to slow down the rate of nutrient loss.
■ Use cooking methods that don't bring food into direct contact with water, such as steaming, pressure cooking, roasting, grilling, stir-frying, baking and microwaving.
■ Don't thaw frozen vegetables before cooking and only reheat them until they are tender.
■ Cook vegetables for the shortest time possible in the least amount of water. If boiling, bring the water to the boil first, cut up the vegetables and then add to the water. Use the remaining cooking water for soups and sauces.
■ Don't use bicarbonate of soda when you are cooking vegetables.
■ Don't cook vegetables in brass or copper saucepans, which can react with them.
■ Minimise the washing and chopping of foods before cooking. Vegetables should not be cut up or cooked until the last minute.
■ Don't soak rice before cooking it.
■ Try to eat fruits and vegetables in larger pieces, rather than smaller pieces, including shredded, puréed, mashed or juiced. The smaller the pieces, the more vitamins you lose.
■ Serve hot foods immediately—keeping them warm destroys vitamin C.
■ Fresh foods don't always contain more nutrients than canned, bottled, frozen or packaged foods. Processed foods can be used with fresh produce to help you make quick, nutritious meals.

THE RECIPE FOR A HEALTHY DIET

Forget about the complicated figures and calculations—health professionals have devised ten simple steps to a healthy diet, which are discussed in detail on the following pages.

To stay healthy now and in the future, nutrition authorities recommend that you consume a variety of nutritious foods each day. These should provide you with 55 to 70 per cent of your daily energy as carbohydrate, 10 to 15 per cent as protein, and 30 per cent or less as fat. Unfortunately, most people in western societies are still eating too much fat and are not getting enough physical activity.

	WHAT WE ARE EATING*	WHAT WE SHOULD BE EATING
Energy from carbohydrate	46%	55% or more
Energy from fat	33%	20–30%
Energy from protein	17%	10–15%

*Source: Selected highlights from the 1995 National Nutrition Survey, Australian Bureau of Statistics

Trying to work out what these numbers mean in terms of the quantities and types of foods we should be eating can be difficult, so health professionals have devised the following general guidelines that highlight the main features of a healthy diet.

It's really not hard to have a healthy balanced diet—it simply means eating more of some foods and less of others. You don't have to give up your favourite indulgences completely, but you might need to treat yourself less frequently, and use healthier versions of your favourite recipes, as seen in this book. No one meal is bad as long as the total mix of foods you consume over a period of days or weeks adds up to an overall healthy diet.

TEN STEPS TO A HEALTHY DIET

1 Eat a variety of nutritious foods each day.
2 Base your diet on grain products, fruits, vegetables and legumes.
3 Eat a diet that is low in fat, particularly saturated fat.
4 Maintain a healthy body weight by balancing food intake with regular exercise.
5 If you drink alcohol, only have moderate amounts.
6 Eat moderate amounts of sugar and foods containing added sugar.
7 Choose low-salt foods and limit your use of table salt.
8 Drink plenty of water throughout the day.
9 Eat calcium-rich foods on a regular basis.
10 Make iron-rich foods a regular part of your diet.

These dietary guidelines have been developed as a result of the findings from scientific studies that have studied the dietary habits of large numbers of people over many years. The diseases that these people developed over time were then examined. Results from careful laboratory experiments and dietary trials have confirmed these findings.

It's clear that a nutritious diet based on a wide range of plant foods (grain products, fruits, vegetables, legumes, nuts and seeds) offers significant protection against the most common diseases in our society.

Breakfast: Banana bread with maple ricotta (page 77)

STEP 1: EAT A VARIETY OF NUTRITIOUS FOODS EACH DAY

Although scientists continue to make new discoveries about the health benefits of different foods, the basic prescription for healthy eating has been the same for the last 20 years and will hardly change in the future. Many nutrients and other food factors are needed by your body to work together and keep it healthy and functioning normally.

Therefore, the basic principle of a healthy diet is to eat a variety of foods from all of the major food groups each day. This will ensure that you consume the entire range of nutrients that your body needs. Even limiting your intake of one major food group, such as dairy products or meats, can lead to a nutrient deficiency, which may affect your health in the future.

Lunch: Low-fat chicken Caesar salad (page 118)

The key to healthy eating is to eat a wide range of foods, in their right proportions, most of the time. Try to eat 30 different foods each day. It's not as difficult as it sounds—muesli, salads, casseroles, stir-fries and sandwiches all contain a variety of foods—yet many people in our society eat less than 15 different foods a day.

Dinner: Tuna with chickpea salad (page 215)

STEP 2: BASE YOUR DIET ON GRAIN PRODUCTS, FRUITS, VEGETABLES AND LEGUMES

The healthy diet pyramid is a good guide to help you achieve the main steps for a healthy balanced diet, and is suitable for all healthy people over the age of two, in all ethnic groups. It's also the model for a healthy weight loss diet, as long as you eat sensible portions and use low-fat dairy products and lean protein foods.

The pyramid guide shows you how to eat a balanced diet by selecting a variety of foods from each of the five major food groups each day (fruits, vegetables, cereal products, dairy products, meats and alternatives). Each food group provides some, but not all, of the nutrients you need, so you need different amounts of servings from each food group. You may also be surprised how much healthy food you can eat each day. This is because healthy foods contain fewer calories than fat-laden take-away meals and snack foods.

The bottom layer of the pyramid shows the foods that we should eat in the largest amounts, because they offer so many health benefits. These foods are important sources of energy, vitamins, minerals and fibre, and they also contain other protective compounds, such as antioxidants, phytoestrogens and resistant starch.

The high nutritional quality of these foods is one reason why people who regularly eat plenty of fresh fruit and vegetables are less likely to develop certain cancers.

Eating plenty of wholegrain foods, legumes, fruits and vegetables can also reduce the risk of heart disease, diabetes and weight gain. These foods contain relatively few calories, so by basing your meals and snacks on these foods, it's possible to lose weight without going hungry (as long as you don't add lots of mayonnaise and sour cream).

Rather than eating the same types of fruits and vegetables each week, try to eat a variety of different-coloured fruits and vegetables. This may help protect you from more diseases.

The recipes in this book will help you explore the wide variety of fruits and vegetables, legumes and grain products that are readily available in supermarkets. Healthy eating isn't about depriving yourself of great-tasting foods. Even if you are sensitive to wheat or certain fruits and vegetables, there are still plenty of foods at the bottom of the pyramid that you can eat.

MINIMUM NUMBER OF DAILY SERVES FROM THE FIVE MAJOR FOOD GROUPS NEEDED TO ACHIEVE AT LEAST 70% OF DAILY REQUIREMENTS OF PROTEIN, VITAMINS AND MINERALS

AGE GROUP	BREAD, CEREALS, RICE, PASTA, NOODLES	VEGETABLES, LEGUMES	FRUIT	DAIRY PRODUCTS	MEAT, FISH, POULTRY, EGGS, NUTS, LEGUMES
Children 4–7 years	2	2	1	2	0.5
Children 8–11 years	3	3	1	2	1
Teenagers 12–18 years*	3.5	4	2.5	2.5	1
Adults 19+ years	4	5	2	2	1
Pregnant women	4	5	4	2	1.5
Breast-feeding women*	6	7.5	5	2.5	2

*Average requirement only. Individual needs may differ.

Adapted from: The Australian Guide to Healthy Eating—Background information for nutrition educators. Commonwealth Department of Health and Family Services, Australia, 1998

THE BALANCED DIET PYRAMID

Eat least:
sugar, fats,
alcohol and salt

Eat moderately:
poultry, meat,
nuts, eggs and
dairy products

Eat most:
vegetables,
seafoods,
legumes,
cereals,
breads,
and
fruits

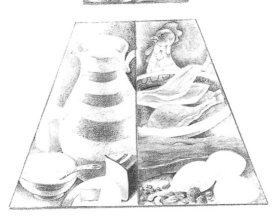

TOP OF PYRAMID: EAT LEAST

INDULGENCES OR EXTRAS   NO MORE THAN 1–2 SERVES PER DAY

1 serve = 1 small doughnut
            4 plain sweet biscuits
            1 small slice of cake
            1/2 small bar (25 g) chocolate
            1 1/2 scoops ice cream
            1 can (375 ml) soft drink
            1/3 meat pie or pasty (60 g)
            12 (60 g) hot chips
            1 small packet (30 g) chips
            2 tablespoons cream or mayonnaise
            1 tablespoon butter, margarine or oil
            200 ml wine, 400 ml beer or 600 ml light beer (1.5 standard drinks)

MIDDLE OF PYRAMID: EAT MODERATELY

LEAN MEATS AND ALTERNATIVES   1–2 SERVES PER DAY

1 serve = 65–100 g cooked meat (2 small chops, 2 slices roast meat, 1/2 cup mince)
            80–120 g cooked fish
            2 small eggs
            1/3 cup nuts
            1/4 cup seeds

LOW-FAT MILK AND DAIRY PRODUCTS   2 SERVES PER DAY (ADULTS)
                                          4 OR MORE SERVES PER DAY (CHILDREN AND TEENAGERS)

1 serve = 1 cup (250 ml) milk
            1/2 cup (125 ml) evaporated milk
            2 slices (40 g) cheese
            1 tub (200 g) yoghurt

BOTTOM OF PYRAMID: EAT MOST

FRUIT   3 OR MORE SERVES PER DAY

1 serve = 1 medium piece fruit (apple, banana, orange, pear)
            2 small pieces fruit (apricots, kiwi fruit, plums)
            1/2 cup grapes
            1 cup diced or canned fruit
            1 1/2 tablespoons sultanas
            4 dried apricots
            1/2 cup (125 ml) fruit juice

VEGETABLES, INCLUDING LEGUMES   4 OR MORE SERVES PER DAY

1 serve = 1 cup salad vegetables
            1/2 cup cooked or raw vegetables
            3/4 cup (185 ml) vegetable juice
            1/2 cup cooked legumes
            1 small potato

GRAIN PRODUCTS   5 OR MORE SERVES PER DAY

1 serve = 2 slices bread (60 g)
            1 medium bread roll
            1 cup cooked rice, pasta or noodles
            1 cup cooked porridge
            1 1/3 cups ready-to-eat breakfast cereal
            1/2 cup natural muesli

The middle layer of the diet pyramid contains protein-rich foods, which should be low in fat and eaten in moderation. All of these foods, except dairy products, contain iron and zinc—minerals that many people don't eat enough of. These foods help to keep your blood, bones, skin and muscles strong and healthy, but large portions are usually not needed (a palm-sized serving of lean meat is generally sufficient).

The foods and drinks at the top of the pyramid should be eaten in the smallest quantities, because they contain many calories but relatively few vitamins and minerals.

Eating the pyramid way isn't difficult because supermarkets are full of healthy food all year round. If you eat well and exercise regularly most of the time, you have room for a small indulgence each day, such as a glass of wine or a small serve of ice cream. Some healthy treats, such as a cup of low-fat frozen yoghurt, can even count as one serve of dairy food. There's room to have your cake and eat it too, particularly if it's a low-fat treat, but by filling up with a regular supply of healthy foods, you probably won't crave the less healthy foods at the top of the pyramid.

DID YOU KNOW?

Legumes or pulses were important foods for our ancestors long before wheat became a dietary staple. Legumes have fewer calories than many foods and are a great source of protein, vitamins and minerals. They also contain soluble fibre and slowly digested carbohydrate, which provides a slow, sustained stream of energy. If eaten regularly, they can help reduce high blood cholesterol levels and will be less likely to cause flatulence.

A HEALTHY MENU FOR A DAY

BREAKFAST	LUNCH	DINNER
Start with an orange, grapefruit, melon or paw paw	Accompany your lunch with a couple of glasses of water	Don't make this the big meal— spread out your eating evenly
A bowl of wholegrain cereal or untoasted muesli and 2 slices of wholegrain toast	A lentil burger on wholegrain bread with salad	Barbecued fillet steak with spicy chutney and chargrilled vegetables
OR	OR	OR
Baked beans and fresh tomato on toast	California rolls with miso soup	Chilli con carne with rice
OR	OR	OR
1 bowl of porridge (use fruit instead of sugar to sweeten)	A bowl of chunky vegetable soup with a bagel	Mushroom risotto
OR	OR	OR
A banana smoothie made with low-fat milk and honey	Niçoise salad with oil-free dressing	Chargrilled tuna or salmon with salsa, steamed potatoes and vegetables
	OR	OR
	Baked potato with salmon, capers and low-fat yoghurt	Spicy vegetables with steamed couscous
BETWEEN-MEAL SNACKS	OR	
	Roll-up with hummus, tabbouleh and skin-free chicken	Finish with poached fruit, a baked apple or a grilled
Keep your energy levels high with low-fat yoghurt, fresh or dried fruit		banana with low-fat yoghurt
	Finish with a piece of fruit	

STEP 3: EAT A DIET THAT IS LOW IN FAT, PARTICULARLY SATURATED FAT

Dietary guidelines advise people to limit their fat intake, because high-fat diets:

■ increase the risk of weight gain (because fat contains more calories per gram than either carbohydrate or protein, and is also less filling)

■ increase the risk of developing certain cancers and adult-onset diabetes

■ increase blood cholesterol levels and the risk of heart disease and stroke—two major causes of death in our society.

Many people in our society are overweight and consume too much fat. Heart disease is a major cause of premature death in  men and women. A high level of cholesterol in your bloodstream can result in fatty deposits building up inside your arteries (atherosclerosis). If these fatty deposits keep growing over time, they can eventually restrict the blood flowing through your arteries.

Are some fats healthier than others?

The fat in foods is a mixture of three types of fat: saturated, monounsaturated and polyunsaturated. These fats vary in the effects they have on blood cholesterol and their relationship to heart disease.

■ **Saturated fats** tend to increase the amount of cholesterol in your blood to a greater extent than dietary cholesterol and their intake should be limited. Saturated fats are found mainly in animal produce, such as dairy products, meat, poultry and lard, and in many processed foods, such as biscuits, pies, cakes, pastries and chocolate. Coconut and palm oil are also high in saturated fat.

■ **Monounsaturated fats** can help lower the level of cholesterol in the blood, if your total and saturated fat intake is low. Monounsaturated fats are found in avocados, olive oil, canola oil, sunola oil, monounsaturated margarines and nuts.

■ **Polyunsaturated fats** can help reduce the level of blood cholesterol if they are used in place of saturated fat as part of a low-fat diet. Polyunsaturated fats are found in sunflower oil, safflower oil, soya bean oil, evening primrose oil, linseed oil, fish oils, polyunsaturated margarines, mackerel, tuna and salmon.

Health professionals recommend that fats provide no more than 30 per cent of your total daily energy intake, with saturated fat providing 7 per cent of the total fat intake, monounsaturated fat 13 per cent and polyunsaturated fat 10 per cent. It's not so important to achieve these exact percentages, but monounsaturated and polyunsaturated fats should be consumed in greater proportions than saturated fat.

An easy way to increase your intake of healthy fats without blowing your daily fat budget is to eat fish that is rich in omega-3 polyunsaturated fatty acids, such as

sardines, herrings, mackerel, tuna and salmon, two to three times a week. These fish are readily available fresh, canned or bottled in brine, so it's easy to eat them regularly. Make sure you use low-fat  cooking methods to prepare them. Regular consumption of fish can also help reduce high blood pressure and triglyceride levels and reduce the risk of blood clots and strokes. It may also help alleviate depression and arthritis.

Tips for reducing your fat intake

■ Cut down your fat intake gradually by making a series of small changes. Stick with each change for a few weeks, and you'll soon like the taste of low-fat foods.

■ Learn to read food labels so you can identify high-fat foods. As a general rule, low-fat snacks contain no more than 5 grams of fat per serve, and low-fat meals contain no more than 10 grams per serve. Food labels will also show you which reduced-fat foods are still relatively high in fat and calories.

■ Switch from full-fat dairy products to low-fat and reduced-fat varieties. Healthy children over the age of five years can switch from full-fat to reduced-fat milk.

■ Substitute added fats (butter, margarine, mayonnaise, salad dressing, sour cream) with low-fat alternatives (vinegar, oil-free dressings, mustard, salsa, lemon juice). Flavour your foods with herbs, spices, low-fat relishes and sauces.

■ Choose fresh fish or fish canned in brine or spring water, not oil.

■ Choose lean cuts of meat and poultry, and remove any skin and visible fat before cooking.

■ Fill up on vegetables and grain products at lunch and dinner, and eat small portions of meat, chicken or fish.

■ Avoid fried foods and fatty snacks.

■ Some healthy-looking foods, such as toasted muesli and muffins, are high in fat. Make your own versions of your favourite foods (low-fat grilled pitta pizzas, hamburgers, burrito wraps) using your imagination or the recipes in this book.

■ Pack low-fat foods to take with you to work or school or when travelling so you have something healthy on hand.

■ Fill sandwiches with plenty of juicy salad vegetables so that you don't need margarine, and add a small serving of lean meat, skinless chicken, fish or reduced-fat cheese.

■ When you have to eat on the run, choose lower-fat foods:
- healthy sandwiches or salads (skip the margarine and fatty dressings; choose filling wholegrain breads)
- Asian food (steamed rice, mixed vegetable dishes, lean meat or seafood stir-fries)
- pasta with tomato-based sauces
- pizza with low-fat toppings
- pitta bread with meat, tabbouleh and fresh salad.

■ At dinner parties and social events, limit your intake of fatty hors d'oeuvres (cream dips, crackers, peanuts, chips, vol au vents). Fill up on fresh vegetables, low-fat dips, and non-alcoholic drinks.

■ When dining out:
- choose low-fat dishes rather than dishes that are crumbed and fried, and dishes with low-fat sauces rather than creamy ones
- trim any fat from meat and poultry
- don't go overboard at a smorgasbord—fill up on salads and clear soup
- skip creamy desserts or share them with someone else
- swap garlic bread for fresh crusty bread with a thin scrape of butter.

Low-fat cooking

Choosing low-fat foods is just one aspect of following a healthy diet—you also have to prepare them in a healthy way. You may think you're doing the right thing when you choose brown rice over white, but if you're making a dish like fried rice with lots of oil and ham, you may still be eating a high-fat meal.

Healthy, carbohydrate-rich foods, like potatoes, bread and pasta, have been falsely accused of being fattening foods, but it's really the accompaniments that are fattening (butter on bread, sour cream on potatoes, creamy pasta sauces).

You have to eat a considerable amount of carbohydrate before it's turned into fat, whereas dietary fat is readily stored as body fat. The secret to tasty low-fat cooking is to use cooking techniques that maintain the flavour of the food without adding any extra, unnecessary fat.

Low-fat ingredients

It's possible to lower the fat content of many dishes without reducing the flavour by using simple substitutions. The table opposite contains alternatives for high-fat ingredients. By using a mix of low-fat substitutes and spices and flavourings, the low-fat recipe can taste even better.

The two main ways to reduce a recipe's fat content are to switch to low-fat cooking techniques and to replace some or all of the high-fat ingredients with low-fat alternatives.

LOW-FAT COOKING TECHNIQUES

Meat, poultry, fish and seafood

- Use non-stick pans and low-fat cooking methods requiring little or no fat or oil (dry-fry, stir-fry, grill, roast on a rack, steam, poach, microwave, simmer in low-fat sauce).
- As little as one tablespoon of oil is enough to brown or stir-fry enough meat for four people. Brush the base of the pan with oil, instead of pouring oil into the pan. Stock can also be used in place of oil for meat dishes.
- Grilling and barbecuing trim meat with low-fat marinades produces flavoursome meals. Marinate chicken breast fillets or lean meat in fruit or wine and herbs before grilling on the barbecue.
- Bake fish fillets or kebabs in foil with seasoning and lemon juice.
- Use a rack when grilling or roasting meat so the fat drips away.
- Cook legs of lamb in a roasting pan with a little water, wine or stock.

Soups, mixed dishes, sauces

- Let home-made soups, casseroles, mince dishes and stews cool until the fat solidifies on top. Then remove the fat before adding vegetables and reheating.
- Substitute low-fat ingredients for high-fat ones in recipes.
- Use low-fat, tomato-based sauces instead of creamy or cheesy ones.
- Use low-fat ricotta cheese with a sprinkle of Parmesan in cheese dishes.
- Use evaporated skim milk for creamy soups.
- Use puréed vegetables to thicken sauces.
- Use barley, lentils or potatoes to thicken casseroles or stews.

Vegetables

- Pre-cook potatoes in the microwave or oven, then crisp on the barbecue.
- Brown microwaved vegetables under the griller for crispness without the fat (if necessary, brush with a little oil first).
- Stir-fry vegetables in a little water and salt-reduced soy sauce.

HIGH-FAT INGREDIENT	REDUCED- OR LOW-FAT ALTERNATIVE
Milk, yoghurt	• Use low-fat varieties.
Whipped cream	• Use evaporated skim milk and chill before whipping. • Whip low-fat ricotta cheese with icing sugar and low-fat milk or fruit juice.
Sour cream	• Use low-fat yoghurt or buttermilk. • Blend cottage cheese with skim milk and lemon juice or vinegar. • Mix low-fat evaporated milk with lemon juice.
Whole eggs	• Use 2 egg whites or $1/4$ cup of egg substitute for 1 egg. If the recipe needs a few eggs, keep at least one or two whole eggs to maintain texture. Replace 3 whole eggs with 1 whole egg and 4 egg whites. Before you add the fresh egg whites, whisk them slightly.
Cream cheese	• Use low-fat cream cheese or low-fat fromage frais. • Use blended low-fat cottage cheese.
Cheese	• Use smaller amounts of lower-fat varieties. • Choose low-fat ricotta or cottage cheese. • Instead of a Cheddar cheese topping, mix a little grated Parmesan with oats, bran or wheat germ.
Butter or margarine	• Use small amounts of reduced-fat varieties (but not for baking). • Use lower-fat alternatives (chutney, cottage cheese, a little avocado) for sandwiches or only butter one slice of bread.
Oil	• Use less oil or use olive oil spray, stocks and juices for stir-frying or sautéing. • In cakes, replace oil with an equal amount of fruit purée and one-third of the oil—use puréed prunes, dried apricots or apple.
Mayonnaise/salad dressings	• Use non-fat varieties. • Make your own low-fat dressings (vinegar, herbs, lemon juice, ricotta, tomato paste) or sauces (low-fat yoghurt, buttermilk, mustard).
Coconut cream or milk	• Use reduced-fat versions. • Use low-fat yoghurt and a little desiccated coconut.
Pastry	• Use filo pastry, brushing every 3–4 layers with oil, juice, low-fat yoghurt or concentrated stock. • Mix cooked rice with egg white and pat onto a lightly oiled pie dish. Bake before using as a pastry base.
Sweet pie crust or slice base	• Combine plain reduced-fat sweet biscuits or wafer biscuits with dried fruit (apricots, prunes or figs) in a food processor until the mixture forms a ball. For 150 g biscuits, you need 75 g fruit. You may need to vary the amounts depending on the fruit's moisture.
Cakes and biscuits	• Minimum fat needed for biscuits is 2 tablespoons per cup of flour. • Replace oil with an equal amount of fruit purée plus one-third of the oil. • Use non-stick pans.
Meat and poultry	• Buy lean cuts and remove any visible fat before cooking. • Remove the skin and fat under the skin from poultry before cooking. • Keep portions small and fill up with vegetables and legumes.

Source: Winning Tastes, National Heart Foundation of Australia, 1993

STEP 4: MAINTAIN A HEALTHY BODY WEIGHT BY BALANCING FOOD INTAKE WITH REGULAR EXERCISE

People come in all shapes and sizes, and there is a range of healthy weights for each height. When deciding whether or not your weight is healthy, you need to consider how much body fat you have and where it's located. Body weight alone isn't always a good indication of body fatness— some thin-looking people can have a lot of fat but little muscle.

Firstly, use the chart opposite to see if your current weight is within the healthy range for your height. Since muscle and bone weigh more than fat, the higher weights in the healthy range typically apply to people with larger, muscular frames, whereas the lower end of the range applies to people with less muscle and smaller frames.

Secondly, for adults aged 20 to 69 years, you can estimate your body fat level by calculating your body mass index (BMI), which is your weight in kilograms divided by your height in metres squared. In general, the greater your BMI, the greater your risk of serious health problems (see example page 36).

Thirdly, using a tape measure, measure the circumference of your waist and hips. People who carry more fat around their mid-section (apple shaped) rather than on their lower body (pear shaped) have a greater risk of heart disease and diabetes.

Although it's often hard for women to lose the fat from their hips and thighs, this lower body fat isn't as detrimental to health as the classic 'beer gut', upper body/abdominal fat. See your doctor or a dietitian if you want a more accurate assessment of your body fat level, particularly if you're very active. Body weight is often a poor indication of body fatness in athletes because changes in their weight, even up to 2 kilograms at a time, can be due to fluid and carbohydrate lost from the body and increased muscle mass.

Weight gain with age is a common problem in our society. Currently, in Australia, it's estimated that half of all men and one-third of women over the age of 18 years are overweight or obese.

Besides being bad for self-esteem and your general feeling of wellbeing, being overweight and inactive increases your

SOME HEALTH PROBLEMS THAT CAN OCCUR AT EITHER EXTREME OF THE WEIGHT RANGE

OVERWEIGHT OR OBESE	UNDERWEIGHT
High blood pressure	Delayed development (children and teenagers)
High blood cholesterol	Decreased immunity
Sleep disorders	Menstrual irregularities
Breathing problems	Increased risk of anaemia and osteoporosis
Arthritis	Malnutrition
Diabetes	Less energy and vitality
Heart disease and stroke	Depression
Cancer (breast, uterus, prostate, colon)	Risk of early death (if very underweight)
Gall bladder disease, gallstones	

risk of many illnesses, including heart disease, diabetes, gallstones, degenerative joint disease and some cancers. You can greatly reduce your risk of these problems by staying active and maintaining your weight within the healthy weight range for your height. The good news is that you don't need to be skinny or at the lowest end of the weight range in order to be healthy—being underweight may also adversely affect your health.

How much weight should I lose?

If you are overweight, you should aim to get your weight into the healthy weight range. Even maintaining your weight at the top end of the healthy range for your height can significantly improve your health, and should be achievable by most overweight adults.

An overweight person who reduces their weight by 2 BMI units and increases their general activity will significantly improve their health relative to when they were overweight.

Losing weight slowly by making gradual changes in your dietary and  exercise habits is the best way to achieve a healthy weight and lifestyle that you can maintain. Gradual weight loss will help you lose body fat rather than muscle. You should aim to lose only 1 to 2 kilograms per week if you are very overweight or 0.5 to 1 kilogram per week if you are only slightly overweight.

It may have taken you years to gain 5 kilograms, so you can't expect to lose it all in a month. This could require drastic measures, such as very restricted diets or liquid-only diets, which could adversely affect your health.

It's also important to remember that the closer you are to your ideal weight, the

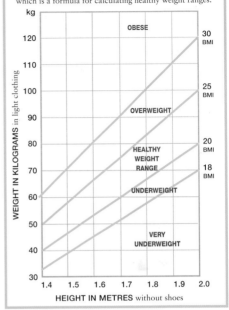

HEALTHY WEIGHT RANGE GRAPH
For men and women from 18 years onwards
Based on the Body Mass Index, or BMI (weight/height^2), which is a formula for calculating healthy weight ranges.

© The Australian Nutrition Foundation Inc

more difficult it can be to lose weight, simply because you've got less to lose. Also, our body shapes are genetically determined—some people naturally need more body fat to remain healthy than others.

If your weight is normal for your height, and you have to diet and exercise excessively to lose even 2 kilograms, it's likely that you're trying to maintain a body weight that's unnaturally low for you. A dietitian can establish an ideal body fat level that you can achieve with a healthy diet and exercise program so that you won't have trouble maintaining these habits over time.

If you decrease your fat intake and begin weight training, you may not lose any body weight (as shown on the scales), but you can lose body fat, which is more important for your health. So instead of spending money on diet pills and powders, take up some active leisure pursuits and purchase fresh, healthy foods.

BODY MASS INDEX	CLASSIFICATION	HEALTH RISK	
less than 18.5	Underweight	Risk of health problems	
18.5–24.9	Healthy		
25–29.9	Overweight	Risk of health problems	(Health risk is further increased
30–39.9	Obese	Significant health risk	if waist circumference is more than
40 or more	Extremely obese	Serious health risk	40 inches for men or 38 inches
			for women.)

Example: A man who weighs 80 kg is 175 cm. BMI = $80 \div 1.75^2 = 80 \div 3.0625 = 26.1$ kg/m^2
By losing 5 kg, he will bring his BMI down to 24.5 ($75 \div 1.75^2$) and reduce his risk of health problems.

What's the best way to lose weight?

To achieve a healthy body weight you have to balance your energy intake with the amount of energy your body needs. So in order to lose weight, you can eat less energy and/or increase your physical activity. However, it's much harder to lose weight simply by eating less, and may even be counterproductive in the long term.

People who have managed to lose a lot of weight and keep it off for many years will tell you that increasing your physical activity is essential for lasting weight loss. Rather than taking up jogging or other difficult forms of exercise, which are hard to stick to and leave you too tired to keep moving the rest of the day, you can burn more calories simply by going for regular long walks (at least 30 minutes a day) and by being generally more active (take the stairs, park your car further from work, go bowling instead of to the movies).

Trying to lose weight by eating less food is difficult and usually doesn't last long, because the body is designed to protect itself against food shortages with increased hunger and a lower metabolic rate, meaning that you feel hungrier but you're burning less energy. The persistent hunger will make even the most resolved dieter constantly think about food, and often within a month people end up breaking their diet by bingeing on their favourite high-calorie foods.

There's no need to feel like a failure if this happens to you, because your body has driven you to eat to increase its chances of survival. The body doesn't know if there's a famine coming so it has developed stronger mechanisms to stop people eating less energy than they need. There's always room to store more fat, so our bodies don't have the same defences against overeating.

These natural mechanisms are a problem for modern people because we have so many opportunities to overeat and under-exercise. Up until the last 50 years, people were generally more active, and fewer people were overweight.

Although there's no single method of losing weight that will suit everyone, there are three habits that will increase your chance of success:

- eating balanced, healthy meals
- limiting fat and alcohol intake
- being physically active.

Is it possible to eat more and still lose weight?

Many of us think that losing weight is a matter of starving yourself, but this isn't true. One of the best things you can do to help control your weight is to give yourself permission to eat three healthy meals a day, which will help stop you craving less nutritious foods. By eating regular low-fat meals and keeping active, you will keep your internal engine running and burning calories.

Rather than trying to restrict your food intake, focus on making better food choices, using the healthy diet pyramid

from carbohydrate and protein, and they are also more effective at increasing body fat stores. It's hardly surprising that many research studies have found that people who eat high-fat diets are more likely to be overweight than people with low fat intakes. So an effective way of reducing your calorie intake without going hungry is to limit your intake of fat and alcohol.

Isn't carbohydrate fattening?

Carbohydrate-rich foods, like bread and potatoes, are often claimed to be fattening, but, as we've said, it's the fat that's added to them that is fattening, not the carbohydrate itself. This extra fat provides lots of calories, but doesn't increase fullness and is readily stored as body fat.

Although it's possible to gain weight if you eat more carbohydrate than you need, it's much easier to overeat high-fat foods.

Some foods that are sweet but rich in fat have wrongly been classified as carbohydrate-rich foods, like cakes, pastries, ice cream and chocolate. Although they contain sugar, fat provides most of the calories in these foods. Refined sugar shouldn't be a major part of your diet, but because sugar contains less energy than fat, you can add small amounts of sugar to your low-fat meals to make them more palatable.

However, if you want to lose weight, it's a good idea to cut back on extra sugar where you can. If you have a craving for something sweet, satisfy it with a sweet low-fat food like fruit or low-fat yoghurt.

(page 27) as a guideline, and eat to a comfortable level of fullness. Basing your diet on the low-fat foods at the bottom of the pyramid means you can control your calorie intake without going hungry. These foods contain fewer calories per gram than fatty foods, so it's possible to eat filling meals and reduce your calorie intake at the same time. You just have to make a conscious effort to choose the right foods and prepare them using low-fat methods.

Limit your fat and alcohol intake

Fat and alcohol contain more energy per gram than carbohydrate or protein, with fat containing over twice as much energy per gram. Even small amounts of fatty foods and alcoholic drinks contain a lot of calories, making it much easier to consume more calories than you need.

Worse still, many research studies have shown that fat and alcohol don't make you feel as full as the same amount of calories

A GUIDE FOR ESTIMATING YOUR DAILY FAT AND KILOJOULE INTAKES
If you want to lose weight, aim to make fat less than 30% of your daily energy intake (not suitable for children).

FOR WOMEN WHO WANT TO LOSE	DAILY ENERGY INTAKE (KJ)	DAILY FAT INTAKE
Less than 5 kg	5000	30–35 g
Between 5 and 15 kg	6000	35–40 g
More than 15 kg	7000	40–50 g

Men add 500 kJ and 5 g fat.

Source: Australian Slimming Magazine, September 2000

Increasing the filling power of your low-fat diet: more fullness for fewer calories
If you eat a low-fat diet but can't lose weight, you're probably still eating more calories than you need. By choosing the most filling low-fat foods, you can reduce your calorie intake without going hungry.

Low-fat foods that are high in fibre or are less refined are more difficult to chew and swallow. Therefore, they take longer to eat, giving your brain time to register the growing level of fullness in your stomach. Not only do these filling foods help you eat less, they tend to keep you full for longer because they are slowly digested.

Many of the foods in modern supermarkets are soft and tasty, and can be eaten and digested very quickly. Perhaps this is one reason why it's now so easy to gain weight. Because you may be used to these soft foods, you may initially find whole foods a little unpalatable. But

if you make small changes and stick with them for a few weeks, you'll soon learn to like their taste. Also, remember to drink plenty of water throughout the day to help fill your stomach.

'Lite' calories still count
The food industry is helping people lower their fat intake by making reduced-fat versions of high-fat products. However, reduced-fat foods are not always lower in calories, because some ingredients that replace fats in foods are also high in calories. Many people believe they can eat larger portions of 'lite' foods and still consume fewer calories than if they had eaten a normal portion of the high-fat version.

Unfortunately, this isn't true and probably explains why some people don't lose weight on a low-fat diet. It's important to learn to interpret the information on food labels because some terms are confusing. A reduced-fat food contains less fat than the regular version, but it may still be high in fat and/or calories. The word 'lite' on a food label can mean that the product either has a light colour or contains less fat than the regular version. A food that is 90 per cent fat-free still contains 10 per cent of its weight or energy content as fat.

Crash diets—not a healthy way to lose weight
In recent times, one fad diet after another has claimed to be the most effective weight loss method, and new diet books are still becoming best sellers. Why are there so

LOW FAT, FEWER CALORIES	HIGH FAT, MORE CALORIES
1 slice of wholegrain bread 255 kJ (60 Cal), 1 g fat	1 slice of wholegrain bread thickly spread with butter 560 kJ (135 Cal), 9 g fat
1 medium potato, boiled 335 kJ (80 Cal), 0 g fat	1 medium potato, boiled, with 1 tablespoon sour cream 640 kJ (155 Cal), 8 g fat 1 small serve of French fries 1155 kJ (275 Cal), 16 g fat
1 cup pasta with 125 g tomato sauce 910 kJ (215 Cal), 1 g fat	1 cup pasta with 125 g creamy sauce 1440 kJ (345 Cal), 14 g fat
1 cup steamed white rice 990 kJ (235 Cal), 0 g fat	1 cup fried rice 1735 kJ (415 Cal), 16 g fat
1 big handful of sultanas 385 kJ (90 Cal), 0 g fat	1 big handful of chocolate-covered sultanas 550 kJ (130 Cal), 5 g fat
1 medium lean pork chop, grilled 715 kJ (170 Cal), 7 g fat	1 medium pork chop, not trimmed of any fat, grilled 975 kJ (235 Cal), 15 g fat

combination of foods, if you keep eating fewer calories than normal. However, fad diets are usually only something you can stick to for a short time, so they don't help you make lasting changes that will improve your health and weight. Many women go on a rapid weight loss diet before an important event, but they may put on even more weight when they start eating normally again. Rapid weight loss diets are not a healthy way of losing weight.

many fad diets? The simple answer is that they don't achieve lasting weight loss. Typically, fad diets require very specific meals and may be deficient in nutrients, especially if they restrict entire food groups, such as grain or dairy products. Although their methods vary, fad diets all produce weight loss by significantly reducing your normal energy intake.

None of these diets magically melt fat away. You can lose weight eating any

Before trying a high-protein diet, liquid meal replacements or any other diet fad, find out if it has any side effects. If you stick to a low-calorie diet for more than a month, you'll lose some weight, but it will be mostly water, not body fat. As time progresses, weight loss will occur more slowly and side effects may appear, such as increased hunger, cravings, irritability, tiredness and light-headedness. High-protein diets can also be harmful to the kidneys, as they have to work harder to remove the extra waste products from the body.

LESS FILLING	MORE FILLING
Foods	
Fruit juice, fruit purée, soft canned fruit, dried fruit	Fresh, crunchy fruit, unpeeled
Soft white or wholemeal bread, crackers, rice cakes	Crunchy or grainy bread
White pasta or white rice	Brown pasta or brown rice
Mashed potatoes, potato chips	Whole boiled or steamed potatoes, unpeeled
Minced or processed meat, thin strips	Large strips, slices or chunks of meat, steaks
Natural muesli	Porridge
Light breakfast cereals and cereal bars	Bran-based breakfast cereals
Fish spread	Fresh or canned fish
Finely strained or puréed soups	Soups with large chunks of meat and vegetables
Canned legumes (baked beans, etc)	Boiled dry legumes
Soft cakes and slices	Crunchy or thicker cakes and slices
Meals	
Cornflakes, skim milk and sugar	Porridge, skim milk and fresh fruit slices
White bread, chicken and lettuce sandwich	Grainy bread, lean beef and crunchy salad sandwich
Mashed potatoes, pork chops, peas	Whole potatoes, grilled pork steak, steamed vegetables

Light or lite   This can refer to the colour or texture of a product or its calorie or nutrient content. Read the food label to check which feature this refers to. If 'lite' refers to the calorie or fat content, then the product must also be reduced or low in energy and fat.

Reduced-fat   The product must contain 25% less fat than the regular version. Some reduced-fat versions of high-fat foods like margarine are still high in fat and calories.

Low-fat   Solid foods must contain no more than 3 grams of fat per 100 grams. Liquids must contain no more than 1.5 grams of fat per 100 grams. Some low-fat foods are not lower in calories because the fat has been replaced with sugar and other high-calorie ingredients. Use the nutrient information on food labels to help you select low-fat, lower-calorie foods.

Be prepared to eat well

We all lead busy, stressful lives and many people come home to find the fridge empty or they are simply too tired to cook. You can make it easier to follow a low-fat diet by stocking your pantry, fridge and freezer with low-fat foods and ingredients that can be quickly prepared to make nutritious meals.

For the pantry

Breads, low-fat crispbreads and crackers, rice cakes, natural muesli, breakfast cereals, porridge oats, low-fat breakfast cereal bars, reduced-fat muesli bars, rice, pasta, noodles, canned spaghetti, couscous, polenta, quick-cooking grain mixes, risotto rice, low-fat muffin and pancake mixes, dried fruit, nuts and seeds, wheat germ, oat bran, potatoes, low-fat microwave popcorn, low-fat pretzels, canned legumes (lentils, beans, baked beans, chickpeas), vacuum-packed legumes, canned vegetables, canned fish in brine, bottled pasta sauces, low-fat casserole sauces, long-life reduced-fat or low-fat milks, light evaporated milk, soy sauce, oyster sauce, vinegar, dried herbs and spices, stock cubes or long-life stocks, low-fat soups (canned, sachets, packets), baking ingredients (flour, sugar), spray oils, olive oil, yeast extract spreads, jam, honey, low-fat drinking chocolate mixes, diet jelly

For the fridge

Fresh fruit and vegetables, juices, mineral water, reduced-fat or low-fat dairy products or soy-alternatives (milk, cheese, yoghurt, custard), tofu, tempeh, smoked salmon, reduced-fat margarine, eggs, reduced-fat processed meat slices, fresh pasta (ravioli, tortellini, lasagne sheets), fresh noodles, sauces, minced herbs, tomato paste, curry paste, mustard, fat-free dressings and mayonnaise

For the freezer

Any type of bread, pitta bread or pizza bases, English muffins, bagels, fruit loaf, filo pastry, skinless chicken fillets, fish fillets, marinara mix, lean meats (mince, steaks, etc), frozen vegetables, frozen vegetable stir-fry mixes, thick-cut 97% fat-free oven fries, grated reduced-fat cheese, frozen berries, sorbet, gelato, low-fat frozen fruit desserts

In addition to low-calorie diet books, many other products are marketed for weight loss. Unfortunately, most of them don't promote fat loss and some may jeopardise your health. Below are some common products that should not be used in place of a healthy balanced diet if you're trying to lose weight.

Laxatives and diuretics

- These don't prevent you from absorbing food.
- They cause water loss rather than fat loss, so your normal weight will return once you drink enough fluid.
- Long-term use of such products can lead to dangerous losses of water, sodium and potassium, which can cause death.

Supplements claimed to suppress appetite, increase fat metabolism or block fat absorption

- As yet, there is no scientific evidence that use of these supplements alone results in weight loss.
- They often contain only minute amounts of the ingredients claimed to produce the beneficial effects.

Fibre supplements

- These are claimed to help reduce appetite by filling the stomach, but must be taken with lots of water.
- They can cause constipation, bloating, and flatulence.
- Excessive use can cause gut problems and reduced absorption of iron, zinc and calcium.
- Natural high-fibre foods may be more beneficial for weight control by decreasing the amount of food that is consumed at meals and increasing fullness between meals.

Meal replacement drinks and bars

- These are often low in calories and/or carbohydrate, and don't contain all important vitamins and minerals.
- They are not as filling as a wholesome low-fat meal and don't contain all the important vitamins and minerals.
- They can lead to hunger between meals and increased risk of snacking.
- There is no scientific evidence that they are useful for long-term weight loss.

Modified fasting (very low-calorie diets) and low-carbohydrate diets

- Due to low calorie intake, these diets can lead to rapid weight loss, but this is mostly water.
- Side effects include dizziness, fatigue, depression, hair loss, nervousness and skin problems.
- With time, loss of muscle mass will cause the body to run on less energy and slow the rate of weight loss.
- They are difficult to maintain due to boredom, hunger and side effects.

■ Make realistic changes to your eating and activity habits in a series of small steps. Set gradual goals you can achieve and measure. For example, first switch from full-fat to reduced-fat dairy products. Once you've mastered this, change to low-fat dairy products. Focus on changes you know you can stick to.

■ Be prepared to eat healthily. Stock your pantry and fridge with healthy foods on hand for fast meals and snacks. Cook extra portions of healthy meals to store in the freezer, so you can reheat them when you don't have time to cook. Plan a menu for the week and take healthy foods with you to eat at work or school.

■ Try to eat regular, balanced meals containing a variety of healthy foods. Focus on what you can eat, rather than what you shouldn't eat. Eat at a slow pace to a comfortable level of fullness. This will give you time to register how much you've eaten. Wait a while before deciding whether or not to eat a second helping.

■ Make your meals as filling as possible by choosing less refined foods. Include a little protein with your high-carbohydrate meals (for example, low-fat milk with breakfast cereal, lean beef and salad on your sandwich).

■ Restrict your alcohol intake. This will help keep your calorie intake and blood pressure down.

■ Become aware of times when you are likely to overeat, such as when you're stressed or bored, or when there is free food around, and check if you're really hungry before you eat anything. Finding tasks to keep you busy can help you feel happier and productive, and you'll have less time to snack.

■ Don't give up if you have problems, just get back on track as soon as you can. Learn to think positively and find ways of dealing with your emotions other than eating. Regular exercise and yoga can be great stress-relievers. Don't weigh yourself every day.

■ Aim for at least 30 minutes of moderate activity on most days. Find activities that you enjoy so you'll look forward to doing them. If you haven't been physically active, build up to 30 minutes gradually and look at ways to increase your general daily activity. It's harder to eat if you're out of the house exercising.

■ Develop a strategy for eating healthily at social occasions. Bring some suitable foods with you, if appropriate, or have a healthy snack beforehand so you're not hungry at the party.

■ Drink plenty of water throughout the day. This can help keep your appetite down, as sometimes it's easy to confuse thirst for hunger.

STEP 5: IF YOU DRINK ALCOHOL, ONLY HAVE MODERATE AMOUNTS

Unlike the other nutrients, we can do without alcohol altogether. Alcoholic drinks provide 'empty calories'—lots of energy, but few vitamins or minerals. However, a low to moderate intake with some alcohol-free days each week appears to be fine for most healthy people.

Another good reason to limit your alcohol intake is that alcohol can cause weight gain, because it provides energy (29 kJ per gram) and suppresses the body's use of carbohydrate and fat as fuel. The body can't store alcohol, because it's a toxin and causes cell damage, so your body has to burn off any alcohol that's in your system. While this is happening, any fat in your system won't be needed for energy and will be stored as body fat.

Unlike the other nutrients, alcohol is also a drug that has short-term effects immediately after ingestion—and being a drug, there are many myths and claims associated with its effects. For example, some people believe that alcoholic drinks will make you feel warm in cold weather. Although some alcoholic drinks can have an initial warming effect, alcohol metabolism increases heat loss from the body, so you may end up feeling colder. Another myth is that alcohol helps fight a cold, but it can actually suppress the body's immune system and interfere with the effects of any medication.

In recent times, wine has been promoted as being helpful for heart health. However, this is a controversial issue. The regular consumption of moderate to high amounts of alcohol may, in fact, cause cardiovascular problems. Even a low to moderate intake of alcohol has some harmful effects, including headaches, disrupted sleep and reduced alertness, coordination and mental activity.

Alcohol consumption at any level tends to raise your blood pressure and can also

raise your blood triglyceride level—both of these factors over time may increase the risk of heart disease. In addition, alcohol can interact with many prescription and over-the-counter medications and can be dangerous if consumed with tranquilisers, sleeping pills, antihistamines and aspirin.

Over time, moderate to heavy alcohol use increases the risk of death from heart attack or stroke, and cancers of the digestive system.

If you choose to drink alcohol, do so only in moderation. You should be particularly careful if you have diabetes, high blood pressure or high cholesterol levels. People taking medication to lower their blood pressure should avoid alcohol or restrict their intake to one or two drinks per day at most. Alcohol should be entirely avoided by children, pregnant or breast-feeding women, and women trying to conceive.

A moderate alcohol intake is defined as two to four standard drinks a day for men and one to two standard drinks a day for women, with some alcohol-free days each week. People over the age of 65 years are advised to consume only one standard drink a day. A standard alcoholic drink contains eight to 10 grams of alcohol.

STEP 6: EAT MODERATE AMOUNTS OF SUGAR AND FOODS CONTAINING ADDED SUGAR

Sugars, like starches, are carbohydrates, which serve as the body's main energy source. Like salt, sugars are found naturally in foods (intrinsic or natural sugars) or can be added to foods (extrinsic or refined sugars).

Taste is only one of the important roles that sugars play in food. They are also used to preserve jams, cereals, cakes, biscuits and drinks, and add texture and colour to baked goods and dairy products. Sugar is also a source of energy for the yeast that causes bread to rise, and helps balance acidity in tomato sauces and salad dressings.

Most of the sugar in our diet comes from processed foods and drinks (biscuits, cakes, breakfast cereals, jams, sauces, cordial, soft drinks), rather than from table sugar that is added to drinks and foods.

There are a number of different sugars that occur naturally in foods:

- glucose
- fructose
- sucrose
- maltose
- lactose.

Once consumed and in the body, there is little difference between most of these sugars in their effects on the body in healthy people. During digestion, all sugars and starches are broken down into glucose and fructose (except lactose, which is broken down into galactose and glucose). Glucose and fructose are small enough to be absorbed through the small intestine into the bloodstream and then delivered to the body's cells for immediate use as energy or storage as glycogen (in muscles or the liver) to be broken down for later fuel needs.

However, in terms of healthy eating, you should be eating most of the sugar in your diet from foods like fruit and dairy products that contain other valuable nutrients, rather than from refined sugar (table or added to processed foods) that doesn't contain any vitamins or minerals.

Sugar: friend or foe?

In the past, refined sugar was thought to be the cause of common western diseases, such as obesity, heart disease and diabetes, and was also thought to be responsible for hyperactivity in children.

Refined sugar was assumed to be responsible for these disorders simply because western societies ate so much of it. Subsequently, a lot of research has been conducted to find out whether these claims are true.

Sugar is one of the most extensively studied nutrients, and we now know that it doesn't cause obesity, heart diease, diabetes, or hyperactivity. Studies in which sugar has been given to children with attention deficit disorder or hyperactivity have consistently shown that sugar does not worsen behaviour or decrease attention span in these children.

However, sugar can contribute to tooth decay when it is consumed in soft drinks, fruit juice, sticky lollies and dried fruit, but not when in the form of fresh fruit like apples.

You may also need to watch your intake of refined sugar if you're trying to lose weight or if you regularly eat a lot of sugary foods that might prevent you consuming all the vitamins and minerals you need.

How much sugar?

For most people, a moderate amount of refined sugar as part of a varied diet won't cause health problems or weight gain. In fact, adding a little sugar to some bland foods, like porridge, may make it easier for you to stick to a healthy low-fat diet. However, table sugar, soft drinks and other sweet 'junk' foods remain at the top of the dietary pyramid and should only be eaten occasionally. Rather than reaching for the table sugar, try to get sweetness from foods containing natural sugars, like fruit or yoghurt, because they also give you other valuable nutrients.

If you want to lose weight, first concentrate on reducing your fat intake and becoming more physically active. Then reduce any unnecessary sugar in your diet (for example, soft drinks, cordials, sugar added to tea or coffee) by using sugar-free products or leaving it out altogether.

Fat contains more than twice the amount of energy per gram (37 kJ or 9 Cal per gram) than sugar does (16 kJ or 4 Cal per gram). So you can cut more calories from your diet by reducing your fat intake than you can by reducing your sugar intake. Limit your intake of foods that are high in both fat and refined sugar, like biscuits, cakes and chocolate. When you feel like a sweet treat, choose a healthy food such as low-fat yoghurt, fruit, fruit loaf or mineral water flavoured with fruit juice.

Honey contains a few more vitamins and minerals than table sugar, but it should be treated in the same way—eaten only in moderation.

Sugar and food labels

The nutrition panel on a label lists the total amount of sugar that is either naturally present or has been added to the food during processing (per average serve and per 100 grams). The ingredient list on the food label will show any sources of sugar that have been added to the food, such as cane sugar, honey, fructose, fruit juice concentrate, treacle, malt/maltose and dextrose. Sugar is not allowed to be added to foods labelled as containing 'no added sugar' or 'without added sugar'. A low-sugar food must contain less than 5 grams of sugar per average serve.

HEALTHIER SOURCES OF SUGAR	LESS DESIRABLE SOURCES OF SUGAR (Sugar with fat or sugar without other nutrients)
EAT IN MODERATION	EAT LESS
Fruit (dried, canned, jellied)	Soft drinks, cordials
Fruit juices	Sweet alcoholic beverages, beer
Yoghurt, custard, flavoured milk	Chocolate, lollies, syrups, topping
Breakfast cereals	Jelly, ice cream, jam, glacé fruit
Fruit and yoghurt snack bars	Biscuits, cakes, pastries, puddings

FAT REDUCTION VERSUS SUGAR REDUCTION

Reducing your fat intake can cut more calories from your diet than reducing your sugar intake because fat contains more calories per gram and is often consumed in larger amounts than sugar. However, if you have a high intake of fat and sugar, particularly sugar-rich drinks, you may need to cut down on both.

HIGH-FAT	LOW-FAT	HIGH-SUGAR	LOW-SUGAR
Regular margarine 2 teaspoons = 250 kJ	Low-fat cottage cheese 35 kJ	Table sugar 2 teaspoons = 134 kJ	Artificial sweetener 17 kJ
Full-cream milk 1 cup = 700 kJ	Skim milk 377 kJ	Regular soft drink 375 ml = 657 kJ	Sugar-free soft drink 8 kJ
Lamb chop, untrimmed, fried 2 small chops = 1340 kJ	Grilled, trimmed of fat 688 kJ	Regular cordial 1 cup = 463 kJ	Sugar-free cordial 15 kJ
Sour cream 2 tablespoons = 605 kJ	Low-fat yoghurt 92 kJ	Regular jam 1 tablespoon = 289 kJ	Sugar-free jam 21 kJ

Sugar substitutes

Many sweet-tasting substances are now used instead of sugar to produce reduced-sugar products for people trying to control their weight or blood sugar levels. These substances are either reduced-calorie sweeteners (isomalt and sugar alcohols) or artificial, non-nutritive sweeteners (for example: aspartame, cyclamate, saccharin, acesulphame-K, sucralose).

Unlike 'nutritive' or sugar-containing sweeteners, such as table sugar, honey and golden syrup, and reduced-energy sweeteners, artificial sweeteners are intensely sweet and don't provide any calories because they are used in very small amounts.

Sugar alcohols (sorbitol, mannitol, xylitol, maltitol, lactitol) and isomalt are mainly used to sweeten 'diet' products because they are not completely absorbed in the intestine and therefore provide fewer calories than normal sugars.

Sugar alcohols occur naturally in plums, apples and other foods, or they can be produced commercially from carbohydrates such as sucrose, glucose and starch. Apart from adding a sweet taste, sugar alcohols also add bulk and texture to foods, provide a cooling effect or aftertaste, and help retain moisture in foods. When consumed in large amounts, sugar alcohols can have a laxative effect, and are only used in small amounts in products, such as sugar-free chewing gum and lollies.

Sucralose is a reduced-calorie sweetener made from a sugar that can't be digested and so passes through the body without being absorbed. It is about 600 times sweeter than sugar, so it's used in tiny amounts, replacing the calories that would normally be provided by sugar, in foods like jams, confectionery and cakes. Sucralose can be used in home cooking to replace sugar in cakes and desserts because it's stable at high temperatures. Foods containing sucralose are safe for consumption in normal-sized portions by healthy adults and children, and people with diabetes.

Sugar substitutes can be purchased from the supermarket in tablet or granule form to be used at home in place of sugar to sweeten drinks and foods. These artificial sweeteners can replace sugar in most foods, resulting in a reduction of the food's calorie content of approximately 67 kilojoules (16 Calories) per teaspoon.

However, sweeteners used as a substitute for table sugar are less popular than the artificial sweeteners that are used in confectionery and soft drinks. Recent surveys indicate that nearly one in three Australian people regularly drink 'diet' soft drinks.

One of the most common sweeteners is aspartame, which is used as an ingredient in breakfast cereals, soft drinks and desserts. Aspartame is about 200 times sweeter than sugar. Tiny amounts of aspartame produce a satisfactory level of sweetness, so calories can be substantially reduced or almost eliminated by using aspartame in place of sugar.

Aspartame also enhances fruit flavours and doesn't increase blood sugar levels or contribute to tooth decay. However, it contains the natural amino acid phenylalanine and, therefore, aspartame-containing products are not suitable for consumption by people with phenylketonuria, who can't metabolise phenylalanine.

Do sugar substitutes have any benefits for weight control or health?

■ Weight control—most people use artificial sweeteners for weight control purposes, but they don't produce weight loss or prevent weight gain in most people who use them. There are three main reasons for this: most people simply add artificially sweetened products to their diet rather than using them instead of sugar-rich versions; some sugar-free products still contain high amounts of fat and calories; and many people wrongly think that by using sugar-free products they have spared enough calories to allow them to eat larger than normal portions of other foods. Sugar substitutes may be helpful for weight control if you use normal portions of them in place of foods you eat regularly in your low-fat diet, such as yoghurts, soft drinks and sugar sprinkled on cereal.

■ Tooth decay—instead of preventing tooth decay by replacing sugar, some artificial sweeteners can erode tooth enamel because they are acidic.

■ Diabetes—people with diabetes don't have to totally avoid sugar because small amounts of sugar won't disturb their blood sugar level. However, if you have diabetes, you still need to eat less sugar than most people consume. If you choose artificially sweetened foods, use a variety of sweeteners and make sure you eat normal-sized portions.

■ Other diseases—there is no strong scientific evidence to suggest that the regular use of artificial sweeteners in normal amounts causes cancer, multiple sclerosis or any other diseases.

STEP 7: CHOOSE LOW-SALT FOODS AND LIMIT YOUR USE OF TABLE SALT

Table salt contains 40 per cent sodium and 60 per cent chloride and its chemical name is sodium chloride. A teaspoon of salt weighs about 5 grams and contains about 2 grams of sodium.

Sodium and chloride are both minerals with important roles in the body. Sodium is needed to regulate the body's fluid balance and blood pressure and for the proper functioning of nerves and muscles. Chloride is also needed to maintain normal fluid balance and blood pressure, and is a component of the stomach's digestive juices.

A certain amount of sodium chloride is needed for the normal functioning of the body, but most people consume far more than they need, mainly because salt is added to so many processed foods. The recommended intake of sodium for adults is between 0.9 and 2.3 milligrams per day or a maximum of one teaspoon of salt per day. However, in western countries many people consume more than 2.5 teaspoons of salt a day.

Health authorities advise against consuming too much salt because a high salt intake increases the risk of developing high blood pressure (hypertension), which in turn increases the risk of early death from heart disease or stroke. Almost half of the population of western countries develop high blood pressure with age. Scientists estimate that if most people  simply cut their salt intake by 30 per cent, there would be a 16 per cent fall in deaths due to heart disease and a 50 per cent reduction in the number of people requiring treatment for hypertension.

In addition to protecting you from hypertension as you get older, there are other good reasons to control your salt intake, even if your blood pressure is normal. An excessive intake of salt will increase your fluid needs and may contribute to osteoporosis and kidney stones. In addition, the drugs that are prescribed to lower blood pressure have adverse side effects, such as nausea, cramps and reduced blood sugar control, so prevention is better than the cure.

The best way to prevent hypertension is to have a healthy diet with a low to moderate salt intake, as well as remaining physically active and maintaining a healthy body weight.

What is high blood pressure?

Blood pressure refers to the amount of force exerted by the blood against artery walls while it is circulating around the body. A blood pressure measurement consists of two numbers. The first number represents systolic blood pressure, which is the pressure in your blood vessels created by the contraction of your heart. The second number represents diastolic blood pressure, which is the pressure in your blood vessels when your heart is relaxing in between heart beats (contractions). Optimal blood pressure is less than 110/70.

You should have your blood pressure

measured when you're feeling calm and relaxed because stress, anxiety or exercise can elevate both systolic and diastolic blood pressure by up to 20 units (mmHg) on both readings. For this reason, a high blood pressure measurement on one occasion should be re-checked on another day, especially before any medication is prescribed.

Risk factors for high blood pressure

- Genetics—if high blood pressure runs in your family, you may have a greater risk
- A high salt intake
- A high alcohol intake (either regularly or infrequent binges)
- Excess body weight
- Older age
- Smoking
- Being inactive
- Regularly feeling stressed

Reducing salt intake

To significantly lower your salt intake you need to choose low-salt foods and stop using the salt shaker at meals and while cooking. You can cut your salt intake significantly if you use reduced-salt versions of foods that you eat regularly, such as bread, spreads, cheese and breakfast cereals.

Gradually switch to using salt-reduced products to give your taste buds time to adjust. After a few weeks you won't miss the salt. Humans are not born with a preference for salt, but we learn to like it by eating salty foods. You can retrain your taste buds to like the natural flavours of healthy foods without the salt.

TIPS FOR REDUCING YOUR SALT INTAKE

Shopping

- Use the nutrient information on food labels to help you compare the sodium or salt content of different foods. Choose 'reduced-salt', 'salt-free' or 'no added salt' products.
- Choose frozen or fresh vegetables rather than canned.
- Choose fish or vegetables canned in water rather than brine.
- Buy unsalted nuts and low-salt snack foods (fresh fruit, yoghurt, rice cakes).

Cooking

- Don't add salt to meals before or after cooking.
- Don't add salt to the water when boiling vegetables, rice or pasta.
- Flavour foods with low-salt seasonings, such as lemon juice and rind, herbs, spices, garlic, chilli, pepper, wine and onions.
- Use unsalted butter or margarine for baking cakes and biscuits.

Eating

- Don't add table salt to your meals.
- Limit your intake of salty take-away foods and snacks. Replace them with healthy salt-free choices.
- Replace processed or smoked meat and fish with freshly roasted meat or poultry slices and fresh fish.
- Limit your intake of gherkins, olives and other pickled vegetables. Replace them with fresh vegetables.
- Squeeze fresh lemon juice on vegetables, fish, rice or pasta for a refreshing taste.
- Limit the amounts of salty sauces, spreads and cheeses you add to foods.
- Add some salt-free garlic-and-herb seasoning to soup to liven up the flavour.
- When eating out, choose freshly made dishes, such as steaks or fish, that aren't swimming in sauce, and ask the chef not to add any salt.

Should I increase my salt intake when I sweat?

Unless recommended by a doctor, there is no need to increase your salt intake in hot weather or when exercising. The body itself carefully adjusts the salt content of sweat according to its own salt balance. Increasing your salt intake under these conditions can, in fact, cause dehydration and cramps. Most people eat far more salt than they need, so it's better to concentrate on drinking more water when you're hot and sweaty.

Only a small number of endurance athletes and people with certain medical conditions that cause excessive sweating or diarrhoea may need to increase their salt intake.

Salt and food labels

Eating less salt is easier than you think. Supermarket shelves contain reduced-salt varieties of many popular foods. You can't always tell if a food is high in salt by its flavour because some sweet-tasting foods contain lots of salt.

Use the nutrient information on food labels to help you choose lower-salt varieties. If a product's salt content has been reduced, one of the following terms will appear on the label:
■ reduced-salt contains less than 75 per cent of the salt in the regular version
■ low-salt contains less than 120 milligrams of sodium per 100 grams of food
■ no added salt or unsalted means no salt has been added during processing, but this doesn't mean that the product is sodium-free
■ reduced-sodium contains at least 25 per cent less sodium than the regular version, but it may still be high in sodium, so use sparingly
■ low-sodium contains 120 milligrams or less of sodium per 100 grams of food
■ sodium-free contains 5 milligrams or less of sodium per serve.

STEP 8: DRINK PLENTY OF WATER THROUGHOUT THE DAY

Water is the second most essential compound for our survival, with oxygen being the first. An average healthy adult can survive for about eight weeks without food, but can only live for a few days without water.

Water accounts for 50 to 70 per cent of our body weight, with the percentage being greater in infants than adults. A loss of as little as 10 per cent of body water due to excessive vomiting or diarrhoea is a serious health risk in adults, and could be fatal in a young child.

There's so much water in your body because it plays a vital role in all bodily processes—it's involved in metabolic reactions and also provides the medium in which these reactions occur.

Water is needed for the digestion and absorption of food, maintaining a normal temperature in the body, and for the lubrication and protection of body joints. As a major component of blood, water helps deliver nutrients to body cells and transports waste to the kidneys for excretion. Water also helps prevent urinary tract infections by flushing toxins out of the body.

Water also contains small amounts of essential minerals, such as sodium, potassium, calcium, copper and magnesium, depending on the mineral content of the rock or soil from where it has come. Hard water contains higher levels of these minerals than soft water.

How much water?

The body can't store water so a regular intake of liquid throughout the day is essential to replace the fluid that's constantly being lost from your body.

In normal conditions, adults need about 2 to 3 litres of water a day (8 to 12 glasses of water), but much more fluid is needed when the body's losses are greater, such as in hot, dry weather, at high altitudes, and during strenuous physical activity.

Sweating is the body's way of getting rid of extra heat, and sweating rates increase as the environment gets drier or when the body's temperature rises (due to exercise or illness). If you don't drink enough fluid to replace your sweat losses, you will become dehydrated.

A loss of only 2 per cent of body weight as water (mild dehydration—1.4 kg for a 70 kg person) will lower your blood volume and reduce your capacity to perform physical and mental tasks, even before you feel badly affected. It's quite easy to lose a litre or more of fluid during an hour or two of hard physical activity.

Unfortunately, thirst isn't a good indication of your body's fluid needs, because you're already slightly dehydrated by the time you feel thirsty. Drinking plenty of water throughout the day is the best way to meet your daily fluid needs and avoid dehydration. You'll also obtain some fluid from the foods and other drinks you consume, such as milk, fruits, vegetables, meats, porridge and bread.

Infants and children need more fluid than adults and therefore have a greater risk of dehydration. Children should take a drink bottle or two to school or sport, and should be encouraged to drink water throughout the day. If they don't like plain water, flavour it with a little juice to encourage drinking.

Factors that increase fluid loss or fluid needs
- Hot, dry temperatures
- Fever, diarrhoea and vomiting
- Exercise and physical labour
- Low-calorie and high-protein diets
- High salt or fibre intake
- Alcohol consumption
- Caffeine consumption
- Pregnancy and breast-feeding

Is bottled water better than tap water?
Bottled water comes in different forms, including mineral, spring and distilled tap water. Although bottled waters are often marketed as being fresh and pure, they may not necessarily be any safer or healthier than tap water.

In several instances, bottled water has been found to contain higher than recommended levels of bromate. Too much bromate can cause a number of health problems, including nausea, diarrhoea, kidney and nerve problems.

If you are concerned about the purity of your tap water, you can use a simple activated charcoal water filter that will remove chlorine and other bad-tasting substances from the water. These simple filters also keep more minerals in the water than complicated filter units, distillation units or water softeners (ion exchange units), which remove contaminants as well as calcium and magnesium and replace them with sodium.

DID YOU KNOW?
The numerous health claims for water ionisers have not yet been proven. Water ionisers are expensive machines claimed to produce ionised water that will give you more oxygen, control the body's acid (pH) balance and protect you from disease. However, these machines cause the electrolysis of water, which produces hydrogen and oxygen atoms, not ions. If you don't want to drink plain tap water, buy a simple activated charcoal filter or boil tap water.

STEP 9: EAT CALCIUM-RICH FOODS ON A REGULAR BASIS

Calcium is needed to maintain the strength of your bones and teeth, is required for normal blood pressure and blood clotting, and for the proper functioning of nerves and muscles. Most of the calcium in your body is found in your skeleton, where it maintains bone strength and acts as a reservoir from which calcium can be drawn when it is needed by other parts of the body.

Bone is a living tissue that is constantly changing. It has a web-like structure, which makes it a strong but light shock-absorbing material. Most of your bone mass is formed during childhood, when the skeleton rapidly increases in thickness and strength.

Our bones generally stop growing in length when we are between 16 and 18 years of age, but continue to grow in strength up until our early thirties. Between the ages of 16 and 30, depending on your genes and dietary habits, your bones will have reached their maximum strength and thickness (peak bone mass). Between the ages of 35 and 45, bone breakdown begins to exceed bone

formation as part of the natural ageing process, but an adequate calcium intake can reduce this rate of bone loss.

If enough bone is lost over time, the skeleton becomes weaker and fractures more easily, resulting in osteoporosis. Even though they may have been losing bone mass for years, many people don't realise they have osteoporosis until they have experienced the first of possibly many fractures.

Many children and adults regularly don't eat the recommended amount of calcium each day and are at risk of developing osteoporosis. Women have a greater risk than men because they generally have a smaller bone mass and have an accelerated rate of bone loss for about five years after menopause. Osteoporosis can also occur in younger people, particularly in young women who have lost a lot of weight and not had their menstrual periods for a while. As with postmenopausal women, the lower level of oestrogen in their body prevents calcium from being retained in their bones.

Reducing the risk of osteoporosis

- Regularly eat calcium-rich foods.
- Get adequate exposure to sunlight (several hours a week). Your body needs vitamin D to absorb calcium.
- Do at least 30 minutes of physical activity each day. Weight-bearing exercise (such as walking, weight training, tennis, low-impact aerobics) helps keep your bones strong.
- Limit your intake of alcohol to one to two standard drinks a day, with alcohol-free days each week.
- Don't smoke.
- Limit your intake of salt and caffeine.
- Don't consume excess protein.
- Women shouldn't lose so much weight that their menstrual periods stop.

Sources of calcium

Dairy products, such as milk, cheese and yoghurt, are the richest sources of dietary calcium, and they also provide the other essential nutrients for healthy bones (protein, magnesium and phosphorous). Just three serves of dairy products a day supplies all the calcium most healthy people need (one serve equals 250 ml of milk; 200 g of yoghurt; or 35 g of hard cheese). There are dairy products to suit everyone's tastes, and low-fat varieties for those trying to reduce their fat and cholesterol intake.

Other sources of calcium include calcium-enriched soy milk and tofu, canned salmon or sardines eaten with their bones, canned crab meat, some green vegetables (broccoli and Chinese cabbage), calcium-enriched drinking powders, dried figs, spinach, sweet potatoes and grains. However, more of the calcium in dairy foods is absorbed by the body than the calcium in cereals and vegetables because absorption is impaired by certain compounds in plant foods (tannins, fibre and oxalates).

Calcium and lactose intolerance

If you have lactose intolerance and can't drink large amounts of cow's milk, try to consume smaller amounts of dairy products throughout the day. Full-cream milk will be easier for you to digest than skim milk. Lactose-reduced milks are also available. Most cheeses don't contain much lactose and you can reduce the amount of lactose in yoghurt by storing it in the fridge for a while.

If you choose to avoid dairy products, you will need to consume larger amounts of the other calcium-containing foods listed above. Include calcium in your main meals and snacks by adding some dried figs or raw almonds to breakfast cereals, desserts and yoghurt, or some cheese, salmon or crab meat to salads.

Calcium supplements

If you can't consume enough calcium on a regular basis, your doctor may recommend a calcium supplement, particularly if you have a higher risk of bone loss. You should look for a calcium-only supplement rather than a multivitamin and mineral tablet, which typically contain small amounts of calcium. Avoid calcium supplements that also contain iron and magnesium—these minerals actually reduce the amount of calcium that your body will absorb. While taking supplements, make sure that you don't take high-dose calcium supplements (more than 800 mg a day) or calcium supplements containing vitamin D on a regular basis (to avoid vitamin D toxicity and imbalances in other minerals).

Increasing calcium intake

■ Read the ingredient list and nutrition information on food labels to compare the calcium content of different products, and choose calcium-enriched breakfast cereals, drinking powders and dairy products.

■ Eat yoghurt instead of ice cream for snacks or dessert—you'll get more calcium as well as less fat and calories.

■ For breakfast, add calcium-enriched low-fat milk and drinking powder to your cereal instead of full-cream milk and sugar.

■ Use low-fat cheese on bread instead of butter and drink a calcium-enriched low-fat milk instead of full-fat milk.

STEP 10: MAKE IRON-RICH FOODS A REGULAR PART OF YOUR DIET

Iron is needed for a healthy immune system, for producing energy from the nutrients you eat, for metabolising drugs and protecting your cells from damage caused by free radicals. Iron is also essential for transporting oxygen around the body, because it is a component of the body's two main oxygen-carrying proteins: haemoglobin and myoglobin.

Haemoglobin is the protein in red blood cells that takes oxygen from the lungs to the body's cells, and then takes carbon dioxide back to the lungs to be exhaled from the body.

Myoglobin is a protein found in muscles. It stores oxygen until needed by the muscles to contract and move.

Iron deficiency

In western countries, people's diets are more likely to be deficient in iron, zinc, calcium or dietary fibre than any other nutrients. Dietary surveys indicate that many people don't eat iron-rich foods on a regular basis, and sales of red meat have fallen over the last three decades. In fact, iron deficiency is the most common nutrient deficiency in the world.

Symptoms of iron deficiency include feeling constantly tired and lethargic, depression, a lack of concentration, and greater difficulty in performing and recovering from exercise. However,

these symptoms could be due to other factors, such as a virus, lack of sleep or lack of carbohydrate. A doctor needs to take a blood test to confirm iron deficiency. Don't self-diagnose iron deficiency because problems can arise from the use of iron supplements when you're not actually deficient.

Although iron deficiency can lead to the serious condition of anaemia, not everybody with iron deficiency is actually anaemic. Anaemia only occurs when the body's iron stores are depleted, which may take several years, because the body tries to compensate for falling iron stores by absorbing more of the iron you eat. As the body's iron stores continue to fall, less haemoglobin is made by the body and the red blood cells that are formed are pale and small and not able to carry as much oxygen.

At this stage, symptoms include fatigue, weakness, headaches, decreased ability to perform physical or mental work, an increased risk of illness and infection, and impaired mental development in infants and young children.

Who's at risk of iron deficiency?

■ Teenage girls and women of reproductive age lose more iron from their bodies than men due to menstruation, and also tend to eat less iron. About one-third of these women consume less than 70 per cent of the recommended daily intake of iron.

■ Pregnant women need much more iron for the growth and development of their baby as well as to increase their own blood supply.

■ Infants and children up to six years old have higher iron needs due to their rapid growth rates. Iron stores at birth are sufficient to meet their needs for the first four to six months, but after this time infants need iron-fortified formula or cereals. Toddlers who are fussy eaters may not consume enough iron.

■ Vegetarians consume iron in plant foods, but the body does not absorb this as efficiently as the iron found in meat.

■ Teenage boys are growing rapidly and may not eat enough iron.

■ Athletes have high iron needs for growing muscle and energy production, and may also be losing iron through sweat. They may have low iron intake due to poor dietary habits, little time to eat or drastic weight loss practices.

Sources of iron

Iron is found in both plant and animal foods, but occurs in two different chemical forms—haem iron and non-haem iron. Most of the iron in animal products is haem iron, which is the same kind of iron found in haemoglobin and myoglobin, and our bodies absorb this more efficiently than non-haem iron.

Good sources of haem iron include meat, poultry, fish and seafood. Red meat, oysters and mussels have particularly high levels of this type of iron.

Non-haem iron is found in eggs, legumes, fortified breakfast cereals and drinking powders, wholegrain bread, leafy green vegetables, nuts and seeds.

It's possible to increase the absorption of non-haem iron by combining it with certain foods. For example, the muscle proteins in meat, poultry and fish increase the absorption of non-haem iron by up to three times. So you can absorb more of the non-haem iron in a plant food, such as rice or bread, by eating it with some meat, chicken or fish. Vitamin C also increases the absorption of non-haem iron up to

three times if eaten in the same meal. So add some strawberries or kiwi fruit to your iron-enriched breakfast cereal, have a glass of orange juice with your sandwich or add lots of capsicum and spinach to your stir-fries.

On the other hand, some substances can reduce the absorption of non-haem iron, such as tannin in tea, phytates in grains and oxalates in spinach, and compounds in soy foods. For example, the tannin in one large cup of black tea reduces non-haem iron absorption by around 50 per cent. The presence of these compounds means that only a small amount of iron in the diet is actually absorbed. This means that you need to be extra careful about eating plenty of iron if you are vegetarian or have higher iron needs. Drink less strong tea or coffee in between meals and look for iron-enriched products in your supermarket, including breakfast cereals, pasta, breads and drinking powders.

Some soy milks may be fortified with iron, but this iron is not well absorbed. However, the iron in processed soy foods, such as miso, tempeh and tofu, tends to be better absorbed.

to eat by using mince or thin strips of meat. Another common misconception is that meat stays in your stomach a long time and can't be broken down, but this is also not true. Your stomach is full of digestive acids, which efficiently break down all food matter, except some fibres.

Including lean meat in your diet is one of the easiest ways to consume all of the iron, zinc, vitamin B12, essential fatty acids and protein you need.

Red meat and iron

During the last three decades, the consumption of red meat in western countries has fallen because people have less time to cook and some people think meat is unhealthy or fattening. However, this isn't the case. There are now many lean cuts of meats available, which can be cooked quickly, and meat is a filling and nutritious food—a factor that is particularly beneficial if you're trying to control your weight. Some people think that meat is heavy or fattening because they eat very large portions, but all you really need is 100 to 150 grams of meat, three to four times a week (two to three slices of roast meat, 1/2 cup of cooked meat strips or mince, or 2 lean lamb chops).

Many people these days are also not used to eating filling foods. They have grown up eating white bread, fruit juice, and other foods that don't need much chewing. You can make meat less difficult

A word of caution

Not everyone needs extra iron. Some people have a genetic disorder called haemochromatosis, which means they have an excessively high iron level in their body. It is the most common genetic disorder in Caucasians living in North America, Europe and Australasia, affecting approximately one in 300 people. The symptoms experienced by these people are related to the amount of iron in their body. Initially they may experience lethargy and fatigue, but rising iron levels can lead to heart and liver damage, diabetes and some types of cancer. Early diagnosis and regular treatment can reduce this risk.

Treatment of haemochromatosis involves regularly donating blood and avoiding a high-iron diet and combinations of foods that enhance iron absorption. If you have a family history of this disorder, see your doctor, who can test whether you or your children are also at risk.

THE IRON CONTENT OF COMMON PROTEIN-RICH FOODS

FOOD (SERVE SIZE)	FAT (GRAMS)	IRON (MILLIGRAMS)	ENERGY (KJ)
Lean beef (100 g)	1.8	2.4	450
Lean lamb (100 g)	4.2	2.3	501
Eggs (2 large = 100 g)	10.9	1.8*	632
Baked beans (100 g)	0.5	1.6*	285
Canned red salmon (100 g)	12.0	1.2	815
Lean pork (100 g)	1.7	1.0	438
Skinless chicken (100 g)	3.3	1.0	466
Tofu (100 g)	0.4	0.4*	107
Cheddar cheese (100 g)	33.8	0.0	1690

*Contain non-haem iron, so not all of this iron will be absorbed.
Adapted from: The Role of Red Meat in Healthy Australian Diets, Meat and Livestock, Australia, 2001

TIPS TO HELP BOOST YOUR IRON INTAKE

- Eat meals containing lean red meat or liver three to four times a week. A small serve (100 to 150 grams) is enough.
- Read the ingredient list and nutrient panel on food labels to help you identify foods with added iron (such as pasta, breakfast cereals, breads and drinking powders). Consume these in place of non-enriched versions.
- Add some vitamin C or haem iron such as meat, poultry, fish or seafood to foods containing non-haem iron, such as legumes, eggs, breakfast cereals, rice, pasta, bread or spinach. For example, add tomatoes and capsicum to a spinach omelette, and sprinkle some dried apricots and fresh fruit on your iron-enriched breakfast cereal and serve with a glass of guava or orange juice. See the lists below to help you mix and match foods containing iron with those containing vitamin C.
- If you are a vegetarian, make sure you eat some good sources of non-haem iron at main meals, such as eggs, legumes, spinach, iron-fortified pasta or breakfast cereals.
- Avoid strongly brewed tea, especially with your meals. Drink weak tea in between meals.
- Don't add unprocessed wheat bran to your meals. Look for bran-rich breakfast cereals with added iron.

COMBINING IRON WITH VITAMIN C

HAEM-IRON	NON-HAEM IRON	VITAMIN C
Lean beef	Nuts, sesame seeds	Orange juice
Lean lamb	Legumes	Guava juice
Lean pork	Muesli	Drinks with added vitamin C
Skinless chicken or turkey	Wholemeal or grain bread	Fresh citrus fruit
(darker meat)	Iron-enriched breakfast cereals	Pawpaw, mangoes
Liver, liverwurst	Iron-enriched pasta	Kiwi fruit
Heart	Dried fruit	Fresh berries
Fish	Spinach	Pineapple
Oysters	Eggs	Capsicum, spinach
Mussels	Cocoa powder	Parsley, tomatoes
Scallops	Iron-enriched drinking powders	Broccoli, cauliflower
Canned crab	Curry powder	Cabbage, Asian greens Sprouts

HEALTHY EATING FOR VEGETARIANS

Vegetarianism has gained popularity over the last 20 years, but many people who claim to be vegetarian still eat fish or chicken and just avoid red meat. This isn't strictly vegetarianism. Although many people go through vegetarian phases or eat meat infrequently, less than five per cent of the population follows a strict vegetarian diet for any extended period of time.

A balanced vegetarian diet has a number of health benefits, such as reduced blood cholesterol levels, help in weight control and a lower risk of heart disease and diabetes, but this also reflects other healthy lifestyle factors, such as lower alcohol intake and less smoking.

Vegetarian diets, however, aren't healthy if they don't provide you with the balance of nutrients that your body needs. It takes a conscious effort to balance a vegetarian diet because the nutrients provided by meat and any other foods that are avoided have to be obtained from other sources. In particular, vitamin B12, iron, zinc and calcium can be lacking in vegetarian diets.

The more foods you eliminate from your diet, the harder you have to work to create a balance. You can't have a balanced vegetarian diet simply by taking meat off your plate and leaving everything else the same. The principles of healthy vegetarian eating are the same as those for the general population— meals should be based on grains, fruits, vegetables and legumes, with moderate amounts of fat and protein. Because it's more difficult to absorb minerals from plant foods, vegetarians need to eat more minerals per mouthful than non-vegetarians just to get enough.

COMMON TYPES OF TRUE VEGETARIAN DIETS
- Ovo-lacto vegetarians eat plant foods, eggs and dairy products.
- Lacto vegetarians eat plant foods and dairy products.
- Vegans eat only plant foods and avoid all animal products.

HOW CAN VEGETARIANS EAT ENOUGH GOOD-QUALITY PROTEIN?
Vegetarians who eat eggs and dairy products usually consume enough protein, and can also obtain the correct balance of essential amino acids by consuming a variety of grain products and legumes.

Vegetable proteins are lacking in one or more essential amino acids, but by combining different protein-containing foods in meals, it's possible to get all the amino acids you need. Vegetarians, particularly vegans, should try to eat a wide variety of different protein-containing foods each day. It's easy to make quick and nutritious meals using fast-cooking varieties of rice, pasta and couscous, canned legumes, nuts and seeds, and meat substitutes (textured vegetable protein).

VITAMIN B12
Vitamin B12 is only found in animal products. Spirulina and fermented soy products (miso and tempeh) are claimed to be good sources of B12, but almost none of it is absorbed by the body. Vegetarians who don't eat eggs or dairy products may have a low intake, and should consume B12-enriched soy milk and check with their doctor to see if they need a B12 supplement. Pregnant vegan women, in particular, who intend to breast-feed, should ask their doctor to check their vitamin B12 status.

ZINC

Zinc is essential for proper growth and a healthy immune system. Like iron, zinc in animal foods occurs in larger amounts and is better absorbed than the zinc in plant foods. Vegetarian sources of zinc include grainy breads, wholegrain breakfast cereals, legumes and nuts, but the absorption of zinc from these foods can be reduced if consumed with bran or soy products.

CALCIUM

Vegetarians should think about including dairy products in their diet, particularly from childhood until their early thirties, when they are still laying down calcium in the bones. Vegetarians who eliminate dairy products may not consume or absorb enough calcium, which could increase their risk of developing osteoporosis.

Non-dairy sources of calcium include calcium-enriched soy milk and tofu, tahini, almonds, brazil nuts, hazelnuts, dried figs, and dark-green leafy vegetables, but the calcium in these foods is not absorbed as well as the calcium in dairy foods.

If you are opposed to eating animal products for ethical reasons, you may feel strongly against eating dairy products. However, if you are eating a vegetarian diet for health reasons, it's a good idea to include dairy products because they are the best dietary source of calcium.

IRON

Iron deficiency due to a low iron intake or poor iron absorption is a common problem for vegetarians, particularly in females and athletes. As well as causing exhaustion and depression, iron deficiency can reduce mental performance and can lead to impaired mental development in children. Because the iron in plant foods is not as well absorbed as the iron in meat, vegetarians need to eat even more iron in order to absorb enough to meet their needs. Vegetarian sources of iron include iron-enriched breakfast cereals and drinking powders, dark-green leafy vegetables (spinach, silverbeet, Chinese broccoli and cabbage), legumes, some soy-based meat alternatives (textured vegetable protein, soy steaks), dried fruit, seeds and nuts. You can improve the absorption of this iron by consuming these foods with a source of vitamin C, such as orange juice, kiwi fruit or capsicum.

Your doctor can perform a blood test to check whether your iron stores are low and you need an iron supplement. Don't self-diagnose an iron deficiency, as regular use of iron supplements can interfere with the absorption of other minerals and cause bowel problems.

Pregnancy, from conception to birth, usually lasts 40 weeks, during which time a single cell has to grow and develop into a fully formed baby. For normal development, the baby needs oxygen and nutrients from the mother in the right amounts at the right time.

HEALTHY BEGINNINGS

To help produce a healthy baby, a woman should be in good nutritional health even before conception because deficiencies of certain nutrients or exposure to toxins at the time of conception and during the early stages of pregnancy can cause birth defects. If you are trying to fall pregnant, it's important that you eat a healthy, balanced diet. Cut down on caffeine and avoid alcohol so that it's not a strain when you fall pregnant. Before conception, you need to take care when you drink alcohol because alcohol in the mother's bloodstream can cause defects or death in a foetus of any age.

You may also need to consult a doctor and dietitian to find out whether you're eating enough folate. An adequate folate intake is crucial during the early stages of pregnancy to prevent neural tube defects, such as spina bifida, which are the most common birth defects causing death and disabilities in infants.

You can reduce the risk of neural tube defects by consuming a minimum of 400 micrograms of folate a day from at least one month before conception until three months after conception. Try to consume a variety of folate-rich foods each day, and see your doctor for advice about taking a folate supplement. Good sources of folate include leafy green vegetables, orange juice, liver, asparagus, legumes, yeast extract spreads and fortified breakfast cereals.

DURING PREGNANCY

During pregnancy, a woman needs to ensure that her diet provides the energy and nutrients she needs to maintain her health and fuel the physiological changes occurring in her own body, as well as providing the nutrients needed by the rapidly developing baby.

Adequate weight gain during pregnancy is necessary for the health of the mother and baby. Although pregnant women need to think of the health of two people when they're eating, they don't need to increase their calorie intake to feed two adults.

The number of calories needed during pregnancy is not much higher than normal (an extra 850 to 1100 kJ per day), but nutrient needs definitely increase, meaning that pregnant women need to take in more nutrients per mouthful. A healthy, balanced diet should supply you with all the energy and nutrients you need.

However, your doctor may recommend an iron-folate supplement if you have low body stores of these nutrients or can't eat much food due to morning sickness or heartburn. If your doctor recommends a general multivitamin and mineral supplement, make sure it doesn't contain greater than RDI amounts and don't take more than recommended. You could also see a dietitian, who will show you how to make your diet more nutritious and give you advice on suitable supplements.

Regularly eating iron-rich foods, like lean red meat, is important during pregnancy and while breast-feeding, when the body's need for iron is much greater than normal. Pregnant and breast-feeding mothers are also recommended to eat fish, like salmon, tuna, mackerel or herrings, two to three times a week to increase their intake of essential fatty acids, needed for the healthy development of the infant's eyes and brain. To avoid constipation, make sure you eat lots of fresh fruit and vegetables and wholegrain cereal products, and drink lots of water throughout the day. Try to eat vegetables that are raw or lightly cooked, so you get more nutrients. Most pregnant women can safely consume a moderate amount of caffeine (up to three cups a day), but some herbal teas should be strictly avoided (comfrey, raspberry leaf, sage, pennyroyal, senna and yarrow) because they may increase the risk of miscarriage.

BREAST-FEEDING

A mother's need for energy and many nutrients, including protein, calcium, vitamin A, folate and other B group vitamins, is even greater while breast-feeding than during pregnancy. She now has to make milk containing all of the nutrients needed for the infant, who is growing faster than when he or she was in the womb. During the first six months of breast-feeding, approximately 600 to

900 ml of milk is produced daily, which requires 2350 to 3530 kJ to produce.

The need for calcium can be met by increasing your intake of dairy products or calcium-enriched alternatives from two to three serves a day. Extra servings of vegetables, grain products and meat can help you get all the nutrients you need.

Due to the energy needed for milk production, most breast-feeding women naturally lose about 0.5 to 1 kilogram of weight per month during the first six months of breast-feeding. Some women will find that they feel much hungrier when breast-feeding, but this is the body's way of making sure you consume more energy.

Dieting to lose weight is not recommended while breast-feeding because you need more nutrients than normal. This is difficult to achieve if you're restricting your food intake.

In order to avoid dehydration and ensure normal milk production, you may need to drink more than one litre of fluid a day. Take a water bottle with you if you go out and have an extra glass of water, milk or juice with meals and after you feed your baby. Some substances consumed by the mother can be secreted into breast milk, including caffeine, alcohol and medications. A moderate intake of caffeine should be fine unless it upsets the baby, but alcohol should be strictly avoided.

APPROXIMATE NUMBER OF DAILY SERVINGS FROM THE FIVE MAIN FOOD GROUPS (INDIVIDUAL NEEDS MAY DIFFER)

FOOD GROUP	NON-PREGNANT WOMEN (DAILY ENERGY NEEDS 5000 KJ)	PREGNANT WOMEN (6000 KJ)	BREAST-FEEDING WOMEN (8000 KJ)
Cereal foods	4	4	6
Vegetables, legumes	5	5	7–8
Fruit	2	4	5
Dairy products	2	2	2–3
Meat and alternatives	1	1.5	2

Source: The Australian Guide to Healthy Eating, Commonwealth Department of Health and Family Services, Australia, 1998

HEALTHY EATING FOR BABIES AND TODDLERS

It is currently recommended that breast milk (or an appropriate formula) is the only food given to an infant for the first four to six months of life. Breast milk can then supplement solid foods up until the age of two.

THE FIRST STEPS

Solid and semi-solid foods should be introduced gradually between four and six months of age when the infant's feeding abilities, kidneys and gastrointestinal tract are mature enough to tolerate food. Food should never be forced into an infant, to prevent choking, and breast milk or formula should remain the most important part of the baby's diet. When introducing solids, they should be offered after a feed or between feeds. At this stage, solid foods are 'extras' for the baby, while milk is the staple food, providing most of the baby's energy and nutrients.

Iron-fortified infant rice cereal is the most commonly recommended food to start feeding your baby, because it can be mixed with breast milk or formula, is easily digested and rarely causes allergic reactions. Wheat should be avoided at this stage because this grain has the greatest potential to cause an allergic reaction.

Other popular foods to begin introducing to your baby include vegetables, such as mashed pumpkin, carrot or potato, and fruit, such as mashed banana, apple or pear.

Some people believe that vegetables should be given first so that the baby doesn't develop a preference for sweet foods. You should not add any sugar or salt to foods that you give your baby.

To check whether an allergic reaction occurs, it's important to introduce only one food at a time to your baby. Stick with this food for two to three days and, if there has been no reaction, it should be safe to introduce another new food. Start with one to two teaspoons of solids and then increase the quantity to two to three tablespoons. Gradually build up to three meals a day at your baby's own pace.

SEVEN TO NINE MONTHS

Once your baby is seven to nine months old and is eating rice cereal and several varieties of fruit and vegetables, foods with a thicker texture can be offered if the baby's teeth have started appearing.

Suitable foods include:

- less blended or small pieces of meat, chicken, fish without bones
- egg yolk (avoid egg white until nine to 12 months)
- baked beans
- yoghurt
- custard
- grated cheese on vegetables
- rolled oats
- baby muesli
- pasta
- rice.

Once the baby is eating a range of food, try to include foods from different groups at each meal. However, products containing wheat should be the last to be introduced to the infant because of the potential for wheat to trigger an allergy.

If you have a family history of allergies, delay the introduction of cow's milk, eggs, peanuts and any foods containing these ingredients, and ask your doctor for advice first.

Always be present and attentive when your baby is eating to check that he or she can chew and swallow the food without choking. Meats that are cooked by long slow heat until they are very soft, such as lamb, veal shanks or gravy beef, are good for infants. Tender pieces of lamb, beef, veal or chicken, and flaked boneless fish are also very nutritious choices.

A regular intake of iron-rich foods is important for infants, who need more iron than 10-year-old children. Combine iron-rich foods with those containing vitamin C, such as kiwi fruit, oranges, rockmelon, tomatoes, broccoli and capsicum, to enhance the absorption of iron.

OLDER BABIES

As babies develop they learn to use their hands and will want to start feeding themselves. These messy, learning-to-feed sessions can be great fun for the baby, and are vital for normal development. Babies who are always spoon-fed on soft foods at this age may not want to learn to chew foods as they get older.

By the age of eight to nine months, a baby can hold a bottle and self-feed finger foods, such as rusks, cheese sticks, pieces of soft fruit and strips of cooked meat or vegetables. Nuts, whole peas, raw or undercooked pieces of fruit or vegetables (such as apple and carrot) should not be given to babies as they can cause choking.

At this relatively late stage, it is still essential to watch your baby eating. By 10 months, most babies can drink from a cup, so water and diluted fruit juices can be offered. Don't give babies juice in a bottle on a regular basis because it can damage their teeth. Large amounts or frequent drinks of undiluted apple and pear juice should also be avoided because they can cause diarrhoea.

Honey should not be offered to children under the age of one year because it can contain bacterial spores that may cause food poisoning.

Although breast milk or formula should still be the main milk consumed until the baby is at least one year old, cow's milk can be used in the preparation of solids before this time. For babies less than nine months old, cow's milk should always be brought to the boil and cooled before use.

APPROXIMATE NUMBER OF SERVES EACH DAY AND PORTION SIZES OF SUITABLE FOODS FOR INFANTS

FOOD	SERVING SIZE	4–6 MONTHS	SERVINGS PER DAY 6–8 MONTHS	9–12 MONTHS
Breast milk or formula*	230 ml	4	4	4
Infant cereal	2 tablespoons	0–2	4	4
Vegetables	2–3 tablespoons	0	2	3
Fruits	2 tablespoons	0	2	4
Fruit juice	115 ml	0	0	1
Meats or egg yolk	1 tablespoon	0	2–4 (puréed)	4–6 (chopped)
Finger foods**		0	1	4

*Includes milk added to cereal
**Except foods that could cause choking (large pieces of meat, raw fruits and vegetables, peas, nuts)

Source: Nutrition and Applied Science (3rd Edition), LA Smolin and MB Grosvenor, Saunders College Publishing, Orlando, USA, 2000

WHAT IS A FOOD ALLERGY?

Although many people claim to suffer from allergies to foods or food ingredients, only a very small number of people actually have a true food allergy. A true food allergy happens when the body's immune system overreacts to an otherwise harmless compound in a food or food ingredient, recognising it instead as a foreign substance, like a virus, that needs to be attacked with antibodies.

The compound in the food that stimulates the immune system of allergic people is called an allergen. A single food can contain several allergens, most of  which are proteins. A few food-allergic individuals are so sensitive that just touching or even smelling the offending food can cause an allergic reaction. Others must actually eat the food before they get an allergic reaction. Symptoms of food allergies include sneezing, a runny nose, asthma, rashes, hives, eczema, vomiting, diarrhoea, and a rapid heart rate. Symptoms can appear immediately or within 24 hours, and can be mild or severe, depending on how much of the allergen was consumed and the individual's sensitivity.

Some people suffer from an extreme reaction where their throat swells up so much that they have trouble breathing. This type of reaction to a food is rare, but life threatening.

Food allergies are most common in people with gastrointestinal disease and in infants. Once an infant's intestinal tract is fully developed, food allergies are less likely to occur. Many children who develop food allergies before three years of age will outgrow them, except for an allergy to peanuts. It's estimated that 5 per cent of infants and 1.5 per cent of young children suffer from a true food allergy, compared to 1 per cent of adults. Food allergies that appear after the age of three years are more likely to be a problem for life.

Although allergic reactions can occur to virtually any food, most reactions are caused by a small number of foods: eggs, cow's milk, nuts, soya beans, wheat, fish and seafood.

WHAT IS A FOOD INTOLERANCE?

Food intolerance (or food sensitivity) is the term used for adverse reactions to foods that are not caused by antibodies produced by the immune system. A food intolerance can be caused by chemicals or toxins that occur naturally in foods, or by substances added to foods during processing and preparation. Usually the more of the offending chemical that is eaten, the worse the symptoms.

Foods that are commonly thought to cause food intolerances include coffee, tea, red wine, beer, cocoa, chocolate, cow's milk, cheese, tomatoes, citrus fruit, processed meats, yeast and wheat. Unless it's obvious which foods cause your symptoms, you may need to use an elimination diet under the supervision of a doctor or dietitian to identify them.

FOOD ALLERGIES VERSUS FOOD INTOLERANCES

Excessive reactions to particular components in foods can be divided into two classes: food allergies and food intolerances.

Food allergies

■ Food allergies are uncommon in adults, more common in children under five years of age and usually disappear with age.

■ Reactions are more immediate and can be mild (rash, itchiness, watery eyes), severe or life threatening (throat closes and swells, breathing difficulties).

■ Skin-prick tests can show which allergens you are sensitive to and blood tests can confirm the production of a specific antibody to the allergen.

Food intolerances

■ Symptoms may develop over hours or even after days and are usually more vague (bloating, headache, flatulence, diarrhoea).

■ Repeated exposure to the culprit chemical in foods may be necessary to reach a threshold level of the compound in the blood before a reaction occurs.

LACTOSE INTOLERANCE

People with lactose intolerance are unable to digest significant amounts of lactose, the main sugar in milk, because they don't produce enough of the enzyme lactase.

Lactase is normally produced in the gut of all humans at birth, so they can digest breast milk. Lactase levels tend to decrease with age and in many people decline so much that lactose can't be completely digested. In these people, any lactose they consume in dairy products will pass through the stomach into the large intestine, where it will be metabolised by bacteria. The undigested lactose, together with acids and gas produced by the bacteria, can result in flatulence, a bloated abdomen, cramping and diarrhoea.

The number of people with lactose intolerance varies in different ethnic groups, ranging from less than 5 per cent in Caucasians to almost 100 per cent of adults in some Asian and African societies that don't consume dairy products. People can also become lactose intolerant after an intestinal infection and other illnesses.

Because dairy products are a rich source of calcium, people with lactose intolerance must consume other sources of calcium to meet their needs. Some foods contain calcium with little or no lactose, such as sardines and salmon (eaten with bones), tofu processed in calcium salts, calcium-enriched soy milk and soy yoghurt, lactose-reduced milk, regular cheese and yoghurt. In most cases, small amounts of cow's milk can be tolerated.

GLUTEN INTOLERANCE (COELIAC DISEASE)

Coeliac disease is an illness in which the lining of the small intestine is damaged by gluten and similar proteins found in wheat, rye, oats, barley and triticale.

The disease tends to run in families, and can begin at any age, from infancy (after cereals have been introduced) until later in life (even if the person has been eating cereal grains for a long time), in response to some kind of physical or emotional stress.

Symptoms of coeliac disease vary depending on how much of the small intestine is affected. Gluten consumption can cause frequent diarrhoea resulting in dehydration and loss of minerals, which can lead to anaemia and osteoporosis. The reduced absorption of fat, carbohydrate and protein usually causes weight loss.

Coeliacs often suffer from other food sensitivities, particularly to lactose, alcohol, soy foods and MSG, which may also respond to a gluten-free diet.

The healthier your diet, the more energy you'll have to enjoy being physically active. And, in turn, the more active you are, the more you will feel like eating healthy foods.

All of the basic principles for a healthy diet apply to athletes and active people. However, very active people may need even higher amounts of carbohydrate, iron and calcium. Carbohydrate is the main fuel for exercising muscles and the brain. The longer and harder you exercise, the more carbohydrate you need to eat. Iron-rich foods are essential for oxygen transport and energy production in the body and a good supply of calcium is needed for muscles to work and for strong healthy bones.

Dietary habits have a big impact on your physical performance, during training and events. The more serious you are about performing, the more attention you will need to pay to your dietary habits.

An athlete's program can be divided into three stages, which may require different dietary strategies: training, before events, and after events. Endurance athletes may also need various dietary strategies during events.

STAGE 1: TRAINING

The foods you eat before and during an event can help sustain your performance, but your everyday dietary habits have an even greater influence on your performance. It is these habits that affect how well you train and recover, and the size and efficiency of your body's energy stores. Just as it takes months to get into top physical condition, it also takes

months to nutritionally condition your body.

The features of an optimal training diet are:

- high carbohydrate intake
- regularly drinking plenty of fluids
- limited fat intake
- restricted alcohol intake
- moderate intake of lean protein
- regular and high intake of iron- and calcium-rich foods.

Base your meals and snacks on high-carbohydrate foods

- Pasta or rice (brown and white), canned spaghetti
- Bread, bread rolls, pitta bread, English muffins, crumpets, fruit loaf, bagels
- Breakfast cereals (not toasted muesli), porridge
- Potato, corn, pumpkin, sweet potato
- Beans, lentils, chickpeas (canned or boiled), baked beans
- Polenta, couscous, barley
- Fruit (fresh, dried, canned, juice)
- Low-fat crispbreads, rice crackers, rice cakes, bread sticks
- Low-fat pancakes, pikelets, muffins
- Low-fat milk and yoghurt

Make water a top priority

Drinking plenty of fluids each day is as important for peak performance as a high carbohydrate intake. Active people need to drink more than eight glasses of fluid a day to replace water lost from the body as sweat. Dehydration is a common problem in all sports and causes headaches and cramps, and even a small level of dehydration will impair mental and physical performance. Muscle contains about 75 per cent water and a loss of just three per cent of this fluid can reduce muscle strength by 10 per cent and speed by 8 per cent. Prevent dehydration by making a conscious effort to drink plenty of fluid before, during and after exercise.

STAGE 2: BEFORE EVENTS

The food and drink you consume before an event can either enhance or impair your performance. However, there are no 'magic' pre-event meals that can overcome bad dietary habits during the months beforehand.

It's important to eat a healthy, high-carbohydrate diet while you're training to keep your muscles' fuel stores high and gain the full benefit of your program. You can top up your muscles' glycogen stores during the 24 to 36 hours before an event by reducing your physical activity and consuming very low-fat, high-carbohydrate meals. The night before your event, base your evening meal on high-carbohydrate foods with a small serve of lean protein. Water and other carbohydrate-containing fluids should be consumed, but alcohol, tea and coffee should be avoided because they have a dehydrating effect.

Start the next day with a high-carbohydrate breakfast to replace the liver glycogen that is used up during the night.

You will also need to drink plenty of water leading up to an event in order to avoid dehydration. Drink larger volumes of fluid two or more hours before the event and then keep topping up with small sips of water at regular intervals, even if you're not thirsty. Take several large water bottles with you to the event, so you'll have plenty of water on hand.

Ideas for pre-event meals or snacks

- Breakfast cereal (not toasted muesli) with low-fat milk and fresh fruit/canned fruit/stewed fruit/fruit juice
- Toasted bread/crumpets/English muffins with jam/honey/banana
- Low-fat pancakes/pikelets with syrup or apple sauce
- Low-fat muffins with jam
- Fruit salad/stewed fruit/canned fruit with low-fat yoghurt and natural muesli
- High-carbohydrate sports bars or low-fat breakfast cereal bars (not muesli bars or health cakes) with sports drink
- Sandwich or bread roll with jam or banana filling
- Pitta bread with low-fat cottage cheese and tomato or banana, and fruit juice
- Pasta with low-fat tomato sauce
- Baked/microwaved potato with low-fat filling
- Baked beans (high-fibre) or canned spaghetti with toast
- Fruit smoothie (low-fat milk with fruit and low-fat yoghurt/ice cream)
- Rice pudding made with low-fat milk
- High-carbohydrate liquid meal supplements

STAGE 3: AFTER EVENTS

An athlete's first priority after training or an event is to start drinking plenty of water as soon as possible to replace the fluid that has been lost. Alcohol should be avoided before and after exercise because it impairs performance and recovery and can make injuries worse by aggravating inflammation. If you do decide to drink alcohol after an event, make sure that you first consume all the water and carbohydrate you need first. Set yourself a limit of one or two drinks, preferably low-alcohol varieties.

BREAKFAST

A healthy, nourishing breakfast is the best start to the day that you can give your body. It will boost your energy levels and help you cope with the challenges of the day ahead.

Breakfast is, literally, the meal that breaks the fast of the previous night. We all know that breakfast is an important meal because it replenishes our fuel stores and recharges the brain and body. And yet it still seems to be the most neglected time, the meal least thought is given to. Many people are on 'autopilot' as they reach for a cup of coffee and grab a cereal bar or piece of toast on the way out the door. However, a healthy breakfast can be tasty, something to look forward to and enjoy before dealing with the demands of a busy day.

Compared to people who regularly skip breakfast, breakfast-eaters tend to consume more vitamins and minerals and less fat, and have lower blood cholesterol and a lower body weight. This is because breakfast-skippers tend to overeat later in the day, and often choose fatty snacks because they are the easiest option.

For everyday breakfasts, try to keep the  fat content down, and include carbohydrates in the form of fruit, cereal or bread. The small amount of time it takes to make up your own Puffed corn cereal (page 72) gives you satisfaction in knowing

exactly what you are eating, and knowing that it contains no added sugar or preservatives. If you soak your Bircher muesli (page 72) overnight, no preparation is needed the next morning.

Weekends may be a more leisurely affair when breakfast becomes brunch, a time to relax and savour food. When stone fruits are in season, enjoy Grilled fruit with cinnamon toast (page 76). When you are 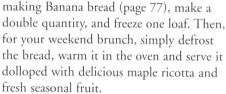 making Banana bread (page 77), make a double quantity, and freeze one loaf. Then, for your weekend brunch, simply defrost the bread, warm it in the oven and serve it dolloped with delicious maple ricotta and fresh seasonal fruit.

Enjoy boiled or poached eggs, not more than twice a week, and serve with lean bacon only as a rare treat. Eggs are an excellent source of nutrients and protein. However, they may need to be eaten in moderation if you are watching your weight or blood cholesterol level.

A great way of incorporating fibre into the diet is to leave the skin on fruit, choose wholegrain breads and cereals, and drink lots of water to enhance the beneficial effects of fibre. Both soluble fibre (found in fruit, vegetables, oats, barley and legumes) and insoluble fibre (found in the skins of fruit and vegetables, wholegrains and nuts) help to lower high blood cholesterol and help prevent bowel disorders and diseases.

When buying cereal from a supermarket, read the nutrition panel on the packet and choose one that is wholegrain, low in fat and added salt and sugar. Often these are the plainer cereals, such as:

- rolled oats
- wheat germ
- natural rather than toasted muesli
- wholewheat breakfast biscuits
- bran flakes
- processed cereals based on whole wheat, oats and barley.

To make these cereals more interesting and nutritious, top them with fresh seasonal fruit, natural yoghurt and low-fat milk. The fruit will add natural sweetness, so you won't need to add sugar, and the yoghurt will add a rich flavour. Instead of milk, you can serve your cereal with a flavoured low-fat drinking yoghurt.

If your preference is toast or muffins, then choose wholegrain varieties, and spread them with only a little butter or margarine, if any. Below are some nutritious toppings for your toast:

- cottage cheese with fresh tomatoes
- ripe avocado with a squeeze of lemon
- low-fat cream cheese and banana
- baked beans
- ricotta and chopped fresh dates.

BREAKFAST DRINKS
Smoothies provide a fast, healthy fix for those who don't have time to sit down to breakfast. Simply blend your favourite combination, including ingredients such as:

- fresh seasonal fruit (berries, bananas, mango, rockmelon)
- natural or low-fat fruit yoghurt

- wheat germ
- an egg
- honey
- oat bran
- a breakfast wheat biscuit.

Fresh fruit juices are another delicious way to include fruit in the diet. Enjoy a freshly squeezed orange juice to start the day, or try a fruit, vegetable and herb combination:

- orange, pineapple and mint
- apple and ginger
- strawberry and pear
- watermelon and passionfruit pulp
- rockmelon and mint
- beetroot, apple and parsley.

Tea and coffee are common breakfast beverage choices. Both contain caffeine (tea about half the amount of coffee). Caffeine stimulates the central nervous system and may increase the heart rate, which can give a 'wake up' jolt in the mornings. However, caffeine is also a diuretic that promotes fluid loss from the body. It is recommended that coffee and tea be enjoyed in moderation—no more than three or four cups a day. There is a large range of caffeine-free and herbal teas available, as well as decaffeinated coffee and coffee substitutes.

MIXED BERRY COUSCOUS

This sweet couscous makes a delicious breakfast or dessert, providing a refreshing mix of carbohydrate, fibre, vitamin C, calcium and antioxidants.

Prep time: 10 minutes + standing + chilling
Cooking time: 5 minutes
Serves 4
EASY

1 cup (185 g) instant couscous
2 cups (500 ml) apple and blackcurrant juice
1 cinnamon stick
250 g raspberries
250 g blueberries
250 g strawberries, halved
2 teaspoons grated lime rind
1 tablespoon finely shredded fresh mint
200 g low-fat plain yoghurt
2 tablespoons maple syrup

1 Place the couscous in a bowl. Pour the apple and blackcurrant juice into a small saucepan and add the cinnamon stick. Bring to the boil, then remove from the heat and pour over the couscous. Cover with plastic wrap and leave for 5 minutes, or until the liquid has been absorbed. Remove the cinnamon stick. Chill.
2 Separate the couscous grains with a fork, add the berries, lime rind and mint, and gently fold through. Spoon the mixture into four bowls. Top with a large dollop of yoghurt and drizzle with the maple syrup. Serve the couscous chilled.

NUTRITION PER SERVE
Protein 8.5 g; Fat 3 g; Carbohydrate 70 g; Dietary Fibre 7 g; Cholesterol 8 mg; 1448 kJ (346 Cal)

VARIATION: Try using orange juice and dried fruits or fresh mango, peach, pear and apple.

PORRIDGE WITH STEWED RHUBARB

This recipe provides a more nutritious version of traditional porridge. It's rich in slowly digested carbohydrate and soluble fibre—great for keeping hunger at bay.

Prep time: 5 minutes
Cooking time: 20 minutes
Serves 4
EASY

6 cups (600 g) rolled oats
1/2 cup (55 g) rolled rice flakes
1/2 cup (60 g) rolled barley
1/2 cup (60 g) rolled rye
1/4 cup (30 g) millet flakes

Stewed rhubarb
350 g rhubarb
1/2 cup (95 g) soft brown sugar
1/4 teaspoon ground mixed spice

1 Place all the porridge ingredients in a large bowl and mix together well. Store in a large airtight jar until ready to use.
2 To make enough porridge for four, place 2 cups (200 g) of the porridge mixture in a saucepan with 1.25 litres water. Bring to the boil, then reduce the heat and simmer over medium heat, stirring frequently, for 15 minutes, or until the porridge is thick. (If it is too thick, add a little skim milk.)
3 To make the stewed rhubarb, cut the rhubarb into 2 cm lengths. Place in a saucepan with the sugar, mixed spice and 1 cup (250 ml) water. Slowly bring to the boil, stirring to dissolve the sugar, then reduce the heat and simmer for 10 minutes, stirring often. Serve hot or cold with the porridge.

NUTRITION PER SERVE
Protein 5.5 g; Fat 3.5 g; Carbohydrate 37 g; Dietary Fibre 4.5 g; Cholesterol 0 mg; 858 kJ (205 Cal)

NOTES: The dry porridge mixture makes about 8 cups (enough for 16 serves). It can be stored in a large airtight jar or container for up to 2 months.
The cooking time of the porridge will decrease considerably if you use quick-cooking oats (one-minute oats), so make sure you check the packet carefully when you buy the rolled oats.

PUFFED CORN CEREAL

The ingredients of this breakfast cereal come from four food groups providing carbohydrate, fibre, B vitamins, vitamin A, and magnesium.

Prep time: 10 minutes
Cooking time: 15 minutes
Serves 20 (Makes about 1.5 kg)
EASY

85 g puffed corn
85 g puffed millet
400 g dried fruit and nut mix
180 g unprocessed natural bran
60 g flaked coconut
1/3 cup (60 g) pepitas
3/4 cup (185 ml) maple syrup
1 cup (70 g) processed bran cereal
400 g dried fruit salad mix, chopped

1 Preheat the oven to moderate 180°C (350°F/Gas 4). Spread out the corn, millet, fruit and nut mix, bran, coconut and pepitas in a large roasting tin.
2 Pour the maple syrup over the puffed corn mixture and stir until the dry ingredients are well coated.
3 Stir in the bran cereal and fruit salad mix and bake for 15 minutes, or until golden, turning the cereal several times during cooking. Cool completely.

NUTRITION PER SERVE
Protein 5 g; Fat 4 g; Carbohydrate 47 g; Dietary Fibre 9 g; Cholesterol 0 mg; 965 kJ (231 Cal)

BIRCHER MUESLI

Place 3 cups (300 g) rolled oats, 1 cup (250 ml) skim milk, 100 g low-fat plain yoghurt, 100 ml orange juice and 1/4 cup (60 g) sugar in a bowl, and mix together well. Cover and refrigerate for 4 hours, or overnight. Serve with 1/2 cup (125 g) low-fat plain yoghurt, 2 grated apples and 2 cups chopped mixed fresh fruit, such as banana, peach, apricot, melon, apple or strawberries. Drizzle with a little honey, if desired. Serves 6

NUTRITION PER SERVE
Protein 9 g; Fat 5 g; Carbohydrate 60 g; Dietary Fibre 6 g; Cholesterol 4.5 mg; 1319 kJ (315 Cal)

FRUIT SALAD IN LEMON GRASS SYRUP

This is a refreshing blend of fresh fruit, providing vitamin C, antioxidants, fibre and potassium. Serve with low-fat yoghurt for a calcium boost.

Prep time: 20 minutes + chilling
Cooking time: 15 minutes
Serves 4
EASY

---

500 g watermelon, cut into large cubes
260 g honeydew melon, cut into large cubes
1/2 small pineapple, cut into large pieces
1 mango, cut into 2 cm cubes
250 g strawberries, halved
1/4 cup (5 g) small fresh mint sprigs

Lemon grass syrup
1/2 cup (125 ml) lime juice
1/4 cup (45 g) soft brown sugar
1 stem lemon grass, white part only,
    thinly sliced
2 tablespoons grated fresh ginger
1 vanilla bean, split

1 Place the fruit and mint in a bowl and mix gently.
2 To make the syrup, place the lime juice, sugar and 1/2 cup (125 ml) water in a small saucepan and stir over low heat until the sugar dissolves. Add the lemon grass, ginger and vanilla bean. Bring to the boil, then reduce the heat and simmer for 10 minutes, or until reduced. Remove the vanilla bean, pour the syrup over the fruit and refrigerate until cold.

NUTRITION PER SERVE
Protein 3.5 g; Fat 0.5 g; Carbohydrate 40 g; Dietary Fibre 6 g; Cholesterol 0 mg; 797 kJ (190 Cal)

NOTE: If you prefer your syrup without the lemon grass pieces but like the flavour, bruise the white part of the lemon grass with a rolling pin. Remove the lemon grass along with the vanilla bean.

Spinach and feta frittatas (top), and Creamed rice with citrus compote

SPINACH AND FETA FRITTATAS

These are lower-fat cheese frittatas, full of protein, calcium, vitamin A and riboflavin. The spinach provides extra taste and minerals.

Prep time: 15 minutes
Cooking time: 20 minutes
Makes 6
EASY

150 g English spinach leaves
1 garlic clove, crushed
2 eggs
2 egg whites
1/4 cup (60 ml) skim milk
2 tablespoons grated Parmesan
70 g low-fat feta, cut into 1 cm cubes (you
  should have 18 cubes)

1 Preheat the oven to moderately hot 200°C (400°F/Gas 6). Place the washed spinach leaves and garlic in a saucepan, cover and steam for 3–5 minutes, or until the spinach is wilted.
2 Cool the spinach slightly and squeeze any excess liquid out of the leaves, then roughly chop. Place the eggs, egg whites, skim milk and Parmesan in a bowl, and whisk to combine. Stir in the spinach. Season with salt and ground black pepper.
3 Spoon the spinach mixture into six 1/2 cup (125 ml) non-stick muffin holes, filling each three-quarters full. Place three cubes of low-fat feta on top and press lightly into the mixture. Bake for 15 minutes, or until the frittatas are golden and set. Serve immediately.

NUTRITION PER FRITTATA
Protein 8 g; Fat 5 g; Carbohydrate 0 g; Dietary Fibre 0.5 g; Cholesterol 100 mg; 336 kJ (80 Cal)

NOTE: The mixture has a soufflé effect and will deflate quite quickly.

CREAMED RICE WITH CITRUS COMPOTE

This is a low-fat version of traditional creamed rice. It's based on slowly digested carbohydrate (rice), topped with vitamin C, fibre, potassium, antioxidants and soothing mint.

Prep time: 15 minutes
Cooking time: 30 minutes
Serves 4
EASY

3/4 cup (150 g) basmati rice
2 cups (500 ml) milk
4 cardamom pods, bruised
1/2 cinnamon stick
1 clove
3 tablespoons honey
1 teaspoon vanilla essence

Citrus compote
2 ruby grapefruit, peeled and segmented
2 oranges, peeled and segmented
3 tablespoons orange juice
1 teaspoon grated lime rind
3 tablespoons honey
8 fresh mint leaves, finely chopped

1 Cook the rice in a large saucepan of boiling water for 12 minutes, stirring occasionally. Drain and cool.
2 Place the rice, milk, cardamom pods, cinnamon stick and clove in a saucepan and bring to the boil. Reduce the heat to low and simmer for 15 minutes, stirring occasionally, until the milk is absorbed and the rice is creamy. Remove the spices, then stir in the honey and vanilla.
3 To make the compote, combine the ruby grapefruit, orange, orange juice, lime rind, honey and mint, and stir until the honey has dissolved. Serve with the rice.

NUTRITION PER SERVE
Protein 9 g; Fat 2.5 g; Carbohydrate 81 g; Dietary Fibre 3 g; Cholesterol 9 mg; 1575 kJ (375 Cal)

GRILLED FRUIT WITH CINNAMON TOAST

More filling and nutritious than toast and jam, and with less fat than French toast, this recipe is a great source of vitamin C, potassium, beta-carotene and fibre.

Prep time: 10 minutes
Cooking time: 10 minutes
Serves 4
EASY

2 tablespoons low-fat margarine
1 1/2 teaspoons ground cinnamon
4 thick slices brioche
4 ripe plums, halved and stones removed
4 ripe nectarines, halved and stones removed
2 tablespoons warmed blossom honey

1 Place the margarine and 1 teaspoon of the ground cinnamon in a bowl and mix until well combined. Grill the brioche on one side until golden. Spread the other side with half the cinnamon spread, then grill until golden. Keep warm in the oven.
2 Brush the plums and nectarines with the remaining spread and cook under a grill until the spread is bubbling and the fruit is tinged at the edges.
3 To serve, place 2 plum halves and 2 nectarine halves on each toasted slice of brioche. Dust with the remaining cinnamon and drizzle with the warmed honey. Dollop with a little fromage frais, if desired.

NUTRITION PER SERVE
Protein 9 g; Fat 13 g; Carbohydrate 66 g; Dietary Fibre 7 g; Cholesterol 41 mg; 1730 kJ (415 Cal)

NOTE: Canned plums or apricots may be used in place of fresh stone fruits.

MAPLE BANANA BREAKFAST

Blend 350 ml fresh or creamy soy milk, 150 g vanilla soy yoghurt, 2 very ripe chopped bananas, 1 large ripe chopped peeled yellow peach and 2 tablespoons maple syrup in a blender until smooth. Pour into glasses to serve. Serves 2

NUTRITION PER SERVE
Protein 12.5 g; Fat 9 g; Carbohydrate 61 g; Dietary Fibre 4.5 g; Cholesterol 0 mg; 1560 kJ (370 Cal)

BANANA BREAD WITH MAPLE RICOTTA

This reduced-fat banana bread provides carbohydrate, protein and minerals, and is topped with calcium, fibre and antioxidants.

Prep time: 10 minutes
Cooking time: 55 minutes
Makes 10–12 slices
EASY

1/3 cup (80 ml) strong coffee
2/3 cup (125 g) soft brown sugar
1 egg
1 egg white
1/4 cup (60 ml) vegetable oil
1 teaspoon vanilla essence
3 ripe bananas, mashed
1 cup (125 g) plain flour
2 cups (250 g) self-raising flour
1/2 teaspoon baking powder
1 teaspoon ground ginger
1/2 teaspoon ground nutmeg
1 teaspoon ground cinnamon
1 teaspoon bicarbonate of soda
200 g low-fat ricotta
2 tablespoons maple syrup
fresh fruit, to serve

1 Preheat the oven to warm 170°C (325°F/Gas 3). Lightly grease a 22 x 12 cm loaf tin and line the base with baking paper. Heat the coffee in a small saucepan over low heat, add the brown sugar and stir until the sugar has dissolved.
2 Place the egg, egg white, oil and vanilla in a bowl and beat until just combined. Add the coffee mixture and banana.
3 Sift the flours, baking powder, ginger, nutmeg, cinnamon and bicarbonate of soda onto the mixture and stir gently to combine—do not overbeat. Spoon the mixture into the prepared loaf tin. Bake for 50 minutes, or until a skewer comes out clean when inserted into the centre. Leave in the tin for 10 minutes before turning out onto a wire rack to cool completely.
4 Combine the ricotta and maple syrup in a small bowl. Cut the banana bread into thick slices and serve with the maple ricotta and fresh fruit.

NUTRITION PER SLICE (12)
Protein 8 g; Fat 7 g; Carbohydrate 45 g; Dietary Fibre 3.5 g; Cholesterol 22.6 mg; 1135 kJ (270 Cal)

DRY-ROASTED GRANOLA MUESLI

Although relatively high in fat, this recipe is a source of polyunsaturated and monounsaturated fat, with fibre, B vitamins and minerals.

Prep time: 5 minutes
Cooking time: 20 minutes
Serves 4
EASY

———

1 1/4 cups (125 g) rolled oats
1/4 cup (30 g) slivered almonds
1/4 cup (35 g) hazelnuts, roughly chopped
1/4 cup (25 g) desiccated coconut
1/3 cup (30 g) wheat germ
2 tablespoons sesame seeds
3 tablespoons sunflower seeds
1/4 cup (45 g) soft brown sugar

1 Place the rolled oats, almonds and hazelnuts in a large heavy-based frying pan over low heat. Cook for 4–5 minutes, stirring constantly, until the mixture begins to darken.
2 Add the coconut, wheat germ, sesame seeds and sunflower seeds to the pan. Stir for 8–10 minutes, or until the mixture develops a golden toasted look. Add the brown sugar and stir for a further 2–3 minutes. Remove from the heat and cool completely before storing in an airtight container. Serve with cold milk.

NUTRITION PER SERVE
Protein 11 g; Fat 22 g; Carbohydrate 26 g; Dietary Fibre 6.5 g; Cholesterol 0 mg; 1420 kJ (340 Cal)

BREAKFAST DELUXE

Cut 12 strawberries into thin slices. Peel 4 kiwi fruit and cut into slices. Divide the strawberry slices, kiwi fruit slices, 160 g low-fat muesli and 400 g 99.8% fat-free natural yoghurt among four glasses. Repeat these layers, finishing with some fruit. Pour 1/3 cup (80 ml) milk into each glass, then drizzle each with 2 teaspoons honey. Serve with a spoon. Serves 4

NUTRITION PER SERVE
Protein 16 g; Fat 6 g; Carbohydrate 54 g; Dietary Fibre 7 g; Cholesterol 11 mg; 1370 kJ (325 Cal)

OATY BUCKWHEAT PANCAKES

These nourishing pancakes contain slowly digested carbohydrate, fibre and protein.

Prep time: 10 minutes
Cooking time: 40 minutes
Serves 4
EASY

———

Berry sauce
1/4 cup (60 g) sugar
2 teaspoons lemon juice
250 g raspberries

1/3 cup (40 g) buckwheat flour
2/3 cup (100 g) wholemeal plain flour
1 1/2 teaspoons baking powder
1/4 cup (25 g) rolled oats
1 egg yolk
1 1/2 cups (375 ml) buttermilk
3 egg whites
raspberries, to serve

1 To make the sauce, place the sugar, lemon juice and 1/4 cup (60 ml) water in a saucepan over medium heat and bring to the boil. Add the raspberries and cook over low heat for 3 minutes. Cool, then purée in a food processor for 10 seconds.
2 Sift the flours into a bowl and return the husks to the bowl. Add the baking powder and rolled oats and combine. Make a well in the centre. Combine the egg yolk and buttermilk and add to the dry ingredients all at once. Stir to form a smooth batter. Whisk the egg whites until firm peaks form, then fold into the batter.
3 Heat a non-stick frying pan over medium–high heat and brush lightly with butter. Pour 1/4 cup (60 ml) batter into the pan and swirl to form a 10 cm circle. Cook for 1–2 minutes, or until bubbles appear on the surface. Turn and cook for 1–2 minutes, or until light brown. Transfer to a plate and keep warm. Repeat to make 8 pancakes. Serve with the berry sauce and raspberries.

NUTRITION PER SERVE
Protein 13 g; Fat 5 g; Carbohydrate 51 g; Dietary Fibre 7.5 g; Cholesterol 53.5 mg; 1255 kJ (300 Cal)

Dry-roasted granola muesli (top), and Oaty buckwheat pancakes

RICOTTA CORN FRITTERS

This delicious, reduced-fat fritter recipe is a great source of protein, calcium, vitamin A and B vitamins.

Prep time: 10 minutes
Cooking time: 25 minutes
Serves 4
EASY

---

200 g low-fat ricotta
1 egg
1 egg white
$1/2$ cup (125 ml) skim milk
$1/2$ cup (75 g) wholemeal self-raising flour
420 g can corn kernels, drained
3 spring onions, chopped
2 tablespoons snipped fresh chives
cooking oil spray
100 g low-fat ricotta, extra
$1/3$ cup (100 g) spicy tomato chutney

1 Place the ricotta, egg, egg white and milk in a bowl, and beat together until smooth. Stir in the flour, corn kernels, spring onion and chives. Season well with salt and ground black pepper.
2 Spray a non-stick frying pan liberally with cooking oil. Add heaped tablespoons of the mixture to the pan, four at a time, and flatten to about 1.5 cm thick. Cook for 3–4 minutes each side. Drain on paper towels. Serve the fritters in a stack of three and top with a tablespoon of ricotta and a tablespoon of spicy tomato chutney.

NUTRITION PER SERVE
Protein 16 g; Fat 9 g; Carbohydrate 40 g; Dietary Fibre
6.5 g; Cholesterol 77 mg; 1305 kJ (311 Cal)

FRUIT COMPOTE WITH CRUMPET FINGERS

High in carbohydrates, this recipe is full of energy and fibre, as well as a wide variety of vitamins and minerals.

Prep time: 10 minutes
Cooking time: 20 minutes
Serves 4
EASY

---

200 g pitted prunes
200 g fresh dates, pitted and halved
400 g dried fruit salad mix
2 cups (500 ml) apple juice
1 tablespoon ground cinnamon
3 tablespoons sugar
4 crumpets
20 g butter
200 g low-fat vanilla fromage frais or
    whipped yoghurt

1 Place the prunes, dates and dried fruit salad mix in a saucepan with the apple juice. Bring to the boil, then reduce the heat and simmer for 15 minutes, or until the fruit is plump and tender.
2 Place the ground cinnamon and sugar in a small bowl, and mix together well.
3 Toast the crumpets for 3 minutes each side, or until golden brown, then spread lightly with the butter. Sprinkle with the combined sugar and cinnamon, then cut into fingers.
4 Spoon the compote into four serving bowls and top with a spoonful of fromage frais. Stack the crumpet fingers on a side plate and serve.

NUTRITION PER SERVE
Protein 7 g; Fat 7 g; Carbohydrate 169 g; Dietary Fibre 16 g; Cholesterol 13 mg; 3255 kJ (775 Cal)

NOTE: Any combination of dried fruits can be used in the compote.

GRILLED MUSHROOMS WITH SCRAMBLED EGGS

This is a more nutritious version of traditional scrambled eggs—a good source of high-quality protein, vitamin A, folate and antioxidants.

Prep time: 10 minutes
Cooking time: 20 minutes
Serves 4
EASY

4 mushrooms
10 g butter
4 Roma tomatoes, halved
3 tablespoons balsamic vinegar
4 eggs, lightly beaten
4 egg whites, lightly beaten
1/4 cup (60 ml) skim milk
2 tablespoons snipped fresh chives
8 slices wholegrain bread

1 Trim the mushroom stalks to 2 cm above the cap. Brush the mushrooms with paper towels to remove any dirt and grit.
2 Melt the butter in a small saucepan over low heat until it begins to foam.
3 Brush both sides of the mushrooms with the melted butter and place on a non-stick baking tray with the tomato halves. Drizzle the mushrooms and tomato with the balsamic vinegar, sprinkle with salt and ground black pepper, then place under a medium grill for 10–15 minutes, or until tender.
4 Meanwhile, place the eggs, egg whites, milk and chives in a bowl, and whisk to combine. Pour the mixture into a non-stick frying pan and cook over low heat for 5 minutes, or until the egg begins to set, then gently stir with a wooden spoon to scramble.
5 Toast the wholegrain bread until golden brown, then cut on the diagonal. Serve with the mushrooms, tomato and scrambled eggs.

NUTRITION PER SERVE
Protein 17 g; Fat 8.5 g; Carbohydrate 26 g; Dietary Fibre 4 g; Cholesterol 187 mg; 1056 kJ (252 Cal)

BAGELS WITH BAKED BEANS

These bagels are a low-fat savoury breakfast, providing slowly released carbohydrate energy, fibre, protein, phytochemicals and calcium—an excellent meal at any time of day.

Prep time: 10 minutes
Cooking time: 10 minutes
Serves 4
EASY

400 g can baked beans
4 cups (200 g) baby English spinach leaves
4 bagels, halved
1 cup (250 g) low-fat cottage cheese

1 Place the baked beans in a small saucepan and cook over medium heat for 3 minutes, or until warmed.
2 Place the washed spinach in a medium saucepan, cover and cook over medium heat for 2 minutes, or until wilted.
3 Toast the bagel halves and top with the cottage cheese and spinach. Spoon the baked beans over the top, and season with ground black pepper.

NUTRITION PER SERVE
Protein 17 g; Fat 2 g; Carbohydrate 58 g; Dietary Fibre 6 g; Cholesterol 18 mg; 1780 kJ (424 Cal)

TROPICAL MORNING SMOOTHIE

Blend 2 chopped mangoes, 350 ml creamy soy milk, 150 ml pineapple juice, 1/4 cup (15 g) chopped fresh mint and 6 ice cubes in a blender until smooth. Garnish with a sprig of fresh mint. Serves 3

NUTRITION PER SERVE
Protein 6 g; Fat 4.5 g; Carbohydrate 28.5 g; Dietary Fibre 3 g; Cholesterol 0 mg; 735 kJ (175 Cal)

Fruit muffins (top), and Waffles with maple syrup and ricotta

FRUIT MUFFINS

Lower in fat and calories than most commercial varieties, these tangy muffins are a great source of fibre, potassium and phosphorus. Serve them with some fruit yoghurt to boost the calcium content.

Prep time: 15 minutes + 5 minutes soaking
Cooking time: 20 minutes
Makes 12
EASY

1 cup (160 g) chopped mixed dried fruit
    (apricots, dates, peaches or fruit medley
    with peel)
1 1/2 cups (225 g) wholemeal self-raising flour
1 teaspoon baking powder
1 cup (150 g) unprocessed oat bran
1/3 cup (60 g) soft brown sugar
300 ml skim milk
1 egg
1 tablespoon oil

1 Preheat the oven to moderate 180°C (350°F/Gas 4). Grease twelve 1/2 cup (125 ml) muffin holes. Soak the dried fruit with 1/4 cup (60 ml) boiling water for 5 minutes.
2 Sift the flour and baking powder into a large bowl, returning the husks to the bowl. Stir in the oat bran and sugar and make a well in the centre.
3 Combine the milk, egg and oil in a jug. Add the soaked fruit and milk mixture all at once to the dry ingredients. Fold in gently using a metal spoon, until just combined—do not overmix.
4 Divide the mixture evenly among the muffin holes. Bake for 20 minutes, or until the muffins are risen and golden, and a skewer inserted into the centre comes out clean. Cool for a few minutes in the tin, then turn out onto a wire rack. Serve warm or at room temperature.

NUTRITION PER MUFFIN
Protein 6 g; Fat 3.5 g; Carbohydrate 28 g; Dietary Fibre 5 g; Cholesterol 16.5 mg; 700 kJ (170 Cal)

WAFFLES WITH MAPLE SYRUP AND RICOTTA

These waffles are a sweet, nutritious breakfast alternative, providing niacin and minerals. Top them with berries or other fruit for a burst of vitamin C and antioxidants.

Prep time: 15 minutes + 1 hour standing
Cooking time: 20 minutes
Serves 6
EASY

200 g plain flour
1 1/2 tablespoons caster sugar
1 tablespoon baking powder
1/2 teaspoon salt
1/2 cup (50 g) rolled oats
1 egg yolk
350 ml reduced-fat milk
2 teaspoons reduced-fat dairy spread, melted
3 egg whites
100 g low-fat ricotta
2 tablespoons low-fat vanilla yoghurt
1/4 cup (60 ml) maple syrup, plus extra to serve

1 Sift the flour, sugar, baking powder and salt into a bowl, then stir in the oats. Add the combined egg yolk and milk with the dairy spread and stir until combined.
2 Whisk the egg whites in a clean, dry bowl until soft peaks form, then gently fold into the batter with a metal spoon. Cover and leave for 1 hour. Beat together the ricotta, yoghurt and maple syrup until smooth.
3 Preheat a waffle maker. Pour one-sixth of the mixture, or enough to fill, into the waffle maker and cook for 2–3 minutes. Repeat with the remaining mixture to make six waffles. To serve, place each waffle on a serving plate, top with some ricotta mixture and drizzle with the extra maple syrup.

NUTRITION PER SERVE
Protein 11 g; Fat 5 g; Carbohydrate 47 g; Dietary Fibre 2 g; Cholesterol 43 mg; 1165 kJ (280 Cal)

NOTE: The number of waffles you make may vary, depending on the size of your waffle maker.

CREPES WITH WARM FRUIT COMPOTE

A wonderful breakfast or winter dessert, these crepes provide energy with fibre, vitamin A, potassium, calcium, phosphorus and a little iron.

Prep time: 30 minutes + 30 minutes standing
Cooking time: 20 minutes
Serves 4
EASY

1/2 cup (60 g) plain flour
2 eggs
1 cup (250 ml) skim milk
canola oil spray
2 teaspoons caster sugar

Compote
100 g whole dried apricots
1/4 cup (60 ml) port or Muscat
2 firm pears, peeled, cored and quartered
1 vanilla bean, split
2 cinnamon sticks
425 g can pitted prunes in syrup, drained, syrup reserved

1 Place the flour in a bowl and gradually add the combined eggs and milk, whisking to remove any lumps. Cover and leave for 30 minutes.
2 Meanwhile, cook the apricots and port in a covered saucepan over low heat for 2–3 minutes, or until softened. Scrape the seeds from the vanilla bean and add to the pan with the pod, cinnamon, pear and prune syrup. Simmer, stirring occasionally, for 4 minutes, or until the pear is soft. Add the prunes and simmer for 1 minute.
3 Heat a 20 cm non-stick crepe pan or frying pan over medium heat. Lightly spray with oil. Pour 1/4 cup (60 ml) batter into the pan and swirl over the base. Cook for 1 minute, or until the underside is golden. Turn and cook for 30 seconds. Transfer to a plate and keep warm. Repeat to make 8 crepes. Fold the crepes into triangles and scatter with the sugar. Serve with the compote.

NUTRITION PER SERVE
Protein 9 g; Fat 4 g; Carbohydrate 59 g; Dietary Fibre 6 g; Cholesterol 92 mg; 1340 kJ (320 Cal)

OMELETTE WITH ASPARAGUS, SMOKED SALMON AND DILL

This recipe is packed full of essential nutrients—high-quality protein, fat-soluble vitamins, calcium, choline, folate and antioxidants.

Prep time: 10 minutes
Cooking time: 10 minutes
Serves 2
EASY

6 egg whites
6 eggs
2 tablespoons low-fat ricotta
2 tablespoons chopped fresh dill
420 g fresh asparagus, cut into 5 cm lengths
100 g smoked salmon, thinly sliced
lemon wedges, to garnish
fresh dill sprigs

1 Whisk the egg whites until foaming. In a separate bowl, whisk the whole eggs and ricotta. Add the whites. Season with salt and pepper, and stir in the dill.
2 Bring a saucepan of lightly salted water to the boil. Add the asparagus and cook for 1–2 minutes, or until just tender. Drain and refresh in iced water.
3 Heat a non-stick 24 cm frying pan over low heat and spray lightly with oil spray. Pour in half the egg mixture and arrange half the asparagus on top. Cook over medium heat until the egg is just setting. Flip one side onto the other and transfer to a serving plate. Repeat with the remaining mixture and asparagus.
4 To serve, top the omelettes with smoked salmon, and garnish with lemon wedges and a sprig of dill.

NUTRITION PER SERVE
Protein 25 g; Fat 9 g; Carbohydrate 2 g; Dietary Fibre 1.5 g; Cholesterol 298 mg; 810 kJ (195 Cal)

MORNING BLENDED FRUIT JUICE

Blend 1/2 chopped fresh pineapple with 1 1/2 cups (375 ml) orange juice, 1 large chopped pear, 1 chopped banana and 40 g chopped pawpaw until smooth. Serve immediately. Serves 4

NUTRITION PER SERVE
Protein 1.5 g; Fat 0.5 g; Carbohydrate 27 g; Dietary Fibre 4 g; Cholesterol 0 g; 500 kJ (120 Cal)

SCRAMBLED TOFU WITH MUSHROOMS

This is a nourishing vegetarian meal. The tofu and bread are a great source of protective phytochemicals, and the mushrooms provide vitamin B12.

Prep time: 10 minutes
Cooking time: 15 minutes
Serves 4
MEDIUM

20 g soy margarine
200 g button mushrooms, sliced
1 clove garlic, crushed
2 spring onions, chopped
400 g firm tofu, drained and crumbled
1 teaspoon tamari
1 tablespoon finely chopped fresh parsley
8 thick slices soy and linseed bread

1 Melt half of the soy margarine in a large frying pan. Add the mushrooms and cook over high heat for 5 minutes, or until they start to lose their moisture. Add the garlic and cook for 5 minutes, or until the liquid has evaporated. Remove from the pan.
2 Melt the remaining soy margarine in the pan. Add the spring onion and cook for 30 seconds, or until just wilted. Add the tofu, tamari and mushrooms and cook, stirring gently, for 2 minutes, or until the tofu is heated through. Stir in the parsley and season with black pepper.
3 Lightly toast the bread and serve with the scrambled tofu.

NUTRITION PER SERVE
Protein 22 g; Fat 13.5 g; Carbohydrate 39 g; Dietary Fibre 7.5 g; Cholesterol 0 mg; 1535 kJ (365 Cal)

SOY PANCAKES WITH MAPLE RASPBERRIES

This is a great recipe for vegetarians. The pancakes are full of protective soy phytochemicals, carbohydrate energy and fibre. Topped with berries, they provide vitamin C and antioxidants.

Prep time: 10 minutes + 15 minutes standing
Cooking time: 20 minutes
Serves 4–6
EASY

1 cup (125 g) plain flour
1/2 cup (50 g) soy flour
1 tablespoon baking powder
1/2 teaspoon salt
2 tablespoons sugar
1/4 cup (65 g) silken tofu
13/4 cups (435 ml) vanilla soy milk
50 g soy spread or margarine, melted and cooled
500 g raspberries
1/2 cup (125 ml) maple syrup
icing sugar, for dusting

1 Sift the flours, baking powder and salt into a large bowl, then stir in the sugar. Place the tofu, soy milk and 1 tablespoon of the melted soy spread in a food processor and combine until smooth. Add to the dry ingredients and mix well. Cover and leave for 15 minutes.
2 Heat some of the soy spread in a frying pan over medium heat. Making two pancakes at a time, drop 2 tablespoons of batter in the pan per pancake and cook for 1–2 minutes, or until bubbles form on the surface. Turn and cook for 1 minute, or until golden. Keep warm and repeat with the remaining batter.
3 Place the raspberries and maple syrup in a saucepan and stir to coat. Gently cook for 1–2 minutes, or until the berries are warm and well coated in the syrup.
4 Place 2 or 3 pancakes on each plate, top with the raspberries and dust with sugar.

NUTRITION PER SERVE (6)
Protein 9 g; Fat 12 g; Carbohydrate 50 g; Dietary Fibre 6 g; Cholesterol 0 mg; 1372 kJ (328 Cal)

Scrambled tofu with mushrooms (top), and Soy pancakes with maple raspberries

CHEESE WAFFLES WITH HERBED RICOTTA AND ROAST TOMATO

This is a savoury waffle recipe containing high-quality protein, calcium, phosphorus (great for bones and teeth), vitamin A, niacin and folate.

Prep time: 20 minutes
Cooking time: 1 hour 15 minutes
Serves 4
MEDIUM

---

4 Roma tomatoes, halved lengthways
1 tablespoon olive oil
1 tablespoon balsamic vinegar
1 teaspoon sugar
1 tablespoon chopped fresh oregano
4 tablespoons chopped fresh herbs (oregano, sage, rosemary, parsley)
1 1/4 cups (310 g) low-fat ricotta
1 1/2 cups (185 g) self-raising flour
1/4 cup (25 g) grated Parmesan
1/4 cup (30 g) grated low-fat Cheddar
3 large spring onions, finely chopped
1 egg
1 cup (250 ml) low-fat milk
2 egg whites
fresh oregano sprigs

1 Preheat the oven to warm 160°C (315°F/Gas 2–3). Place the tomato halves on a lightly greased baking tray and drizzle with olive oil and balsamic vinegar. Sprinkle with the sugar, oregano and some salt. Bake for 1 hour, or until very soft.

2 Fold the chopped herbs into the ricotta. Season with salt and black pepper. Using two tablespoons, shape the ricotta into quenelle shapes. Refrigerate until needed.

3 Place the flour, Parmesan, Cheddar, spring onion, egg and milk in a bowl. Season, then mix well. Whisk the egg whites until soft peaks form, then gently fold into the cheese and egg mixture.

4 Preheat a waffle maker and brush lightly with oil. Pour in 1/3 cup (80 ml) batter and cook until golden on both sides. Keep warm while you cook the remaining waffles. Arrange two waffle halves on each plate with two tomato halves and two ricotta quenelles. Garnish with oregano.

NUTRITION PER SERVE
Protein 28 g; Fat 14 g; Carbohydrate 42 g; Dietary Fibre 3.5 g; Cholesterol 93 mg; 1800 kJ (430 Cal)

EGGS EN COCOTTE

This delicious and satisfying meal is densely packed with nutrients from the eggs, vitamin C and antioxidants from the sauce, and B vitamins and carbohydrate from the bread.

Prep time: 15 minutes
Cooking time: 30 minutes
Serves 4
EASY

Tomato sauce
1 tablespoon olive oil
1 clove garlic, crushed
3 vine-ripened tomatoes (about 300 g), peeled, seeded and chopped

1/2 teaspoon olive oil
4 eggs
Tabasco sauce, to taste
2 tablespoons snipped fresh chives
4 slices thick multigrain bread
20 g margarine

1 Preheat the oven to moderate 180°C (350°F/Gas 4). To make the tomato sauce, heat the oil in a heavy-based frying pan. Add the garlic and cook for 1 minute, or until it begins to turn golden. Add the tomato and season with salt and ground black pepper. Cook over medium heat for 15 minutes, or until thickened.
2 Grease four 1/2 cup (125 ml) ramekins with the oil, then break 1 egg into each, trying not to break the yolk. Pour the sauce around the outside of each egg so the yolk is still visible. Add a little Tabasco, sprinkle with the chives and season.
3 Place the ramekins in a deep baking dish and pour in enough hot water to come halfway up the side of the ramekins. Bake for 10–12 minutes, or until the egg white is set. Toast the bread and lightly spread with the margarine, then cut into thick fingers. Serve immediately with the egg.

NUTRITION PER SERVE
Protein 11 g; Fat 15 g; Carbohydrate 20 g; Dietary Fibre 3 g; Cholesterol 187.5 mg; 1075 kJ (255 Cal)

SNACKS AND DRINKS

Following a healthy diet doesn't mean giving up snacks and tasty drinks, it just means making better choices when hunger strikes or you crave a sweet treat.

Sometimes you may feel too hungry to wait for your next main meal before you eat again, or you may start to feel a little sluggish and in need of an energy boost. Because this often happens when you don't have a lot of time to prepare food, an easy alternative is to reach for a packaged snack food like potato chips or a chocolate bar to satisfy your hunger or craving. However, these processed snack foods are generally high in fat, sugar and salt. They may provide a quick-fix for your hunger, but they don't supply you with many nutrients or a lasting energy supply.

There are many healthier alternatives to processed snack foods, which will satisfy your hunger and taste cravings, and provide you with energy until your next main meal.

One of the best and easiest to prepare snack foods is fresh fruit. Most fruit is easy to transport, and the only preparation needed is washing or chopping. Leave the skin on fruit such as apples or pears to increase dietary fibre, and choose fruit at the peak of its season, when its flavour is fully developed and the taste and texture are at their best. If you've got a little more time to prepare your snack, try a fresh fruit salad topped with low-fat yoghurt and a handful of sunflower seeds.

Among the less healthy processed foods, there are plenty of low-fat snack foods in supermarkets and health food stores that you can choose for a quick, healthy snack. Use the nutritional information on food labels to help you choose products that contain relatively low amounts of fat. Not only is it important to be aware of what you are eating, you might be surprised by the amount of fat, sugar and salt some supposedly healthy foods contain.

Some examples of healthy snacks on the run are:
- reduced-fat muesli bars
- dried fruit
- rice crackers
- puffed rice/corn cakes
- breakfast cereal bars
- low-fat yoghurt
- low-fat frozen yoghurt
- low-fat fruit muffins
- pretzels
- microwave popcorn.

For a snack to accompany fresh vegetable sticks, take one of your favourite dip recipes and make it with less fat:
- make hummus by blending the chickpeas with water or vegetable stock rather than oil
- use low-fat plain yoghurt rather than

full-fat yoghurt to make tzatziki
- use light sour cream and reduced-salt French onion soup mix to make French onion dip
- use Indian or Moroccan spice blends to add flavour to vegetable and bean purées and serve them as a dip, such as sweet potato with ras el hanout, or red lentil dahl with garam masala

- make use of fresh herbs to enhance the flavour of your dips or tomato salsas
- serve the dips with rice crackers, crisp wedges of pitta bread, or thinly sliced toasted Italian bread.

HEALTHY SNACK IDEAS

There are many ways of making your favourite snack foods a little more healthy, simply by using different cooking methods, and reducing the fat while adding different seasonings to make up for any changes in texture and flavour.
- Wash and dry potatoes, cut them into wedges, leaving the skin on (which contains nutrients and dietary fibre), lightly spray them with olive oil and sprinkle with Cajun spice powder or lemon pepper, then bake in a hot oven until cooked through and crisp.
- Cook popcorn without any oil in a paper bag in the microwave, or in a saucepan on the stove using a minimum of oil. Instead of seasoning the popcorn with salt, try chilli powder, garlic and dried herbs, or a light sprinkling of grated Parmesan cheese.
- Mix diced fresh tomato with balsamic vinegar, chopped fresh basil and cracked black pepper, then pile it onto toasted Italian bread.
- Spread toasted crumpets with low-fat ricotta, top with sliced banana and drizzle with honey.

- Spoon some hot baked beans onto toasted English muffins.
- Make your own pizzas using pitta bread topped with tomato paste, fresh basil and slices of roasted vegetables such as eggplant, sweet potato and zucchini. Sprinkle the pizzas with a little grated light mozzarella cheese and bake or grill until the pizzas are golden and crisp.
- Marinate chicken wings with soy sauce, grated fresh ginger and crushed garlic, then bake on a rack in a baking dish until cooked through. Serve hot or cold.
- Fill triangles of wholemeal filo pastry with leftover curry, seal and lightly spray with olive oil, then bake until golden and heated through. Serve with low-fat natural yoghurt flavoured with ground coriander.

DRINK UP

Drinking plenty of fluid regularly throughout the day is a great way of keeping your brain and tissues well hydrated and functioning at their best, and can help keep hunger at bay.

This is especially important if you are exercising. While exercising, you should regularly replace any fluid lost as sweat, to avoid cramps, fatigue and headaches. As a general guideline, drink lots of water, limit your consumption of drinks containing caffeine, avoid soft drinks that contain large quantities of sugar, and limit your consumption of alcohol.

If you're looking for some taste as well as refreshment, try:
- fresh fruit juices
- low-fat fruit smoothies
- soda water flavoured with fresh fruit purée
- sports drinks (for a long exercise session)
- herbal tea—hot or iced
- mineral water flavoured with fresh lemon or lime juice.

PUFFED CORN SNACK MIX

More nutritious than regular popcorn, this snack provides good amounts of fibre, vitamin E and beta-carotene.

Prep time: 10 minutes
Cooking time: 20 minutes
Serves 20
EASY

170 g puffed corn
400 g packet dried fruit and nut mix
1 1/4 cups (95 g) unprocessed natural bran
1 cup (55 g) flaked coconut, toasted
1/3 cup (60 g) pepitas
3/4 cup (260 g) honey

1 Preheat the oven to moderate 180°C (350°F/Gas 4). Line four baking trays with baking paper. Place the puffed corn, dried fruit and nut mix, bran, coconut and pepitas in a large bowl, and mix together well.

2 Heat the honey in a small saucepan over low heat for 3 minutes, or until it thins to a pouring consistency. Pour over the puffed corn mixture and stir until all the dry ingredients are well coated with the honey.

3 Spread the mixture onto the lined baking trays in a single layer and bake for 15 minutes, or until golden, turning the cereal several times during cooking. Cool completely before storing in an airtight container in a cool, dark place.

NUTRITION PER SERVE
Protein 4 g; Fat 7.5 g; Carbohydrate 28.5 g; Dietary Fibre 4.5 g; Cholesterol 0 mg; 820 kJ (195 Cal)

PUMPKIN AND SWEET POTATO DIP

This low-fat dip tastes great alone or with fresh carrot and celery sticks, and is an excellent source of potassium, folate and antioxidants.

Prep time: 15 minutes
Cooking time: 30 minutes
Serves 3–4
EASY

500 g pumpkin, cut into 2 cm cubes
300 g orange sweet potato, cut into 2 cm cubes
2 teaspoons honey
1 teaspoon ground cumin
1 teaspoon ground coriander
1/2 teaspoon ground cinnamon
1 clove garlic
2 tablespoons chopped fresh flat-leaf parsley
2 tablespoons chopped fresh coriander leaves
1/2 teaspoon grated orange rind
2 teaspoons white vinegar

1 Preheat the oven to moderate 180°C (350°F/Gas 4). Line a large baking tray with baking paper, place the pumpkin and sweet potato on the tray, drizzle with the honey and sprinkle the cumin, coriander and cinnamon over the top. Cook in the oven for 5 minutes, then turn the vegetables, making sure they are well coated, and cook for another 25 minutes, or until soft and golden brown. Cool.
2 Place the roasted vegetables, garlic, parsley, coriander leaves, orange rind and vinegar in a food processor, and process until smooth. With the motor still running, slowly add 1/4 cup (60 ml) hot water to the processor in a thin stream until the mixture is smooth and 'dippable'. Serve at room temperature with crudités and pitta crisps.

NUTRITION PER SERVE (4)
Protein 4.5 g; Fat 1 g; Carbohydrate 22 g; Dietary Fibre 3.5 g; Cholesterol 0 mg; 470 kJ (110 Cal)

PEACH AND ROCKMELON JUICE

A refreshing thirst quencher, this drink provides sweet natural sugar for energy and a boost of vitamin C, beta-carotene, folate, potassium and fibre.

Prep time: 10 minutes
Cooking time: Nil
Serves 2
EASY

1/2 rockmelon
4 peaches
600 ml orange juice
12 ice cubes
1 tablespoon lime juice

1 Peel the rockmelon, remove the seeds and roughly chop the flesh into bite-sized pieces. Cut a cross in the base of the peaches. Place them in a heatproof bowl and cover with boiling water. Leave for 1–2 minutes, then remove with a slotted spoon, cool slightly and peel. Halve, remove the stone, and chop the flesh into bite-sized pieces.
2 Place the fruit in a blender with the orange juice and ice cubes, and blend until smooth. If the juice is too thick, add a little iced water. Stir in the lime juice and serve immediately.

NUTRITION PER SERVE
Protein 3 g; Fat 0.5 g; Carbohydrate 23 g; Dietary Fibre 5 g; Cholesterol 0 mg; 465 kJ (110 Cal)

BANANA AND BERRY SMOOTHIE

A nutritious snack or breakfast, this drink provides carbohydrate energy, soluble fibre, vitamin C, calcium and flavonoids.

Prep time: 5 minutes
Cooking time: Nil
Serves 2–3
EASY

---

2 ripe bananas, roughly chopped
200 g fresh or frozen mixed berries
1 tablespoon oat bran
3 tablespoons low-fat vanilla fromage frais or whipped yoghurt
2 cups (500 ml) skim milk

1 Place the chopped banana, berries, oat bran, vanilla fromage frais and skim milk in a blender, and blend for 2 minutes, or until thick and creamy.

NUTRITION PER SERVE (3)
Protein 8 g; Fat 1 g; Carbohydrate 30 g; Dietary Fibre 3.5 g; Cholesterol 5 mg; 660 kJ (155 Cal)

NOTE: The smoothie will be thicker if you use frozen berries. You may need to add an extra 1/2 cup (125 ml) skim milk to thin it down.

FRUIT FRAPPE

This drink is a refreshing antioxidant cocktail, which makes a substantial snack or light meal, rich in vitamin C, vitamin A, vitamin B6, fibre and flavonoid antioxidants.

Prep time: 5 minutes + 10 minutes soaking
Cooking time: Nil
Serves 4
EASY

---

10 dried apricot halves
200 g fresh or frozen raspberries
1 banana, roughly chopped
1 mango, chopped
2 cups (500 ml) orange juice
1 tablespoon fresh mint leaves
6 ice cubes

1 Place the dried apricots in a heatproof bowl. Cover with 1/4 cup (60 ml) boiling water for 10 minutes, or until plump. Drain, then roughly chop.
2 Place the chopped apricots, raspberries, banana, mango, orange juice, mint leaves and ice cubes in a blender, and blend until thick and smooth.

NUTRITION PER SERVE
Protein 2 g; Fat 1 g; Carbohydrate 33 g; Dietary Fibre 5 g; Cholesterol 0 mg; 615 kJ (145 Cal)

Peach and rockmelon juice (left), Banana and berry smoothie (top), and Fruit frappé (right)

FALAFEL ROLLS

*If plain sandwiches don't tempt you, then satisfy
your hunger with this nutritious dish. These rolls
provide plenty of fibre, and good amounts of folate,
vitamin C and iron.*

Prep time: 20 minutes + 45 minutes refrigeration
Cooking time: 10 minutes
Serves 4
MEDIUM

8 spring onions, chopped
1 cup (30 g) roughly chopped fresh flat-leaf
    parsley
1/2 cup (15 g) fresh coriander leaves
2 teaspoons ground coriander
2 teaspoons ground cumin
1/4 teaspoon chilli powder
2 cloves garlic, crushed
300 g can chickpeas, rinsed and drained
plain flour, for coating
oil, for deep-frying
4 tablespoons ready-made hummus
4 rounds Lebanese bread
200 g ready-made tabbouleh

1 Place the spring onion, parsley and fresh
coriander in a food processor, and process
until finely chopped.
2 Add the spices, garlic and chickpeas,
and process to a smooth paste. Shape into
12 patties. Coat lightly in flour and
refrigerate for 45 minutes.
3 Fill a deep heavy-based saucepan one-
third full of oil and heat to 180°C (350°F),
or until a bread cube browns in 15 seconds
when dropped into the oil. Cook the
falafel in batches for 2–3 minutes, or until
dark gold and cooked through. Drain.
4 To serve, spread the hummus over the
four rounds of Lebanese bread, top with
the tabbouleh and three falafel each. Roll
up securely and serve wrapped in paper.

NUTRITION PER SERVE
Protein 15 g; Fat 21.5 g; Carbohydrate 63 g; Dietary
Fibre 10.5 g; Cholesterol 0 mg; 2095 kJ (500 Cal)

NOTE: You can reduce the fat content of
this dish by using reduced-fat hummus,
and salad rather than tabbouleh.

PIZZETTE

With much less fat per mouthful than commercial pizzas, this is a good source of protein.

Prep time: 20 minutes + 30 minutes rising
Cooking time: 15 minutes
Makes 4
EASY

1 cup (125 g) plain flour
1 cup (150 g) wholemeal plain flour
2 teaspoons dried yeast
1/2 teaspoon sugar
2 tablespoons natural yoghurt
2 tablespoons tomato paste
1 clove garlic, crushed
1 teaspoon dried oregano
80 g lean shaved ham
2 tablespoons grated light mozzarella
rocket leaves, chopped, to serve
extra virgin olive oil, to drizzle

1 Sift the plain flour into a bowl, then add the wholemeal plain flour, yeast, sugar and 1/2 teaspoon salt. Make a well in the centre, add 1/2 cup (125 ml) water and the yoghurt, and mix to a dough. Knead on a lightly floured surface for 5 minutes, or until smooth and elastic. Cover with a tea towel and rest in a warm place for 20–30 minutes, or until doubled in size.
2 Preheat the oven to moderately hot 200°C (400°F/Gas 6). Punch down the dough and knead for 30 seconds, then divide into four portions. Roll each portion into a 15 cm round and place on a baking tray. Combine the tomato paste, garlic, oregano and 1 tablespoon water. Spread over each base, then top with the ham and mozzarella. Bake for 12–15 minutes, or until crisp and golden on the edges.
3 Just before serving, top with rocket and drizzle with the oil.

NUTRITION PER PIZZETTE
Protein 17 g; Fat 5 g; Carbohydrate 45 g; Dietary Fibre 6 g; Cholesterol 23 mg; 1235 kJ (295 Cal)

ISLAND SHAKE

This refreshing tropical blend will boost your vitamin C, beta-carotene and antioxidant intake.

Prep time: 10 minutes + chilling
Cooking time: Nil
Serves 2
EASY

---

400 g fresh mango pulp
1/2 cup (125 ml) lime juice
1/2 cup (125 ml) light coconut milk
2 teaspoons honey
3 teaspoons finely chopped fresh mint
200 g ice cubes

1 Place the mango pulp, lime juice, coconut milk, honey, mint and ice in a blender and blend until smooth.
2 Chill well and serve.

NUTRITION PER SERVE
Protein 3 g; Fat 6.5 g; Carbohydrate 33 g; Dietary Fibre 3 g; Cholesterol 0 g; 875 kJ (210 Cal)

ICED HONEYED COFFEE

This drink increases your alertness as well as increasing your calcium, phosphorus and riboflavin intake.

Prep time: 10 minutes + chilling + freezing time
Cooking time: Nil
Serves 2
EASY.

---

1 1/2 cups (375 ml) very strong (double
   strength) fresh coffee
2 tablespoons honey
1 1/2 cups (375 ml) reduced-fat milk
caster sugar, to taste

1 Pour the hot coffee into a heatproof jug and add the honey. Stir until the honey has dissolved, then chill in the refrigerator.
2 Add the milk and taste for sweetness. Add a little caster sugar if necessary. Pour about 1/2 cup (125 ml) of the mixture into eight holes of an ice-cube tray and freeze. Meanwhile, chill the remaining mixture in the refrigerator.

3 When ready to serve, place four coffee ice cubes in each glass, then pour in the iced coffee.

NUTRITION PER SERVE
Protein 8 g; Fat 2.5 g; Carbohydrate 34 g; Dietary Fibre 0.2 g; Cholesterol 13.5 mg; 775 kJ (185 Cal)

NOTE: You can make this using instant coffee, just use twice as many granules as you would for a normal cup of coffee.

FRUIT SPRITZER

More nutritious than soft drink, this sparkling drink provides vitamin C, potassium and beta-carotene.

Prep time: 5 minutes
Cooking time: Nil
Serves 4
EASY

---

2 cups (500 ml) apricot nectar, chilled
2 cups (500 ml) soda water, chilled
1 cup (250 ml) apple juice, chilled
1 cup (250 ml) orange juice, chilled
8 ice cubes

1 Place the apricot nectar, soda water, apple juice, orange juice and ice cubes in a large jug and stir until combined.
2 Pour into glasses and serve.

NUTRITION PER SERVE
Protein 0.5 g; Fat 0.2 g; Carbohydrate 30 g; Dietary Fibre 0 g; Cholesterol 0 g; 505 kJ (120 Cal)

Island shake (left), Iced honeyed coffee (top), and Fruit spritzer (right)

Rice paper rolls with dipping sauce (top), and Cannellini bean and chickpea dip

RICE PAPER ROLLS WITH DIPPING SAUCE

This vegetarian snack is full of vitamin C, folate and beta-carotene, with some iron and calcium.

Prep time: 40 minutes + 5 minutes soaking
Cooking time: 2 minutes
Serves 4
MEDIUM

50 g dried rice vermicelli
200 g frozen soya beans
16 square (15 cm) rice paper wrappers
1 zucchini, julienned
1 Lebanese cucumber, julienned
1 carrot, grated
1 cup (20 g) fresh mint, julienned
100 g tofu, cut into 1 cm wide batons

Dipping sauce
1/3 cup (80 ml) fish sauce
2 tablespoons chopped fresh coriander leaves
2 small red chillies, finely chopped
2 teaspoons soft brown sugar
2 teaspoons lime juice

1 Soak the vermicelli in hot water for 5 minutes, or until soft. Drain and cut into 5 cm lengths. Bring a saucepan of water to the boil, add the soya beans and cook for 2 minutes. Drain well.
2 Working with no more than two wrappers at a time, dip each rice paper wrapper in warm water for 10 seconds. Drain, then lay out on a flat work surface.
3 Place a small amount of vermicelli on the bottom third of each wrapper, leaving a 2 cm border either side. Top with a little zucchini, cucumber, carrot, soya beans, mint and 2 batons of tofu. Keeping the filling compact and neat, fold in the sides and roll up tightly. Seal with a little water. Cover with a damp cloth.
4 To make the dipping sauce, combine the fish sauce, coriander, chilli, sugar, lime juice and 2 tablespoons water in a small bowl. Serve with the rice paper rolls.

NUTRITION PER SERVE
Protein 13 g; Fat 5.5 g; Carbohydrate 46.5 g; Dietary Fibre 5.5 g; Cholesterol 0 mg; 1200 kJ (285 Cal)

CANNELLINI BEAN AND CHICKPEA DIP

This filling dip is an excellent source of fibre and slowly digested starch. Eat it with fresh vegetables for an antioxidant boost.

Prep time: 10 minutes
Cooking time: Nil
Serves 3–4
EASY

400 g can cannellini beans, rinsed and drained
400 g can chickpeas, rinsed and drained
1 1/2 teaspoons ground cumin
3 cloves garlic, crushed
2 tablespoons chopped fresh flat-leaf parsley
1/4 cup (60 ml) lemon juice
1 teaspoon grated lemon rind
1 tablespoon tahini

1 Place all the ingredients in a food processor and process for 30 seconds. With the motor still running, slowly add 1/4 cup (60 ml) hot water to the processor in a thin stream until the mixture is smooth and 'dippable'. Serve at room temperature with crudités and pitta crisps.

NUTRITION PER SERVE (4)
Protein 11 g; Fat 5 g; Carbohydrate 19 g; Dietary Fibre 9 g; Cholesterol 0 mg; 675 kJ (160 Cal)

STRAWBERRY AND WATERMELON SLUSHY

Peel and seed a large watermelon to give 2 kg flesh and place it in a bowl. Add 250 g hulled strawberries and 2 teaspoons caster sugar. Blend in batches in a blender or food processor until smooth, then pour into a shallow metal tray. Cover with plastic wrap and freeze for 2–3 hours, or until the mixture begins to freeze. Remove from the freezer and return to the blender. Whiz quickly to break up the ice, pour into a jug and serve immediately. Serves 4–6

NUTRITION PER SERVE (6)
Protein 1.5 g; Fat 0.5 g; Carbohydrate 19 g; Dietary Fibre 3 g; Cholesterol 0 mg; 375 kJ (90 Cal)

PEACHY KEEN

This drink is a great dessert or snack. It's low in fat but high in flavour, vitamin C, beta-carotene and healthy flavonoids.

Prep time: 15 minutes
Cooking time: Nil
Serves 2
EASY

─────

3/4 cup (185 g) low-fat peach and mango
    yoghurt
3/4 cup (185 ml) apricot nectar, chilled
1/2 cup (60 g) fresh or frozen raspberries
11/2 cups (300 g) diced fresh peaches
8 large ice cubes
fresh peach wedges, to serve

1 Place the yoghurt, apricot nectar, raspberries, peaches and ice in a blender and blend until smooth.
2 Serve with the peach wedges.

NUTRITION PER SERVE
Protein 6.5 g; Fat 0.5 g; Carbohydrate 36 g; Dietary Fibre 4.5 g; Cholesterol 3 g; 750 kJ (180 Cal)

PASSIONFRUIT LIME CRUSH

More nutritious than a regular cordial drink, this tangy mix provides a burst of sweet energy with fibre, beta-carotene and small amounts of minerals.

Prep time: 10 minutes
Cooking time: Nil
Serves 4
EASY

─────

1/2 cup (125 g) passionfruit pulp
3/4 cup (185 ml) lime juice cordial
3 cups (750 ml) ginger ale
crushed ice

1 Combine the passionfruit pulp, lime juice cordial and ginger ale in a large jug. Mix well.
2 Pour into glasses filled with crushed ice. Serve immediately.

NUTRITION PER SERVE
Protein 0.5 g; Fat 0 g; Carbohydrate 40 g; Dietary Fibre 1.7 g; Cholesterol 0 g; 700 kJ (170 Cal)

BANANA SOY LATTE

This drink has less fat than a chocolate smoothie and more nutrients than iced coffee, plus good amounts of calcium, phosphorus and potassium.

Prep time: 10 minutes
Cooking time: Nil
Serves 4
EASY

─────

13/4 cups (440 ml) coffee-flavoured soy milk,
    chilled
2 bananas, sliced
8 large ice cubes
1 teaspoon drinking chocolate
1/4 teaspoon ground cinnamon

1 Place the soy milk and sliced bananas in a blender and process until smooth.
2 With the blender running, add the ice cubes one at a time until well incorporated and the desired consistency is reached.
3 Pour into tall chilled glasses and sprinkle generously with the drinking chocolate and ground cinnamon.

NUTRITION PER SERVE
Protein 4 g; Fat 3.5 g; Carbohydrate 19 g; Dietary Fibre 1.5 g; Cholesterol 0 g; 520 kJ (125 Cal)

CRUNCHY WEDGES

Preheat the oven to moderately hot 200°C (400°F/Gas 6). Cut 6 potatoes into eight wedges each. Dry, then toss with 1 tablespoon oil. Combine 1/2 teaspoon chicken or vegetable stock powder, 1/4 cup (25 g/3/4 oz) dry breadcrumbs, 2 teaspoons chopped fresh chives, 1 teaspoon celery salt, 1/4 teaspoon garlic powder and 1/2 teaspoon chopped fresh rosemary. Add the wedges and toss. Spread on greased baking trays and bake for 40 minutes, or until golden. Serves 6

NUTRITION PER SERVE
Protein 4 g; Fat 2.5 g; Carbohydrate 22.5 g; Dietary Fibre 3 g; Cholesterol 0 mg; 555 kJ (135 Cal)

Peachy keen (left), Passionfruit lime crush (top), and Banana soy latte (right)

DOLMADES

This snack provides monounsaturated fat, some beta-carotene, niacin and minerals.

Prep time: 1 hour + cooling
Cooking time: 1 hour 5 minutes
Makes 20–25
DIFFICULT

1/2 cup (125 ml) olive oil
6 spring onions, chopped
3/4 cup (150 g) long-grain rice
1/4 cup (15 g) chopped fresh mint
2 tablespoons chopped fresh dill
2/3 cup (170 ml) lemon juice
1/4 cup (35 g) currants
1/4 cup (40 g) pine nuts
240 g (about 50) packaged vine leaves
2 tablespoons olive oil, extra

1 Heat the oil in a pan over medium heat. Cook the spring onion for 1 minute. Stir in the rice, mint, dill and half the lemon juice, then season. Add 1 cup (250 ml) water and bring to the boil. Reduce the heat, cover and simmer for 20 minutes.

Remove the lid, fork through the currants and pine nuts, cover with a paper towel, then the lid, and leave to cool.
2 Rinse and separate the vine leaves. Drain, then dry on paper towels. Trim any thick stems. Line the base of a 20 cm pan (with a lid) with any torn or misshapen leaves.
3 Place each leaf shiny side down. Spoon a tablespoon of filling into the centre, bring in the sides and roll up tightly from the stem end. Place seam side down with the stem end closest to you in pan, tightly, in a single layer.
4 Pour in the remaining lemon juice, extra oil and 3/4 cup (185 ml) water to just cover the dolmades. Cover with an inverted plate. Place a can on the plate to compress the dolmades. Cover with the lid.
5 Bring to the boil, then reduce the heat and simmer for 45 minutes. Allow to cool in the pan. Serve at room temperature.

NUTRITION PER DOLMADE (25)
Protein 1.5 g; Fat 7.5 g; Carbohydrate 6 g; Dietary Fibre 1 g; Cholesterol 0 mg; 380 kJ (90 Cal)

FRUIT BARS

A great snack when you're on the run, these fruit bars provide carbohydrate, unsaturated fat, beta-carotene, vitamin E and minerals.

Prep time: 10 minutes + cooling
Cooking time: 25 minutes
Makes 16–20
EASY

2 cups (60 g) puffed rice cereal
1 1/2 cups (150 g) rolled oats
1/4 cup (30 g) sunflower seeds
1/4 cup (40 g) sesame seeds
200 g packet dried fruit medley
1/3 cup (60 g) rice flour
1/2 cup (125 ml) liquid glucose
1/4 cup (90 g) honey

1 Preheat the oven to moderate 180°C (350°F/Gas 4). Line the base and two long sides of a 29 x 19 cm tin with baking paper. Place the puffed rice cereal, rolled oats, sunflower seeds, sesame seeds, dried fruit and rice flour in a bowl, and mix together well.

2 Place the liquid glucose and honey in a small saucepan and heat gently over medium heat for 2 minutes, or until runny. Stir the syrup into the dry ingredients and mix well to coat.

3 Press the mixture firmly into the tin. Place a sheet of baking paper over the mixture and use the back of a spoon or a measuring cup to spread it evenly. Remove the top sheet of baking paper. Bake for 20 minutes, or until golden brown. Leave to cool and crisp in the tin, before lifting out and cutting into fingers. Store in an airtight container in the refrigerator.

NUTRITION PER BAR (20)
Protein 2.5 g; Fat 3 g; Carbohydrate 25 g; Dietary Fibre 1.5 g; Cholesterol 0 mg; 560 kJ (135 Cal)

NOTE: Liquid glucose is available from health food stores.
VARIATION: Any low-fat sports breakfast cereal can be used in this recipe.

CARROT COCKTAIL

This drink is rich in vitamin C and beta-carotene, and also provides some folate and niacin.

Prep time: 10 minutes
Cooking time: Nil
Serves 2
EASY

10–12 carrots, quartered lengthways
1/2 cup (125 ml) pineapple juice
1/2 cup (125 ml) orange juice
1–2 teaspoons honey, to taste
8 ice cubes

1 Using the plunger, push the carrot pieces through a juicer.
2 Combine the carrot juice with the pineapple juice, orange juice, honey and ice cubes in a jug and serve.

NUTRITION PER SERVE
Protein 3 g; Fat 0.5 g; Carbohydrate 34 g; Dietary Fibre 10 g; Cholesterol 0 g; 640 kJ (150 Cal)

GINGER AND LEMON SOOTHER

This drink provides vitamin C and potassium, and may help ease a cold or stomach ache.

Prep time: 10 minutes + infusing + chilling time
Cooking time: Nil
Serves 4
EASY

2 cm piece fresh ginger, thinly sliced
1/2 cup (125 ml) lemon juice
21/2 tablespoons honey
1 tablespoon fresh mint leaves

1 Place the ginger, lemon juice, honey and mint in a heatproof jug and cover with 3 cups (750 ml) boiling water. Leave to infuse for 2–3 hours, or until cold.
2 When the mixture is cold, strain into another jug and chill in the refrigerator.
3 Serve in tall, chilled glasses over ice.

NUTRITION PER SERVE
Protein 0.2 g; Fat 0 g; Carbohydrate 15 g; Dietary Fibre 0 g; Cholesterol 0 mg; 260 kJ (60 Cal)

NOTE: This drink is delicious served the next day as all the flavours will have time to infuse.

PINEAPPLE WITH MANDARIN SORBET

This sweet snack is low in fat but high in fibre, vitamin C and potassium.

Prep time: 10 minutes + chilling
Cooking time: Nil
Serves 2
EASY

1 (2.4 kg) pineapple, peeled and cored
1 cup (250 ml) ginger ale
4 scoops mandarin sorbet

1 Roughly chop the pineapple flesh, then push it through a juicer.
2 Combine the pineapple juice and the ginger ale in a large jug; chill.
3 Pour the juice into chilled glasses and top with scoops of the mandarin sorbet.

NUTRITION PER SERVE
Protein 3.5 g; Fat 0.5 g; Carbohydrate 64 g; Dietary Fibre 5 g; Cholesterol 0 g; 1115 kJ (265 Cal)

GRILLED PIDE SANDWICHES

Cut a Turkish pide bread into quarters and split each piece in half horizontally. Spread each piece of bread with 1 teaspoon Dijon mustard. Combine 100 g low-fat cottage cheese and 2 tablespoons finely shredded fresh basil and spread over the mustard. Divide 200 g shaved light ham, 30 g baby English spinach leaves and 2 large sliced tomatoes among the sandwiches. Spray a sandwich grill or toasted sandwich maker with olive oil spray and cook each sandwich for 3 minutes, or until crisp and golden. Serves 4

NUTRITION PER SERVE
Protein 15 g; Fat 4 g; Carbohydrate 13 g; Dietary Fibre 1.5 g; Cholesterol 37.5 mg; 675 kJ (160 Cal)

Carrot cocktail (left), Ginger and lemon soother (top), and Pineapple with mandarin sorbet (right)

VEGETABLE FRITTATA

A nourishing snack or meal with a greater range of nutrients than scrambled eggs, this dish is a good source of vitamin A, folate, vitamin B12 and high-quality protein.

Prep time: 25 minutes
Cooking time: 25 minutes
Serves 6
EASY

200 g zucchini, cubed
250 g pumpkin, cubed
300 g potato, cubed
100 g broccoli florets
3 teaspoons oil
1 small onion, chopped
1 small red capsicum, chopped
2 tablespoons finely chopped fresh parsley
3 eggs
2 egg whites

1 Steam the zucchini, pumpkin, potato and broccoli until tender, then transfer to a bowl.

2 Heat 2 teaspoons of the oil in a non-stick frying pan, about 22 cm in diameter. Add the onion and capsicum, and cook for 3 minutes, or until tender. Transfer to the bowl of steamed vegetables, along with the chopped parsley.

3 Brush the pan with the remaining oil. Return all the vegetables to the pan and spread out with a spatula to an even thickness. Beat the eggs and whites together and pour into the pan, tilting to distribute evenly.

4 Cook over medium heat until the egg is almost set, but still runny on top. Wrap the handle of the pan in a damp tea towel to protect it and place the pan under the grill to cook the frittata top (pierce gently with a fork to make sure it is cooked through). Cut into wedges and serve.

NUTRITION PER SERVE
Protein 8 g; Fat 5 g; Carbohydrate 10.5 g; Dietary Fibre 3 g; Cholesterol 93.5 mg; 510 kJ (120 Cal)

BEETROOT HUMMUS

Beetroot adds colour, flavour, carotene and folate to this delicious, fibre-rich dip.

Prep time: 15 minutes
Cooking time: 40 minutes
Serves 8 (Makes 2 cups)
EASY

500 g beetroot, trimmed
1/4 cup (60 ml) olive oil
1 large onion, chopped
1 tablespoon ground cumin
400 g can chickpeas, drained
1 tablespoon tahini
1/3 cup (90 g) low-fat plain yoghurt
3 cloves garlic, crushed
1/4 cup (60 ml) lemon juice
1/2 cup (125 ml) vegetable stock

1 Scrub the beetroot well. Bring a large saucepan of water to the boil and cook the beetroot for 35–40 minutes over high heat, or until soft and cooked through. Drain and cool slightly before peeling.

2 Meanwhile, heat 1 tablespoon of the oil in a frying pan over medium heat and cook the onion for 2–3 minutes, or until soft. Add the cumin and cook for a further 1 minute, or until fragrant.
3 Chop the beetroot and place in a food processor or blender with the onion mixture, chickpeas, tahini, yoghurt, garlic, lemon juice and stock, and process until smooth. With the motor running, add the remaining oil in a thin steady stream. Process until the mixture is thoroughly combined, adding a little water if it is too thick. Serve the hummus with Lebanese or Turkish bread.

NUTRITION PER SERVE
Protein 5.5 g; Fat 9 g; Carbohydrate 13 g; Dietary Fibre 4.5 g; Cholesterol 0.5 mg; 640 kJ (155 Cal)

VARIATION: You can use 500 g of any vegetable to make the hummus. Try carrot or pumpkin.

RUBY GRAPEFRUIT FIZZ

This sweet, fizzy drink provides carbohydrate energy, vitamin C and potassium.

Prep time: 5 minutes
Cooking time: Nil
Serves 4
EASY

2 cups (500 ml) ruby grapefruit juice
1 cup (250 ml) soda water
1 tablespoon caster sugar
4 scoops lemon sorbet

1 Combine the ruby grapefruit juice, soda water and caster sugar in a large jug, stir, then refrigerate.
2 Pour into chilled glasses and top with a scoop of lemon sorbet.

NUTRITION PER SERVE
Protein 1 g; Fat 0 g; Carbohydrate 26 g; Dietary Fibre 0 g; Cholesterol 0 g; 460 kJ (110 Cal)

APPLE AND CINNAMON INFUSION

This delicious combination will provide a sweet burst of energy, fibre and potassium.

Prep time: 10 minutes + chilling
Cooking time: 15 minutes
Serves 2
EASY

4 (600 g) golden delicious apples, roughly chopped
1 cinnamon stick
3–4 tablespoons soft brown sugar
ice cubes, to serve

1 Place the apple, cinnamon stick, brown sugar and 1 litre water in a pan. Bring to the boil, then reduce the heat and simmer for 10–15 minutes, or until the flavours have infused and the apple has softened.
2 Remove from the heat, cool slightly, then chill in the refrigerator until cold.
3 When cold, strain the infusion and serve it over lots of ice.

NUTRITION PER SERVE
Protein 1 g; Fat 0.5 g; Carbohydrate 53.5 g; Dietary Fibre 5 g; Cholesterol 0 g; 885 kJ (210 Cal)

BLUE MAPLE

More nutritious than a regular milkshake, this smoothie is very low in fat, yet rich in calcium and phosphorus. The berries provide vitamin C, flavonoids and fibre.

Prep time: 10 minutes
Cooking time: Nil
Serves 2
EASY

200 g low-fat blueberry fromage frais
3/4 cup (185 ml) low-fat milk
1 tablespoon maple syrup
1/2 teaspoon ground cinnamon
300 g frozen blueberries

1 Combine the fromage frais, milk, maple syrup, cinnamon and 250 g blueberries in a blender until smooth.
2 Pour into chilled glasses and top with the remaining blueberries.

NUTRITION PER SERVE
Protein 11 g; Fat 0.5 g; Carbohydrate 0 g; Dietary Fibre 2.7 g; Cholesterol 7 g; 940 kJ (225 Cal)

PINEAPPLE AND MINT ICE BLOCKS

Purée 500 g pineapple flesh and 10 fresh mint leaves in a blender or food processor until smooth. Sweeten with 1–2 teaspoons caster sugar. Pour the pineapple purée into six plastic ice-block moulds. Freeze for 30 minutes, add the ice-block sticks, and return to the freezer. Freeze for 2 1/2–3 hours, or until the ice blocks are frozen solid. Makes 6

NUTRITION PER SERVE
Protein 1 g; Fat 0 g; Carbohydrate 7.5 g; Dietary Fibre 2 g; Cholesterol 0 mg; 150 kJ (35 Cal)

Ruby grapefruit fizz (left), Apple and cinnamon infusion (top), and Blue maple (right)

POLENTA WITH MUSHROOMS

This dish contains mostly monounsaturated fat and good amounts of fibre, B vitamins and folate.

Prep time: 20 minutes + 10 minutes soaking +
   30 minutes refrigeration
Cooking time: 40 minutes
Serves 4
EASY

1 litre vegetable stock
1 cup (150 g) polenta
40 g low-fat margarine
1 tablespoon grated fresh Parmesan
rocket, to serve
Parmesan shavings, to serve

Mushroom sauce
10 g dried porcini mushrooms
1 tablespoon olive oil
800 g mixed mushrooms, thickly sliced
4 cloves garlic, finely chopped
2 teaspoons chopped fresh thyme
3/4 cup (185 ml) dry white wine
1/2 cup (125 ml) vegetable stock
1/2 cup (30 g) chopped fresh parsley

1 Bring the stock to the boil in a large saucepan. Add the polenta in a thin stream, stirring constantly. Simmer for 20 minutes over very low heat, stirring frequently, until the mixture starts to leave the side of the pan. Add the margarine and Parmesan, and season with salt and ground black pepper. Grease a shallow 20 cm square cake tin. Pour in the polenta, smooth the surface and refrigerate for 30 minutes, or until set.
2 To make the mushroom sauce, soak the porcini mushrooms in 1/2 cup (125 ml) boiling water for 10 minutes, or until softened. Drain, reserving 1/3 cup (80 ml) of the liquid.
3 Heat the oil in a large frying pan. Add the mixed mushrooms and cook over high heat for 4–5 minutes, or until softened. Add the porcini, garlic and thyme, then season and cook for 2–3 minutes. Add the wine and cook until it has evaporated.

Add the vegetable stock, then reduce the heat and cook for a further 3–4 minutes, or until the stock has reduced and thickened. Add the parsley.
4 Cut the polenta into 4 squares and grill until golden on both sides. Place one square on each serving plate and top with the mushrooms. Garnish with rocket and Parmesan shavings.

NUTRITION PER SERVE
Protein 14.5 g; Fat 11 g; Carbohydrate 31.5 g; Dietary Fibre 7 g; Cholesterol 1.5 mg; 1335 kJ (320 Cal)

HERBED COTTAGE CHEESE POTATO

This is a very sustaining snack that will give you more nutrients than potato crisps. It is a great source of B vitamins, vitamin C, beta-carotene, potassium and phosphorus.

Prep time: 20 minutes
Cooking time: 40 minutes
Serves 4
EASY

4 large potatoes or orange sweet potatoes
200 g blanched, chopped spinach leaves
1 cup (250 g) low-fat cottage cheese
2 tablespoons chopped, mixed fresh herbs
   (basil, parsley, oregano)
1/2 cup (80 g) rinsed, chopped sun-dried
   capsicum
125 g diced mushrooms

1 Preheat the oven to moderately hot 200°C (400°F/Gas 6). Bake the potatoes for 40 minutes, or until cooked through.
2 Place the spinach leaves, cottage cheese, herbs, sun-dried capsicum and mushrooms in a bowl, and mix together well. Divide among the baked potatoes. Serve hot.

NUTRITION PER SERVE
Protein 15.5 g; Fat 1 g; Carbohydrate 21.5 g; Dietary Fibre 3.5 g; Cholesterol 8 mg; 665 kJ (160 Cal)

NOTE: Sun-dried capsicum can be bought dehydrated. To reconstitute, soak in warm water for 20 minutes, then drain. Otherwise, buy sun-dried capsicum in oil and rinse well before using.

Polenta with mushrooms (top), and Herbed cottage cheese potato

Yoghurt and honey smoothie (left), Summer fruit drink (top), and Orange sorbet soda (right)

YOGHURT AND HONEY SMOOTHIE

A soothing, sweet drink, this smoothie is rich in calcium, potassium and phosphorus, with a little vitamin A and B2.

Prep time: 10 minutes
Cooking time: Nil
Serves 4
EASY

1 cup (250 g) thick plain low-fat yoghurt
3 tablespoons honey
1 cup (250 ml) reduced-fat milk
3 scoops low-fat vanilla ice cream

1 Blend the yoghurt and honey in a blender for 10 seconds, or until well combined. Add the milk and ice cream and blend until smooth.
2 Serve in chilled glasses.

NUTRITION PER SERVE
Protein 7 g; Fat 1.5 g; Carbohydrate 28 g; Dietary Fibre 0 g; Cholesterol 9.5 g; 640 kJ (155 Cal)

SUMMER FRUIT DRINK

This refreshing drink is bursting with vitamin C, folate, potassium and fibre.

Prep time: 15 minutes
Cooking time: Nil
Serves 2
EASY

3 oranges
250 g strawberries
300 g seedless grapes
2 peaches

1 Peel the oranges and cut to fit a juicer. Push through with the plunger.
2 Wash and hull the strawberries. Push the strawberries and grapes through the juicer with the plunger.
3 Place the peaches in a heatproof bowl and cover with boiling water. Leave for 30 seconds, then transfer to cold water. Peel away the skin. Cut the flesh from the stone and push through the juicer.
4 Pour the drink into two glasses and serve with long spoons.

NUTRITION PER SERVE
Protein 6 g; Fat 0.5 g; Carbohydrate 50.5 g; Dietary Fibre 10 g; Cholesterol 0 g; 985 kJ (235 Cal)

ORANGE SORBET SODA

This low-fat, fizzy spider drink provides vitamin C, folate, beta-carotene and potassium.

Prep time: 10 minutes
Cooking time: Nil
Serves 2
EASY

2 cups (500 ml) freshly squeezed orange juice
1 cup (250 ml) lemonade
2–4 scoops lemon sorbet

1 Combine the orange juice and lemonade in a jug. Pour into large, chilled glasses, allowing enough room for the sorbet.
2 Add 1–2 scoops sorbet per glass.

NUTRITION PER SERVE
Protein 2 g; Fat 0.5 g; Carbohydrate 57 g; Dietary Fibre 0 g; Cholesterol 0 g; 980 kJ (235 Cal)

WILD BERRIES

Combine 1 cup (250 g) low-fat strawberry yoghurt and 1/2 cup (125 ml) chilled cranberry juice in a blender. Add 250 g hulled, quartered strawberries and 80 g frozen raspberries. Blend until smooth. Pour into chilled glasses and divide 45 g frozen raspberries among the glasses. Serve with a spoon. Serves 4

NUTRITION PER SERVE
Protein 4 g; Fat 0.5 g; Carbohydrate 10 g; Dietary Fibre 3.5 g; Cholesterol 1.5 g; 295 kJ (70 Cal)

LOW-FAT CHICKEN CAESAR SALAD

A lower-fat version of a popular salad, this dish provides good amounts of B vitamins and minerals.

Prep time: 25 minutes
Cooking time: 35 minutes
Serves 4
EASY

---

100 g thickly sliced white bread, crusts removed
8 rashers lean bacon, rind removed (about 90 g)
500 g chicken breast fillet
3/4 teaspoon garlic salt
1 cos lettuce (reserve some leaves for serving and tear the remaining leaves into small pieces)
2 tablespoons grated fresh Parmesan
4 anchovies, drained and chopped

Dressing
2 cloves garlic, crushed
2 teaspoons Worcestershire sauce
1 tablespoon Dijon mustard
1 1/2 tablespoons lemon juice
2 anchovies, drained and finely chopped
2 tablespoons olive oil
1/2 teaspoon caster sugar
Tabasco sauce, to taste

1 Preheat the oven to moderate 180°C (350°F/Gas 4). Cut the bread slices into 1.5 cm cubes then spread evenly on a baking tray. Bake for 12–15 minutes, or until golden brown. Allow to cool.
2 Cut the bacon into 5 mm strips and place on a foil-lined baking tray. Cook for 10–12 minutes, or until lightly browned. Drain on paper towels and allow to cool.
3 Cut the chicken breast in half lengthways to form two thin schnitzels. Coat the chicken in the garlic salt, pressing firmly into the flesh. Cook under a hot grill for 3–4 minutes each side, or until just cooked. Remove and cool slightly.
4 To make the dressing, whisk all the ingredients until combined.
5 Arrange the reserved lettuce leaves in serving bowls, then divide the torn leaves among them. Slice the chicken breast on the diagonal and arrange on top of the lettuce. Pour the dressing over the chicken, then scatter the croutons and bacon on top. Sprinkle with the Parmesan and garnish with the chopped anchovy.

NUTRITION PER SERVE
Protein 37 g; Fat 20 g; Carbohydrate 14 g; Dietary Fibre 2 g; Cholesterol 102 mg; 1590 kJ (380 Cal)

BEAN ENCHILADAS

Although relatively high in fat, this filling snack is a great choice for vegetarians, providing soluble fibre, slow-release carbohydrate, B vitamins, folate, iron and zinc.

Prep time: 20 minutes
Cooking time: 25 minutes
Serves 4
MEDIUM

---

1 tablespoon light olive oil
1 onion, thinly sliced
3 cloves garlic, crushed
1 bird's eye chilli, finely chopped
2 teaspoons ground cumin
1/2 cup (125 ml) vegetable stock
3 tomatoes, peeled, seeded and chopped
1 tablespoon tomato paste
2 x 430 g cans three-bean mix
2 tablespoons chopped fresh coriander leaves
8 flour tortillas
1 avocado, peeled and chopped
3/4 cup (185 g) light sour cream
1/2 cup (10 g) fresh coriander sprigs
2 cups (160 g) shredded lettuce

1 Heat the oil in a deep frying pan over medium heat. Add the onion and cook for 3–4 minutes, or until just soft. Add the garlic and chilli and cook for a further 30 seconds. Add the cumin, vegetable stock, tomato and tomato paste and cook for 6–8 minutes, or until the mixture is quite thick and pulpy. Season with salt and ground black pepper.

2 Preheat the oven to warm 170°C (325°F/ Gas 3). Drain and rinse the beans, add to the sauce and cook for 5 minutes to heat through, then add the chopped coriander.

3 Meanwhile, wrap the tortillas in foil and warm in the oven for 3–4 minutes.

4 Place a tortilla on a plate and spread with 1/4 cup of the bean mixture. Top with some avocado, sour cream, coriander sprigs and lettuce. Roll the enchiladas up, tucking in the ends. Cut each one in half to serve.

NUTRITION PER SERVE
Protein 20 g; Fat 26 g; Carbohydrate 53 g; Dietary Fibre 16 g; Cholesterol 29.5 mg; 2190 kJ (525 Cal)

RASPBERRY AND APPLE JUICE

This drink will satisfy your thirst and your daily vitamin C needs.

Prep time: 5 minutes + chilling
Cooking time: Nil
Serves 2
EASY

---

6 Granny Smith apples, quartered
150 g fresh raspberries
ice cubes, to serve
mint sprigs, to garnish

1 Using the plunger, push the apple pieces and raspberries through a juicer and into a jug. Chill.
2 Stir well before serving. Add ice and garnish with mint sprigs.

NUTRITION PER SERVE
Protein 1.5 g; Fat 0.5 g; Carbohydrate 30 g; Dietary Fibre 8 g; Cholesterol 0 g; 515 kJ (125 Cal)

ICED LEMON AND PEPPERMINT TEA

Enjoy this refreshing tea with few calories and small amounts of many vitamins and minerals.

Prep time: 10 minutes + infusing + chilling
Cooking time: Nil
Serves 2
EASY

---

2 peppermint tea bags
6 strips lemon rind (2 x 5 cm)
1 tablespoon sugar
ice cubes, to serve
fresh mint leaves, to garnish

1 Place the tea bags and lemon rind strips in a large bowl. Cover with 3¹/3 cups (830 ml) boiling water and leave to infuse for 5 minutes.
2 Squeeze out the tea bags and discard. Stir in the sugar to taste.

3 Pour into a jug and chill. Serve in chilled glasses with the ice cubes and fresh mint leaves.

NUTRITION PER SERVE
Protein 0.5 g; Fat 0.5 g; Carbohydrate 8.5 g; Dietary Fibre 0 g; Cholesterol 0 g; 165 kJ (40 Cal)

HAWAIIAN CRUSH

This tropical drink is a good source of beta-carotene, potassium and healthy plant compounds.

Prep time: 10 minutes + chilling
Cooking time: Nil
Serves 2
EASY

---

1 cup (250 ml) apple juice
100 g papaya, peeled, seeded, chopped
200 g watermelon, seeded, chopped
100 g ice cubes

1 Blend the apple juice, papaya, watermelon and ice cubes in a blender until smooth.
2 Chill well. Pour into glasses and serve.

NUTRITION PER SERVE
Protein 0.5 g; Fat 0.25 g; Carbohydrate 21.5 g; Dietary Fibre 2 g; Cholesterol 0 g; 375 kJ (90 Cal)

MELON FREEZIE

Remove the rind and seeds from 500 g rockmelon and 500 g honeydew melon. Cut the flesh into pieces, place in a blender and blend for 1 minute, or until smooth. Add 12 ice cubes and 2 cups (500 ml) orange juice and blend for 30 seconds. Transfer to a large shallow plastic dish and freeze for 3 hours. Return the mixture to the blender and blend quickly until smooth. Serve immediately. Serves 4

NUTRITION PER SERVE
Protein 2 g; Fat 0.5 g; Carbohydrate 21.5 g; Dietary Fibre 2.5 g; Cholesterol 0 mg; 415 kJ (100 Cal)

Raspberry and apple juice (left), Iced lemon and peppermint tea (top), and Hawaiian crush (right)

LAYERED COBS

These filling rolls provide carbohydrate, B vitamins, folate and minerals.

Prep time: 45 minutes + overnight refrigeration
Cooking time: 30 minutes
Makes 6
MEDIUM

---

1 red capsicum, cut into large pieces
1 large zucchini, thinly sliced on the diagonal
2 slender eggplants, thinly sliced on the diagonal
70 g English spinach leaves
100 g ricotta
6 round bread rolls
1 tablespoon olive oil
1 clove garlic, crushed
1 tablespoon snipped fresh chives
90 g sliced light leg ham, cut into quarters

1 Cook the capsicum, skin side up, under a hot grill until blackened and blistered. Place in a plastic bag, cool, then remove the skin. Cut into strips.
2 Lightly spray a non-stick frying pan with oil. Cook the zucchini and eggplant in batches until golden. Steam the spinach until just wilted. Cool, squeeze and chop. Combine with the ricotta, and season.
3 Cut the tops from the rolls and remove the bread inside, leaving a 1 cm border. Combine the oil, garlic and chives, and brush inside each roll. Add a layer of capsicum and zucchini, spread with the ricotta mixture, then top with the ham and eggplant. Lightly press down, then replace the lids.
4 Cover with plastic wrap and place tightly in a baking dish. Place a tray on top and weigh down with heavy cans or weights. Refrigerate overnight.
5 Preheat the oven to hot 220°C (425°F/ Gas 7). Remove the plastic wrap from the rolls, place on a baking tray and bake for 10–15 minutes, or until crisp.

NUTRITION PER COB
Protein 15 g; Fat 8 g; Carbohydrate 45 g; Dietary Fibre 4.5 g; Cholesterol 16 mg; 1330 kJ (320 Cal)

SPINACH PIE

Lower in fat than many commercial varieties, this pie also contains B vitamins, fibre and iron.

Prep time: 25 minutes
Cooking time: 50 minutes
Serves 6
MEDIUM

1.5 kg English spinach, trimmed and washed
2 teaspoons olive oil
1 onion, chopped
4 spring onions, chopped
750 g reduced-fat cottage cheese
2 eggs, lightly beaten
2 cloves garlic, crushed
pinch of ground nutmeg
1/4 cup (15 g) chopped fresh mint
8 sheets filo pastry
30 g butter, melted
1/2 cup (40 g) fresh breadcrumbs

1 Preheat the oven to moderate 180°C (350°F/Gas 4). Lightly spray a square 1.5 litre ovenproof dish with oil. Place the spinach in a large pan. Cover and cook for 2–3 minutes, or until just wilted. Drain, cool, then squeeze dry and chop.
2 Heat the oil in a small pan. Cook the onion and spring onion for 2–3 minutes, or until softened. Combine with the spinach. Stir in the cheese, egg, garlic, nutmeg and mint. Season, and mix thoroughly.
3 Brush a sheet of filo pastry with a little butter. Fold in half widthways and line the base and sides of the dish. Repeat with three more sheets. Keep the unused sheets moist by covering with a damp tea towel.
4 Sprinkle the breadcrumbs over the pastry. Spread the filling in the dish. Fold over any overlapping pastry. Brush and fold another sheet and place on top. Repeat with three more sheets. Tuck the pastry in. Brush the top with any leftover butter. Score squares on top. Bake for 40 minutes, or until golden.

NUTRITION PER SERVE
Protein 33.5 g; Fat 10 g; Carbohydrate 20.5 g; Dietary Fibre 8 g; Cholesterol 91.5 mg; 1295 kJ (310 Cal)

Layered cobs (top), and Spinach pie

SOUPS

Soups are a wonderful option for a healthy diet, and are a versatile way of incorporating the freshest seasonal ingredients into a one-pot meal that can be as simple or elaborate as you like.

There are many different types of soups that can be made to suit every occasion and season. Many traditional soups are naturally very healthy, or with a few simple changes can be made with relatively little fat, but still plenty of flavour.

Soup may be served as a starter, a light meal with some crusty bread and a green salad, or a hearty vegetable and bean soup can be a complete meal on a chilly winter evening.

Every cuisine around the world embraces soup, whether it be chunky Mediterranean soups flavoured with fresh basil or rosemary, the delicate miso of Japan, or the spicy noodle soups so popular in Southeast Asian cooking.

STOCKS

The making of a delicious soup begins with a flavoursome stock base. Stocks are readily available from the supermarket in waxed cardboard packs, and as stock cubes and powders, and these are great to keep in the pantry, although some brands are high in salt. However, it's very economical and simple to prepare your own stocks at home. Home-made stocks are full of flavour and contain very little fat and salt. They can be made and then frozen until you are ready to use them.

Beef stock

Roast 1.5 kg beef bones on a rack over a large roasting tin in a 220°C (425°F/ Gas 7) oven for 20 minutes. Add a quartered onion, 2 chopped carrots, 1 chopped leek and 1 chopped celery stick and roast for 20 minutes. Transfer to a stockpot with 10 peppercorns, a bouquet garni (a sprig of parsley, a sprig of thyme and a bay leaf wrapped together in a small piece of muslin) and 4 litres water. Bring to the boil, then reduce the heat and simmer for 6–8 hours, skimming regularly to remove any scum. Strain the stock and leave it to cool in the fridge. Lift off any fat that congeals on the top.

Chicken stock

Put 1 kg chicken carcasses in a stockpot with a bouquet garni, a quartered onion, 1 chopped carrot and 10 peppercorns. Add 4 litres water and bring to the boil, then reduce the heat and simmer, skimming regularly to remove any scum. Strain the stock, and remove any fat by dragging a piece of paper towel over the surface. Cool in the fridge. When cool, lift off any congealed fat.

Fish stock

Put 2 kg fish bones and heads, a bouquet garni, 1 chopped onion and 10 peppercorns in a stockpot. Add 2.5 litres water, bring to the boil, then reduce the heat and simmer the mixture  for 20–30 minutes. Skim off any scum. Strain the stock, then cool in the fridge. When cool, lift off any congealed fat. (When making a fish stock, it is better to use the bones from a white-fleshed fish such as cod, snapper or flounder rather than an oily fish such as salmon, tuna or mackerel.)

Vegetable stock

Put 500 g mixed chopped carrots, celery, onions and leeks in a stockpot with a bouquet garni and 10 peppercorns. Add 2.5 litres water and bring to the boil. Skim off any scum. Simmer for 1–2 hours, pressing the solids to extract all the flavour, then strain and cool in the fridge.

MAKING LOW-FAT SOUPS

When it comes to preparing soup, it is quite easy to reduce the amount of fat without sacrificing texture or flavour.

■ Instead of sautéing any vegetables in butter and oil, combine the vegetables with water or stock, and gently simmer until they are tender.

■ While the soup is gently simmering away on the stove, use a metal spoon to skim any fat that rises to the surface.

■ Many vegetable purée soups contain cream, but you can reduce their fat content simply by omitting the cream or using low-fat yoghurt. If you purée the soup in a blender, it will be so smooth and creamy that you won't miss the cream.

■ If you are looking for a rich, creamy flavour, stir through a spoonful of low-fat sour cream before serving. Don't boil the soup after the sour cream has been added or the soup may curdle. Sour cream is especially delicious in chunky bean soups or spicy Mexican-style soups.

■ Add a spoonful of low-fat plain yoghurt to add a delicious tang to Indian spiced bean and lentil soups. Don't boil the soup after adding yoghurt or it will curdle.

■ Make croutons for soup by simply dicing a sourdough loaf and baking the bread on a baking tray until crisp, instead of frying the bread in oil or butter. Croutons add a crunchy texture to puréed vegetables soups.

HEALTHY TIPS FOR TASTY SOUPS

■ If you are making a stock for an Asian-style soup, add some grated ginger, garlic, star anise, coriander roots and lemon grass.

■ Add a spoonful of finely diced tomato and cucumber on top of gazpacho or chilled cucumber soup.

■ Gremolata, a mixture of finely chopped fresh parsley, garlic and lemon rind, is a simple and tasty garnish to use on tomato-based soups.

■ Use chopped fresh herbs to add flavour.

■ Adding dried legumes to chunky soups is an easy way to add more fibre and minerals.

■ Turn a simple chicken broth into a meal by adding egg noodles, fresh herbs and shredded poached chicken breast.

■ Add some Chinese greens to a ginger-flavoured chicken broth. Try some baby bok choy, Chinese broccoli or Chinese cabbage, which are all very nutritious.

■ Clear soups or broths are suitable if you are unwell, as they are easily digested and are an excellent way of getting nourishment when you can't eat solid foods.

PEA AND HAM SOUP

The combination of slowly digested carbohydrate, fibre and protein makes this an extremely filling soup, which also contains B vitamins, folate and vitamin A.

Prep time: 15 minutes + overnight soaking
Cooking time: 2 hours 10 minutes
Serves 8
EASY

500 g yellow or green split peas
1 leek
1 tablespoon oil
2 carrots, chopped
1 celery stick, chopped
2 cloves garlic, crushed
750 g meaty ham bone

1 Put the split peas in a large bowl, cover with water and soak overnight.
2 Cut the leek in half lengthways and wash thoroughly to remove any dirt. Slice thickly. Heat the oil in a large heavy-based pan and add the leek, carrot, celery and garlic. Cook, stirring, for 2–3 minutes, then add the drained peas, the ham bone and 2.5 litres water. Bring to the boil, then reduce the heat and simmer for 2 hours, stirring occasionally.
3 Remove the ham bone and set it aside to cool. Cool the soup a little, then purée in batches in a blender or food processor and return to the pan. Remove the meat from the bone, chop and return the meat to the soup. Season to taste with salt and cracked black pepper, reheat gently and serve hot.

NUTRITION PER SERVE
Protein 17 g; Fat 8 g; Carbohydrate 8.5 g; Dietary Fibre 4 g; Cholesterol 30 mg; 725 kJ (175 Cal)

NOTE: If you forget to soak the split peas overnight, rinse them and cook the soup for longer until the peas are tender.

ROAST PUMPKIN SOUP

Roasted pumpkin gives a stronger flavour to this classic soup—rich in beta-carotene and potassium, with a little folate and vitamin C.

Prep time: 20 minutes
Cooking time: 55 minutes
Serves 6
EASY

1.25 kg pumpkin, peeled and cut into chunks
2 tablespoons olive oil
1 large onion, chopped
2 teaspoons ground cumin
1 large carrot, chopped
1 celery stick, chopped
1 litre chicken or vegetable stock
sour cream, to serve
finely chopped fresh parsley, to serve
ground nutmeg, to serve

1 Preheat the oven to moderate 180°C (350°F/Gas 4). Put the pumpkin on a greased baking tray and lightly brush with half the olive oil. Bake for 25 minutes, or until softened and slightly browned.

2 Heat the remaining oil in a large pan. Cook the onion and cumin for 2 minutes, then add the carrot and celery and cook for 3 minutes more, stirring frequently. Add the roasted pumpkin and stock. Bring to the boil, then reduce the heat and simmer for 20 minutes.

3 Allow to cool a little, then purée in batches in a blender or food processor. Return the soup to the pan and gently reheat without boiling. Season to taste with salt and cracked black pepper. Top with sour cream and sprinkle with chopped parsley and ground nutmeg before serving.

NUTRITION PER SERVE
Protein 5 g; Fat 8.5 g; Carbohydrate 15 g; Dietary Fibre 3.5 g; Cholesterol 4.5 mg; 665 kJ (160 Cal)

NOTE: Butternut pumpkin is often used in soups as it has a sweeter flavour than other varieties.
HINT: If the soup is too thick, thin it down with a little stock.

CHICKEN AND CORN SOUP

This soup is quick to prepare—great for a meal or snack. It provides niacin, vitamin B6 and a little folate and iron.

Prep time: 15 minutes
Cooking time: 20 minutes
Serves 6
EASY

---

3 corn cobs
1 tablespoon vegetable oil
4 spring onions, finely chopped
2 teaspoons grated fresh ginger
1 litre chicken stock
1 tablespoon rice wine, mirin or sherry
1 tablespoon light soy sauce
1/2 small barbecued chicken, shredded
1 tablespoon cornflour
1 teaspoon sesame oil
420 g can creamed corn
fresh thyme sprigs, to garnish

1 Cut the corn kernels from the cobs—you will need about 2 cups (400 g). Heat the oil in a large pan, and add the spring onion and ginger. Cook for 1 minute, or until softened, then add the corn, stock, rice wine and soy sauce. Bring slowly to the boil, then reduce the heat and simmer for 10 minutes, or until the kernels are cooked through. Add the chicken.

2 In a bowl, blend the cornflour with 1/4 cup (60 ml) water or stock to make a smooth paste. Add to the soup with the sesame oil and simmer, stirring continuously, until slightly thickened. Stir in the creamed corn and heat for 2–3 minutes without allowing to boil. Season with salt and pepper, and serve hot, garnished with thyme sprigs.

NUTRITION PER SERVE
Protein 14 g; Fat 8 g; Carbohydrate 30 g; Dietary Fibre 5 g; Cholesterol 45 mg; 1075 kJ (255 Cal)

NOTE: If fresh corn is unavailable, use a 440 g can of drained corn kernels.

CHUNKY VEGETABLE SOUP

An easy way to eat a variety of healthy vegetables, this soup provides a range of phytochemicals, folate, beta-carotene and carbohydrate.

Prep time: 25 minutes
Cooking time: 1 hour 30 minutes
Serves 6
EASY

---

50 g butter
1 leek, chopped
1 celery stick, chopped
1 large carrot, peeled and chopped
1 large potato, peeled and chopped
1 parsnip, peeled and chopped
1 swede or turnip, peeled and chopped
225 g sweet potato, peeled and chopped
1/2 cup (115 g) soup mix (see Note)
2 litres vegetable stock or water
1 cup (155 g) frozen peas
125 g green beans, chopped
1/4 cup (15 g) chopped fresh mint
1/3 cup (20 g) chopped fresh parsley

1 Heat the butter in a large heavy-based pan, and cook the leek, celery, carrot, potato, parsnip, swede or turnip and sweet potato, stirring, for 5 minutes.
2 Add the soup mix and stock or water. Bring slowly to the boil, then reduce the heat and simmer, covered, for 11/4 hours, or until the soup mix has softened.
3 Add the peas and beans, and cook for a further 10 minutes, or until tender. Stir in the chopped mint and parsley. Season with salt and cracked black pepper. Serve hot. Delicious with crusty bread.

NUTRITION PER SERVE
Protein 3 g; Fat 7 g; Carbohydrate 15 g; Dietary Fibre 4 g; Cholesterol 20 mg; 555 kJ (135 Cal)

NOTE: Soup mix is a combination of dried beans and pulses.

Osso buco and vegetable soup (top), and Seafood chowder

OSSO BUCO AND VEGETABLE SOUP

This is a very filling soup, providing protein, slow-release carbohydrate, B vitamins, soluble fibre and beta-carotene.

Prep time: 25 minutes
Cooking time: 50 minutes
Serves 6
EASY
___

500 g veal shanks with bones (osso buco), cut into 5 cm pieces (ask your butcher to do this)
2 tablespoons olive oil
1 onion, diced
1–2 cloves garlic, crushed
425 g can chopped tomatoes
1 tablespoon tomato paste
1/2 teaspoon dried oregano
1.5 litres beef stock
300 g potatoes, cubed
300 g pumpkin, cubed
3/4 cup (165 g) pearl barley
200 g zucchini, sliced

1 Trim the meat from the bones and cut it into cubes. Scrape out the marrow from the bones, if you want to use it, and discard the bones. Heat the oil in a heavy-based pan and brown the meat and marrow, in batches if necessary, until rich brown. Remove and drain on paper towels. Set the fried marrow aside.
2 Add the onion to the pan and cook for 4–5 minutes over low heat, then add the garlic and cook for 1 minute longer. Add the meat, tomato, tomato paste, oregano, stock, potato and pumpkin.
3 Wash the barley in a sieve until the water runs clean, then drain and add to the soup. Bring to the boil, reduce the heat to low and simmer, covered, for 20 minutes. Add the zucchini and cook, covered, for 10 minutes, or until the barley is cooked. Serve topped with the fried marrow.

NUTRITION PER SERVE
Protein 25 g; Fat 10 g; Carbohydrate 30 g; Dietary Fibre 6 g; Cholesterol 70 mg; 1310 kJ (315 Cal)

SEAFOOD CHOWDER

This nutritious broth is full of flavour and is a great source of protein, vitamin A and minerals, including selenium and iron.

Prep time: 30 minutes
Cooking time: 30 minutes
Serves 4–6
EASY
___

60 g butter
3 rashers bacon, chopped
2 onions, chopped
2 cloves garlic, finely chopped
2 celery sticks, sliced
3 potatoes, diced
1.25 litres fish or chicken stock
3 teaspoons chopped fresh thyme
1 tablespoon tomato paste
425 g can chopped tomatoes
375 g boneless white fish fillets, cut into chunks
12 large raw prawns, peeled, deveined and halved
310 g can baby clams, undrained
2 tablespoons chopped fresh parsley
grated orange rind, to garnish

1 Melt the butter in a large pan and cook the bacon, onion, garlic and celery over low heat, stirring occasionally, for 5 minutes, or until soft but not brown. Add the potato, stock and thyme and bring to the boil.
2 Reduce the heat and simmer, covered, for 15 minutes. Stir in the tomato paste and tomato and return to the boil. Add the fish pieces, prawns and clams, and simmer for 3 minutes.
3 Season with salt and ground black pepper, and stir in the parsley. Serve garnished with grated orange rind.

NUTRITION PER SERVE (6)
Protein 35 g; Fat 10 g; Carbohydrate 15.5 g; Dietary Fibre 3 g; Cholesterol 166 mg; 1270 kJ (300 Cal)

CHICKEN LAKSA

This laksa is easy to make and provides niacin, potassium, phosphorus, iron and folate.

Prep time: 30 minutes
Cooking time: 25 minutes
Serves 4
EASY

---

500 g chicken breast fillets
1 large onion, roughly chopped
5 cm piece ginger, chopped
8 cm piece galangal, peeled and chopped
1 stem lemon grass, white part only, roughly
　　chopped
2 cloves garlic
1 fresh red chilli, seeded and chopped
2 teaspoons vegetable oil
2 tablespoons mild curry paste
2 cups (500 ml) chicken stock
60 g rice vermicelli
50 g dried egg noodles
400 ml light coconut milk
10 snow peas, halved
3 spring onions, finely chopped
1 cup (90 g) bean sprouts
1/2 cup (15 g) fresh coriander leaves

1 Cut the chicken into bite-sized cubes. Process the onion, ginger, galangal, lemon grass, garlic and chilli in a food processor until finely chopped. Add the oil and process until the mixture has a paste-like consistency. Spoon into a large wok, add the curry paste and stir over low heat for 1–2 minutes, or until aromatic. Take care not to burn.

2 Increase the heat to medium, add the chicken and stir for 2 minutes, or until the chicken is well coated. Stir in the chicken stock and mix well. Bring slowly to the boil, then simmer for 10 minutes, or until the chicken is cooked through.

3 Meanwhile, cut the vermicelli into shorter lengths using scissors. Cook the vermicelli and egg noodles separately in large pans of boiling water for 5 minutes each. Drain and rinse under cold water.

4 Just prior to serving, add the light coconut milk and snow peas to the chicken and heat through. To serve, divide the vermicelli and noodles among four warmed serving bowls. Pour the hot laksa over the top and garnish with the spring onion, bean sprouts and coriander leaves.

NUTRITION PER SERVE
Protein 30 g; Fat 8 g; Carbohydrate 4.5 g; Dietary Fibre 3 g; Cholesterol 65 mg; 945 kJ (225 Cal)

WON TON SOUP

Low in fat, with plenty of taste, this Asian soup is a great source of folate, calcium, iron, niacin and vitamin C.

Prep time: 25 minutes
Cooking time: 25 minutes
Serves 4
MEDIUM

———

70 g raw prawns
70 g veal mince
1/4 cup (60 ml) soy sauce
1 tablespoon finely chopped spring onion
1 tablespoon finely chopped water chestnuts
1 teaspoon finely chopped ginger
2 cloves garlic, finely chopped
24 gow gee wrappers
1.25 litres chicken stock
2 tablespoons mirin
500 g baby bok choy, finely shredded
8 spring onions, sliced

1 Peel, devein and finely chop the prawns. Mix with the veal mince, 2 teaspoons soy sauce, spring onion, water chestnuts, ginger and garlic. Lay the round wrappers out on a work surface and place a teaspoon of mixture in the middle of each.
2 Moisten the edges of the wrappers and bring up the sides to form a pouch. Pinch together to seal. Cook in batches in a large pan of rapidly boiling water for 4–5 minutes. Drain and divide among soup bowls.
3 Bring the stock, remaining soy sauce and mirin to the boil in a pan. Add the bok choy, cover and simmer for 2 minutes, or until the bok choy has just wilted. Add the sliced spring onion and season with salt and pepper. Ladle the stock, bok choy and spring onion over the won tons.

NUTRITION PER SERVE
Protein 18.5 g; Fat 3.5 g; Carbohydrate 34 g; Dietary Fibre 3.5 g; Cholesterol 44.5 mg; 1075 kJ (255 Cal)

VEGETABLE AND PASTA SOUP

This low-fat soup is a good source of fibre, beta-carotene and potassium.

Prep time: 20 minutes
Cooking time: 40 minutes
Serves 6
EASY

2 teaspoons olive oil
1 onion, chopped
1 carrot, chopped
2 celery sticks, chopped
350 g sweet potato, chopped
400 g can corn kernels, drained
1 litre vegetable stock
1 cup (90 g) pasta spirals

1 Heat the oil in a large pan and add the onion, carrot and celery. Cook over low heat, stirring regularly, for 10 minutes, or until soft.

2 Add the sweet potato, corn kernels and stock. Bring to the boil, reduce the heat and simmer for 20 minutes, or until the vegetables are tender.

3 Add the pasta to the pan and return to the boil. Reduce the heat and simmer for 10 minutes, or until the pasta is tender. Serve immediately.

NUTRITION PER SERVE
Protein 7.5 g; Fat 3 g; Carbohydrate 34.5 g; Dietary Fibre 4.5 g; Cholesterol 0 mg; 825 kJ (200 Cal)

SPINACH AND PEA SOUP

Heat 2 teaspoons oil in a large saucepan, add 4 roughly chopped spring onions and cook, stirring, over medium heat for 2 minutes, or until soft. Add 200 g English spinach leaves, 3 cups (390 g) minted peas and 1 litre chicken stock. Bring to the boil and cook for 10 minutes, or until the spinach and peas are soft. Transfer to a blender or food processor and blend until smooth. Season and serve with a dollop of low-fat plain yoghurt. Serves 4

NUTRITION PER SERVE
Protein 7.5 g; Fat 3 g; Carbohydrate 7.5 g; Dietary Fibre 7.5 g; Cholesterol 0.5 mg; 365 kJ (85 Cal)

MINESTRONE

This nourishing meal is rich in carbohydrate, fibre, folate and beta-carotene.

Prep time: 30 minutes
Cooking time: 2 hours 30 minutes
Serves 8
EASY

---

1 tablespoon olive oil
1 onion, finely chopped
2 cloves garlic, crushed
2 carrots, diced
2 potatoes, diced
2 celery sticks, finely chopped
2 zucchini, finely chopped
125 g green beans, chopped
2 cups (150 g) shredded cabbage
2 litres beef stock
425 g can chopped tomatoes
1/2 cup (80 g) macaroni
440 g can borlotti or red kidney beans, drained
fresh thyme sprigs, to serve
grated Parmesan, to serve

1 Heat the oil in a large heavy-based saucepan. Add the onion and garlic, and cook over low heat for 5 minutes. Add the carrot, potato and celery, and cook, stirring, for a further 5 minutes.
2 Add the zucchini, green beans and cabbage to the pan and cook, stirring, for 5 minutes. Add the stock and chopped tomatoes. Bring slowly to the boil, then reduce the heat, cover and leave to simmer for 2 hours.
3 Add the macaroni and beans, and cook for 15 minutes, or until the pasta is tender. Serve hot, sprinkled with the thyme sprigs and Parmesan.

NUTRITION PER SERVE
Protein 9 g; Fat 3.5 g; Carbohydrate 22.5 g; Dietary Fibre 6.5 g; Cholesterol 0 mg; 660 kJ (160 Cal)

NOTE: Any type of pasta can be used for minestrone, although smaller shapes are easier to manage on a soup spoon. The Milanese version uses rice.

CHILLED MINTED PEA SOUP

This cool soup provides a boost of vitamin C, folate, phosphorus, potassium and some B vitamins.

Prep time: 15 minutes + 3 hours refrigeration
Cooking time: 50 minutes
Serves 4–6
EASY
———

2 tablespoons olive oil
1 onion, chopped
1 leek, sliced
1 celery stick, chopped
2 cloves garlic, crushed
2 rashers bacon, trimmed of fat, chopped
1 litre chicken or vegetable stock
500 g frozen peas
2 tablespoons chopped fresh mint
1 1/2 tablespoons lemon juice
1/3 cup (90 g) low-fat plain yoghurt

1 Heat the oil in a large saucepan and add the onion, leek, celery, garlic and bacon. Cook, stirring, over medium heat for 4–5 minutes, or until the vegetables are softened.
2 Add the stock, bring to the boil, then reduce the heat and simmer for 25 minutes. Stir in the frozen peas and mint, return to the boil over high heat, then reduce the heat and simmer for a further 15 minutes.
3 Leave the soup to cool slightly (for safety reasons) before transferring to a blender and blending until smooth. Season to taste with salt and cracked black pepper, then stir in the lemon juice. Refrigerate for at least 3 hours, or until well chilled.
4 Serve the chilled pea soup in individual soup bowls with a generous dollop of plain yoghurt and some crusty bread.

NUTRITION PER SERVE (6)
Protein 11 g; Fat 8.5 g; Carbohydrate 12.5 g; Dietary Fibre 6 g; Cholesterol 10 mg; 720 kJ (170 Cal)

GAZPACHO

A refreshingly cold summer soup originally from Spain, Gazpacho contains monounsaturated fat, vitamin C and beta-carotene.

Prep time: 40 minutes + 3 hours refrigeration
Cooking time: Nil
Serves 4–6
EASY
———

750 g ripe tomatoes
1 Lebanese cucumber, chopped
1 green capsicum, chopped
2–3 cloves garlic, crushed
1–2 tablespoons finely chopped black olives (optional)
1/3 cup (80 ml) red or white wine vinegar
1/4 cup (60 ml) olive oil
1 tablespoon tomato paste

Accompaniments
1 onion, finely chopped
1 red capsicum, finely chopped
2 spring onions, finely chopped
1 Lebanese cucumber, finely chopped
2 hard-boiled eggs, chopped
chopped mint or parsley

1 Score a cross in the base of each tomato. Cover with boiling water for 1 minute, plunge into cold water, drain and peel away the skins. Chop the flesh so finely that it is almost a purée.
2 Mix together the tomato, cucumber, capsicum, garlic, olives, vinegar, oil and tomato paste, and season with salt and ground black pepper. Cover and refrigerate for 2–3 hours.
3 Use 2–3 cups (750 ml) of chilled water to thin the soup to your taste. Serve chilled, with the chopped onion, capsicum, spring onion, cucumber, boiled egg and herbs served separately for diners to add to their own bowls.

NUTRITION PER SERVE (6)
Protein 4.5 g; Fat 11 g; Carbohydrate 6.5 g; Dietary Fibre 3 g; Cholesterol 73 mg; 610 kJ (145 Cal)

Chilled minted pea soup (top), and Gazpacho

MEDITERRANEAN FISH SOUP

This nutritious soup contains a mix of filling fish protein, fibre and good amounts of niacin, vitamin C, potassium and lycopene.

Prep time: 30 minutes
Cooking time: 45 minutes
Serves 4
EASY

1/2 teaspoon saffron threads
3 teaspoons oil
2 large onions, thinly sliced
1 leek, white part only, chopped
4 cloves garlic, finely chopped
1 bay leaf, torn
1/2 teaspoon dried marjoram
1 teaspoon grated orange rind
2 tablespoons dry white wine
1 red capsicum, cut into chunks
500 g tomatoes, chopped
1/2 cup (125 ml) tomato purée
2 cups (500 ml) fish stock
2 tablespoons tomato paste
2 teaspoons soft brown sugar
500 g firm white fish, cut into bite-sized pieces
1/4 cup (15 g) chopped fresh parsley

1 Soak the saffron in 2 tablespoons boiling water; set aside. Heat the oil in a large heavy-based pan, over low heat. Add the onion, leek, garlic, bay leaf and marjoram. Cover and cook for 10 minutes, shaking the pan occasionally, until the onion is soft. Add the rind, wine, capsicum and tomato. Cover and cook for 10 minutes.
2 Stir in the purée, stock, tomato paste, sugar and saffron (with liquid). Bring to the boil, reduce the heat and simmer, uncovered, for 15 minutes.
3 Add the fish to the soup, cover and cook for 8 minutes, or until tender. Add salt and pepper and half the parsley. Garnish with the remaining parsley.

NUTRITION PER SERVE
Protein 31 g; Fat 7 g; Carbohydrate 14.5 g; Dietary Fibre 5 g; Cholesterol 74 mg; 1065 kJ (255 Cal)

SPLIT PEA SOUP

A great way to include legumes in your diet, this delicious soup provides carbohydrate energy, soluble fibre, folate, B vitamins and minerals.

Prep time: 20 minutes
Cooking time: 1 hour 20 minutes
Serves 6–8
EASY

2 tablespoons olive oil
1 large brown onion, chopped
1 large carrot, cut into 1 cm cubes
1 large celery stick, cut into 1 cm cubes
2 bay leaves
1 tablespoon fresh thyme, finely chopped
6 cloves garlic, finely chopped
2 cups (440 g) yellow split peas
1 litre chicken stock
1/4 cup (60 ml) lemon juice
olive oil, extra

1 Heat the oil in a large saucepan over medium heat. Add the onion, carrot and celery, and cook for 4–5 minutes, or until starting to brown. Add the bay leaves, thyme and garlic, and cook for 1 minute.
2 Stir in the split peas, then add the chicken stock and 1 litre water. Cook for 1 hour 15 minutes, or until the split peas and vegetables are soft. Stir often during cooking to prevent the soup from sticking to the bottom of the pan, and skim any scum from the surface. Add a little extra water if the soup is too thick.
3 Remove the soup from the heat and discard the bay leaves. Stir in the lemon juice and season with salt and ground black pepper. Drizzle with a little olive oil before serving.

NUTRITION PER SERVE (8)
Protein 14.5 g; Fat 6.5 g; Carbohydrate 29 g; Dietary Fibre 6.5 g; Cholesterol 0 mg; 960 kJ (230 Cal)

LAMB HOT POT

This thick vegetable and lamb soup is rich in vitamins A, B and C, folate and minerals.

Prep time: 40 minutes + 1 hour refrigeration
Cooking time: 2 hours
Serves 4
MEDIUM

2 tablespoons olive oil
8 lamb shanks
2 onions, sliced
4 cloves garlic, finely chopped
3 bay leaves, torn in half
1–2 teaspoons hot paprika
2 teaspoons sweet paprika
1 tablespoon plain flour
1/4 cup (60 g) tomato paste
1.5 litres vegetable stock
4 potatoes, chopped
4 carrots, sliced
3 celery sticks, thickly sliced
3 tomatoes, seeded and chopped

1 Heat 1 tablespoon of the oil in a large, heavy-based pan over medium heat. Brown the lamb shanks well in two batches and drain on paper towels.

2 Add the remaining oil to the pan and cook the onion, garlic and bay leaves over low heat for 10 minutes, stirring regularly. Add the paprika and flour, and cook, stirring continuously, for 2 minutes. Gradually add the combined tomato paste and stock. Bring to the boil, stirring continuously, and return the shanks to the pan. Reduce the heat to low and simmer, covered, for 1 1/2 hours, stirring occasionally.

3 Remove and discard the bay leaves. Remove the shanks, allow to cool slightly and then cut the meat from the bone. Discard the bones. Cut the meat into pieces and refrigerate. Refrigerate the stock for about 1 hour, or until fat forms on the surface and can be spooned off.

4 Return the meat to the soup along with the potato, carrot and celery and bring to the boil. Reduce the heat and simmer for 15 minutes. Season with salt and pepper, and add the chopped tomato to serve.

NUTRITION PER SERVE
Protein 70 g; Fat 15 g; Carbohydrate 30 g; Dietary Fibre 8 g; Cholesterol 170 mg; 2200 kJ (525 Cal)

LENTIL AND VEGETABLE SOUP

This flavoursome, aromatic soup provides a great range of nutrients, including carbohydrate, soluble fibre, vitamins A, B and C, calcium and iron.

Prep time: 30 minutes
Cooking time: 40 minutes
Serves 6
EASY

2 tablespoons olive oil
1 small leek (white part only), chopped
2 cloves garlic, crushed
2 teaspoons curry powder
1 teaspoon ground cumin
1 teaspoon garam masala
1 litre vegetable stock
1 fresh bay leaf
1 cup (185 g) brown lentils
450 g butternut pumpkin, peeled and cut into
    1 cm cubes
400 g can chopped tomatoes
2 zucchini, cut in half lengthways and sliced
200 g broccoli, cut into small florets
1 small carrot, diced
1/2 cup (80 g) peas
1 tablespoon chopped fresh mint

Spiced yoghurt
1 cup (250 g) low-fat thick plain yoghurt
1 tablespoon chopped fresh coriander leaves
1 clove garlic, crushed
3 dashes Tabasco sauce

1 Heat the oil in a saucepan over medium heat. Add the leek and garlic and cook for 4–5 minutes, or until soft and golden. Add the curry powder, cumin and garam masala, and cook for 1 minute.
2 Add the stock, bay leaf, lentils and pumpkin. Bring to the boil, then reduce the heat and simmer for 10–15 minutes, or until the lentils are tender. Season.
3 Add the tomato, zucchini, broccoli, carrot and 2 cups (500 ml) water, and simmer for 10 minutes, or until the vegetables are tender. Add the peas and simmer for 2–3 minutes.
4 Combine the yoghurt, coriander, garlic and Tabasco. Serve the soup with the yoghurt and mint.

NUTRITION PER SERVE
Protein 17 g; Fat 9 g; Carbohydrate 26.5 g; Dietary Fibre 9.5 g; Cholesterol 4 mg; 1055 kJ (255 Cal)

Scotch broth (top), and Leek and potato soup

SCOTCH BROTH

*This broth is a good source of soluble fibre,
B vitamins, beta-carotene, iron and zinc.*

Prep time: 40 minutes + 1 hour soaking +
   overnight refrigeration
Cooking time: 4 hours
Serves 8
MEDIUM

1 kg lamb shanks, cut in half through the bone
   (ask your butcher to do this)
3 onions, chopped
3 turnips, chopped
2 carrots, chopped
1 tablespoon black peppercorns
1/2 cup (110 g) pearl barley
1 carrot, diced, extra
2 onions, finely chopped, extra
2 turnips, diced, extra
1 leek, chopped
1 celery stick, diced
chopped fresh flat-leaf parsley

1 To make the stock, put the lamb shanks,
onion, turnip, carrot, peppercorns and
2 litres of water in a large pan. Bring to the
boil, reduce the heat and simmer, covered,
for 3 hours. Skim the surface as required.
2 Remove the shanks and any meat that
has fallen off the bones and cool slightly.
Remove the meat from the bones and
finely chop, then cover and refrigerate.
Strain the stock, discarding the vegetables.
Cool the stock and refrigerate overnight,
or until the fat has set on top and can be
spooned off. Cover the barley with water
and soak for 1 hour, then drain.
3 Put the stock in a large pan and gently
reheat. Add the barley, extra carrot, onion
and turnip, and the leek and celery. Bring
to the boil, reduce the heat and simmer
for 30 minutes, or until the barley and
vegetables are just cooked. Return the meat
to the pan and simmer for 5 minutes.
Season well and serve with the parsley.

NUTRITION PER SERVE
Protein 35 g; Fat 3 g; Carbohydrate 20 g; Dietary Fibre
6 g; Cholesterol 80 mg; 970 kJ (230 Cal)

LEEK AND POTATO SOUP

*Leeks add a delicate flavour to this nourishing
soup, which is a good source of calcium, potassium,
niacin, vitamin C and folate.*

Prep time: 15 minutes
Cooking time: 30 minutes
Serves 4
EASY

4 leeks, trimmed and quartered lengthways
30 g butter
3 floury potatoes, chopped
3 cups (750 ml) chicken or vegetable stock
1 cup (250 ml) reduced-fat milk
1/4 teaspoon ground nutmeg
cream and chopped fresh spring onions, to serve

1 Wash the leeks thoroughly in cold water
to remove any dirt, then cut into small
chunks. Heat the butter in a large heavy-
based pan. Add the leek and cook for
3–4 minutes, stirring frequently, until
softened. Add the potato and stock. Bring
slowly to the boil, then reduce the heat
and simmer for 20 minutes, or until the
vegetables are tender.
2 Cool the mixture slightly then transfer
to a blender or food processor and purée
in batches. Return to the pan, stir in the
milk and nutmeg, and season well with
salt and cracked black pepper. Reheat
gently and serve garnished with a swirl of
cream and a scattering of spring onion.

NUTRITION PER SERVE
Protein 9 g; Fat 8 g; Carbohydrate 21.5 g; Dietary Fibre
4 g; Cholesterol 23.5 mg; 815 kJ (195 Cal)

NOTE: Old floury potatoes such as sebago
will give the best results for this dish.

SALADS AND VEGETABLES

Vegetables are an important part of a healthy diet, and with such a wide variety and different ways of serving them, they need never be boring or bland.

SALADS

Salads are a naturally healthy and versatile way of incorporating many vegetables and fruits into your diet, either as a complete meal or an accompaniment. Almost any raw or cooked ingredient can be made into a salad, ranging from vegetables and fruits to seafood, poultry, meat, noodles, legumes and pasta.

Salads should make use of the best seasonal ingredients available, and many variations of flavour, texture and temperature are possible by simply using a different dressing, different herbs, cooked rather than raw, and warm rather than cold ingredients.

A salad can be a light starter, or a complex combination of ingredients that provides all the nutrients you need, in one bowl. It can be as simple as some dressed green leaves, or as complicated as a tuna niçoise, which includes a variety of raw and cooked ingredients.

When choosing salad greens, buy them as fresh and green as possible, wash them well in cold water, then dry them with paper towel or in a salad spinner. To create interesting flavours and texture, use a combination of leaves:

- raddichio is colourful and crisp, and has quite a bitter flavour
- rocket has peppery leaves
- watercress is small and delicate looking, but has a mustardy bite
- cos lettuce is crisp, with a sweet flavour
- snow pea sprouts are crunchy and sweet.

Dressings add flavour to salads, but be aware that many salad dressings contain lots of hidden fat. Different salad leaves are suited to different dressings. Leaves that are full flavoured and crisp are ideal for strong, thick dressings, such as cos lettuce with Caesar dressing, while more delicate leaves are better with light dressings, such as butter lettuce with a simple lemon vinaigrette.

Simple, healthy salads

- When tomatoes are at the peak of their season, they are best treated simply—sliced, seasoned and drizzled with some balsamic vinegar and extra virgin olive oil.
- Use a Thai-style dressing of chilli, garlic, ginger, lime juice and fish sauce on a coleslaw salad as a low-fat alternative to the traditional mayonnaise dressing.
- Mix some salad vegetables with pasta and canned tuna for a complete meal.

- A low-fat yoghurt dressing flavoured with fresh herbs and a little honey, thinned slightly with lemon juice or warm water, is a tasty alternative dressing, and goes well with legumes such as chickpeas, lentils, cannellini beans, new potatoes, green beans, roasted beetroot, and chargrilled sweet potatoes.
- Asian-style dressings tend to be lower in fat because they contain a minimum of oil or no oil, but the delicate balance of flavours makes them tasty and delicious.
- Dress warm potatoes with a zesty herb vinaigrette rather than mayonnaise.
- Save the juices from roasting red capsicums, lightly season and use to dress the skinned capsicums.
- If you marinate seafood, poultry or meat before you cook it, you will only need a very light dressing or squeeze of lemon for a delicious salad.
- Toss leftover diced meats or legumes with a spicy salsa of diced tomato, avocado, chilli, baby corn and lime juice.
- Use a slightly sweeter vinegar such as balsamic, or rice wine vinegar, or sherry for a more mellow dressing that will require less oil to balance the flavours.

VEGETABLES

Vegetables can be eaten raw or cooked, made into salads, soups, starters, main meals, accompaniments or snacks. They may be steamed, grilled, roasted, braised, boiled or barbecued.

Vegetables provide carbohydrates, dietary fibre, vitamins and minerals. The most delicious, ecconomical and nutritious way of enjoying fresh vegetables is to use them at the peak of their season.

Modern storage methods mean that there is an abundance of fresh vegetables available all year round, but often they are at their peak to complement the season. For example, hearty root vegetables that are perfect for soups or roasting are autumn or winter vegetables, while tomatoes and salad greens are perfect in spring and summer.

When vegetables are at the peak of their season, they are so full of flavour and texture that they need little preparation or dressings.

Healthy tips for cooking vegetables

- Steam rather than boil vegetables, so that they retain nutrients that may otherwise be leached out into the cooking water.
- Leave the skin on boiled potatoes for a potato salad, for maximum fibre.
- Cook vegetables for the minimum time so they retain more nutrients.
- For flavour and variety, a stir-fry is a great way of incorporating a healthy variety of vegetables into your diet.
- Salting eggplant before cooking will draw out excess moisture, leaching away any bitterness, and less oil will be needed for cooking.
- Spinach and silverbeet need only minimum cooking. Simply wash the leaves and then put them in a saucepan with only the water clinging to the leaves. Place the pan over heat and toss gently until wilted.
- Dress steamed green leafy vegetables with an Asian-style soy and ginger dressing for a highly nutritious dish.
- When roasting vegetables, lightly spray them with olive oil before cooking rather than filling the dish with oil.
- Leave the skin on when roasting pumpkin, carrots, parsnips and potatoes. Be sure to wash them thoroughly first.
- Bake a layered potato dish using vegetable or chicken stock rather than cream.

TOMATO AND BASIL SALAD

This fragrant, healthy side salad provides vitamin C, beta-carotene and other antioxidants, with some potassium and folate.

Prep time: 10 minutes + 10 minutes standing
Cooking time: Nil
Serves 4
EASY

6 ripe Roma tomatoes
1 red onion
1 clove garlic, crushed
1 cup (60 g) finely shredded basil leaves
1–2 tablespoons balsamic vinegar

1 Cut the tomatoes into quarters, and thinly slice the red onion. If you find raw onion too strong, put it in a bowl and cover it with boiling water for 5 minutes. Drain well.

2 Combine the tomato, red onion, garlic, basil and balsamic vinegar, and toss to combine. Season with salt and ground black pepper, then set aside for 10 minutes to allow the flavours to develop. Transfer the salad to a shallow dish.

NUTRITION PER SERVE
Protein 1.5 g; Fat 0.2 g; Carbohydrate 3 g; Dietary Fibre 2 g; Cholesterol 0 mg; 90 kJ (20 Cal)

STUFFED MUSHROOMS

Peel and remove the stalks from 8 field mushrooms, then grill top side up. Place 1/2 cup (95 g) instant couscous, 1 tablespoon extra virgin olive oil, 1 teaspoon ground cumin, 1/4 teaspoon cayenne pepper and 2 teaspoons finely grated lemon rind in a bowl. Season. Stir the flavourings through the couscous. Stir in 1/2 cup (125 ml) boiling chicken stock, and cover. Leave for 5 minutes, then fluff the grains with a fork. Stir in 1 finely chopped tomato, 1 tablespoon lemon juice, 2 tablespoons chopped fresh parsley and 2 tablespoons chopped fresh mint. Fill each of the mushrooms with the couscous mixture and pack down firmly. Grill until the couscous is golden. Serve hot or cold. Makes 8

NUTRITION PER MUSHROOM
Protein 3 g; Fat 2 g; Carbohydrate 11 g; Dietary Fibre 1 g; Cholesterol 0 mg; 317 kJ (75 Cal)

HOT BEAN SALAD

A satisfying combination of high-fibre beans and nutritious vegetables and herbs, rich in slow-release carbohydrate and soluble fibre, this salad is ideal if you are watching your blood sugar and cholesterol levels.

Prep time: 15 minutes + overnight soaking
Cooking time: 1 hour 15 minutes
Serves 8
EASY

100 g dried chickpeas
100 g dried pinto beans
100 g dried red kidney beans
100 g dried black-eyed beans
2 onions, sliced
2 teaspoons ground cumin
1 teaspoon ground coriander
420 g can corn kernels, drained
2 tomatoes, chopped
1/3 cup (80 ml) lemon juice
1/4 cup (15 g) chopped fresh
    coriander leaves
1 Lebanese cucumber, grated
1 cup (250 g) low-fat plain yoghurt

1 Combine the chickpeas, pinto beans, red kidney beans and black-eyed beans in a large bowl. Cover with water and soak overnight. Drain, place in a large saucepan and cover with water. Bring to the boil, then reduce the heat and simmer for 45 minutes, or until tender. Don't overcook or the beans will be mushy.
2 Meanwhile, in a large, deep non-stick frying pan, cook the onion over low heat for 25 minutes, or until golden. Add the cumin and coriander with the beans, and toss to combine. Add the corn kernels, tomato, lemon juice and coriander. Season with salt and black pepper, and stir.
3 Squeeze out the moisture from the cucumber. Combine the cucumber with the yoghurt, and season. Stir to combine.
4 Put the hot bean mixture on a serving plate, and top with the yoghurt mixture.

NUTRITION PER SERVE
Protein 10 g; Fat 2 g; Carbohydrate 25 g; Dietary Fibre 8.5 g; Cholesterol 1.5 mg; 745 kJ (180 Cal)

CITRUS SALAD WITH HONEY DRESSING

This tangy salad is rich in vitamin C, with some folate, fibre and potassium. Eat it with red meat to increase iron absorption.

Prep time: 20 minutes
Cooking time: Nil
Serves 6
EASY

1 grapefruit
2 small red grapefruit
4 oranges
1 red onion, sliced
1/3 cup (10 g) fresh coriander leaves
2 tablespoons honey
1/3 cup (80 ml) raspberry vinegar
rocket leaves, to serve

1 Remove the rind from the grapefruit and oranges. Remove and discard all the pith from a few slices of the rind from each fruit and cut the rind into long thin strips. Remove any remaining pith from the fruit and slice between each section. Segment the fruits over a bowl to catch any juice; set the juice aside. Put the citrus segments and rind in a bowl with the onion and coriander.

2 Add the honey and raspberry vinegar to the reserved fruit juice and whisk to combine. Pour over the salad and toss. Serve on a bed of rocket.

NUTRITION PER SERVE
Protein 2 g; Fat 0.5 g; Carbohydrate 20 g; Dietary Fibre 2.5 g; Cholesterol 0 mg; 395 kJ (95 Cal)

RAVIOLI SALAD WITH SPRING VEGETABLES

The vegetables in this dish provide many beneficial phytochemicals and fibre. The regular intake of cruciferous vegetables, such as broccoli, is associated with a reduced risk of bowel cancer.

Prep time: 20 minutes
Cooking time: 30 minutes
Serves 4
EASY

375 g fresh spinach and ricotta ravioli
200 g cauliflower, cut into florets
200 g broccoli, cut into florets
155 g asparagus, cut into
   5 cm lengths
1 cup (155 g) fresh peas
100 g baby English spinach leaves

Dressing
2 cloves garlic, finely chopped
1 tablespoon sugar
$1/3$ cup (80 ml) lime juice
$1/4$ cup (60 ml) raspberry vinegar
1 cup (50 g) chopped fresh coriander

1 Bring a large saucepan of lightly salted water to the boil. Add the ravioli and cook until *al dente*. Drain well.
2 Steam or microwave the cauliflower, broccoli, asparagus and peas separately until just tender and bright. Rinse under cold water and drain well.
3 Place the ravioli, blanched vegetables and spinach in a bowl, and toss to combine.
4 To make the dressing, place the garlic, sugar, lime juice and vinegar in a bowl, and whisk together. Stir in the coriander, pour over the salad and toss to coat.

NUTRITION PER SERVE
Protein 15 g; Fat 5 g; Carbohydrate 25 g; Dietary Fibre 8.5 g; Cholesterol 19 mg; 960 kJ (230 Cal)

HOKKIEN NOODLE SALAD

The noodles and marinade add a zesty Asian flavour to this nutritious salad, bursting with vitamin C, folate, fibre, beta-carotene and potassium. It is also low in fat.

Prep time: 20 minutes
Cooking time: 5 minutes
Serves 4
EASY

450 g Hokkien noodles
200 g broccoli, cut into florets
4 spring onions, sliced
1 red capsicum, thinly sliced
1 green capsicum, thinly sliced
1 carrot, diagonally sliced
100 g snow peas, sliced
100 g fresh baby corn, halved lengthways
1/4 cup (15 g) chopped fresh coriander leaves
1 teaspoon sesame oil
1/4 cup (60 ml) sweet chilli sauce
1/4 cup (60 ml) light soy sauce
2 tablespoons lime juice

1 Gently separate the noodles, place in a heatproof bowl and cover with boiling water. Leave to stand for 2 minutes, then rinse under cold water and drain well.
2 Boil or steam the broccoli for 3 minutes, or until bright green and tender. Rinse under cold water and drain.
3 Place the noodles, vegetables and coriander in a large bowl, and mix well.
4 Combine the sesame oil, sweet chilli sauce, soy sauce and lime juice. Pour over the salad and toss to coat.

NUTRITION PER SERVE
Protein 12.5 g; Fat 5.5 g; Carbohydrate 40.5 g; Dietary Fibre 8 g; Cholesterol 1 mg; 1100 kJ (265 Cal)

TABBOULEH WITH SOY GRITS

Soy grits and chickpeas add protein, fibre and isoflavones to this version of the traditional Middle-Eastern salad, which provides vitamin C, beta-carotene, folate and potassium.

Prep time: 20 minutes + soaking
Cooking time: Nil
Serves 6–8
EASY

150 g fresh flat-leaf parsley
1 cup (180 g) soy grits
2 tablespoons chopped fresh mint
1 small red onion, cut into thin wedges
3 ripe tomatoes, chopped
400 g can chickpeas, rinsed and drained
1/4 cup (60 ml) lemon juice
2 tablespoons extra virgin olive oil
Lebanese or pitta bread, to serve

1 Remove all the parsley leaves from the stalks, roughly chop and place in a large serving bowl.
2 Place the soy grits in a heatproof bowl and pour in 2/3 cup (170 ml) boiling water. Leave to soak for 3 minutes, or until all the water has been absorbed.
3 Add the soy grits to the parsley, along with the mint, onion, tomato and chickpeas. Drizzle with the lemon juice and olive oil. Season well with salt and ground black pepper and toss together. Serve with Lebanese or pitta bread or as an accompaniment to barbecued meat, chicken or fish.

NUTRITION PER SERVE (8)
Protein 12 g; Fat 11 g; Carbohydrate 13 g; Dietary Fibre 6.5 g; Cholesterol 0 mg; 820 kJ (195 Cal)

Hokkien noodle salad (top), and Tabbouleh with soy grits

CHICKEN AND SWEET POTATO SALAD

Tender pieces of chicken are mixed with nutritious vegetables in this light meal, providing good amounts of protein, B vitamins, vitamin E, folate and beta-carotene.

Prep time: 30 minutes
Cooking time: 40 minutes
Serves 6
EASY

---

4 Roma tomatoes, quartered lengthways
300 g eggplant, quartered lengthways, thickly sliced
olive oil spray
500 g orange sweet potato, cut into 2 cm slices
1 large red onion, sliced into thin wedges
1 barbecued chicken
2 tablespoons chopped fresh coriander leaves
2–3 tablespoons balsamic vinegar
100 g rocket leaves

1 Preheat the oven to moderately hot 200°C (400°F/Gas 6). Place the tomato and eggplant on a non-stick baking tray, spray with a little oil and season with salt and ground black pepper. Bake, turning the eggplant halfway through, for 25–30 minutes.
2 Meanwhile, steam the sweet potato for 15 minutes, or until just tender. Place in a large bowl with the tomato and eggplant.
3 Lightly spray a small non-stick frying pan with oil, add the onion and cook over low heat for 6 minutes, or until golden. Set aside.
4 Remove and discard the skin and bones from the chicken. Cut the chicken into bite-sized pieces and add to the vegetables with the coriander and 1 tablespoon balsamic vinegar. Toss gently.
5 Place the rocket on a platter, then the chicken mixture, and top with the onion. Drizzle with the remaining balsamic vinegar to taste. Serve.

NUTRITION PER SERVE
Protein 19.5 g; Fat 6 g; Carbohydrate 15 g; Dietary Fibre 3.5 g; Cholesterol 62.5 mg; 825 kJ (195 Cal)

COUSCOUS SALAD

This salad is a good source of carbohydrate energy, fibre, B vitamins and folate.

Prep time: 20 minutes + 5 minutes standing
Cooking time: 10 minutes
Serves 4
EASY

300 g orange sweet potato, cubed
100 g green beans, halved
350 g instant couscous
2 cups (500 ml) boiling chicken stock
200 g cherry tomatoes, halved
1 cup (150 g) frozen corn kernels, thawed
1 cup (155 g) frozen peas, thawed
1 red capsicum, chopped
1 cup (60 g) chopped fresh parsley
1/2 cup (25 g) chopped fresh mint

Dressing
2 cloves garlic, crushed
1/4 cup (60 ml) lemon juice
1 tablespoon oil
1 tablespoon white wine vinegar
1 teaspoon honey mustard

1 Boil or steam the sweet potato and beans in separate saucepans until tender, then drain. Place the couscous in a large bowl and pour on the boiling stock. Cover and leave for 5 minutes, or until all the liquid has been absorbed. Fluff with a fork to separate the grains.
2 Add the sweet potato, beans, tomato, corn, peas, capsicum and herbs to the couscous, and mix together well.
3 Place the garlic, lemon juice, oil, vinegar and mustard in a bowl, and whisk together. Pour the dressing over the salad and toss well.

NUTRITION PER SERVE
Protein 20 g; Fat 6.5 g; Carbohydrate 92 g; Dietary Fibre 9 g; Cholesterol 0 mg; 2155 kJ (515 Cal)

THAI BEEF SALAD

Tender strips of lean meat mixed with herbs, vegetables and a tangy aromatic dressing provide good amounts of complete protein, iron, zinc and B vitamins.

Prep time: 15 minutes
Cooking time: 10 minutes
Serves 4
EASY

400 g lean beef fillet steaks
75 g mixed salad leaves
1/2 small red onion, thinly sliced
100 g cherry tomatoes, halved
1 small Lebanese cucumber, thinly sliced
1/3 cup (20 g) chopped fresh coriander
  leaves
1/3 cup (20 g) chopped fresh mint

Dressing
1 1/2 tablespoons fish sauce
2 tablespoons lime juice
1 tablespoon soft brown sugar
1 small fresh red chilli, seeded and finely
  chopped

1 Season the beef well on both sides with salt and ground black pepper. Spray a chargrill or hotplate with oil spray and, when very hot, sear the beef fillets on each side for 3–4 minutes. Remove and leave to rest for 10 minutes before slicing thinly—the meat should still be quite pink in the middle.

2 While the meat is resting, combine the fish sauce, lime juice, brown sugar, chilli and 2 tablespoons water in a small saucepan. Stir over low heat until the sugar has dissolved. Remove from the heat and keep warm.

3 Place the mixed salad leaves, onion, tomato, cucumber, coriander leaves and mint in a large bowl and toss together. Arrange the salad on a large platter, top with the beef slices and pour the warm dressing on top. Serve immediately.

NUTRITION PER SERVE
Protein 22.5 g; Fat 5 g; Carbohydrate 6 g; Dietary Fibre 2 g; Cholesterol 67 mg; 670 kJ (160 Cal)

GRILLED VEGETABLES

The nutrients you get from this recipe will depend on which combination of vegetables you choose, but you'll obtain folate, vitamin C and beta-carotene from the other ingredients.

Prep time: 20 minutes
Cooking time: 30 minutes
Serves 4
EASY

1.5 kg thickly sliced vegetables (such as
    pumpkin, potato, parsnip, eggplant and
    zucchini)
2 tablespoons olive oil
4 cloves garlic, finely chopped
cooking oil spray
300 g baby spinach leaves
1/2 red capsicum, thinly sliced
2 tablespoons balsamic vinegar
snipped fresh chives

1 Preheat the oven to moderate 180°C (350°F/Gas 4). Place the vegetables in a baking dish with the olive oil and garlic. Toss to combine.
2 Heat a large flat grill or barbecue plate and spray lightly with cooking oil. Grill the vegetables separately (they will cook at different rates), turning until charred.
3 Place the vegetables on a lightly greased baking tray and bake for 15 minutes, or until cooked.
4 Arrange the baby spinach leaves on a platter and top with the vegetables and capsicum. Drizzle with the balsamic vinegar and chives.

NUTRITION PER SERVE
Protein 9 g; Fat 10 g; Carbohydrate 25 g; Dietary Fibre 10 g; Cholesterol 0 mg; 1000 kJ (240 Cal)

Tandoori lamb salad (top), and Scallop and spinach salad

TANDOORI LAMB SALAD

The tender pieces of lean lamb marinated in yoghurt and spices make a nutritious meal that is rich in iron, zinc, B vitamins and potassium.

Prep time: 20 minutes + overnight marinating
Cooking time: 15 minutes
Serves 4
EASY

1 cup (250 g) low-fat natural yoghurt
2 cloves garlic, crushed
2 teaspoons grated ginger
2 teaspoons ground turmeric
2 teaspoons garam masala
1/4 teaspoon paprika
2 teaspoons ground coriander
red food colouring, optional
500 g lean lamb fillets
1/3 cup (80 ml) lemon juice
1 1/2 teaspoons chopped fresh coriander
1 teaspoon chopped fresh mint
150 g mixed salad leaves
1 large mango, cut into strips
2 cucumbers, cut into matchsticks

1 Mix the yoghurt, garlic, ginger and spices in a bowl, add a little colouring and toss with the lamb to thoroughly coat. Cover and refrigerate overnight.
2 Grill the lamb on a foil-lined baking tray under a hot grill for 7 minutes each side, or until the marinade starts to brown. Set aside for 5 minutes before serving.
3 Mix the lemon juice, coriander and mint, then season. Toss with the salad leaves, mango and cucumber, then arrange on plates. Slice the lamb and serve over the salad.

NUTRITION PER SERVE
Protein 31 g; Fat 5 g; Carbohydrate 12 g; Dietary Fibre 2.5 g; Cholesterol 84.5 mg; 935 kJ (225 Cal)

SCALLOP AND SPINACH SALAD

Serve this recipe as a light meal or with rice or noodles for a main course. It is a good source of selenium, sulphur, chromium, iodine and vitamin C.

Prep time: 10 minutes
Cooking time: 5 minutes
Serves 4
EASY

300 g fresh scallops, without roe
2 cups (100 g) baby English spinach leaves
1 small red capsicum, cut into very thin strips
50 g bean sprouts
25 ml sake
1 tablespoon lime juice
2 teaspoons shaved palm sugar
1 teaspoon fish sauce

1 Remove any veins, membrane or hard white muscle from the scallops. Lightly brush a chargrill plate with oil. Cook the scallops in batches on the chargrill plate for 1 minute each side, or until cooked.
2 Divide the English spinach leaves, capsicum and bean sprouts among four serving plates. Arrange the scallops over the top.
3 To make the dressing, place the sake, lime juice, palm sugar and fish sauce in a small bowl, and mix together well. Pour over the salad and serve immediately.

NUTRITION PER SERVE
Protein 10 g; Fat 0.5 g; Carbohydrate 3.5 g; Dietary Fibre 1.5 g; Cholesterol 25 mg; 275 kJ (65 Cal)

NOTE: Sprinkle with toasted sesame seeds, for extra minerals.

WARM CHICKEN SALAD

This aromatic salad provides good amounts of B vitamins, vitamins A and E, folate and iron.

Prep time: 30 minutes + overnight marinating
Cooking time: 20 minutes
Serves 4
EASY

---

500 g chicken thigh fillets, fat removed
2 teaspoons Thai red curry paste
1 teaspoon chopped red chilli
1 clove garlic, crushed
1 stem lemon grass, white part only,
    finely chopped
cooking oil spray
1 red onion, thinly sliced
2 tomatoes, cut in wedges
1/2 cup (25 g) chopped fresh mint
1/4 cup (15 g) chopped fresh coriander
400 g mixed salad leaves
2 tablespoons dry-roasted peanuts

Dressing
1 1/2 tablespoons soft brown sugar
2 tablespoons fish sauce
2 tablespoons lime juice
2 kaffir lime leaves, shredded
2 teaspoons oil

1 Cut the chicken into thin strips and mix with the curry paste, chilli, garlic and lemon grass. Cover and refrigerate for several hours or overnight.
2 Lightly spray a non-stick frying pan with oil and cook the chicken in batches until tender and lightly browned; set aside. Add the onion to the pan and cook for 1 minute, or until just soft. Return the chicken and any juices to the pan, and add the tomato, mint and coriander, stirring until heated. Set aside until just warm.
3 To make the dressing, thoroughly mix the ingredients in a jug. In a large bowl, toss the chicken mixture with the salad leaves and dressing, and serve sprinkled with the peanuts.

NUTRITION PER SERVE
Protein 28.5 g; Fat 17 g; Carbohydrate 10.5 g; Dietary Fibre 5 g; Cholesterol 109 mg; 1300 kJ (310 Cal)

ROAST PUMPKIN AND ONION WITH ROCKET

This quick recipe is an excellent source of beta-carotene. One serve provides your daily requirement of vitamin A, and also delivers good amounts of folate, vitamin C and potassium.

Prep time: 15 minutes
Cooking time: 35 minutes
Serves 4
EASY

800 g jap pumpkin, peeled
2 small red onions
2 cloves garlic, finely chopped
150 g rocket leaves
1–2 tablespoons balsamic vinegar

1 Preheat the oven to moderately hot 200°C (400°F/Gas 6). Cut the pumpkin into 3 cm cubes. Cut the onions into small wedges.

2 Line a small baking dish with baking paper, add the vegetables and sprinkle with the garlic. Lightly spray with oil. Season with salt and ground black pepper.

3 Bake for 30–35 minutes, or until the pumpkin is just tender. Set aside.

4 Tear the rocket leaves into pieces. Arrange on a platter, then top with the pumpkin and onion. Drizzle all over with the balsamic vinegar. Serve warm.

NUTRITION PER SERVE
Protein 5.5 g; Fat 1 g; Carbohydrate 15 g; Dietary Fibre 3.5 g; Cholesterol 0 mg; 395 kJ (95 Cal)

ASPARAGUS AND MUSHROOM SALAD

This tangy combination delivers a good dose of vitamin C, folate and potassium.

Prep time: 20 minutes
Cooking time: 10 minutes
Serves 4
EASY

---

155 g asparagus spears
1 tablespoon wholegrain mustard
1/4 cup (60 ml) orange juice
2 tablespoons lemon juice
1 tablespoon lime juice
1 tablespoon orange zest
2 teaspoons lemon zest
2 teaspoons lime zest
2 cloves garlic, crushed
1/4 cup (90 g) honey
400 g button mushrooms, halved
150 g rocket
1 red capsicum, cut into strips

1 Trim the woody ends from the asparagus spears and cut in half on the diagonal. Place the asparagus in a saucepan of boiling water and cook for 1 minute, or until just tender. Drain, plunge into cold water and set aside.

2 Place the mustard, citrus juice and zest, garlic and honey in a large saucepan and season with pepper. Bring to the boil, then reduce the heat and add the mushrooms, tossing for 2 minutes. Cool.

3 Remove the mushrooms from the sauce with a slotted spoon. Return the sauce to the heat, bring to the boil, then reduce the heat and simmer for 3–5 minutes, or until reduced and syrupy. Cool slightly.

4 Toss the mushrooms, rocket leaves, capsicum and asparagus. Place on a plate and drizzle with the sauce.

NUTRITION PER SERVE
Protein 6.5 g; Fat 1 g; Carbohydrate 24 g; Dietary Fibre 4.5 g; Cholesterol 0 mg; 555 kJ (130 Cal)

TUNA AND BEAN SALAD

Based on fish and beans, this salad contains filling protein, slow-release carbohydrate and fibre, with good amounts of B vitamins, folate, vitamin C, potassium and some beneficial fish oils.

Prep time: 20 minutes + 10 minutes refrigeration
Cooking time: 5 minutes
Serves 4
EASY

100 g green beans, chopped
400 g can butter beans, rinsed and
    drained
425 g can tuna in brine, drained
200 g cherry tomatoes, quartered
1 red onion, thinly sliced
100 g mixed salad leaves
100 g baby rocket leaves

Dressing
1 tablespoon extra virgin olive oil
1/4 cup (60 ml) lemon juice
1 teaspoon honey
2 cloves garlic, crushed
2 tablespoons chopped fresh dill

1 Steam the green beans until tender, rinse under cold water and drain. Place the green and butter beans, tuna, tomato and onion in a bowl, and toss well.
2 To make the dressing, whisk all the ingredients together. Pour the dressing over the tuna mixture, cover and refrigerate for 10 minutes.
3 Combine the salad leaves and rocket, and arrange on a salad platter. Top with the tuna mixture and serve.

NUTRITION PER SERVE
Protein 24.5 g; Fat 7 g; Carbohydrate 7.5 g; Dietary Fibre 4.5 g; Cholesterol 43 mg; 815 kJ (195 Cal)

PESTO BEEF SALAD

The pesto sauce and capsicum provide vitamin C, which will increase the amount of iron you'll absorb from the beef.

Prep time: 30 minutes
Cooking time: 25 minutes
Serves 4
EASY

---

1 large yellow capsicum, quartered
1 large red capsicum, quartered
cooking oil spray
100 g lean beef fillet steak
135 g penne
100 g button mushrooms, quartered

Pesto
1 cup (50 g) fresh basil leaves
2 cloves garlic, chopped
2 tablespoons pepitas
1 tablespoon olive oil
2 tablespoons orange juice
1 tablespoon lemon juice

1 Grill the capsicum, skin side up, until the skin blackens and blisters. Cool under a damp tea towel, then peel and dice the flesh.
2 Spray a non-stick frying pan with oil and cook the steak over high heat for 3–4 minutes each side. Remove and leave for 5 minutes before cutting into thin slices. Season with a little salt.
3 To make the pesto, finely chop the basil leaves, garlic and pepitas in a food processor. With the motor running, add the oil, orange and lemon juice. Season with salt and pepper.
4 Meanwhile, cook the penne in a large pan of rapidly boiling salted water until *al dente*. Drain, then toss with the pesto in a large bowl.
5 Add the capsicum pieces, steak slices and mushroom quarters to the penne and toss to distribute evenly. Serve immediately.

NUTRITION PER SERVE
Protein 12.5 g; Fat 10 g; Carbohydrate 27.5 g; Dietary Fibre 3.5 g; Cholesterol 17 mg; 1065 kJ (255 Cal)

GREEK SALAD

This Mediterranean side dish provides monounsaturated fat, some B vitamins, calcium and phosphorus.

Prep time: 20 minutes
Cooking time: Nil
Serves 6–8
EASY

---

6 tomatoes, cut into thin wedges
1 red onion, cut into thin rings
2 Lebanese cucumbers, sliced
185 g Kalamata olives
200 g reduced-fat feta
1 tablespoon extra virgin olive oil
dried oregano, to garnish

1 Combine the tomato, onion, cucumber and olives in a bowl. Season to taste.
2 Break the feta into large pieces and scatter over the top. Drizzle with the olive oil and sprinkle with the oregano.

NUTRITION PER SERVE (8)
Protein 8 g; Fat 6.5 g; Carbohydrate 9 g; Dietary Fibre 2 g; Cholesterol 15 mg; 520 kJ (125 Cal)

NOTE: What is widely known as Greek salad is but one of the numerous salads served in Greece. Its Greek name, *salata horiatiki*, translates as Greek country or village salad. It is a rustic salad with tomato, cucumber, feta cheese and olives as its staple ingredients, although cos lettuce, capsicums, anchovy fillets, flat-leaf parsley, capers and a sprinkle of oregano are not unusual additions.

Pesto beef salad (top), and Greek salad

BAKED VEGETABLES

With less fat than regular roast vegetables, this healthy combination provides carbohydrate energy, fibre, beta-carotene, folate and potassium.

Prep time: 15 minutes
Cooking time: 40 minutes
Serves 4
EASY

2 carrots
2 parsnips
2 large potatoes
300 g pumpkin
cooking oil spray
2 finger eggplants
chopped fresh parsley

1 Preheat the oven to moderately hot 200°C (400°F/Gas 6). Cut the carrots and parsnips in half lengthways, then crossways. Quarter the potatoes. Cut the pumpkin into chunks.

2 Put the carrot, parsnip, potato and pumpkin in a baking dish and spray lightly with cooking oil. Sprinkle with salt and ground black pepper. Bake for 20 minutes, turning occasionally.
3 Meanwhile, cut the eggplants in half lengthways and make thin shallow cuts through the skin. Add to the baking dish and cook, turning occasionally, for 20 minutes, or until all of the vegetables are tender. Sprinkle with the parsley.

NUTRITION PER SERVE
Protein 5.5 g; Fat 1 g; Carbohydrate 25 g; Dietary Fibre 6 g; Cholesterol 0 mg; 535 kJ (130 Cal)

SAUTEED MUSHROOMS

Fresh thyme adds some flavour and flavonoids to this delicious side dish, which also provides some B vitamins, potassium and a little vitamin A, but few calories.

Prep time: 10 minutes
Cooking time: 10 minutes
Serves 4
EASY

15 g butter
3 spring onions, chopped
2 teaspoons chopped fresh thyme
2 cloves garlic, crushed
270 g Swiss brown mushrooms, sliced
1 tablespoon red wine vinegar

1 Heat the butter in a large saucepan. Add the spring onion, thyme and garlic, and cook for 2 minutes. Add the mushrooms and cook, stirring frequently, until the mushrooms are very soft and most of the liquid has evaporated.
2 Add the red wine vinegar to the saucepan, and season well with salt and ground black pepper. Cook for another 2 minutes, then serve. Delicious with grilled meats.

NUTRITION PER SERVE
Protein 3 g; Fat 3.5 g; Carbohydrate 1.5 g; Dietary Fibre 2 g; Cholesterol 9.5 mg; 205 kJ (50 Cal)

LOW-FAT POTATO MASH

Place 750 g peeled, chopped desiree potatoes in a large saucepan with 2 cups (500 ml) chicken stock and enough water to cover. Bring to the boil and cook for 15 minutes, or until tender. Remove from the heat and drain, reserving $1/3$ cup (80 ml) of the liquid. Mash the potatoes with a potato masher, then add 1 crushed clove garlic, the reserved cooking liquid and 2 tablespoons low-fat sour cream. Season well with salt and white pepper, and serve with chicken, steak or fish.
Serves 4

NUTRITION PER SERVE
Protein 5 g; Fat 2.5 g; Carbohydrate 24.5 g; Dietary Fibre 3 g; Cholesterol 6.5 mg; 595 kJ (140 Cal)

STEAMED ASIAN GREENS

This recipe is an excellent way to include nutritious greens in your diet. It is an excellent source of folate, protective phytochemicals and vitamin C.

Prep time: 10 minutes
Cooking time: 10 minutes
Serves 4
EASY

___

1 lime, thinly sliced
3 x 3 cm piece fresh ginger, chopped
400 g trimmed mixed Asian greens (bok choy, choy sum, Chinese broccoli)
2 tablespoons oyster sauce
1 tablespoon Chinese rice wine
1 teaspoon sesame oil
1 clove garlic, crushed
1 teaspoon toasted sesame seeds

1 Bring 3 cups (750 ml) water to the boil in a wok or large saucepan. Add the lime slices and ginger. Place a bamboo steamer lined with baking paper over the wok or saucepan, and add the vegetables. Steam, covered, for 2–3 minutes, or until tender.
2 Combine the oyster sauce, rice wine, sesame oil and garlic in a small saucepan. Bring to the boil, then reduce the heat and simmer for 1–2 minutes.
3 Place the steamed greens on a large plate, drizzle the sauce over the top and sprinkle with the sesame seeds. Serve immediately.

NUTRITION PER SERVE
Protein 2.5 g; Fat 2 g; Carbohydrate 4 g; Dietary Fibre 2.5 g; Cholesterol 0 mg; 195 kJ (45 Cal)

BOULANGERE POTATOES

Chicken stock and garlic add flavour but no fat to this delicious potato dish. It is a good source of potassium and carbohydrate energy, with some B vitamins, vitamin C and folate.

Prep time: 35 minutes
Cooking time: 1 hour
Serves 4–6
EASY

---

1 kg potatoes, peeled and very
   thinly sliced
2 cloves garlic, crushed
400 ml chicken or vegetable stock

1 Preheat the oven to moderately hot
200°C (400°F/Gas 6).

2 Thoroughly grease a 1 litre gratin dish and arrange a layer of overlapping potato slices in the base of the dish. Add a little of the crushed garlic and season with salt and pepper. Repeat the layers with the remaining potatoes.

3 Pour the stock over the potato and bake for 1 hour, uncovered, or until the potato is tender and the top crisp and brown.

NUTRITION PER SERVE (6)
Protein 5 g; Fat 0.5 g; Carbohydrate 22.5 g; Dietary Fibre 3 g; Cholesterol 0 mg; 490 kJ (115 Cal)

NOTE: This is a French name meaning 'baker's potatoes'. Last century, when many didn't have an oven, women prepared it and left it to be cooked at the local bakery during the day.

Asparagus and beans with almonds (top), and Creamy mushroom and potato bake

ASPARAGUS AND BEANS WITH ALMONDS

Asparagus has a diuretic effect and has been used in traditional medicine to treat arthritis, rheumatism and fluid retention. This variety of ingredients provides a good serve of folate.

Prep time: 10 minutes
Cooking time: 5 minutes
Serves 4
EASY

---

150 g young asparagus, trimmed
100 g baby green beans
2 teaspoons butter
1¹/2 tablespoons toasted flaked almonds

1 Add the asparagus and beans to a large saucepan of rapidly boiling water. Cook for 1 minute, or until just tender.
2 Drain the vegetables and toss with the butter and almonds. Season with ground black pepper, and serve immediately.

NUTRITION PER SERVE
Protein 2.5 g; Fat 4 g; Carbohydrate 1.5 g; Dietary Fibre 1.5 g; Cholesterol 6 mg; 215 kJ (50 Cal)

BRUSCHETTA

Chop 4 Roma tomatoes. Combine the tomato with 2 tablespoons olive oil, 1 tablespoon balsamic vinegar and 2 tablespoons chopped fresh basil. Season well. Toast 8 slices of crusty Italian bread on one side. Rub the toasted side lightly with a peeled clove of garlic. Top with the tomato mixture and garnish with extra chopped basil. Serve immediately. Makes 8

NUTRITION PER BRUSCHETTA
Protein 3.5 g; Fat 9 g; Carbohydrate 17 g; Dietary Fibre 2 g; Cholesterol 0 mg; 710 kJ (170 Cal)

CREAMY MUSHROOM AND POTATO BAKE

A delicious creamy treat for cold winter nights, this recipe provides folate, vitamin C and potassium.

Prep time: 25 minutes
Cooking time: 55 minutes
Serves 4–6
MEDIUM

---

1 kg potatoes
1 tablespoon cream
20 g butter
1 egg yolk
¹/4 teaspoon nutmeg

Mushroom filling
40 g butter
125 g mushrooms, finely chopped
2 spring onions, finely chopped
50 g ham, finely chopped
60 g Gruyère cheese, grated
1 cup (80 g) fresh breadcrumbs

1 Peel the potatoes and cut them into even pieces. Cook in boiling salted water for 15 minutes, or until tender. Drain the potatoes, then mash thoroughly. Gradually beat in the cream, butter, egg yolk and nutmeg. Season with salt and pepper.
2 To make the filling, melt half the butter in a pan and cook the mushrooms and spring onion for 2–3 minutes, or until softened. Stir in the ham and pepper.
3 Preheat the oven to moderately hot 200°C (400°F/Gas 6). Divide the mashed potato in half. Spread the first half evenly into a well-greased 23 cm ovenproof pie dish. Spread the mushroom filling over the top, sprinkle with the grated cheese, then spread the remaining potato over the top.
4 Melt the remaining butter and stir it through the breadcrumbs, mixing well. Spread the breadcrumbs evenly over the mashed potato, then bake for 30 minutes, or until lightly browned. Serve at once.

NUTRITION PER SERVE (6)
Protein 12 g; Fat 14.5 g; Carbohydrate 33 g; Dietary Fibre 4 g; Cholesterol 73.5 mg; 1315 kJ (315 Cal)

RATATOUILLE

This Mediterranean-style dish provides monounsaturated fat and healthy phytochemicals.

Prep time: 30 minutes
Cooking time: 40 minutes
Serves 4–6
MEDIUM

6 vine-ripened tomatoes
1/3 cup (80 ml) olive oil
500 g eggplant, cut into 2 cm cubes
375 g zucchini, cut into 2 cm slices
1 green capsicum, cut into 2 cm cubes
1 red onion, cut into 2 cm wedges
3 cloves garlic, finely chopped
1/4 teaspoon cayenne pepper
2 teaspoons chopped fresh thyme
2 bay leaves
1 tablespoon red wine vinegar
1 teaspoon caster sugar
1/4 cup (15 g) shredded fresh basil

1 Score a cross in the base of each tomato. Place in a bowl of boiling water for 1 minute, then plunge into cold water and peel the skin away from the cross. Roughly chop the flesh.

2 Heat 2 tablespoons oil in a large saucepan and cook the eggplant over medium heat for 4–5 minutes, or until soft but not browned. Remove. Add 1 tablespoon oil to the pan and cook the zucchini for 3–4 minutes, or until softened. Remove from the pan. Add the capsicum to the pan, cook for 2 minutes, then remove.

3 Heat the remaining oil, add the onion and cook for 2–3 minutes, or until softened. Add the garlic, cayenne, thyme and bay leaves, and cook, stirring, for 1 minute. Return the eggplant, zucchini and capsicum to the pan, and add the tomato, vinegar and sugar. Simmer for 20 minutes, stirring occasionally. Stir in the basil and season with salt and black pepper. Serve hot or cold.

NUTRITION PER SERVE (6)
Protein 4 g; Fat 12.5 g; Carbohydrate 8 g; Dietary Fibre 5.5 g; Cholesterol 0 mg; 660 kJ (160 Cal)

CREAMY POTATO AND PARSNIP MASH

An easy way to increase the variety of vegetables in your diet, this recipe provides folate, potassium, fibre and some vitamin A and C. Parsnips add a creamy texture without adding extra fat.

Prep time: 10 minutes
Cooking time: 20 minutes
Serves 4–6
EASY

2 large potatoes
5 large parsnips
30 g butter
1 tablespoon milk
2 tablespoons sour cream
snipped fresh chives

1 Peel the potatoes and parsnips, then chop into evenly sized pieces. Cook them in a large pan of lightly salted boiling water for about 20 minutes, or until soft.
2 Drain well, then transfer to a bowl and mash with the butter, milk and sour cream until smooth and fluffy. Season generously with salt and ground black pepper. Sprinkle with chives and serve at once.

NUTRITION PER SERVE (6)
Protein 5 g; Fat 7 g; Carbohydrate 30 g; Dietary Fibre 5 g; Cholesterol 25 mg; 800 kJ (190 Cal)

NOTE: Sebago, bison, coliban, nicola, pontiac and King Edward are some good all-purpose potatoes that give successful results in this recipe.

SPICY BAKED SWEET POTATO

These spicy sweet potatoes provide plenty of carbohydrate energy, beta-carotene, vitamin C and potassium.

Prep time: 15 minutes
Cooking time: 45 minutes
Serves 4
EASY

800 g orange sweet potato, peeled
2 teaspoons olive oil
2 tablespoons honey, warmed
2 teaspoons cumin seeds
2 teaspoons coriander seeds, crushed
2 tablespoons fresh coriander sprigs
1/2 teaspoon ground cinnamon

1 Preheat the oven to moderately hot 190°C (375°F/Gas 5). Cut the sweet potato into small wedges or rounds, then place in a bowl and toss with the olive oil, honey, cumin seeds, crushed coriander seeds, coriander sprigs and cinnamon.
2 Transfer the sweet potato wedges to a lightly greased baking tray and bake for 45 minutes. Serve immediately. If desired, top the sweet potato wedges with a dollop of low-fat yoghurt.

NUTRITION PER SERVE
Protein 4 g; Fat 2.5 g; Carbohydrate 40 g; Dietary Fibre 3.5 g; Cholesterol 0 mg; 820 kJ (195 Cal)

STIR-FRIED VEGETABLES

Stir-frying preserves the crisp texture and fresh flavour of the vegetables, and helps retain water-soluble vitamins. This combination of vegetables provides vitamin C and phytochemicals.

Prep time: 20 minutes
Cooking time: 5 minutes
Serves 6
EASY

---

2 tablespoons oil
4 spring onions, cut into 3 cm lengths
3 cloves garlic, crushed
1 fresh red chilli, seeded and sliced
75 g button mushrooms, quartered
100 g Chinese cabbage, roughly chopped
2 tablespoons soy sauce
1 teaspoon fish sauce
1 tablespoon oyster sauce
1/4 cup (60 ml) vegetable stock
1/2 teaspoon grated palm sugar
150 g snow peas
150 g cauliflower, cut into small florets
150 g broccoli, cut into small florets
fresh coriander leaves, chopped, to garnish

1 Heat a wok until very hot, add the oil and swirl to coat. Add the spring onion, garlic and chilli. Stir-fry for 20 seconds. Add the mushrooms and cabbage, and stir-fry for 1 minute.
2 Stir in the sauces, stock, palm sugar, snow peas, cauliflower and broccoli. Cook for 2 minutes, or until tender. Garnish with the coriander leaves.

NUTRITION PER SERVE
Protein 4.5 g; Fat 6.5 g; Carbohydrate 5.5 g; Dietary Fibre 3.5 g; Cholesterol 0 mg; 430 kJ (100 Cal)

RICE

For centuries, rice has been an important part of Asian diets, but it is now a popular staple around the world due to its nutritient content and versatility.

Rice is a staple food in Asian countries, but it also features significantly in the cooking of the Middle East and the Mediterranean.

Rice is a cereal grain with a high starch content, and there are thousands of varieties cultivated across the world. It is eaten as an accompaniment to many Asian dishes, but can also be the main ingredient of a meal, flavoured in various ways, such as in a risotto, paella or pilaf.

Rice by itself is quite healthy, being rich in carbohydrate, but some rice dishes may contain large amounts of fat. Brown rice in particular is a good source of vitamins, minerals, protein and fibre. White rice has fewer nutrients than brown rice because the outer bran layer, which includes the embryo of the seed, is removed during the milling process.

There are three broad classifications of rice—long-grain rice, medium-grain rice and short-grain rice. The different types of rice are suited to different styles and methods of cooking.

TYPES OF RICE

■ Basmati rice is a fragrant Indian extra-long-grain rice, great for curries.
■ Jasmine rice is a long-grain aromatic rice, very popular in Southeast Asia.
■ Long-grain rice can be either white or brown.
■ Arborio rice is a short-grain Italian rice, grown specifically for making risotto. Its high starch content gives risotto dishes their characteristic creamy texture.
■ Short-grain rice has a sticky, plump texture when cooked, making it ideal for paella and sushi. It is also used for making rice desserts.
■ Wild rice is not actually a rice at all, but a type of grass. It is cooked in a similar way to brown rice, and has a chewy texture and a nutty flavour.

FLAVOURING RICE

On its own, rice has quite a bland flavour, but it is usually served as an accompaniment to spiced or highly flavoured dishes. To add more flavour to rice, cook it in vegetable or chicken stock instead of water.

There are many ingredients that can be added to rice during cooking that will subtly add flavour and enhance the overall meal (some will need to be removed before serving):

- slices of fresh ginger
- slices of garlic
- pieces of lemon grass
- a cinnamon stick
- whole cloves
- crushed cardamom pods

  - star anise
  - saffron strands or a little turmeric
  - fresh or dried chilli
  - fresh thyme
  - bay leaves
  - lime leaves
  - pandanus leaf
  - crumbled nori.

HEALTHY RICE HINTS AND TIPS

- When making fried rice, use the same combination of vegetables that you would normally use, but steam or blanch them instead of frying, and add them to steamed rice with lots of finely chopped garlic chives and spring onion. Scatter with toasted sesame seeds and sprinkle with salt-reduced soy sauce.
- Use dried wild forest mushrooms in a risotto. Soak them in warm water, drain them and set aside to add to the risotto. Reserve the soaking liquid to add to the stock for cooking the risotto. It will have a delicious, earthy flavour.
- Add some drained and rinsed red kidney beans to white rice while it is cooking, along with some crushed garlic and chilli powder. Stir through lots of chopped fresh parsley and chives, and serve as an accompaniment, or rolled up in a tortilla.
- Nori rolls are simple to make and construct, and are a tasty, low-fat and nutritious lunch, snack or hors d'oeuvre. The base is short-grain rice flavoured with rice wine vinegar, sugar and salt (see page 191), and fillings can be added to suit your requirements. Serve the rolls with a salt-reduced soy sauce, wasabi and some pickled ginger. Try these suggestions as individual fillings, or combine them to suit your taste:
- strips of omelette flavoured with Japanese soy sauce
- simple combinations of vegetables, such as cucumber, blanched carrot and capsicum
- the classic sashimi tuna and salmon
- smoked salmon
- hot smoked trout
- avocado
- cooked prawns
- Chinese mushrooms sprinkled with sesame seeds
- Japanese smoked eel.
- Cooked brown or white rice can be seasoned and flavoured with herbs, toasted nuts, lemon zest, onion, garlic and ginger, and then used as a tasty and filling stuffing. Try it as a stuffing for:
- vine leaves, braised in the oven with stock
- cabbage leaves, braised with a light tomato and herb sauce
- red capsicums
- banana chillies
- a boned leg of lamb for roasting
- a whole chicken for roasting
- chicken breast fillets.

CHICKEN AND MUSHROOM RISOTTO

This creamy Italian risotto provides a light yet satisfying meal with good amounts of B vitamins, pantothenic acid, iron, zinc, folate, potassium and phosphorus.

Prep time: 15 minutes
Cooking time: 35 minutes
Serves 4
EASY

1 litre chicken stock
1 tablespoon oil
30 g butter
1 leek, thinly sliced
200 g Swiss brown mushrooms, sliced
200 g button mushrooms, sliced
1/4 cup (60 ml) balsamic vinegar
500 g chicken tenderloins, halved
1/2 cup (125 ml) white wine
1 1/4 cups (275 g) arborio rice
2 tablespoons snipped fresh chives

1 Place the stock in a saucepan and heat until the stock is simmering.
2 Heat the oil and butter in a separate saucepan, add the leek and cook over medium heat for 5 minutes, or until golden. Add the mushrooms and 2 tablespoons balsamic vinegar, and cook until tender and the liquid is absorbed.
3 Add the chicken and cook until browned. Stir in the wine and bring to the boil. Add the rice and stir to coat.
4 Add 1/2 cup (125 ml) stock, stirring constantly over medium heat until all the liquid is absorbed. Continue adding the stock, 1/2 cup (125 ml) at a time, stirring for 25 minutes, or until all the stock is absorbed and the rice is tender. Stir in the remaining vinegar and chives, and season with salt and ground black pepper.

NUTRITION PER SERVE
Protein 37 g; Fat 15 g; Carbohydrate 54 g; Dietary Fibre 4 g; Cholesterol 82 mg; 2090 kJ (500 Cal)

SILVERBEET PARCELS

A delicious blend of risotto, cheese and vegetables in nutritious silverbeet delivers carbohydrate, B vitamins, folate, vitamin C and potassium.

Prep time: 40 minutes
Cooking time: 1 hour
Serves 6
DIFFICULT

---

2 cups (500 ml) vegetable stock
1 tablespoon olive oil
1 onion, chopped
2 cloves garlic, crushed
1/2 cup (110 g) arborio rice
1 red capsicum, chopped
250 g mushrooms, chopped
60 g reduced-fat Cheddar, grated
1/4 cup (15 g) shredded fresh basil
6 large silverbeet leaves
2 x 400 g cans chopped tomatoes
1 tablespoon balsamic vinegar
1 teaspoon soft brown sugar

1 Heat the stock in a pan and maintain at simmering point. Heat the oil in a large pan, add the onion and garlic and cook until softened. Add the rice, capsicum and mushrooms, and stir until well combined. Gradually add 1/2 cup (125 ml) hot stock, stirring until the liquid is absorbed. Add the stock, a little at a time, until it is all absorbed and the rice is tender (about 20 minutes). Remove from the heat, add the cheese and basil, and season well.
2 Trim the stalks from the silverbeet and cook the leaves, a few at a time, in a large pan of boiling water for 30 seconds, or until wilted. Drain on a tea towel. Cut away any tough white veins from the leaves. Place a portion of mushroom filling in the centre of each leaf, fold in the sides and roll up carefully. Tie with string.
3 Put the tomato, vinegar and sugar in a large, deep non-stick frying pan and stir to combine. Add the silverbeet parcels, cover and simmer for 10 minutes. Remove the string and serve with tomato sauce.

NUTRITION PER SERVE
Protein 8.5 g; Fat 6 g; Carbohydrate 22.5 g; Dietary Fibre 4 g; Cholesterol 6 mg; 755 kJ (180 Cal)

TOMATO AND HAM PILAF

This quick and easy meal provides carbohydrate energy, B vitamins, folate, vitamin C and iron.

Prep time: 15 minutes
Cooking time: 30 minutes
Serves 4
EASY

1 tablespoon olive oil
1 large onion, chopped
2 cloves garlic, crushed
1 large green capsicum, cut into 2 cm cubes
2 celery sticks, cut into 1 cm slices
3 teaspoons paprika
1 1/2 cups (300 g) long-grain rice
3 cups (750 ml) chicken stock
400 g can diced tomatoes
200 g light ham, chopped
2 bay leaves
1/4 cup (7 g) chopped fresh flat-leaf parsley
1/2 cup (80 g) frozen peas

1 Heat the oil in a large saucepan over medium heat, add the onion and cook for 3 minutes, or until soft. Add the garlic, capsicum, celery and paprika, and cook for 3–4 minutes, or until softened.
2 Add the rice and stir to coat. Add the stock, tomato, ham and bay leaves, and bring to the boil. Reduce the heat and simmer, covered, for 15 minutes, or until the rice is tender.
3 Add the parsley and peas, stir well and simmer, uncovered, for 5 minutes. Season with salt and ground black pepper.

NUTRITION PER SERVE
Protein 19.5 g; Fat 9 g; Carbohydrate 69 g; Dietary Fibre 5 g; Cholesterol 26 mg; 1835 kJ (440 Cal)

GREEN PILAU WITH CASHEWS

Cashews complement the rice and improve the amino acid content of this vegetarian dish. Top it with low-fat yoghurt for extra calcium.

Prep time: 15 minutes
Cooking time: 1 hour 10 minutes
Serves 6
MEDIUM

200 g baby English spinach leaves
2/3 cup (100 g) raw cashew nuts, chopped
2 tablespoons olive oil
6 spring onions, chopped
1 1/2 cups (300 g) long-grain brown rice
2 cloves garlic, finely chopped
1 teaspoon fennel seeds
2 tablespoons lemon juice
2 1/2 cups (625 ml) vegetable stock
1/4 cup (15 g) chopped fresh mint
1/4 cup (7 g) chopped fresh flat-leaf parsley

1 Preheat the oven to moderate 180°C (350°F/Gas 4). Wash the English spinach leaves, then shred them into 1 cm slices.

2 Place the cashew nuts on a baking tray and roast for 5–10 minutes, or until golden brown—watch carefully.

3 Heat the oil in a large frying pan and cook the spring onion over medium heat for 2 minutes, or until soft. Add the rice, garlic and fennel seeds, and cook, stirring frequently, for 1–2 minutes, or until the rice is evenly coated. Increase the heat to high, add the lemon juice, stock and 1 teaspoon salt, and bring to the boil. Reduce to low, cover and cook for 45 minutes without lifting the lid. Remove from the heat and sprinkle with the spinach and herbs. Stand, covered, for 8 minutes, then fork the spinach and herbs through the rice. Season. Serve sprinkled with the cashews.

NUTRITION PER SERVE
Protein 9 g; Fat 16 g; Carbohydrate 43.5 g; Dietary Fibre 4 g; Cholesterol 0 mg; 1490 kJ (355 Cal)

SEAFOOD AND HERB RISOTTO

This nutritious and aromatic risotto is an excellent
source of lean protein.

Prep time: 40 minutes
Cooking time: 50 minutes
Serves 4
MEDIUM

150 g boneless white fish fillet such as sea perch
8 black mussels (200 g)
8 raw prawns (250 g)
1.75 litres chicken stock
cooking oil spray
2 onions, finely chopped
2 cloves garlic, finely chopped
1 celery stick, finely chopped
2 cups (440 g) arborio rice
2 tablespoons chopped fresh parsley
1 tablespoon chopped fresh oregano
1 tablespoon chopped fresh thyme leaves
2 tablespoons grated Parmesan

1 Cut the fish into small cubes. Scrub the mussels and remove the beards. Discard any mussels that are open. Peel and devein the prawns, leaving the tails intact. Put the seafood in a bowl and refrigerate.
2 Put the stock in a saucepan and bring to the boil, then reduce the heat until gently simmering.
3 Lightly spray a large saucepan with oil and heat over medium heat. Cook the onion, garlic and celery for 2–3 minutes. Add 2 tablespoons water, cover and cook for 5 minutes, or until the vegetables are beginning to soften. Add the rice and 2 tablespoons water, cover and cook for 3–4 minutes, or until the rice is coated.
4 Gradually add 1/2 cup (125 ml) of the hot stock to the rice mixture, stirring constantly over low heat, until all the stock has been absorbed. Repeat the process, adding 1/2 cup (125 ml) of liquid each time until all but a small amount of stock is left and the rice is just tender.
5 Meanwhile, bring a small amount of water to the boil in a saucepan. Add the mussels, cover and cook for 3 minutes,

shaking the pan occasionally, until the mussels have opened. Drain the mussels and discard any that have not opened.
6 Add the fish and prawns and the remaining stock to the rice. Stir and cook for 5–10 minutes, or until the seafood is just cooked and the rice is tender and creamy. Remove from the heat, add the mussels, cover and set aside for 5 minutes. Stir the herbs and Parmesan through the risotto, then season well with salt and cracked pepper. Serve immediately.

NUTRITION PER SERVE
Protein 40 g; Fat 5 g; Carbohydrate 90 g; Dietary Fibre 4 g; Cholesterol 175 mg; 2395 kJ (570 Cal)

COCONUT RICE

This rice dish is a good source of carbohydrate,
with small amounts of niacin and minerals.

Prep time: 35 minutes + 40 minutes standing
Cooking time: 15 minutes
Serves 6
EASY

2 cups (400 g) long-grain white rice
1 pandan leaf, tied in a knot (see Note)
3/4 cup (185 ml) coconut cream

1 Rinse the rice and cover with 1 litre water. Set aside for 30 minutes. Drain. Bring 3 cups (750 ml) water to the boil. Add the rice, pandan leaf and salt, to taste. Reduce the heat and cook, covered, for 12 minutes, or until the rice is just cooked.
2 Remove from the heat and add the coconut cream. Stir gently to avoid breaking the grains. Cover and set aside for 10 minutes or until the rice absorbs the coconut cream. Discard the pandan leaf before serving.

NUTRITION PER SERVE
Protein 5 g; Fat 6.5 g; Carbohydrate 54 g; Dietary Fibre 1 g; Cholesterol 0 mg; 1245 kJ (295 Cal)

NOTE: Pandan leaves, also known as pandanus or screw pine leaves. They are available in Asian grocery stores.

Seafood and herb risotto (top), and Coconut rice

JAMBALAYA

This thick, stew-like dish contains a wide range of ingredients and delivers many nutrients. It is a good source of carbohydrate, B vitamins, vitamin C and plant antioxidants.

Prep time: 30 minutes
Cooking time: 50 minutes
Serves 4–6
EASY

2 tablespoons olive oil
1 large red onion, finely chopped
1 clove garlic, crushed
2 rashers bacon, trimmed of fat, finely chopped
1 1/2 cups (300 g) long-grain rice
1 red capsicum, diced
150 g ham, chopped
425 g can tomatoes, chopped
425 g can tomato purée
1 teaspoon Worcestershire sauce
dash Tabasco sauce
1/2 teaspoon dried thyme leaves
1/2 cup (30 g) chopped fresh parsley
50 g cooked, peeled, small prawns
4 spring onions, thinly sliced

1 Heat the oil in a large saucepan over medium heat. Add the onion, garlic and bacon, and cook, stirring, for 5 minutes, or until soft. Stir in the rice and cook for 2 minutes.

2 Add the red capsicum, ham, tomato, tomato purée, sauces and thyme. Stir for 1 minute. Bring to the boil, then reduce the heat to low. Cook, covered, for 40 minutes, or until the rice is tender.

3 Stir in the parsley and prawns. Season with salt and ground black pepper, and serve, sprinkled with the spring onion.

NUTRITION PER SERVE (6)
Protein 14.5 g; Fat 9.5 g; Carbohydrate 48 g; Dietary Fibre 3.5 g; Cholesterol 37 mg; 1415 kJ (340 Cal)

RICE AND LENTIL PILAU

Highly aromatic and full of protein and slow-release carbohydrate, this dish will satisfy your energy needs. It's a good choice for vegetarians.

Prep time: 15 minutes
Cooking time: 25 minutes
Serves 4–6
EASY

1 tablespoon coriander seeds
1 tablespoon cardamom pods
1 tablespoon cumin seeds
1 teaspoon black peppercorns
1 teaspoon cloves
1 small cinnamon stick, crushed
1/4 cup (60 ml) oil
1 onion, chopped
3 cloves garlic, chopped
1 cup (200 g) basmati rice
1 cup (250 g) red lentils
3 cups (750 ml) hot vegetable stock
spring onions, thinly sliced on the diagonal,
    to garnish

1 To make the garam masala, place the coriander seeds, cardamom pods, cumin seeds, peppercorns, cloves and cinnamon in a dry frying pan. Shake over medium heat for 1 minute, or until the mixture is fragrant. Blend in a spice grinder or blender until a fine powder.

2 Heat the oil in a large saucepan. Add the onion, garlic and 3 teaspoons of the garam masala. Cook over medium heat for 3 minutes, or until the onion is soft.

3 Stir in the rice and lentils, and cook for 2 minutes. Add the hot stock and stir well. Slowly bring to the boil, then reduce the heat, and simmer, covered, for 15–20 minutes, or until the rice is cooked and all the stock has been absorbed. Gently fluff the rice with a fork. Garnish with spring onion.

NUTRITION PER SERVE (6)
Protein 14 g; Fat 10.5 g; Carbohydrate 45 g; Dietary
Fibre 7 g; Cholesterol 0 mg; 1370 kJ (330 Cal)

VEGETARIAN PAELLA

This vegetarian version of the classic Spanish recipe is an excellent source of slow-release carbohydrate, fibre, folate and iron.

Prep time: 20 minutes + overnight soaking
Cooking time: 40 minutes
Serves 6
MEDIUM

---

1 cup (200 g) dried haricot beans
1/4 teaspoon saffron threads
2 tablespoons olive oil
1 onion, diced
1 red capsicum, cut into 1 cm x 4 cm strips
5 cloves garlic, crushed
1 1/4 cups (275 g) paella rice or arborio
1 tablespoon sweet paprika
1/2 teaspoon mixed spice
3 cups (750 ml) vegetable stock
400 g can diced tomatoes
1 1/2 tablespoons tomato paste
1 cup (150 g) fresh or frozen soya beans
100 g silverbeet leaves (no stems), shredded
400 g can artichoke hearts, drained, quartered
1/3 cup (20 g) chopped fresh coriander leaves

1 Cover the haricot beans in cold water and soak overnight. Drain and rinse well.
2 Dry-fry the saffron in a small frying pan over medium–low heat for 1 minute, or until darkened. Remove from the heat and crumble into a small bowl. Pour in 1/2 cup (125 ml) warm water and allow to steep.
3 Heat the oil in a large frying pan. Cook the onion and capsicum over medium–high heat for 4–5 minutes, or until soft. Stir in the garlic and cook for 1 minute. Reduce the heat and stir in the beans, rice, paprika, mixed spice and 1/2 teaspoon salt. Add the saffron water, stock, tomato and tomato paste, and bring to the boil. Cover, reduce the heat and simmer for 20 minutes.
4 Stir in the soya beans, silverbeet and artichokes. Cook, covered, for 8 minutes, or until the liquid is absorbed and the rice and beans are tender. Turn off the heat. Leave for 5 minutes, then stir in the coriander.

NUTRITION PER SERVE
Protein 16.5 g; Fat 9.5 g; Carbohydrate 56.5 g; Dietary Fibre 12 g; Cholesterol 0 mg; 1565 kJ (375 Cal)

KITCHEREE

The combination of rice and lentils in this quick vegetarian dish provides complete protein, slow-release carbohydrate and fibre.

Prep time: 15 minutes
Cooking time: 25 minutes
Serves 6
EASY

1¹/2 cups (300 g) basmati rice
1¹/2 cups (300 g) split mung beans (mung lentils)
2 tablespoons oil
1 onion, sliced
3 bay leaves
1 teaspoon cumin seeds
2 pieces cassia bark
1 tablespoon cardamom seeds
6 cloves
¹/4 teaspoon black peppercorns

1 Wash the rice and lentils, then drain and set aside.
2 Heat the oil in a frying pan, add the onion, bay leaves and spices, and cook over low heat for 5 minutes, or until the onion is softened and the spices are fragrant. Add the rice and lentils, and cook, stirring, for 2 minutes.
3 Pour in 1.25 litres water and season with salt. Bring to the boil, then reduce the heat and cook, covered, over low heat for 15 minutes. Stir gently to avoid breaking the grains and cook, uncovered, over low heat for 3 minutes, or until all the moisture has evaporated. Serve hot with Indian curries.

NUTRITION PER SERVE
Protein 15 g; Fat 7.5 g; Carbohydrate 59 g; Dietary Fibre 7.5 g; Cholesterol 0 mg; 1500 kJ (360 Cal)

Nasi goreng (top), and Salmon balls

NASI GORENG

This recipe will help you on your way to eating the recommended 30 different foods a day.

Prep time: 25 minutes
Cooking time: 15 minutes
Serves 4–6
EASY

5–8 long red chillies, seeded and chopped
2 teaspoons shrimp paste
8 cloves garlic, finely chopped
oil, for cooking
2 eggs, lightly beaten
350 g chicken thigh fillets, cut into thin strips
200 g peeled raw prawns, deveined
8 cups (1.5 kg) cooked rice
1/3 cup (80 ml) kecap manis
1/3 cup (80 ml) soy sauce
2 small Lebanese cucumbers, finely chopped
1 large tomato, finely chopped
lime wedges, to serve

1 Mix the chilli, shrimp paste and garlic in a food processor to make a paste.
2 Heat 1 tablespoon of the oil in a wok and swirl it around to coat the side. Add the egg and push the egg up the side of the wok to form a large omelette. Cook for 1 minute over medium heat, or until the egg is set, then flip it over and cook the other side for 1 minute. Remove from the wok and cool before slicing into strips.
3 Reheat the wok, add 1 tablespoon of the oil and stir-fry the chicken and half the chilli paste over high heat until just cooked. Remove from the wok.
4 Reheat the wok, add 1 tablespoon of the oil and stir-fry the prawns and remaining chilli paste until the prawns are cooked. Remove from the wok.
5 Reheat the wok, add 1 tablespoon of the oil and the rice, and toss over medium heat for 4–5 minutes, or until the rice is heated through. Add the kecap manis and soy sauce, and toss until the rice is coated in the sauces. Return the chicken and prawns to the wok, and toss until heated through. Season with salt and pepper.

Transfer to a large deep serving bowl and top with the omelette strips, cucumber and tomato. Serve with the lime wedges.

NUTRITION PER SERVE (6)
Protein 29 g; Fat 10.5 g; Carbohydrate 74.5 g; Dietary Fibre 3.5 g; Cholesterol 170.5 mg; 2160 kJ (515 Cal)

SALMON BALLS

These lightly spiced salmon balls provide protein, slow-release carbohydrate, fibre and B vitamins.

Prep time: 35 minutes + 30 minutes refrigeration
Cooking time: 55 minutes
Makes 8 balls
EASY

3 potatoes
1/2 cup (100 g) long-grain rice
1/2 cup (50 g) rolled oats
415 g can red salmon, drained and flaked
1 egg, lightly beaten
3 spring onions, chopped
2 tablespoons lemon juice
2 tablespoons sweet chilli sauce
1 cup (80 g) fresh breadcrumbs
2 eggs, lightly beaten
2 cups (200 g) dry breadcrumbs
cooking oil spray

1 Steam or microwave the potatoes until tender. Drain and mash. Boil the rice for 15 minutes, or until tender. Cool.
2 Place the potato, rice, oats, salmon, egg, spring onion, lemon juice, sweet chilli sauce and breadcrumbs in a bowl, and mix together well. Season with salt and pepper.
3 Divide the mixture into eight portions and shape into balls. Dip in the egg, then the dry breadcrumbs. Refrigerate on a lined baking tray for 30 minutes.
4 Preheat the oven to moderately hot 200°C (400°F/Gas 6). Spray the salmon balls lightly with oil and bake for 30 minutes, or until crisp, golden and heated through. Serve with lemon juice.

NUTRITION PER BALL
Protein 18.5 g; Fat 9 g; Carbohydrate 44.5 g; Dietary Fibre 3 g; Cholesterol 102.5 mg; 1415 kJ (340 Cal)

RISOTTO WITH SCALLOPS

This dish has a creamy texture without too much fat. It provides carbohydrate, protein, niacin, folate and monounsaturated fat.

Prep time: 15 minutes
Cooking time: 35 minutes
Serves 4–6
MEDIUM

1 litre chicken, fish or vegetable stock
2³/4 cups (360 g) fresh or frozen baby peas
2 tablespoons light sour cream
2 tablespoons finely shredded fresh mint
1 tablespoon olive oil
1 small onion, finely chopped
2 cloves garlic, finely chopped
150 g arborio rice
16 large scallops (without roe)
1 tablespoon grated Parmesan
4 fresh mint leaves, to garnish
lemon wedges, to serve

1 Put the stock in a saucepan and bring to the boil. Simmer the peas for 1–2 minutes, or until tender, then remove with a slotted spoon. Keep the stock at a low simmer. Blend 1³/4 cups (230 g) of the peas with the sour cream in a food processor until smooth. Season and stir in half the mint.
2 Heat the oil in a large saucepan. Cook the onion over low heat for 4–5 minutes, or until soft. Add the garlic and cook for 30 seconds. Stir in the rice and increase the heat to medium.
3 Add 1 cup (250 ml) stock to the rice and cook, stirring, until all the liquid has evaporated. Add ¹/2 cup (125 ml) stock at a time, until the rice is cooked and the mixture is creamy (about 20 minutes).
4 Lightly season the scallops. Sear the scallops on both sides in a chargrill pan.
5 Fold the pea purée through the risotto with the whole peas and Parmesan. Serve the risotto topped with the scallops, remaining mint, a fresh mint leaf and a wedge of lemon.

NUTRITION PER SERVE (6)
Protein 12.5 g; Fat 6 g; Carbohydrate 27.5 g; Dietary Fibre 5 g; Cholesterol 17 mg; 910 kJ (215 Cal)

FRIED RICE

A reduced-fat fried rice, this version is high in protein and carbohydrate, with good amounts of vitamin C, B vitamins, potassium and phosphorus.

Prep time: 20 minutes
Cooking time: 15 minutes
Serves 6
EASY

―――

cooking oil spray
4 egg whites, lightly beaten
2 cloves garlic, crushed
350 g raw prawns, peeled, deveined and halved
    lengthways
100 g cooked chicken, shredded
1/2 cup (80 g) frozen peas
180 g sliced light ham, cut into small strips
1 red capsicum, diced
4 spring onions, sliced
4 cups (750 g) cooked white and wild rice
    blend (see Note)
1 1/2 tablespoons soy sauce
3 teaspoons fish sauce
1 1/2 teaspoons soft brown sugar

1 Lightly spray a non-stick wok with oil and pour in the egg white. Cook over low heat, stirring until the egg is just cooked and slightly scrambled, then remove and set aside.

2 Add the garlic, prawns, chicken, peas, ham and capsicum to the wok, and stir-fry for 3–4 minutes, or until the prawns are cooked.

3 Add the spring onion, rice, soy sauce, fish sauce and sugar, and toss for 30 seconds, or until heated through. Add the egg, toss lightly and serve.

NUTRITION PER SERVE
Protein 25 g; Fat 3.5 g; Carbohydrate 39 g; Dietary Fibre 2 g; Cholesterol 91 mg; 1225 kJ (295 Cal)

NOTE: You will need to cook 1 1/3 cups (260 g) white and wild rice blend for this recipe.

ASIAN BARLEY PILAU

Once an important dietary staple, barley is often overlooked in modern societies, even though it's a highly nutritious food. This satisfying recipe is a great choice for those trying to control their weight.

Prep time: 10 minutes + 15 minutes soaking
Cooking time: 35 minutes
Serves 4
MEDIUM

15 g dried sliced mushrooms
2 cups (500 ml) vegetable stock
$^{1}/_{2}$ cup (125 ml) dry sherry
1 tablespoon oil
3 large French shallots, thinly sliced
2 large cloves garlic, crushed
1 tablespoon grated fresh ginger
1 teaspoon Sichuan peppercorns, crushed
1$^{1}/_{2}$ cups (330 g) pearl barley
500 g choy sum, cut into
     5 cm lengths
3 teaspoons kecap manis
1 teaspoon sesame oil

1 Place the mushrooms in a bowl and cover with boiling water, then leave for 15 minutes. Strain, reserving $^{1}/_{2}$ cup (125 ml) of the liquid.
2 Bring the stock and sherry to the boil in a saucepan, then reduce the heat, cover and simmer until needed.
3 Heat the oil in a large saucepan and cook the shallots over medium heat for 2–3 minutes, or until soft. Add the garlic, ginger and peppercorns, and cook for 1 minute. Add the barley and mushrooms and mix well. Stir in the stock and mushroom liquid, then reduce the heat and simmer, covered, for 25 minutes, or until the liquid evaporates.
4 Meanwhile, steam the choy sum until wilted. Add to the barley mixture. Stir in the kecap manis and sesame oil.

NUTRITION PER SERVE
Protein 9.5 g; Fat 8.5 g; Carbohydrate 48 g; Dietary Fibre 10.5 g; Cholesterol 0 mg; 1415 kJ (340 Cal)

NORI CONES

Add some smoked salmon to these nutritious cones for extra protein, iron and essential fatty acids.

Prep time: 45 minutes + 20 minutes standing
Cooking time: 15 minutes
Makes 40
DIFFICULT

2 cups (440 g) short-grain white rice
2 tablespoons rice vinegar
2 tablespoons caster sugar
10 g dried sliced Chinese mushrooms
250 g choy sum, shredded and blanched
1 tablespoon pickled ginger, shredded
1 tablespoon toasted sesame seeds
1 tablespoon kecap manis
1/2 teaspoon wasabi paste
2 teaspoons mirin
1 tablespoon salt-reduced soy sauce
10 nori sheets
purchased dipping sauce for sushi, to serve

1 Rinse the rice until the water runs clear. Put in a saucepan with 2 cups (500 ml) water. Bring to the boil, then reduce the heat and simmer for 10 minutes. Remove from the heat, and cover for 15 minutes.
2 Spread the rice in a shallow dish. Place the vinegar, sugar, 1/2 teaspoon salt and 2 tablespoons water in a saucepan, and stir over low heat until the sugar dissolves. Pour over the rice, fork it through and cool.
3 Soak the mushrooms in boiling water for 5 minutes. Drain, squeeze out the excess liquid and roughly chop.
4 Place the rice in a large bowl and stir in the mushrooms, choy sum, ginger, sesame seeds and the combined kecap manis, wasabi, mirin and soy sauce.
5 Place the nori sheets shiny-side down and cut each sheet into four squares. Brush the edge with water and place 1 tablespoon of the mixture in the centre of each square. Roll up to form a cone and top up with 2 teaspoons of filling. Serve immediately with the dipping sauce.

NUTRITION PER CONE
Protein 1.5 g; Fat 0 g; Carbohydrate 20 g; Dietary Fibre 1 g; Cholesterol 0 mg; 390 kJ (95 Cal)

PASTA

With over 300 varieties of pasta to choose from, and possibly as many pasta sauces, it's easy to incorporate many nutritious pasta meals into your diet without becoming bored.

Pasta is a simple preparation of flour, water and sometimes eggs. It is readily available in either fresh or dried form, is economical and very easy to cook, even for beginners. On its own, pasta is a healthy source of carbohydrate energy. However, it is the sauce with which the pasta is served that dictates how healthy the dish will be.

There are many delicious rich, creamy and cheesy pasta sauces that are all relatively high in fat. The sauces that are low in fat, but are still very tasty, are mostly tomato-based sauces—a great choice for healthy cooking, or for healthy eating when dining out.

It is generally agreed that chunky, thick pasta sauces are best when served with one of the short pastas such as penne, spirali or farfalle, and that saucy, creamy or oil-based sauces go well with one of the long pastas such as spaghetti, linguine or tagliatelle. Small pasta shapes such as orzo or stelline are a delicious addition to vegetable soups—simply add them to the soup in the last 10 minutes of cooking.

Pasta sauces are another easy way to eat a variety of healthy vegetables. They should be of a consistency and quantity to coat the pasta, not leave it swimming in excess sauce in the bottom of the bowl.

LOW-FAT PASTA SAUCES

- If you can't resist a rich, creamy pasta sauce, one way of reducing the fat is to substitute low-fat evaporated milk for cream. To get the desired creamy and saucey consistency, you will need to simmer the sauce until reduced.
- When making a pasta sauce, instead of using olive oil to sauté the ingredients, give your pan a light spray with cooking oil. If more moisture is needed, add a tablespoon of water or stock to help soften the ingredients.
- If you are using bacon as an ingredient in the sauce, be sure to remove as much of the fat as possible before cooking.
- When purchasing mince for bolognese sauce, choose one of the lean or low-fat varieties that are often available from butchers or supermarkets.
- Read the labels on filled pastas such as ravioli or tortellini to check for high salt or cheese contents.
- Crisp prosciutto or pancetta on a grill tray in the oven, so that any excess fat drips off. Drain on paper towels, then crumble over the top of your pasta dish.

When draining cooked pasta, reserve a little of the cooking water to stir through the sauce. This will add a little flavour, moisture and starch to the dish and,

particularly for pasta dishes with an olive oil sauce, this will reduce the amount of oil needed to moisten the pasta. For example, when tossing pesto through pasta, a tablespoon of the cooking water will help distribute the sauce evenly and smoothly.

■ A simple sauce made with puréed, skinned roasted red capsicum, thinned with a little vegetable stock, seasoned and tossed with chopped fresh herbs, is delicious tossed through hot linguine with some roughly chopped rocket. Add any juices that come from the capsicums while roasting to the purée for a flavour boost.

■ When making lasagne, instead of the béchamel sauce, use a layer of ricotta whisked until smooth with some low-fat evaporated milk and low-fat cream cheese.

SIMPLE AND HEALTHY PASTA SAUCE IDEAS

■ Roast pumpkin pieces until they are soft and caramelised, then toss them through pasta with some low-fat ricotta, garlic chives and a little extra virgin olive oil.

■ Combine capers, diced fresh tomato flesh, chopped fresh parsley and canned tuna in springwater (with the juices), and stir through hot spaghetti.

■ Add some diced bocconcini to pasta that has been dressed with a simple fresh tomato and basil sauce and leave it for 2 minutes so that the bocconcini melts into strands.

■ Instead of tossing pasta with pesto, use half pesto and half tomato passata, chicken or vegetable stock to reduce the amount of oil.

■ Add chickpeas, lentils or other cooked legumes or pulses to your favourite pasta sauce for added texture and fibre.

■ Make a purée with fresh seasonal vegetables, such as pumpkin, sweet potato, asparagus, artichokes, cauliflower, broccoli, peas, broadbeans, spinach and mushrooms (fresh and dried, using the soaking liquid in the purée for added flavour). Cook the vegetables with some garlic, blend with vegetable or chicken stock until the mixture reaches the required consistency, then season well and add plenty of chopped fresh herbs. Serve the sauce with your favourite pasta shape. If you prefer a richer, slightly creamier sauce, blend the sauce with some low-fat ricotta until smooth.

■ Make a risotto-style dish using orzo instead of rice, cooked with stock, and add your favourite seasonings.

■ Stir some low-fat ricotta through a tomato and chilli pasta sauce for a creamier taste.

■ Take advantage of the best green spring vegetables, blanch them in vegetable stock until just tender in vegetable stock, and then toss with some hot pasta and fresh herbs, and enough of the stock to moisten. A light dust with finely grated Parmesan is all that is needed for the perfect pasta Primavera.

SPAGHETTI BOLOGNESE

This low-fat pasta dish is topped with a thick, meat and vegetable sauce. It is packed with good-quality protein, slow-release carbohydrate, iron, zinc, vitamin B12 and niacin.

Prep time: 30 minutes
Cooking time: 1 hour 20 minutes
Serves 4–6
EASY

———

cooking oil spray
2 onions, finely chopped
2 cloves garlic, finely chopped
2 carrots, finely chopped
2 celery sticks, finely chopped
400 g lean beef mince
1 kg tomatoes, chopped
1/2 cup (125 ml) red wine
350 g spaghetti
1/4 cup (15 g) finely chopped fresh parsley

1 Lightly spray a large saucepan with oil. Heat over medium heat, and add the onion, garlic, carrot and celery. Stir for 5 minutes, or until the vegetables have softened. If you find the vegetables are sticking, add 1 tablespoon water.
2 Increase the heat to high, add the mince and cook for 5 minutes, or until browned. Stir constantly to prevent the meat sticking. Add the tomato, wine and 1 cup (250 ml) water. Bring to the boil, then reduce the heat and simmer, uncovered, for 1 hour, or until the sauce has thickened.
3 Cook the spaghetti in a large pan of rapidly boiling water for 10–12 minutes, or until *al dente*. Drain, stir the parsley through the sauce and season well with salt and cracked black pepper. Divide the spaghetti among pasta bowls and top with the bolognese sauce. Garnish with a little chopped fresh parsley.

NUTRITION PER SERVE (6)
Protein 22.5 g; Fat 6.5 g; Carbohydrate 46.5 g; Dietary Fibre 5.5 g; Cholesterol 34 mg; 1470 kJ (350 Cal)

LINGUINE WITH BACON, MUSHROOMS AND PEAS

This dish tastes so good you won't even realise it's relatively low in fat. It's also a good source of B vitamins, folate, potassium, phosphorus and calcium.

Prep time: 20 minutes
Cooking time: 25 minutes
Serves 4
EASY

———

3 rashers bacon
2 teaspoons olive oil
2–3 cloves garlic, crushed
1 red onion, chopped
185 g field mushrooms, sliced
1/3 cup (20 g) chopped fresh parsley
1 cup (155 g) peas
11/2 cups (375 ml) low-fat light evaporated milk
2 teaspoons cornflour
325 g dried linguine
25 g Parmesan shavings

1 Remove the fat and rind from the bacon and chop roughly. Heat the oil in a medium pan, add the garlic, onion and bacon, and cook over low heat for 5 minutes, stirring frequently, until the onion and bacon are soft. Add the sliced mushrooms and cook, stirring, for another 5 minutes, or until soft.
2 Add the parsley, peas and milk to the pan. Mix the cornflour with 1 tablespoon of water until smooth, add to the mixture and stir over medium heat until slightly thickened.
3 Meanwhile, cook the pasta in a large pan of rapidly boiling water for 8 minutes, or until *al dente*. Drain and serve with the hot sauce and Parmesan shavings.

NUTRITION PER SERVE
Protein 31.5 g; Fat 9 g; Carbohydrate 74.5 g; Dietary Fibre 6 g; Cholesterol 44.5 mg; 2140 kJ (510 Cal)

NOTE: Parmesan adds a nice flavour to this dish, but leave it out if you want to achieve a lower fat content.

Spaghetti bolognese (top), and Linguine with bacon, mushrooms and peas

BEEF SAUSAGE PASTA

This quick-to-prepare meal provides good amounts of iron, zinc, vitamin A, B vitamins and fibre.

Prep time: 20 minutes
Cooking time: 15 minutes
Serves 4
EASY

2 cups (160 g) spiral pasta
4 thick beef sausages
2 teaspoons olive oil
2 red onions, cut into wedges
1 1/3 cups (340 g) ready-made chunky tomato
   pasta sauce
4 small ripe tomatoes, peeled, seeded and
   chopped
1/3 cup (20 g) chopped fresh flat-leaf parsley

1 Bring a large saucepan of water to the boil and cook the pasta until *al dente*. Drain, reserving 1/4 cup (60 ml) of the cooking water.

2 Meanwhile, prick the sausages all over with a fork. Heat a non-stick frying pan and cook the sausages over medium heat, turning often, for 5 minutes, or until cooked. Cut into thick diagonal slices and set aside.

3 Clean the frying pan and heat the oil. Cook the onion wedges over medium heat for 3 minutes, or until soft. Add the tomato pasta sauce and the tomato. Cook for 3–4 minutes, or until the tomato has softened. Add the sliced sausage and heat through for 1 minute.

4 Toss the pasta through the sauce, adding a little of the reserved pasta water, if necessary. Sprinkle with parsley and serve.

NUTRITION PER SERVE
Protein 12 g; Fat 18 g; Carbohydrate 44 g; Dietary Fibre
7.5 g; Cholesterol 17 mg; 1605 kJ (385 Cal)

RAVIOLI WITH CAPSICUM SAUCE

Bright red capsicums and leeks add colour and nutritional value to this dish, which is a good source of vitamin C, beta-carotene, folate, B vitamins, potassium, iron and zinc.

Prep time: 15 minutes
Cooking time: 15 minutes
Serves 4
MEDIUM

6 red capsicums
6 slices prosciutto
625 g chicken or ricotta ravioli
2 tablespoons olive oil
3 cloves garlic, crushed
2 leeks, white part only, thinly sliced
1 tablespoon chopped fresh oregano
2 teaspoons soft brown sugar
1 cup (250 ml) hot chicken stock

1 Cut the capsicums into large pieces, removing the seeds and membrane. Place, skin side up, under a hot grill until the skin blackens and blisters. Cool in a plastic bag, then peel away the skin. Place the prosciutto under the hot grill and cook for 1 minute each side, or until crisp. Break into pieces and set aside.

2 Cook the pasta in a large saucepan of boiling water until *al dente*. Meanwhile, heat the oil in a frying pan and cook the garlic and leek over medium heat for 3–4 minutes, or until softened. Add the oregano and sugar, and stir for 1 minute.

3 Place the capsicum and leek mixture in a food processor or blender, season with salt and pepper, and process until combined. Add the chicken stock and process until smooth. Drain the pasta and return to the saucepan. Gently toss the sauce through the ravioli over low heat until warmed through. Divide among four serving bowls and sprinkle with the prosciutto.

NUTRITION PER SERVE
Protein 25 g; Fat 19.5 g; Carbohydrate 58.5 g; Dietary Fibre 8.5 g; Cholesterol 56 mg; 2125 kJ (510 Cal)

VEGETABLE LASAGNE WITH ROCKET

With less fat than meat lasagne, this colourful vegetarian dish is packed with vitamin C, beta-carotene, folate, potassium, calcium, iron and zinc. The vitamin C will enhance iron absorption.

Prep time: 20 minutes
Cooking time: 20 minutes
Serves 4
MEDIUM

Balsamic syrup
1/3 cup (80 ml) balsamic vinegar
1 1/2 tablespoons brown sugar

1 cup (150 g) fresh or frozen peas
16 asparagus spears, cut into 5 cm lengths
2 large zucchini, cut into thin ribbons
2 fresh lasagne sheets (200 g), (each sheet 24 cm x 35 cm)
100 g rocket leaves
1 cup (30 g) fresh basil, torn
2 tablespoons extra virgin olive oil
150 g semi-dried tomatoes
250 g low-fat ricotta
Parmesan shavings, to garnish

1 To make the syrup, place the vinegar and brown sugar in a small saucepan and stir over medium heat until the sugar dissolves. Reduce the heat and simmer for 3–4 minutes, or until the sauce becomes syrupy. Remove from the heat.
2 Bring a large saucepan of water to the boil. Blanch the peas, asparagus and zucchini in separate batches until just tender, removing each batch with a slotted spoon and refreshing in cold water. Reserve the cooking liquid and return to the boil.
3 Cook the lasagne sheets in the boiling water for 1–2 minutes, or until *al dente*. Refresh in cold water and drain well. Cut each lasagne sheet in half lengthways (12 cm x 35 cm).
4 Toss the vegetables and the rocket with the basil and olive oil. Season with salt and ground black pepper.

5 To assemble, place one strip of pasta on a serving plate—one-third on the centre of the plate and two-thirds overhanging one side. Place a small mound of the salad on the centre third, topped with some tomatoes and ricotta. Season lightly and fold over one-third of the lasagne sheet. Top with another layer of salad, tomato and ricotta. Fold back the final layer of pasta and garnish with salad and tomato. Repeat with the remaining pasta strips, salad, tomato and ricotta to make four individual lasagne. Just before serving, drizzle with the balsamic syrup and garnish with Parmesan.

NUTRITION PER SERVE
Protein 18 g; Fat 16 g; Carbohydrate 36 g; Dietary Fibre 6 g; Cholesterol 63 mg; 1515 kJ (360 Cal)

PUTTANESCA SAUCE

Heat 1 tablespoon oil in a large frying pan, add 1 crushed clove garlic and 1 finely chopped onion. Cook over medium heat for 3 minutes, or until golden. Add 6 chopped anchovies, 2 tablespoons chopped capers and 3 tablespoons chopped marinated black olives. Cook for 2 minutes, then stir in two 400 g cans chopped tomatoes, 1 tablespoon balsamic vinegar and 2 teaspoons sugar. Boil, then reduce the heat and simmer for 10 minutes, or until the sauce has reduced and thickened slightly. Toss through spaghetti. Serves 4

NUTRITION PER SERVE
Protein 17 g; Fat 7 g; Carbohydrate 97 g; Dietary Fibre 9.5 g; Cholesterol 3.5 mg; 2220 kJ (530 Cal)

TAGLIATELLE WITH PEAS AND ASPARAGUS

Based on a medley of crisp spring vegetables and aromatic herbs, this dish is highly nutritious. It's an excellent source of folate, vitamin C, plant antioxidants, fibre, potassium and carbohydrate.

Prep time: 20 minutes
Cooking time: 25 minutes
Serves 4
EASY

375 g dried (or 500 g fresh) tagliatelle
1 cup (250 ml) chicken or vegetable stock
2 leeks, white part only, thinly sliced
3 cloves garlic, crushed
1 1/2 cups (235 g) shelled fresh peas
1 tablespoon finely chopped fresh mint
400 g asparagus spears, cut into 5 cm lengths
1/4 cup (15 g) finely chopped fresh parsley
1/2 cup (30 g) shredded fresh basil
1/3 cup (80 ml) light cream
pinch of nutmeg
1 tablespoon grated Parmesan
1 1/2 tablespoons extra virgin olive oil, to drizzle

1 Cook the pasta in a large saucepan of boiling water until *al dente*. Drain well.
2 Place 1/2 cup (125 ml) of the stock and the leek in a large, deep frying pan. Cook over low heat, stirring often, for 4–5 minutes. Stir in the garlic, peas and mint, and cook for 1 minute. Add the remaining stock and 1/2 cup (125 ml) water and bring to the boil. Simmer for 5 minutes. Add the asparagus, parsley and basil, and season well with salt and ground black pepper. Simmer for a further 3–4 minutes, or until the asparagus is just tender. Gradually increase the heat to reduce the sauce to a light coating consistency, if necessary. Stir in the cream, nutmeg and Parmesan, and adjust the seasonings if necessary.
3 Add the tagliatelle to the sauce and toss lightly to coat. Divide among individual serving bowls and drizzle with the extra virgin olive oil. Garnish with extra grated Parmesan, if desired.

NUTRITION PER SERVE
Protein 21 g; Fat 14 g; Carbohydrate 76 g; Dietary Fibre 9 g; Cholesterol 32 mg; 2160 kJ (515 Cal)

SPAGHETTI MARINARA

This low-fat dish is a wonderful way to enjoy the goodness of seafood. It contains filling protein, slow-release carbohydrate, B vitamins, potassium, iron, iodine, selenium and sulphur.

Prep time: 40 minutes
Cooking time: 1 hour
Serves 4–6
MEDIUM

12 black mussels, scrubbed clean, beards
    removed
1/2 cup (125 ml) white wine
2 tablespoons olive oil
1 onion, finely chopped
2–3 cloves garlic, finely chopped
2 x 400 g cans peeled tomatoes, chopped
50 g tomato paste
500 g spaghetti
250 g raw medium prawns, peeled and
    deveined, tails intact
250 g scallops, with coral intact, cleaned
250 g boneless fish fillets, cubed
12 calamari rings
grated rind and juice of half a lemon
1/4 cup (15 g) chopped fresh parsley

1 Place the mussels (discarding any open ones) in a large saucepan with the wine and 1/2 cup (125 ml) water. Cook, covered, over high heat for 2–3 minutes, or until the mussels open. Discard any unopened mussels and reserve the liquid.
2 Heat the oil in a large frying pan. Add the onion and garlic, and cook over medium heat for 3 minutes, or until the onion is soft. Add the tomato, tomato paste and reserved liquid. Simmer for 30 minutes, or until the sauce thickens.
3 Cook the pasta in a large saucepan of boiling water until *al dente*. Drain.
4 Add all the seafood to the sauce. Cook over low heat for 3–4 minutes, or until cooked through. Add the lemon rind, juice and parsley. Toss the sauce and mussels through the pasta and serve immediately.

NUTRITION PER SERVE (6)
Protein 40 g; Fat 9.5 g; Carbohydrate 65 g; Dietary Fibre 5.5 g; Cholesterol 150.5 mg; 2200 kJ (525 Cal)

RED LENTIL AND RICOTTA LASAGNE

An excellent choice for vegetarians, this recipe provides complete protein and plenty of slow-release carbohydrate energy, fibre and good amounts of vitamins and minerals.

Prep time: 30 minutes + soaking
Cooking time: 2 hours 10 minutes
Serves 6
EASY

1/2 cup (125 g) red lentils
2 teaspoons olive oil
2–3 cloves garlic, crushed
1 large onion, chopped
1 small red capsicum, chopped
2 zucchini, sliced
1 celery stick, sliced
2 x 425 g cans chopped tomatoes
2 tablespoons tomato paste
1 teaspoon dried oregano
350 g ricotta
12 instant or fresh lasagne sheets
60 g reduced-fat cheese, grated

White sauce
1/3 cup (40 g) cornflour
3 cups (750 ml) skim milk
1/4 onion
1/2 teaspoon ground nutmeg

1 Soak the lentils in boiling water to cover, for at least 30 minutes, then drain. Meanwhile, heat the oil in a large pan, add the garlic and onion, and cook for 2 minutes. Add the capsicum, zucchini and celery, and cook for 2–3 minutes.
2 Add the lentils, tomato, tomato paste, oregano and 1 1/2 cups (375 ml) water. Bring slowly to the boil, reduce the heat and simmer for 30 minutes, or until the lentils are tender. Stir occasionally.
3 To make the white sauce, blend the cornflour with 2 tablespoons of the milk in a saucepan until smooth. Add the remaining milk and the onion, and stir over low heat until the mixture boils and thickens. Add the nutmeg and some ground black pepper, then cook over low heat for 5 minutes. Remove the onion.
4 Beat the ricotta with about 1/2 cup (125 ml) of the white sauce. Preheat the oven to moderate 180°C (350°F/Gas 4). Spread one-third of the lentil mixture over the base of a 3 litre ovenproof dish. Cover with a layer of lasagne sheets. Spread another third of the lentil mixture over the pasta, then spread the ricotta evenly over the top. Follow with another layer of lasagne, then the remaining lentils. Pour the white sauce evenly over the top and sprinkle with the grated cheese. Bake for 1 hour, covering loosely with foil if the top starts to brown too much. Leave for 5 minutes before cutting.

NUTRITION PER SERVE
Protein 24.5 g; Fat 11 g; Carbohydrate 54 g; Dietary Fibre 7 g; Cholesterol 37 mg; 1725 kJ (410 Cal)

BOSCAIOLA SAUCE

Heat 1 tablespoon oil in a non-stick frying pan, add 1 crushed clove garlic and 6 sliced spring onions. Cook over medium heat for 3 minutes, stir in 100 g chopped light ham, 100 g sliced cap mushrooms and 1/4 cup (60 ml) chicken stock. Bring to the boil and boil until the liquid has evaporated. Add another 1 cup (250 ml) chicken stock and 1/2 cup (125 ml) light cream, and bring to the boil. Boil for 5 minutes, or until thickened slightly. Season to taste with salt and ground black pepper, and serve tossed through farfalle. Garnish with extra sliced spring onions. Serves 4

NUTRITION PER SERVE
Protein 20 g; Fat 14 g; Carbohydrate 90 g; Dietary Fibre 7.5 g; Cholesterol 34 mg; 2405 kJ (575 Cal)

PENNE WITH MEATBALLS

This delicious dish is rich in slow-release carbohydrate and complete protein.

Prep time: 40 minutes
Cooking time: 1 hour 45 minutes
Serves 6
EASY

---

500 g lean veal mince
1 onion, very finely chopped
4 cloves garlic, finely chopped
1 egg white, lightly beaten
1 cup (80 g) fresh breadcrumbs
1/2 cup (30 g) finely chopped fresh parsley
1/4 cup (7 g) finely chopped fresh oregano
cooking oil spray
1.5 kg ripe tomatoes, peeled, roughly chopped
2 onions, thinly sliced
1/2 cup (125 g) tomato paste
1/2 teaspoon sugar
350 g penne

1 Combine the veal mince, onion, half the garlic, the egg white, breadcrumbs, two-thirds of the parsley and 1 tablespoon of the oregano. Season well. Mix with your hands until well combined. Shape into small balls. Spray a large non-stick frying pan with oil. Cook the meatballs in three batches over high heat for 4–5 minutes, or until browned, turning constantly. Remove from the pan.

2 Lightly spray the base of a large, deep non-stick saucepan with oil. Add the sliced onion and remaining garlic. Cook over low heat for 2–3 minutes, stirring. Add 2 tablespoons water, cover and cook for 5 minutes. Stir in the tomato and tomato paste. Simmer, covered, for 10 minutes, then uncover and simmer gently for 40 minutes. Add the meatballs, and simmer, covered, for 15–20 minutes, or until just cooked. Add the sugar, remaining parsley and oregano, and season.

3 Cook the penne in a large saucepan of rapidly boiling water until *al dente*, then drain. Serve with the hot meatballs.

NUTRITION PER SERVE
Protein 31 g; Fat 8 g; Carbohydrate 57.5 g; Dietary Fibre 7.5 g; Cholesterol 68.5 mg; 1805 kJ (430 Cal)

ORECCHIETTE WITH PUMPKIN AND YOGHURT

Pumpkin and yoghurt give this dish a creamy texture. It is rich in beta-carotene, potassium, calcium and B vitamins.

Prep time: 15 minutes
Cooking time: 35 minutes
Serves 6
EASY

1 kg pumpkin, cut into 2 cm cubes
$1/3$ cup (80 ml) olive oil
500 g orecchiette
2 cloves garlic, crushed
1 teaspoon dried chilli flakes
1 teaspoon coriander seeds, crushed
1 tablespoon cumin seeds, crushed
200 g Greek-style natural yoghurt
$1/4$ cup (15 g) chopped fresh coriander leaves

1 Preheat the oven to moderately hot 200°C (400°F/Gas 6). Toss the pumpkin in 2 tablespoons of the oil, place in a roasting tin and bake for 30 minutes, or until golden, tossing halfway through.
2 Meanwhile, cook the pasta in a large saucepan of boiling water until *al dente*. Drain, then return to the saucepan.
3 Heat the remaining oil in a saucepan. Add the garlic, chilli, coriander and cumin, and cook for 30 seconds, or until fragrant. Toss the spice mix and pumpkin through the pasta, then stir in the yoghurt and fresh coriander. Season with salt and cracked black pepper. Divide among serving bowls and serve.

NUTRITION PER SERVE
Protein 15 g; Fat 13.5 g; Carbohydrate 71.5 g; Dietary Fibre 5.5 g; Cholesterol 9.5 mg; 1960 kJ (470 Cal)

LASAGNE

This reduced-fat version of the traditional recipe makes a healthy family meal. One serve provides good amounts of protein, B vitamins, vitamin A, potassium, phosphorus, calcium, iron and zinc.

Prep time: 40 minutes
Cooking time: 1 hour 35 minutes
Serves 8
EASY

___

2 teaspoons olive oil
1 large onion, chopped
2 carrots, finely chopped
2 celery sticks, finely chopped
2 zucchini, finely chopped
2 cloves garlic, crushed
500 g lean beef mince
2 x 400 g cans crushed tomatoes
1/2 cup (125 ml) beef stock
2 tablespoons tomato paste
2 teaspoons dried oregano
375 g instant or fresh lasagne sheets

Cheese sauce
3 cups (750 ml) skim milk
1/3 cup (40 g) cornflour
100 g reduced-fat Cheddar, grated

1 Heat the olive oil in a large non-stick frying pan. Add the onion and cook for 5 minutes, or until soft. Add the carrot, celery and zucchini, and cook, stirring constantly, for 5 minutes, or until the vegetables are soft. Add the crushed garlic and cook for another minute. Add the beef mince and cook over high heat, stirring, until well browned. Break up any lumps of meat with a wooden spoon.
2 Add the crushed tomato, beef stock, tomato paste and dried oregano to the pan and stir to thoroughly combine. Bring the mixture to the boil, then reduce the heat and simmer gently, partially covered, for 20 minutes, stirring occasionally to prevent the mixture sticking to the pan.
3 Preheat the oven to moderate 180°C (350°F/Gas 4). Spread a little of the meat sauce into the base of a 23 x 30 cm ovenproof dish. Arrange a layer of lasagne sheets in the dish, breaking some of the sheets, if necessary, to fit in neatly.
4 Spread half the meat sauce over the top to cover evenly. Cover with another layer of lasagne sheets, a layer of meat sauce, then a final layer of lasagne sheets.
5 To make the cheese sauce, blend a little of the milk with the cornflour, to form a smooth paste, in a small pan. Gradually blend in the remaining milk and stir constantly over low heat until the mixture boils and thickens. Remove from the heat and stir in the grated cheese until melted. Spread evenly over the top of the lasagne and bake for 1 hour.
6 Check the lasagne after 25 minutes. If the top is browning too quickly, cover loosely with non-stick baking paper or foil. Take care when removing the baking paper or foil that the topping does not come away with the paper. For serving, cut the lasagne into eight portions and garnish with fresh herbs.

NUTRITION PER SERVE
Protein 27.5 g; Fat 8.5 g; Carbohydrate 48.5 g; Dietary Fibre 5 g; Cholesterol 41.5 mg; 1585 kJ (380 Cal)

CREAMY PUMPKIN SAUCE

Preheat the oven to moderately hot 200°C (400°F/Gas 6). Peel 500 g butternut pumpkin and chop into 4 cm cubes. Place in a baking dish with 4 unpeeled cloves garlic. Spray lightly with olive oil and bake for 20 minutes, or until soft. Peel the garlic and place in a food processor with the pumpkin, 1 cup (250 ml) chicken stock and 2 tablespoons low-fat plain yoghurt. Process until smooth. Stir in 2 tablespoons snipped fresh chives and season with salt, ground black pepper and nutmeg. Serve over penne. Serves 4

NUTRITION PER SERVE
Protein 18 g; Fat 2 g; Carbohydrate 98 g; Dietary Fibre 8.5 g; Cholesterol 0.5 mg; 2055 kJ (490 Cal)

PENNE WITH RICOTTA AND BASIL SAUCE

An aromatic and creamy sauce, this recipe contains less fat than most cheesy sauces. It provides plenty of carbohydrate energy, with some B vitamins, potassium, phosphorus, calcium and vitamin A.

Prep time: 20 minutes
Cooking time: 15 minutes
Serves 4
EASY

2 teaspoons olive oil
2 rashers bacon, chopped, rind and fat removed
2–3 cloves garlic, crushed
1 onion, finely chopped
2 spring onions, finely chopped
250 g ricotta
1/2 cup (30 g) finely chopped fresh basil
325 g penne
8 cherry tomatoes, halved

1 Heat the oil in a pan, add the bacon, garlic, onion and spring onion, and stir over medium heat for 5 minutes, or until cooked. Remove from the heat, stir in the ricotta and chopped basil, and beat until smooth.

2 Meanwhile, cook the pasta in a large saucepan of rapidly boiling water for 10 minutes, or until *al dente*. Just prior to draining the pasta, add 1 cup (250 ml) of the pasta water to the ricotta mixture to thin the sauce. Add more water if you prefer an even thinner sauce. Season well with salt and ground black pepper.

3 Drain the pasta and stir the sauce through with the tomato halves. Garnish with small basil leaves, if desired.

NUTRITION PER SERVE
Protein 22 g; Fat 12.5 g; Carbohydrate 60.5 g; Dietary Fibre 3.5 g; Cholesterol 56 mg; 1865 kJ (445 Cal)

BUCATINI POMODORO

*This low-fat dish is quick and easy to prepare.
It is packed with carbohydrate energy and
good amounts of fibre, potassium and some
plant antioxidants.*

Prep time: 15 minutes
Cooking time: 35 minutes
Serves 4–6
EASY

---

2 tablespoons olive oil
1 onion, finely chopped
2 cloves garlic, finely chopped
2 tablespoons finely chopped fresh flat-leaf
    parsley
2 x 400 g cans peeled tomatoes, chopped, or
    1 kg ripe romatoes, peeled and chopped
1 tablespoon tomato paste
1 teaspoon caster sugar
500 g bucatini
1/4 cup (15 g) shredded fresh basil

1 Heat the oil in a large frying pan. Cook the onion, garlic and parsley over low heat for 3 minutes, or until the onion is soft.
2 Add the canned or fresh tomato, tomato paste and sugar. Partially cover and simmer for 30 minutes, or until the sauce thickens. Season with salt and ground black pepper.
3 Cook the pasta in a large saucepan of boiling water until *al dente*. Drain.
4 Toss the sauce through the pasta and garnish with shredded basil. Serve with grated Parmesan, if desired.

NUTRITION PER SERVE (6)
Protein 11 g; Fat 3 g; Carbohydrate 63 g; Dietary Fibre 5 g; Cholesterol 0 mg; 1365 kJ (325 Cal)

PAN-FRIES AND BARBECUES

Pan-fries and barbecues are ideal for quick, healthy cooking, particularly if you are entertaining guests. It's easy to add extra flavour and interest with a simple marinade or rub.

Because pan-frying and barbecuing are relatively quick cooking methods using an intense application of heat, they are well suited to cooking tender and smaller cuts of meat. Steaks, chops, sausages, chicken pieces or fillets, rissoles or patties, and skewers are all suitable for these methods of cooking.

Pan-frying and barbecuing are also excellent methods for cooking fish and other seafood, as they provide the high heat necessary to cook it quickly. Try fish fillets, fish cutlets, fish steaks, prawns (in or out of the shell), octopus and scallops. Shellfish such as oysters, mussels or clams can be placed directly on the barbecue and will be ready when the shells open.

Vegetables are also ideal for pan-frying and barbecuing. The surface of the vegetables will caramelise as they cook, and the inside will be moist and tender. Slice the vegetables so that they will cook through quickly, then brush or spray them with olive oil before cooking. Vegetables suited to this method of cooking include: zucchini, eggplant, capsicum, pumpkin, mushrooms, sweet potato, cauliflower, fennel and squash.

After cooking the vegetables, lightly season them with salt and cracked black pepper, a drizzle of balsamic vinegar or a splash of lemon juice, and sprinkle with some finely chopped fresh herbs.

PAN-FRIES

The benefit of pan-frying is that the food is cooked over a relatively high heat, so the outside browns, forming a delicious caramelised crust, and the inside can be cooked to whatever stage you desire.

To make your pan-fried dishes as healthy as possible, use a non-stick frying pan sprayed with a light spray of olive oil rather than oil or butter.

When pan-frying meats that naturally contain a lot of fat, such as lamb chops, pork chops or bacon, it is unnecessary to add any fat while cooking. The fat that is contained within the  meat will melt on heating and be sufficient to cook with.

After pan-frying foods, drain them on crumpled paper towels to remove any excess fat.

Ridged chargrill pans are also perfect for giving a barbecued appearance and smoky barbecue flavour.

BARBECUES

Barbecuing is also a healthy method of cooking. The grill bars simply need a light spray of oil to make sure the food doesn't stick. If the food is cooked on the grill bars rather than on the barbecue plate, any  fat that comes out of the food while cooking will simply drip away. An alternative method of barbecuing is cooking in a kettle barbecue, which is a covered barbecue. This type of cooking is more suited to larger joints of meat and vegetables. It will give the meat a delicious crust while helping the internal flesh to stay moist and tender.

RUBS AND MARINADES

Rubs and marinades are simple ways of adding flavour, tenderising and in some cases even preserving foods.

Rubs are mixtures of dry spices that can be used to 'rub' onto meat, chicken or fish for flavour and variety. You can make up your own combination or they can be purchased already blended from the supermarket. When purchasing prepared mixes, try to avoid brands that have a high salt content. Rub the spice mixture all over the food, then pan-fry or barbecue it.

Marinades are usually liquid, and may contain ingredients such as oil, wine, vinegar, citrus juices, herbs, spices, aromatics (such as garlic, chilli and ginger), and vegetables such as carrot and celery. Different types of marinades are suitable for different types of ingredients. They are not only used to add flavour to the cooked dish, but marinades that contain an acidic ingredient such as citrus juice or vinegar also aid in tenderising. While this may be desirable for some tougher cuts of meat, the same marinade would start to 'cook' the flesh of fish,

altering the texture. It is important to drain marinated food before cooking or the excess liquid will cause the food to stew.

Rubs
■ Cajun spice mix is a spicy blend from the south of the USA, ideal for chicken.
■ Garam masala is a mixture of Indian spices, which is great with lamb.
■ Lemon pepper is a subtle, spiced pepper blend, perfect for coating fish or chicken.
■ Sumac is a lemony North African crushed berry, which goes well with red meats.
■ Smoked paprika is made from dried and crushed smoked peppers, and also goes well with red meats.

Marinades
■ Combine some chopped fresh parsley, crushed garlic and finely grated lemon rind, moisten the mixture with a little olive oil, and use it to marinate fish fillets or chicken pieces or fillets before pan-frying or barbecuing.
■ Mix together some Dijon mustard, lemon juice, rosemary and a little olive oil, and use the mixture to marinate lamb or pork chops or whole joints that are to be roasted in a kettle barbecue.
■ Use red wine, bay leaves, fresh parsley, and diced onion, carrot and celery to marinate beef steak and more robust gamey meats.
■ Soy, ginger and garlic can be used to marinate chicken pieces, skewers of lamb and beef steaks for an Asian-style flavour.
■ Blend chopped coriander with garlic, ginger, finely chopped chilli and ground turmeric to marinate chicken pieces, lamb loins or salmon steaks.
■ Low-fat natural yoghurt mixed with tandoori spices is delicious with lamb.

LAMB BURGER

This burger provides good-quality protein and well-absorbed iron and zinc.

Prep time: 30 minutes
Cooking time: 1 hour
Serves 4
MEDIUM

1 red capsicum, quartered
1 yellow capsicum, quartered
1 green capsicum, quartered
400 g baking potatoes (pontiac or desiree)
garlic oil spray
300 g lean lamb mince
2 teaspoons chopped fresh thyme
2 tablespoons chopped fresh parsley
2 tomatoes, seeded and finely chopped
1 large onion, finely chopped
1/3 cup (25 g) fresh breadcrumbs
1 egg white, lightly beaten
1 teaspoon ground black pepper
4 slices low-fat cheese
1 large red onion, thinly sliced
2 teaspoons olive oil
4 hamburger buns, toasted
40 g rocket

1 Grill the capsicum, skin side up, until the skin blackens and blisters. Place it in a plastic bag until cool enough to handle, then peel off the skin and cut the flesh into strips.

2 Preheat the oven to moderately hot 200°C (400°F/Gas 6). Line a baking tray with foil. Cut the potatoes into wedges. Spray with the oil, then season. Spread out on the tray. Bake for 40 minutes, or until crisp and golden, turning once.

3 Meanwhile, combine the mince, thyme, parsley, tomato, onion, breadcrumbs, egg white and pepper. Form into four patties. Heat a non-stick frying pan over medium heat and cook the patties for 5 minutes on each side, or until cooked. Remove from the pan and put a slice of cheese on top. Cook the onion in the olive oil for 4–5 minutes over medium heat until the onion is softened.

4 To assemble, layer the buns with rocket, the patty with cheese, onion, a strip each of red, yellow and green capsicum, and top with rocket and the top of the bun. Cut in half and serve with the wedges.

NUTRITION PER SERVE
Protein 34.5 g; Fat 14 g; Carbohydrate 52 g; Dietary Fibre 5.5 g; Cholesterol 65.5 mg; 1995 kJ (475 Cal)

HONEY AND MUSTARD CHICKEN

A low-fat recipe, this chicken provides lots of lean protein, phosphorus and potassium, as well as some iron and zinc. The tomatoes add extra vitamin A and C, and the antioxidant lycopene.

Prep time: 20 minutes + 2 hours marinating
Cooking time: 50 minutes
Serves 4
EASY

4 chicken breast fillets
2 tablespoons honey
1 tablespoon wholegrain mustard
1 tablespoon soy sauce
2 red onions, cut into wedges
8 Roma tomatoes, halved lengthways
2 tablespoons soft brown sugar
2 tablespoons balsamic vinegar
cooking oil spray
snow pea sprouts, to serve

1 Preheat the oven to moderate 180°C (350°F/Gas 4). Trim the chicken of any excess fat and place in a shallow dish. Combine the honey, mustard and soy sauce, and pour over the chicken, tossing to coat. Cover and refrigerate for 2 hours, turning once.
2 Place the onion wedges and tomato halves on a baking tray covered with baking paper. Sprinkle with the sugar and drizzle with the balsamic vinegar. Bake for 40 minutes.
3 Heat a chargrill pan and lightly spray it with oil. Remove the chicken from the marinade and cook for 4–5 minutes on each side, or until cooked through. Slice the chicken and serve it with the snow pea sprouts, tomato halves and onion wedges.

NUTRITION PER SERVE
Protein 25 g; Fat 2.5 g; Carbohydrate 30 g; Dietary Fibre 3 g; Cholesterol 50 mg; 990 kJ (235 Cal)

Tandoori pork kebabs (top), and Tuna with chickpea salad

TANDOORI PORK KEBABS

The pork in this meal is an excellent source of niacin, thiamin, zinc and iron, while the rice provides slowly digested carbohydrate, fibre and niacin.

Prep time: 30 minutes + overnight marinating
Cooking time: 40 minutes
Serves 4
MEDIUM

1 cup (250 g) low-fat plain yoghurt
2 cloves garlic, crushed
2 tablespoons tandoori paste
1 tablespoon lemon juice
2 tablespoons chopped fresh coriander leaves
600 g pork fillet, cubed
1 teaspoon olive oil
1 onion, chopped
2 cloves garlic, crushed
2 teaspoons ground cumin
1/2 teaspoon paprika
1 teaspoon ground coriander
2 cups (380 g) basmati and wild rice blend
1 litre vegetable stock
3/4 cup (185 g) low-fat plain yoghurt, extra
1 tablespoon chopped fresh coriander, extra

1 Combine the yoghurt, garlic, tandoori paste, lemon juice and coriander. Add the pork and stir to coat. Refrigerate, covered, overnight.
2 Heat the oil in a saucepan, add the onion, garlic and spices, and cook for 5 minutes, or until golden. Add the rice and stir to coat. Add the stock, bring to the boil, then simmer for 10 minutes, or until tunnels appear in the rice. Reduce the heat to low, cover and cook for 10 minutes.
3 Thread the pork onto eight skewers. Heat a chargrill plate and cook for 3–5 minutes on each side, or until tender.
4 Combine the extra yoghurt and coriander, and serve with the pork and spiced rice.

NUTRITION PER SERVE
Protein 48 g; Fat 9 g; Carbohydrate 88 g; Dietary Fibre 3 g; Cholesterol 75 mg; 2670 kJ (640 Cal)

TUNA WITH CHICKPEA SALAD

This is a highly filling mix of fish protein, fibre and slowly digested carbohydrate.

Prep time: 10 minutes + overnight soaking + 30 minutes marinating
Cooking time: 1 hour 25 minutes
Serves 4
MEDIUM

1 cup (220 g) dried chickpeas
6 Roma tomatoes, quartered lengthways
2 tablespoons olive oil
4 tuna steaks (about 150 g each)
2 tablespoons lemon juice
1 red onion, chopped
1 clove garlic, crushed
1 teaspoon ground cumin
1 cup (30 g) chopped fresh flat-leaf parsley
fresh flat-leaf parsley, extra, to garnish

1 Cover the chickpeas with water and soak overnight, then drain. Place the chickpeas in a saucepan with enough water to cover them and bring to the boil. Cook for 25–30 minutes, or until tender. Drain, then rinse well under cold water.
2 Preheat the oven to moderate 180°C (350°F/Gas 4). Combine the tomato, 2 teaspoons of the oil, salt and pepper. Bake on a baking tray for 35–40 minutes.
3 Brush the tuna with 2 teaspoons of the oil and 1 tablespoon of the lemon juice, and season. Refrigerate for 30 minutes.
4 Heat the remaining olive oil in a frying pan over medium heat. Add the onion and garlic and cook, stirring, for 4–5 minutes, or until softened. Add the ground cumin and cook for 1 minute, then add the chickpeas. Cook for 5 minutes, stirring occasionally. Add the tomato, parsley and remaining lemon juice. Season to taste.
5 Heat a non-stick chargrill plate to high. Cook the tuna steaks on each side for 1–2 minutes. Serve on top of the warm salad and garnish with parsley.

NUTRITION PER SERVE
Protein 47.5 g; Fat 20 g; Carbohydrate 21 g; Dietary Fibre 8 g; Cholesterol 54 mg; 1930 kJ (460 Cal)

CALAMARI WITH SPICY SAUCE

Although high in cholesterol, this meal is relatively low in fat. It is an excellent source of vitamin C, beta-carotene, potassium and phosphorus.

Prep time: 50 minutes + 3 hours marinating
Cooking time: 10 minutes
Serves 4
MEDIUM

---

500 g calamari tubes, cleaned
2 stems lemon grass, white part only, chopped
3 teaspoons grated ginger
3 cloves garlic, finely chopped
1/2 teaspoon chopped red chilli
1 tablespoon vegetable oil
2 very ripe tomatoes
150 g mixed lettuce
1/4 cup (7 g) fresh coriander leaves
2 tablespoons lime juice
1 teaspoon finely grated lime rind
1 red capsicum, cut into strips

Lime, chilli and garlic sauce
1/4 cup (60 ml) lime juice
1 tablespoon lemon juice
2 tablespoons fish sauce
1 tablespoon caster sugar
2 teaspoons chopped red chilli
2 cloves garlic, finely chopped
1 tablespoon finely chopped fresh coriander

1 Cut the calamari tubes open, wash and pat dry. Cut shallow slashes about 5 mm apart on the soft inside, in a diamond pattern, then cut into 3 cm strips. Mix in a bowl with the lemon grass, ginger, garlic, chilli and oil. Cover and refrigerate for 3 hours.

2 Cut the tomatoes in half, scoop out the seeds and finely chop them, retaining the juice. Cut the flesh into cubes. Arrange the lettuce and coriander in serving bowls.

3 Just before serving, lightly grease and heat a solid barbecue plate or large, heavy non-stick pan until very hot. Quickly cook the calamari in batches, tossing for 2–3 minutes, until just tender and curled, sprinkling the lime juice and rind over the top. Remove the calamari, toss with the chopped tomato seeds and arrange on the salad. Scatter the tomato and capsicum over the top. Season well.

4 Stir the sauce ingredients together until the sugar dissolves. Drizzle the sauce over the calamari.

NUTRITION PER SERVE
Protein 25 g; Fat 6.5 g; Carbohydrate 5 g; Dietary Fibre 3 g; Cholesterol 250 mg; 755 kJ (180 Cal)

PORK ROLLS WITH CAPSICUM

This dish provides a delicious blend of flavours, and is an excellent source of potassium, vitamin C, niacin and thiamin.

Prep time: 40 minutes
Cooking time: 30 minutes
Serves 4
MEDIUM

Sauce
3/4 cup (185 ml) beef stock
2 teaspoons soy sauce
2 tablespoons red wine
2 teaspoons wholegrain mustard
2 teaspoons cornflour

1 red capsicum, quartered
4 x 150 g lean pork leg steaks
1/3 cup (90 g) ricotta
2 spring onions, finely chopped
1 clove garlic, crushed
75 g rocket
4 small lean slices prosciutto
cooking oil spray

1 To make the sauce, put the beef stock, soy sauce, red wine and mustard in a pan. Blend the cornflour with 1 tablespoon water and add to the pan. Stir until the mixture boils and thickens.
2 Grill the capsicum until the skin blisters and blackens. Place in a plastic bag until cool enough to handle, then peel and cut the flesh into thin strips.
3 Flatten the steaks with a mallet. Combine the ricotta, onion and garlic, then spread over the pork. Top with a layer of rocket and prosciutto. Place some capsicum at one end and roll up to enclose the capsicum. Tie with string at even intervals.
4 Lightly spray a non-stick pan with oil and fry the pork rolls over medium heat for 5 minutes, or until well browned. Add the sauce and simmer over low heat for 10–15 minutes, or until the rolls are cooked through. Serve sliced with the sauce.

NUTRITION PER SERVE
Protein 40 g; Fat 5 g; Carbohydrate 3.5 g; Dietary Fibre 1 g; Cholesterol 95 mg; 925 kJ (220 Cal)

LEMON GRASS CHICKEN SKEWERS

This is a high-protein dish, and a good source of monounsaturated fat, niacin, potassium and some vitamin A.

Prep time: 20 minutes + overnight marinating
Cooking time: 15 minutes
Serves 4
EASY

4 chicken thigh fillets
1 1/2 tablespoons soft brown sugar
1 1/2 tablespoons lime juice
2 teaspoons green curry paste
18 kaffir lime leaves
2 stems lemon grass

Mango salsa
1 small mango, finely diced
1 teaspoon grated lime rind
2 teaspoons lime juice
1 teaspoon soft brown sugar
1/2 teaspoon fish sauce

1 Discard any excess fat from the chicken fillets and cut them in half lengthways. Combine the brown sugar, lime juice, curry paste and two of the kaffir lime leaves, shredded, in a bowl. Add the chicken and mix well. Cover and refrigerate for several hours or overnight.
2 Trim the lemon grass to measure about 20 cm, leaving the root end intact. Cut each stem lengthways into four pieces. Cut a slit in each of the remaining lime leaves and thread one onto each skewer. Cut two slits in each piece of chicken and thread onto a piece of lemon grass, followed by another lime leaf. Pan-fry or barbecue the skewers until the chicken is cooked through.
3 To make the mango salsa, put all the ingredients in a bowl and stir gently to combine. Serve with the chicken skewers.

NUTRITION PER SERVE
Protein 19.5 g; Fat 8 g; Carbohydrate 11 g; Dietary Fibre 1 g; Cholesterol 87 mg; 810 kJ (195 Cal)

MUSTARD-CRUSTED STEAKS

Many beef-based meals are easy to prepare, and are a valuable addition to healthy diets. This meal provides well-absorbed iron and zinc, as well as plenty of protein, potassium, niacin and Vitamin C.

Prep time: 20 minutes + 10 minutes standing
Cooking time: 55 minutes
Serves 4
EASY

4 potatoes, thinly sliced
1 onion, thinly sliced
1 cup (250 ml) chicken stock
1/4 cup (60 ml) light cream
ground nutmeg, to taste
4 lean beef eye-fillet steaks
1/3 cup (90 g) wholegrain mustard
olive oil spray

1 Preheat the oven to moderately hot 200°C (400°F/Gas 6). Layer the slices of potato and onion in four 1 cup (250 ml) ramekins.

2 Combine the stock and cream in a jug. Season with salt, ground black pepper and nutmeg. Pour over the potato and leave for 10 minutes. Place the ramekins on a baking tray and bake for 55 minutes, or until the potato is tender.

3 Meanwhile, spread each side of the steaks with the mustard. Lightly spray a large non-stick frying pan with the oil and heat over high heat. Add the steaks and cook for 3–4 minutes each side, or until cooked to your liking.

4 Remove the gratin from the dishes and serve with the steaks and some steamed green vegetables.

NUTRITION PER SERVE
Protein 24.5 g; Fat 8.5 g; Carbohydrate 20 g; Dietary Fibre 3 g; Cholesterol 72.5 mg; 1080 kJ (260 Cal)

STUFFED EGGPLANTS

Eggplants have been used in traditional medicine for thousands of years. This is an excellent meal for vegetarians, with slowly digested carbohydrate, protein, vitamin C, B vitamins and antioxidants.

Prep time: 20 minutes
Cooking time: 1 hour
Serves 4
MEDIUM

1/3 cup (60 g) brown lentils
2 large eggplants
cooking oil spray
1 red onion, chopped
2 cloves garlic, crushed
1 red capsicum, finely chopped
1/4 cup (40 g) pine nuts, toasted
440 g can chopped tomatoes
3/4 cup (140 g) cooked short-grain rice
2 tablespoons chopped fresh coriander
1 tablespoon chopped fresh parsley
2 tablespoons grated Parmesan

1 Simmer the brown lentils in a pan of water for 25 minutes, or until soft; drain. Slice the eggplants in half lengthways and scoop out the flesh, leaving a 1 cm shell. Chop the flesh finely.
2 Spray a deep, large non-stick frying pan with oil, add 1 tablespoon water to the pan, then add the onion and garlic, and stir until softened. Add the cooked lentils to the pan with the capsicum, pine nuts, tomato, rice and eggplant flesh. Stir over medium heat for 10 minutes, or until the eggplant has softened. Add the fresh coriander and parsley. Season, then toss until well mixed.
3 Cook the eggplant shells in boiling water for 4–5 minutes, or until tender. Spoon the filling into the eggplant shells and sprinkle with the Parmesan. Grill for 5–10 minutes, or until golden. Serve immediately.

NUTRITION PER SERVE
Protein 15 g; Fat 10 g; Carbohydrate 50 g; Dietary Fibre 8.5 g; Cholesterol 9.5 mg; 1490 kJ (355 Cal)

FISH BURGERS

These burgers are a great source of iron, B vitamins, vitamin C, potassium and good-quality protein.

Prep time: 30 minutes + refrigeration
Cooking time: 25 minutes
Serves 4
EASY

---

500 g white fish fillets
2 tablespoons finely chopped fresh parsley
2 tablespoons finely chopped fresh dill
2 tablespoons lemon juice
1 tablespoon capers, finely chopped
2 finely chopped gherkins
350 g potatoes, cooked and mashed
plain flour, for dusting
2 teaspoons olive oil
4 hamburger buns, toasted
lettuce leaves
2 Roma tomatoes, sliced

Tartare sauce
1/3 cup (90 g) low-fat mayonnaise
1/2 gherkin, finely chopped
2 teaspoons capers, finely chopped
1/2 teaspoon malt vinegar
2 teaspoons finely chopped fresh parsley
2 teaspoons lemon juice

1 Place the fish in a frying pan and cover with water. Slowly heat the water, without boiling. Cover and cook over low heat until just cooked. Drain, transfer to a bowl and flake with a fork. Add the parsley, dill, lemon juice, capers, gherkin and potato, season, and combine well. Divide into four portions and shape into patties. Dust with flour, then refrigerate for 1 hour.
2 Meanwhile, make the tartare sauce by mixing all the ingredients in a bowl.
3 Heat the oil in a large non-stick frying pan. Cook the patties for 5–6 minutes on each side, or until well browned.
4 Place some lettuce leaves, tomato slices, a fish patty and a quarter of the tartare sauce on each bun.

NUTRITION PER SERVE
Protein 33.5 g; Fat 10.5 g; Carbohydrate 46.5 g; Dietary Fibre 4.5 g; Cholesterol 78.5 mg; 1745 kJ (415 Cal)

Stuffed eggplants (top), and Fish burgers

BEEF TERIYAKI

The salad turns this dish into a light and nutritious meal, providing high-quality protein, iron and zinc, with vitamin C and potassium.

Prep time: 20 minutes + 30 minutes refrigeration
+ 10 minutes resting
Cooking time: 20 minutes
Serves 4
EASY

4 scotch fillet steaks
1/3 cup (80 ml) soy sauce
2 tablespoons mirin
1 tablespoon sake (optional)
1 clove garlic, crushed
1 teaspoon grated ginger
1 teaspoon sugar
1 teaspoon toasted sesame seeds

Cucumber salad
1 large Lebanese cucumber, peeled, seeded
    and diced
1/2 red capsicum, diced
2 spring onions, sliced thinly on the diagonal
2 teaspoons sugar
1 tablespoon rice wine vinegar

1 Place the steaks in a non-metallic dish. Combine the soy, mirin, sake, garlic and ginger, and pour over the steaks. Cover and refrigerate for at least 30 minutes.
2 To make the salad, place the cucumber, capsicum and spring onion in a bowl. Place the sugar, rice wine vinegar and 1/4 cup (60 ml) water in a small saucepan and stir over medium heat until the sugar dissolves. Simmer rapidly for 3–4 minutes, or until thickened. Pour over the salad, stir to combine and leave to cool completely.
3 Spray a chargrill plate with oil and heat until very hot. Drain the steaks, reserving the marinade. Cook for 3–4 minutes on each side. Remove and rest before slicing.
4 Place the sugar and reserved marinade in a small saucepan and heat, stirring, until the sugar has dissolved. Bring to the boil, then simmer for 2–3 minutes.
5 Slice each steak and arrange on serving plates. Spoon on some of the marinade and salad, and sprinkle with sesame seeds.

NUTRITION PER SERVE
Protein 23 g; Fat 5 g; Carbohydrate 6 g; Dietary Fibre
1 g; Cholesterol 67 mg; 720 kJ (170 Cal)

GRILLED LAMB PITTAS

This is a refreshing and satisfying lunch or dinner, rich in protein, iron, zinc, potassium and B vitamins. The soothing mint enhances the lamb's flavour, and adds some vitamin C and minerals.

Prep time: 20 minutes + 30 minutes refrigeration
Cooking time: 15 minutes
Serves 4
MEDIUM

1 kg lean minced lamb
1 cup (60 g) finely chopped fresh parsley
1/2 cup (25 g) finely chopped fresh mint
1 onion, finely chopped
1 clove garlic, crushed
1 egg
1 teaspoon chilli sauce
4 small wholemeal pitta pockets

Mint salad
3 small tomatoes
1 small red onion, thinly sliced
1 cup (20 g) fresh mint
1 tablespoon olive oil
2 tablespoons lemon juice

1 Place the lamb, parsley, mint, onion, garlic, egg and chilli sauce in a large bowl and mix together. Shape into eight patties. Chill for 30 minutes. Preheat the oven to warm 160°C (315°F/Gas 2–3).
2 To make the mint salad, slice the tomatoes into thin rings and place in a bowl with the onion, mint, olive oil and lemon juice. Season well with salt and pepper. Gently toss to coat.
3 Wrap the pitta breads in foil and warm in the oven for 5–10 minutes.
4 Heat a chargrill or hot plate and brush with a little oil. When very hot, cook the patties for 3 minutes on each side. Do not turn until a crust has formed on the base or they will fall apart.
5 Remove the pitta breads from the oven. Cut the pockets in half, fill each half with some mint salad and a lamb patty. Serve with some low-fat yoghurt, if desired.

NUTRITION PER SERVE
Protein 59 g; Fat 24 g; Carbohydrate 29 g; Dietary Fibre 8 g; Cholesterol 211 mg; 2390 kJ (570 Cal)

VEGETABLE SKEWERS WITH SALSA VERDE

Just one serve of this recipe meets your daily vitamin A needs, and provides potassium.

Prep time: 20 minutes + 30 minutes soaking
Cooking time: 40 minutes
Serves 8
EASY

Salsa verde
1 clove garlic
1 tablespoon drained capers
1 cup (20 g) fresh flat-leaf parsley
1/2 cup (15 g) fresh basil
1/2 cup (10 g) fresh mint
1/3 cup (80 ml) olive oil
1 teaspoon Dijon mustard
1 tablespoon red wine vinegar

16 small yellow squash
16 French shallots, peeled
16 baby zucchini
16 baby carrots, peeled
1 large red capsicum, halved and cut into 2 cm
    thick slices
2 cloves garlic, crushed
1 teaspoon chopped fresh thyme

1 tablespoon olive oil
16 fresh bay or sage leaves

1 Soak 16 wooden skewers in cold water for 30 minutes.
2 To make the salsa verde, combine the garlic, capers and herbs in a food processor until roughly chopped. With the motor running, slowly pour in the olive oil until incorporated. Combine the mustard with the red wine vinegar and stir through the salsa verde. Season. Cover and refrigerate.
3 Blanch the vegetables separately in a large pot of boiling, salted water until just tender. Drain in a colander, then toss with the garlic, thyme and oil. Season well.
4 Thread the vegetables onto the skewers starting with a squash, then a shallot, a bay leaf, zucchini, carrot and capsicum.
5 Cook the skewers on a hot barbecue grill for 3 minutes on each side, or until cooked and browned. Arrange on couscous or rice and serve with the salsa verde.

NUTRITION PER SERVE
Protein 3 g; Fat 11 g; Carbohydrate 5 g; Dietary Fibre 3.5 g; Cholesterol 0 mg; 525 kJ (125 Cal)

LEMON PEPPER TUNA BURGER

This delicious fish recipe provides some omega-3 and monounsaturated fats, with good amounts of fibre, niacin, thiamin, folate, calcium and vitamin C. It is a good choice for women who are trying to fall pregnant.

Prep time: 20 minutes
Cooking time: 15 minutes
Serves 4
EASY

2 x 185 g cans lemon pepper tuna, drained
1 large onion, chopped
2/3 cup (65 g) dry breadcrumbs
1 egg, lightly beaten
2 tablespoons chopped fresh lemon thyme
1 tablespoon chopped fresh parsley
2 teaspoons grated lemon rind
1 tablespoon oil
1 loaf Turkish bread
1/3 cup (80 g) 97% fat-free mayonnaise
150 g rocket
4 slices low-fat cheese
2 tomatoes, sliced
1 cucumber, sliced
1/2 red onion, sliced

1 Combine the tuna, onion, breadcrumbs, egg, thyme, parsley and lemon rind in a bowl and mix well. Form into four patties and flatten slightly. Heat the oil in a non-stick frying pan. Cook the patties over medium heat for 5 minutes on each side, or until browned.
2 Cut the bread into 4 portions. Split each portion in half horizontally and place under a grill to lightly brown.
3 Spread both cut sides of the bread with mayonnaise. Top with some rocket and layer with a patty, a slice of cheese and slices of tomato, cucumber and onion. Place the other half of the Turkish bread on top, cut in half and serve.

NUTRITION PER SERVE
Protein 30.5 g; Fat 9.5 g; Carbohydrate 56 g; Dietary Fibre 5.5 g; Cholesterol 73 mg; 1825 kJ (435 Cal)

Salmon with bean purée (top), and Pork skewers on rice noodle cakes

SALMON WITH BEAN PUREE

This nourishing meal is an easy and delicious way to include fish in your diet. It provides slowly released carbohydrate energy, filling protein and fibre, monounsaturated fat, niacin, folate, potassium and iron.

Prep time: 20 minutes + 10 minutes marinating
Cooking time: 30 minutes
Serves 4
EASY

---

4 salmon fillets
1 tablespoon oil
1 clove garlic, crushed
2 tablespoons white wine vinegar
1 teaspoon finely grated lime rind
2 tablespoons chopped fresh dill
600 g can cannellini beans, rinsed and drained
1 bay leaf
1 cup (250 ml) chicken stock
100 g baby English spinach leaves

1 Place the salmon in a non-metallic dish. Combine the oil, garlic, vinegar, lime and dill, pour over the fish, then cover and leave for 10 minutes.
2 Place the beans, bay leaf and stock in a saucepan, and simmer for 10 minutes. Remove the bay leaf. Place in a food processor and purée. Season.
3 Drain the salmon, reserving the marinade. Cook in a non-stick frying pan over high heat for 3–5 minutes each side, or until crisp and golden. Remove, add the marinade to the pan and bring to the boil.
4 Steam the spinach until wilted. Serve the salmon on the purée and spinach, and drizzle with the marinade.

NUTRITION PER SERVE
Protein 28 g; Fat 14 g; Carbohydrate 16 g; Dietary Fibre 10 g; Cholesterol 70 mg; 1405 kJ (335 Cal)

PORK SKEWERS ON RICE NOODLE CAKES

This spicy pork dish will supply you with your daily niacin and thiamin needs.

Prep time: 20 minutes + 30 minutes soaking + overnight marinating
Cooking time: 30 minutes
Serves 4
MEDIUM

1 kg pork fillet, cut into 2 cm cubes
8 spring onions, cut into 3 cm lengths
2 tablespoons rice wine vinegar
2 teaspoons chilli bean paste
1/4 cup (60 ml) char siu sauce
400 g fresh flat rice noodles
1 cup (30 g) fresh coriander leaves, chopped
3 spring onions, extra, sliced
1 tablespoon vegetable oil
fresh coriander sprigs, to garnish

1 Soak eight bamboo skewers in water for 30 minutes. Thread the pork and spring onion alternately on the skewers. Combine the vinegar, bean paste and char siu sauce in a shallow non-metallic dish. Add the skewers and coat. Refrigerate overnight.
2 Drain the skewers, reserving the marinade. Heat a grill plate until very hot. Cook the skewers for 1–2 minutes on each side, or until brown and cooked through. Remove and keep warm. Place the marinade in a saucepan and bring to the boil.
3 Separate the noodles with your hands, and toss with the coriander and extra spring onion. Divide into four portions. Heat the oil in a non-stick frying pan over medium heat. Place one portion in the pan, pressing down with a spatula to form a pancake. Cook for 3–4 minutes on each side, or until golden. Remove and keep warm. Repeat with the remaining noodles.
4 Place each noodle cake on a plate and top with two skewers. Drizzle with the marinade and garnish with the coriander.

NUTRITION PER SERVE
Protein 59.5 g; Fat 11.5 g; Carbohydrate 46.5 g; Dietary Fibre 3 g; Cholesterol 237.5 mg; 2240 kJ (535 Cal)

SWORDFISH SKEWERS WITH BEAN PUREE

This recipe is rich in potassium, phosphorus, niacin, fibre and protein.

Prep time: 25 minutes + 30 minutes soaking + 30 minutes marinating
Cooking time: 20 minutes
Serves 4
EASY

1 kg swordfish steaks, cut into 3 cm cubes
1 tablespoon olive oil
2 tablespoons lemon juice
1 clove garlic, crushed
1 tablespoon chopped fresh rosemary
1 tablespoon chopped fresh thyme
2 tablespoons chopped fresh flat-leaf parsley

Bean purée
2 x 400 g cans cannellini beans, rinsed
1 1/2 cups (375 ml) chicken stock
2 fresh bay leaves
2 cloves garlic, crushed
1 teaspoon chopped fresh thyme
1/2 teaspoon finely grated lemon rind
1/4 cup (60 ml) extra virgin olive oil

1 Soak eight wooden skewers in water for 30 minutes. Thread the swordfish cubes onto the skewers. Place in a large non-metallic dish and pour on the combined oil, lemon juice, garlic, rosemary and thyme; season. Refrigerate for 30 minutes.
2 To make the bean purée, place the beans in a large saucepan. Add the stock, bay leaves and 1/2 cup (125 ml) water. Bring to the boil, then reduce the heat and simmer for 10 minutes. Remove from the heat and drain, reserving 2 tablespoons of liquid.
3 Place the beans and liquid in a food processor with the garlic, thyme and rind. Season, and process until smooth. With the motor running, gradually pour in the oil. Process until well combined; keep warm.
4 Cook the skewers on a very hot chargrill or hot plate, turning regularly and basting with the marinade, for 3–4 minutes, or until cooked through and golden. Serve with parsley and a spoonful of the purée.

NUTRITION PER SERVE
Protein 62 g; Fat 21 g; Carbohydrate 18 g; Dietary Fibre 9 g; Cholesterol 147 mg; 2115 kJ (505 Cal)

THAI CHICKEN BURGERS

A lower-fat chicken burger, this dish provides flavonoids, potassium, vitamin A, fibre and monounsaturated fat.

Prep time: 25 minutes + 30 minutes refrigeration
Cooking time: 15 minutes
Serves 4
EASY

400 g lean chicken mince
1 cup (80 g) fresh breadcrumbs
1 clove garlic, crushed
1/2 cup (15 g) chopped fresh coriander leaves
1/4 cup (60 ml) sweet chilli sauce
1 teaspoon ground coriander
3 spring onions, finely chopped
1/4 cup (60 g) sugar
2 tablespoons white vinegar
2 tablespoons finely chopped peanuts
1 tablespoon chopped fresh coriander leaves, extra
1 large carrot
1 large Lebanese cucumber
4 hamburger buns
70 g mixed lettuce leaves
1 large vine-ripened tomato, sliced

1 Place the mince, breadcrumbs, garlic, fresh coriander, sweet chilli sauce, ground coriander and spring onion in a large bowl, and mix together with your hands. Shape into four patties. Refrigerate, covered, for 30 minutes.
2 Place the sugar, vinegar and 1/4 cup (60 ml) water in a small saucepan, and stir over low heat until the sugar dissolves. Simmer for 5 minutes, or until slightly thickened. Cool and stir in the peanuts and extra coriander. Peel strips of carrot and cucumber to make 'ribbons'.
3 Heat a chargrill plate and grill the burgers for 4 minutes each side, or until tender. Serve on hamburger buns, with the dressing, lettuce leaves, tomato, carrot and cucumber.

NUTRITION PER SERVE
Protein 28 g; Fat 5 g; Carbohydrate 63 g; Dietary Fibre 5.5 g; Cholesterol 40 mg; 1710 kJ (410 Cal)

STIR-FRIES AND STEAMED DISHES

When it comes to simple, quick and healthy cooking, stir-fried and steamed meals are hard to beat. All you need is a wok or steamer basket, your favourite ingredients, and a little imagination.

STIR-FRYING

Stir-frying is a fast, easy and healthy cooking method, which combines the best of fresh produce with exotic flavours. Stir-frying is Asian in origin, but recipes can be varied to suit your individual tastes or the ingredients you have.

It is important that all the preparation of ingredients is done before you begin cooking, because once the cooking starts, there's no time to stop. For the best tasting stir-fries, the ingredients should be added at various stages of the process, according to how long they take to cook.

Stir-frying involves cooking in a wok over high heat. It needs only a minimum of oil, and if you use a non-stick wok, you can stir-fry with just a light spray of oil.

A stir-fry served with noodles or rice is a healthy, convenient, complete and filling meal. It can be a simple dish of meat, poultry, seafood or vegetables tossed with a sauce, or a complex combination of flavours and ingredients.

Firm tofu or tofu puffs are a great vegetarian choice for stir-fries, and add protein and minerals to the dish.

Preparing ingredients

■ Meat and poultry should be from a cut that will be tender after only a short cooking time. Cut the meat into thin, even-sized strips across the grain. Marinating the food before cooking will tenderise it and also add to the flavour of the whole dish.

■ Seafood such as prawns, scallops and squid need only the briefest time to cook through. If cooking fish, use firm-fleshed pieces that won't break up, and move them gently around the wok to cook, without breaking up.

■ Vegetables are perfect for stir-frying, and the quick cooking helps them to retain texture, colour and nutrients. Different vegetables require different cooking times, and should be cut and added to the dish accordingly:
- cauliflower, potatoes and carrots will take longer to cook, so slice them thinly and add them at the beginning of cooking
- peas, asparagus and mushrooms should be added towards the end of cooking
- bean sprouts, herbs and leafy vegetables such as bok choy and spinach should be tossed through at the end, because they need only to be heated through until they are just wilted.

Stir-frying tips

- Make sure that the wok is very hot before you begin. Add a minimum of oil and swirl to coat the bottom and side of the wok, or give a light spray of oil.
- Drain any marinade from the

ingredients before you begin to stir-fry, otherwise they will tend to steam or stew in the juices.
- Cook meat in batches over high heat. This will allow each batch to cook evenly and quickly, and will help to maintain the heat throughout cooking. Reheat the wok after cooking each batch.
- Set the cooked meat aside, then cook the aromatics such as garlic, ginger, onion and chilli, followed by the slower-cooking ingredients. Return the meat to the wok just before adding the sauce ingredients, and then any leafy greens and herbs.
- Keep all the ingredients moving constantly around the wok to make sure they cook evenly.
- If the stir-fry looks a little dry, add a little water or stock to moisten and prevent sticking.
- Serve the stir-fry immediately so the ingredients don't go soggy.

STEAMING

Steaming is an efficient and extremely healthy cooking method. It is particularly suitable for cooking most types of vegetables and seafood. The ingredient is placed in a bamboo or metal steamer basket, covered and then placed directly above simmering water in a wok or saucepan. The rising steam becomes trapped by the steamer basket and cooks the food.

Steaming allows food to cook without any fat and, because it doesn't come into contact with the water, more water-soluble nutrients are retained. Several steamer baskets may be stacked on top of each other to cook large quantities of food, or for cooking different types of food that require different cooking times.

Aromatics can be added to the steaming liquid, which will impart a subtle flavour to the food being steamed. Try:
- garlic
- ginger
- lemon grass
- lemon or lime zest
- lime leaves
- coriander roots
- star anise.

Steaming ideas

- Lightly marinate skinless chicken breast fillets with garlic, ginger and soy sauce, and steam until cooked through. Serve sliced with sweet chilli dipping sauce over jasmine rice.
- Steam baby bok choy or Chinese broccoli until tender, then drizzle with oyster sauce.
- Top an Atlantic salmon steak with finely shredded spring onion and coriander leaves, steam until cooked to your liking, and serve with lemon wedges and a green salad.
- Steam mussels in a spicy Thai-flavoured broth until they just open, and serve with crusty bread.
- Leave scallops in their half shell, pour over a little miso broth, top with a few thinly sliced spring onions and steam on the shell until they are just cooked.
- Steam prawns in their shells until they are pink and cooked through, and serve with a Vietnamese lime and chilli dipping sauce.
- Steam fresh summer sweet corn chunks, asparagus and sugar snap peas, and serve as a delicious side dish.

SESAME CHICKEN AND NOODLE STIR-FRY

This high-protein dish is an excellent source of B vitamins, fibre, potassium, phosphorus and iron.

Prep time: 20 minutes
Cooking time: 15 minutes
Serves 4
EASY

600 g Shanghai noodles
1 tablespoon olive oil
1 tablespoon julienned fresh ginger
1 long red chilli, seeded and finely chopped
500 g chicken breast fillets, cut crossways into 1 cm slices
2 cloves garlic, crushed
1/4 cup (60 ml) salt-reduced soy sauce
3 teaspoons sesame oil
700 g baby bok choy, sliced lengthways into eighths
2 tablespoons sesame seeds, toasted

1 Cook the noodles in a saucepan of boiling water for 4–5 minutes, or until tender. Drain and rinse under cold water. Drain again.

2 Heat the oil in a wok and swirl to coat. Add the ginger and chilli, and stir-fry for 1 minute. Add the chicken and stir-fry for a further 3–5 minutes, or until browned and almost cooked.

3 Add the garlic and cook for 1 minute. Pour in the soy sauce and sesame oil, and toss to coat. Add the bok choy and noodles, and stir-fry until the bok choy is tender and the noodles are warmed through. Place in individual serving bowls, sprinkle with sesame seeds and serve.

NUTRITION PER SERVE
Protein 45 g; Fat 19 g; Carbohydrate 80 g; Dietary Fibre 6 g; Cholesterol 102 mg; 2850 kJ (680 Cal)

BEEF AND NOODLE STIR-FRY

High in top-quality protein and B vitamins, this dish also provides significant amounts of fibre, iron, zinc, potassium and vitamin A.

Prep time: 15 minutes + 10 minutes soaking
Coking time: 15 minutes
Serves 4
EASY

350 g lean beef fillet, partially frozen
100 g snow peas
600 g fresh Hokkien noodles
1 tablespoon peanut oil
1 large onion, cut into thin wedges
1 large carrot, sliced thinly on the diagonal
1 medium red capsicum, cut into thin strips
2 cloves garlic, crushed
1 teaspoon grated fresh ginger
200 g fresh shiitake mushrooms, sliced
1/4 cup (60 ml) oyster sauce
2 tablespoons light soy sauce
1 tablespoon soft brown sugar
1/2 teaspoon five-spice powder

1 Cut the steak into thin slices. Top and tail the snow peas and slice in half diagonally. Soak the noodles in a large bowl with enough boiling water to cover for 10 minutes.
2 Spray a large wok with oil spray and, when very hot, cook the steak in batches until brown. Remove and keep warm.
3 Heat the oil in the wok and, when very hot, stir-fry the onion, carrot and capsicum for 2–3 minutes, or until tender. Add the garlic, ginger, snow peas and shiitake mushrooms, and cook for another minute before returning the steak to the wok.
4 Separate the noodles with a fork, then drain. Add to the wok, tossing well. Combine the oyster sauce with the soy sauce, brown sugar, five-spice powder and 1 tablespoon water, and pour over the noodles. Toss until warmed through, then serve immediately.

NUTRITION PER SERVE
Protein 37.5 g; Fat 10 g; Carbohydrate 91.5 g; Dietary Fibre 6.5 g; Cholesterol 78 mg; 2555 kJ (610 Cal)

MA POR TOFU

This dish is a great choice for people who don't eat dairy products as it contains calcium, magnesium, phosphorus, protein and potassium.

Prep time: 15 minutes + 10 minutes marinating
Cooking time: 15 minutes
Serves 4
EASY
———

3 teaspoons cornflour
2 teaspoons soy sauce
1 teaspoon oyster sauce
1 clove garlic, finely chopped
250 g pork mince
1 tablespoon oil
3 teaspoons red bean chilli paste
3 teaspoons preserved bean curd
750 g firm tofu, drained, cubed
2 spring onions, sliced
3 teaspoons oyster sauce, extra
2 teaspoons soy sauce, extra
1 1/2 teaspoons sugar

1 Put the cornflour, soy sauce, oyster sauce and garlic in a bowl, and mix well. Add the mince and toss to coat. Set aside for 10 minutes.
2 Heat a wok until very hot, add the oil and swirl to coat. Add the mince and stir-fry for 5 minutes, or until browned. Add the chilli paste and bean curd, and cook for 2 minutes, or until fragrant.
3 Add the remaining ingredients and stir for 3–5 minutes, or until the tofu is heated through. Serve with rice.

NUTRITION PER SERVE
Protein 26 g; Fat 12 g; Carbohydrate 5 g; Dietary Fibre 0 g; Cholesterol 30 mg; 1090 kJ (260 Cal)

THAI-STYLE STEAMED FISH WITH SPICY TOMATO SAUCE

This meal of filling tender fish is rich in protein, potassium, phosphorus and niacin, and is topped with a spicy tomato sauce.

Prep time: 25 minutes + 30 minutes standing
Cooking time: 40 minutes
Serves 4
MEDIUM
———

6 cloves garlic
3 red Asian shallots
3 vine-ripened tomatoes
2 long red chillies
1 1/2 tablespoons lime juice
70 ml fish sauce
2 cloves garlic, extra
4 coriander roots
6 whole black peppercorns
4 snapper (about 300 g each), fins trimmed, cleaned and gutted
3/4 cup (25 g) fresh coriander leaves

1 Chargrill the skins of the garlic, shallots, tomatoes and chillies over a gas flame, using a pair of metal tongs, or roast in a preheated very hot 230°C (450°F/Gas 8) oven for 15–20 minutes. When cool, peel and discard the skins of the vegetables. Roughly chop the vegetables and combine with the lime juice and 2 tablespoons of the fish sauce. Leave for 30 minutes.
2 Place the extra garlic, coriander roots and peppercorns in a mortar and pestle, and grind to a smooth paste. Add the remaining fish sauce and stir to combine. Score each fish on both sides in a crisscross pattern. Rub the paste on both sides.
3 Line the bottom of a large bamboo steamer with baking paper. Place the fish on the paper and place the steamer over a wok of boiling water. Cover and steam for 15–20 minutes, or until the flesh flakes easily. Slide the fish onto a plate, spoon over the sauce and sprinkle with coriander.

NUTRITION PER SERVE
Protein 64 g; Fat 5 g; Carbohydrate 4.5 g; Dietary Fibre 3 g; Cholesterol 183 mg; 1365 kJ (325 Cal)

Ma por tofu (top), and Thai-style steamed fish with spicy tomato sauce

PEPPERED LAMB AND ASPARAGUS STIR-FRY

Like most stir-fries, this dish shows how easy it is to combine a delicious and highly nutritious variety of foods without unnecessary fat. It is an excellent source of protein, iron, zinc, folate, niacin and vitamin C.

Prep time: 35 minutes + 20 minutes marinating
Cooking time: 20 minutes
Serves 4
EASY

400 g lamb fillets
2 teaspoons green peppercorns, finely chopped
3 cloves garlic, finely chopped
1 tablespoon vegetable oil
1 onion, cut into small wedges
1/3 cup (80 ml) dry sherry
1 green capsicum, cut into strips
1/2 teaspoon sugar
16 small asparagus spears, cut into bite-sized
   pieces
200 g broccoli florets
2 tablespoons oyster sauce
garlic chives, cut into short lengths, to garnish

1 Trim away any sinew from the lamb and cut the lamb into bite-sized pieces. Combine in a bowl with the green peppercorns, garlic and oil, then toss well and set aside for 20 minutes.
2 Heat a wok over high heat until slightly smoking. Add the pieces of lamb and stir-fry in batches until brown and just cooked. Remove, cover and keep warm.
3 Reheat the wok and stir-fry the onion and 2 teaspoons of the sherry for 1 minute. Add the capsicum, sugar and a large pinch of salt. Cover, steam for 2 minutes, add the asparagus, broccoli, then remaining sherry, and stir-fry for 1 minute. Cover and steam for 3 minutes, or until the vegetables are just tender. Return the lamb to the pan, add the oyster sauce and stir to combine with the vegetables. Serve garnished with the garlic chives.

NUTRITION PER SERVE
Protein 25 g; Fat 12 g; Carbohydrate 8 g; Dietary Fibre 4 g; Cholesterol 65 mg; 1100 kJ (265 Cal)

MUSHROOM NOODLES

Suitable for vegetarians, this dish provides fibre, some minerals, B vitamins and folate.

Prep time: 30 minutes + 20 minutes soaking
Cooking time: 15 minutes
Serves 4–6
EASY

25 g dried Chinese mushrooms
1 tablespoon oil
$1/2$ teaspoon sesame oil
1 tablespoon finely chopped fresh ginger
4 cloves garlic, crushed
100 g fresh shiitake mushrooms, trimmed,
    sliced
150 g oyster mushrooms, sliced
150 g shimeji mushrooms, trimmed, pulled
    apart
$3/4$ cup (185 ml) dashi (see Note)
$1/4$ cup (60 ml) soy sauce
$1/4$ cup (60 ml) mirin
$1/4$ teaspoon white pepper
25 g butter
2 tablespoons lemon juice
100 g enoki mushrooms, trimmed, pulled apart
500 g thin Hokkien noodles, separated
1 tablespoon chopped fresh chives

1 Soak the dried Chinese mushrooms in $11/2$ cups (375 ml) boiling water for 20 minutes, or until soft. Drain, reserving the liquid. Discard the stems. Slice the caps.
2 Heat a wok until very hot, add the oils and swirl to coat. Add the ginger, garlic, shiitake, oyster and shimeji mushrooms, and stir-fry for 1–2 minutes, or until the mushrooms have wilted. Remove.
3 Combine the dashi, soy sauce, mirin, white pepper and $3/4$ cup (185 ml) of the reserved liquid, add to the wok and cook for 3 minutes. Add the butter, juice and 1 teaspoon salt, and cook for 1 minute, or until thickened. Return the mushrooms to the wok, cook for 2 minutes, then stir in the enoki and Chinese mushrooms.
4 Add the noodles and stir for 3 minutes, or until heated through. Sprinkle with the chives and serve immediately.

NUTRITION PER SERVE (6)
Protein 15 g; Fat 8.5 g; Carbohydrate 60 g; Dietary Fibre 5 g; Cholesterol 25 mg; 1610 kJ (385 Cal)

NOTE: Dissolve $11/2$ teaspoons dashi powder in $3/4$ cup (185 ml) water to make the dashi.

STEAMED CHICKEN WITH ASIAN GREENS

This light, low-fat chicken dish provides good-quality protein, potassium and niacin.

Prep time: 10 minutes + 20 minutes soaking +
    1 hour marinating
Cooking time: 20 minutes
Serves 4
MEDIUM

8–10 g dried Chinese mushrooms
2 tablespoons light soy sauce
2 tablespoons rice wine
1/2 teaspoon sesame oil
1 tablespoon thinly sliced fresh ginger
4 chicken breast fillets (about 200 g each),
    trimmed
450 g bok choy, ends removed, cut lengthways
    into quarters
1/2 cup (125 ml) chicken stock
1 tablespoon cornflour

1 Soak the dried mushrooms in 1/4 cup (60 ml) boiling water for 20 minutes. Drain and reserve the liquid. Discard the stalks and thinly slice the caps.

2 Combine the soy sauce, wine, sesame oil and ginger in a non-metallic dish. Add the chicken to the marinade and turn to coat. Cover and marinate for 1 hour.

3 Line a bamboo steamer with baking paper. Place the chicken on top, reserving the marinade. Bring water to the boil in a wok, then place the steamer in the wok. Cover and steam for 6 minutes, then turn the chicken over and steam for a further 6 minutes. Place the bok choy on top of the chicken and steam for 2–3 minutes.

4 Meanwhile, place the reserved marinade, mushrooms and liquid in a small saucepan and bring to the boil. Add enough stock to the cornflour to make a smooth paste. Add the cornflour paste and remaining stock, and stir for 2 minutes over medium heat, or until the sauce thickens.

5 Place some bok choy and a chicken fillet on each plate, then pour on some sauce. Serve with rice.

NUTRITION PER SERVE
Protein 45.5 g; Fat 5.5 g; Carbohydrate 4.5 g; Dietary Fibre 2 g; Cholesterol 95 mg; 1085 kJ (260 Cal)

PORK AND BOK CHOY STIR-FRY

This dish is bursting with potassium, vitamin C and niacin, and provides good amounts of thiamin, iron and folate.

Prep time: 20 minutes
Cooking time: 15 minutes
Serves 4
EASY

---

400 g lean pork leg steaks
1 tablespoon canned salted black beans, rinsed
500 g baby bok choy
2 teaspoons sesame oil
2 onions, thinly sliced
2 cloves garlic, finely chopped
2–3 teaspoons chopped fresh ginger
1 red capsicum, cut into strips
1/2 cup (80 g) water chestnuts, thinly sliced
2 tablespoons oyster sauce
1 tablespoon soy sauce
2 teaspoons fish sauce

1 Slice the pork steaks into strips, cutting across the grain. Roughly chop the beans. Cut the ends off the bok choy, separate the leaves and shred.

2 Heat half the sesame oil in a large non-stick frying pan or wok. Cook the onion, garlic and ginger over high heat for 3–4 minutes, add the capsicum, and cook for 2–3 minutes. Remove from the pan. Heat the remaining sesame oil and stir-fry the pork in batches over high heat.

3 Return the pork to the pan along with the onion mixture, black beans, shredded bok choy, water chestnuts and oyster, soy and fish sauces. Toss quickly to combine the ingredients, lower the heat, cover and steam for 3–4 minutes, or until the bok choy is just wilted. Serve immediately.

NUTRITION PER SERVE
Protein 30 g; Fat 3 g; Carbohydrate 20 g; Dietary Fibre 3.5 g; Cholesterol 55 mg; 910 kJ (215 Cal)

Mee grob (top), and Barbecue pork with Asian greens

MEE GROB

This noodle dish is a delicious combination of nutritious foods, providing good amounts of niacin, potassium and protein.

Prep time: 35 minutes + 20 minutes soaking
Cooking time: 15 minutes
Serves 4–6
MEDIUM

4 dried Chinese mushrooms
oil, for deep-frying
100 g dried rice vermicelli
100 g fried tofu, cut into matchsticks
4 cloves garlic, crushed
1 onion, chopped
200 g lean pork fillet, thinly sliced
1 chicken breast fillet, thinly sliced
8 green beans, sliced on the diagonal
6 spring onions, thinly sliced on the diagonal
8 raw prawns, peeled, deveined
30 g bean sprouts
fresh coriander leaves, to garnish

Sauce
1 tablespoon soy sauce
1/4 cup (60 ml) white vinegar
1/4 cup (60 g) sugar
1/4 cup (60 ml) fish sauce
1 tablespoon chilli sauce

1 Cover the mushrooms with hot water and soak for 20 minutes. Drain, discard the stems and thinly slice.
2 Fill a wok one-third full of oil and heat to 180°C (350°F), or until a cube of bread dropped into the oil browns in 15 seconds. Cook the vermicelli in batches for 20 seconds, or until puffed and crispy. Drain and cool.
3 Add the tofu to the wok in batches and cook for 1 minute, or until crisp. Drain. Carefully ladle out all but 2 tablespoons of the oil.
4 Reheat the wok until very hot. Stir-fry the garlic and onion for 1 minute. Add the pork and stir-fry for 3 minutes. Add the chicken, beans, mushrooms and half the spring onion, and stir-fry for 2 minutes, or until the chicken has almost cooked

through. Add the prawns and stir-fry for 2 minutes, or until just tender.
5 Combine the sauce ingredients, add to the wok and stir-fry for 2 minutes, or until the meat and prawns are tender.
6 Remove from the heat and stir in the bean sprouts, tofu and noodles. Garnish with the coriander and the remaining spring onion.

NUTRITION PER SERVE (6)
Protein 25 g; Fat 10 g; Carbohydrate 17 g; Dietary Fibre 2.5 g; Cholesterol 72 mg; 1055 kJ (255 Cal)

BARBECUE PORK WITH ASIAN GREENS

Very simple, but highly nutritious, this dish is loaded with vitamin C, folate, niacin, potassium, iron and zinc—even before you add rice or noodles.

Prep time: 10 minutes
Cooking time: 10 minutes
Serves 4
EASY

1.6 kg Chinese broccoli, cut into 5 cm lengths
1 tablespoon peanut oil
2 cm piece fresh ginger, julienned
2 cloves garlic, crushed
500 g Chinese barbecue pork, thinly sliced
1/4 cup (60 ml) chicken or vegetable stock
1/4 cup (60 ml) oyster sauce
1 tablespoon kecap manis

1 Place the broccoli in a steamer over a saucepan or wok of simmering water and cook for 5 minutes, or until just tender but still crisp.
2 Heat a wok until very hot, add the oil and swirl to coat. Add the ginger and garlic, and stir-fry for 30 seconds, or until fragrant. Add the broccoli and pork, and toss to coat.
3 Pour in the combined stock, oyster sauce and kecap manis, and stir-fry until heated through. Serve with rice or noodles.

NUTRITION PER SERVE
Protein 30 g; Fat 7 g; Carbohydrate 4.5 g; Dietary Fibre 6 g; Cholesterol 60 mg; 885 kJ (210 Cal)

EGGPLANT WITH HOT BEAN SAUCE

The eggplant in this spicy vegetarian dish provides a number of protective compounds.

Prep time: 20 minutes
Cooking time: 15 minutes
Serves 4–6
EASY

1/4 cup (60 ml) peanut oil
800 g eggplant, cut into 2 cm cubes
4 spring onions, chopped
3 cloves garlic, crushed
1 tablespoon finely chopped fresh ginger
1 tablespoon hot bean paste
1/2 cup (125 ml) vegetable stock
1/4 cup (60 ml) Chinese rice wine
2 tablespoons rice vinegar
1 tablespoon tomato paste
2 teaspoons soft brown sugar
2 tablespoons soy sauce
1 teaspoon cornflour
2 tablespoons shredded fresh basil

1 Heat a wok until very hot, add 1 tablespoon of the oil and swirl to coat. Stir-fry the eggplant in batches for 3–4 minutes, or until browned. Remove.
2 Reheat the wok, add the remaining oil and swirl to coat. Stir-fry the spring onion, garlic, ginger and bean paste for 30 seconds. Add the stock, rice wine, rice vinegar, tomato paste, sugar and soy sauce, and stir-fry for 1 minute.
3 Blend the cornflour with 1 tablespoon water, add to the wok and bring to the boil. Return the eggplant to the wok and stir-fry for 2–3 minutes, or until cooked through. Sprinkle with basil.

NUTRITION PER SERVE (6)
Protein 2 g; Fat 10 g; Carbohydrate 5.5 g; Dietary Fibre 3.5 g; Cholesterol 0 mg; 550 kJ (130 Cal)

BEEF AND VEGETABLE STIR-FRY

This beef stir-fry features an array of different coloured vegetables and healthy elements, including vitamin C, beta-carotene, fibre, phytochemicals, iron and zinc.

Prep time: 30 minutes
Cooking time: 15 minutes
Serves 4
EASY

2 tablespoons peanut oil
350 g beef fillet, thinly sliced
1 large onion, cut into thin wedges
1 large carrot, thinly sliced on the diagonal
1 red capsicum, cut into thin strips
100 g snow peas, halved diagonally
150 g baby corn, halved diagonally
200 g can straw mushrooms, drained
2 tablespoons oyster sauce
1 clove garlic, crushed
1 teaspoon grated fresh ginger
2 tablespoons light soy sauce
2 tablespoons medium sherry
1 tablespoon honey
1 teaspoon sesame oil
2 teaspoons cornflour

1 Heat a wok over high heat, add 1 tablespoon of the peanut oil and swirl it around to coat the side of the wok. Cook the meat in batches for 2–3 minutes, or until nicely browned. Remove the meat from the wok and keep warm.

2 Heat the remaining peanut oil in the wok, add the onion, carrot and capsicum, and cook, stirring, for 2–3 minutes, or until the vegetables are just tender. Add the snow peas, corn and straw mushrooms, cook for a further minute, then return all the meat to the wok.

3 Combine the oyster sauce with the garlic, ginger, soy sauce, sherry, honey, sesame oil and 1 tablespoon water in a small bowl, then add the mixture to the wok. Mix the cornflour with 1 tablespoon of water, add to the wok and cook for 1 minute, or until the sauce thickens. Season with salt and ground black pepper. Serve immediately with rice or thin egg noodles.

NUTRITION PER SERVE
Protein 25 g; Fat 16 g; Carbohydrate 24 g; Dietary Fibre 5 g; Cholesterol 59 mg; 1445 kJ (345 Cal)

SINGAPORE NOODLES

This popular dish is tasty as well as being healthy. It contains good amounts of monounsaturated fat, protein, niacin, potassium and phosphorus.

Prep time: 20 minutes + 30 minutes soaking + 30 minutes marinating
Cooking time: 10 minutes
Serves 4–6
EASY

---

400 g dried rice vermicelli
2 cloves garlic, crushed
2 teaspoons grated fresh ginger
1/4 cup (60 ml) oyster sauce
1/4 cup (60 ml) soy sauce
250 g chicken breast fillet, thinly sliced
2 tablespoons oil
2 celery sticks, julienned
1 large carrot, julienned
3 spring onions, diagonally sliced
1 1/2 tablespoons Asian curry powder
1/2 teaspoon sesame oil
65 g bean sprouts

1 Cover the vermicelli with cold water and leave for 30 minutes, or until soft. Drain.
2 Place the garlic, ginger, 1 tablespoon oyster sauce and 2 teaspoons soy sauce in a bowl and mix well. Add the chicken, toss to coat and marinate for 30 minutes.
3 Heat a wok until very hot, add the oil and swirl to coat. Stir-fry the chicken until browned. Add the celery, carrot and half the spring onion, and stir-fry for 2–3 minutes, or until slightly softened. Add the curry powder and stir-fry for 2 minutes, or until aromatic.
4 Add the noodles and mix well to coat and heat through. Stir in the remaining oyster sauce, soy sauce, spring onion, sesame oil and bean sprouts. Serve hot.

NUTRITION PER SERVE (6)
Protein 14.5 g; Fat 9.5 g; Carbohydrate 47.5 g; Dietary Fibre 2.5 g; Cholesterol 28.5 mg; 1405 kJ (335 Cal)

LEMON GRASS PRAWNS

This quick-cooking, aromatic prawn dish gives you valuable selenium and iodine, with good amounts of vitamin C, folate, niacin and potassium.

Prep time: 30 minutes
Cooking time: 10 minutes
Serves 4
EASY

---

1 tablespoon peanut oil
2 cloves garlic, crushed
1 tablespoon finely grated fresh ginger
2 tablespoons finely chopped lemon grass
8 spring onions, cut into 4 cm pieces
1 kg raw prawns, peeled, deveined, tails intact
2 tablespoons lime juice
1 tablespoon soft brown sugar
2 teaspoons fish sauce
1/4 cup (60 ml) chicken stock
1 teaspoon cornflour
500 g baby bok choy, halved lengthways
1/4 cup (15 g) chopped fresh mint

1 Heat a wok until very hot, add the oil and swirl to coat. Add the garlic, ginger, lemon grass and spring onion, and stir-fry for 1 minute, or until fragrant. Add the prawns and stir-fry for 2 minutes.
2 Place the lime juice, sugar, fish sauce, chicken stock and cornflour in a small bowl. Mix well, then add to the wok and stir until the sauce boils and thickens. Cook for a further 1–2 minutes, or until the prawns are pink and just tender.
3 Add the bok choy and stir-fry for 1 minute, or until wilted. Stir in the mint and serve.

NUTRITION PER SERVE
Protein 60 g; Fat 8.5 g; Carbohydrate 8 g; Dietary Fibre 1.6 g; Cholesterol 373 mg; 1435 kJ (340 Cal)

STEWS AND CURRIES

Nothing is more welcoming on a cold winter's night than a steaming stew or spicy curry, and it's not difficult to transform your old favourites into healthy meals with some simple substitutions.

STEWS

A stew is a meal that is simmered on the stove top in an enclosed dish, unlike a casserole, which is cooked in the oven. It is cooked with very little fat, in a liquid usually consisting of a stock base seasoned with aromatics, and is cooked until the ingredients are tender. It is best to use tougher cuts of meat for stews because the long, slow cooking process will break down the connective tissue of these cuts, and develop a deep, succulent flavour.

A stew can be mainly meat based; it may be a combination of meat, poultry, seafood, and vegetables; or perhaps vegetables with spices and legumes. It may simply have a stock base, or include wine (red or white), tomatoes or cream.

One of the most important steps to creating a full-flavoured stew is the initial browning of the ingredients. It is at this stage that you may need to use fat to caramelise the ingredients. This, however, can be kept to a minimum if you use a non-stick frying pan, sprayed with a little oil. Make sure the pan is very hot before you add the ingredients to brown so that they will sear, and develop colour without cooking in their own juices. Once the ingredients are browned, the liquid is added and the dish is covered, the stew simply simmers gently until dinner time. It may be necessary to skim the surface of the stew as it cooks to remove any fat that rises to the surface during cooking.

Tips for healthy stews

■ Add some soaked dried beans or legumes to a vegetable stew to add fibre, minerals and complete protein.

■ When simmering your stew, be sure to have the heat as low as possible, so that the bubbles are gentle and barely break the surface. This will ensure that the stew cooks without any of the ingredients breaking up.

■ For extra flavour, add finely chopped fresh herbs at the very end of cooking. Either stir them through before serving, or scatter them over the dish. This way, they will retain their colour and fresh flavour.

■ If your stew still has a lot of liquid towards the end of cooking, instead of thickening the sauce, add some uncooked pasta 10 minutes before the end of the cooking time, or rice 20 minutes before the end. The pasta or rice will absorb the delicious flavours of the stew and become a one-pot meal.

■ If the stew needs thickening, dissolve 1 teaspoon of cornflour in 1 tablespoon of cold water. Add a little at a time to the hot stew, stirring well, until the stew begins to thicken.

■ The flavours of a stew will develop if it is allowed to sit overnight. Crockpots are good for this.

Stew accompaniments

■ Serve rich red wine beef stews with garlic mashed potato or soft polenta.

■ Couscous is traditionally served with North African-style tagines and stews.

■ Serve Asian-flavoured stews with steamed jasmine or basmati rice.

■ Risotto is delicious with osso bucco and rich, meaty stews.

■ Try short pasta such as penne or maccheroni for added carbohydrate.

■ Serve meaty stews with a green salad.

CURRIES

The main distinction between a curry and a stew is in the use of curry paste or spices that are used to give curries their distinctive flavour. Curries can be either wet or quite dry in texture.

Curries may be made from virtually any kind of meat, poultry, seafood or vegetable. They are usually Indian or Southeast Asian in origin, and the spices and heat will vary according to the region they are from.

Indian curries generally use a blend of dry spices. Traditionally, the whole spices are dry-roasted to enhance the flavour, and then ground to a powder. There are many spice blends available in supermarkets that are simple to use and make a fragrant and authentically flavoured curry.

The spices that are used in Indian spice blends are chilli powder, cumin, cardamom, cinnamon, mustard seeds, turmeric, fenugreek, coriander seeds, curry leaves, cloves and black pepper.

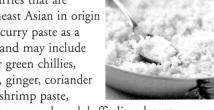

Curries that are Southeast Asian in origin use a curry paste as a base, and may include red or green chillies, garlic, ginger, coriander root, shrimp paste, lemon grass, galangal, kaffir lime leaves, tamarind, palm sugar and basil.

Tips for healthy curries

■ Use a heavy-based non-stick deep frying pan or saucepan. When you are browning the meat, use a light spray of oil in the pan. Add the dry spice mix to the meat so that any fat in the meat will help to sauté the spices, reducing the need to add any fat.

■ Use stock or tomatoes as the liquid base for the curry instead of coconut milk or cream. For a little creaminess, stir through some low-fat yoghurt just before serving. Alternatively, use low-fat evaporated milk in place of coconut milk.

■ Skim off any fat that rises to the surface during cooking.

■ If you use a curry paste, don't add any oil for frying the ingredients, as the paste itself contains enough oil.

CHICKEN CACCIATORE

This popular Italian dish provides protein, monounsaturated fat, potassium, niacin mixed with vitamin C, and antioxidants.

Prep time: 25 minutes
Cooking time: 40 minutes
Serves 4
EASY

500 g chicken breast fillets
plain flour, for dusting
2 teaspoons olive oil
2 onions, thinly sliced
2 cloves garlic, finely chopped
2 anchovy fillets, chopped
440 g can chopped tomatoes
1/2 cup (125 ml) dry white wine
1/4 cup (60 g) tomato paste
1 teaspoon soft brown sugar
6 Kalamata olives, pitted and chopped
chopped fresh parsley, to garnish

1 Trim the fat from the chicken and lightly dust the chicken in plain flour. Heat the oil in a large, heavy-based non-stick frying pan and cook the chicken over high heat for 10 minutes, turning until golden and almost cooked. (If the chicken begins to stick, sprinkle with water and reduce the heat.) Remove, cover and set aside.
2 Add the onion to the pan with the garlic, anchovies and 1 tablespoon of water. Cover and cook for 5 minutes, stirring. Add the tomato, wine, tomato paste, sugar and 200 ml water. Bring to the boil, then reduce the heat and simmer for 20 minutes. Season with salt and pepper.
3 Return the chicken and juices to the pan. Add the olives and simmer for 5 minutes, or until the chicken is heated through. Garnish with parsley. Delicious with fusilli or other pasta.

NUTRITION PER SERVE
Protein 31 g; Fat 5.5 g; Carbohydrate 3 g; Dietary Fibre 3 g; Cholesterol 64 mg; 1000 kJ (240 Cal)

VEGETABLE CURRY

This is a nutritious vegetarian meal that is low in fat, but loaded with protective plant compounds, fibre, vitamin A, vitamin C and potassium. Serve the curry with rice and extra yoghurt for a complete protein meal.

Prep time: 30 minutes
Cooking time: 45 minutes
Serves 6
EASY

2 teaspoons olive oil
1 onion, chopped
2 cloves garlic, crushed
2 teaspoons ground cumin
2 teaspoons ground coriander
3 teaspoons Madras curry powder
500 g potatoes, cut into bite-sized pieces
500 g pumpkin, cut into bite-sized pieces
2 large zucchini, thickly sliced
2 large carrots, thickly sliced
400 g can chopped tomatoes
1 cup (250 ml) vegetable stock
100 g broccoli florets
150 g green beans, cut into short lengths
1/4 cup (15 g) chopped fresh coriander
1 cup (250 g) low-fat natural yoghurt

1 Heat the oil in a large deep pan, add the onion and garlic, and cook until softened. Add the ground cumin, coriander and curry powder, and cook for 1–2 minutes, or until fragrant. Add the potato, pumpkin, zucchini and carrot, and toss to coat in the spices.
2 Stir in the tomato and stock, bring to the boil, then reduce the heat and simmer, covered, for 30 minutes, or until the vegetables are tender, stirring frequently. Add the broccoli florets and chopped beans, and simmer, uncovered, for 5 minutes, or until all the vegetables are tender. Stir in the chopped coriander and serve with yoghurt. Can be served with steamed rice.

NUTRITION PER SERVE
Protein 8.5 g; Fat 4 g; Carbohydrate 25 g; Dietary Fibre 6 g; Cholesterol 7 mg; 715 kJ (170 Cal)

Chicken cacciatore (top), and Vegetable curry

LAMB KOFTA CURRY

Although higher in fat than other recipes, most of the fat in this curry is monounsaturated. The lamb provides top-quality protein.

Prep time: 25 minutes
Cooking time: 35 minutes
Serves 4
MEDIUM

500 g minced lean lamb
1 onion, finely chopped
1 clove garlic, finely chopped
1 teaspoon grated fresh ginger
1 small red chilli, finely chopped
1 teaspoon garam masala
1 teaspoon ground coriander
1/4 cup (25 g) ground almonds
2 tablespoons chopped fresh coriander leaves

Sauce
1 tablespoon oil
1 onion, finely chopped
3 tablespoons Korma curry paste
400 g can chopped tomatoes
1/2 cup (125 g) low-fat plain yoghurt
1 teaspoon lemon juice

1 Combine the lamb, onion, garlic, ginger, chilli, garam masala, ground coriander, ground almonds and 1 teaspoon salt in a bowl. Shape into walnut-sized balls with your hands.
2 Heat a large non-stick frying pan and cook the koftas in batches until brown on both sides—they don't have to be cooked all the way through.
3 Meanwhile, to make the sauce, heat the oil in a saucepan over low heat. Add the onion and cook for 6–8 minutes, or until soft and golden. Add the curry paste and cook until fragrant. Add the chopped tomatoes and simmer for 5 minutes. Stir in the yoghurt (1 tablespoon at a time) and the lemon juice until combined.
4 Place the lamb koftas in the tomato sauce. Cook, covered, over low heat for 20 minutes. Serve over steamed rice and garnish with the chopped coriander.

NUTRITION PER SERVE
Protein 32.5 g; Fat 25.5 g; Carbohydrate 10.5 g; Dietary Fibre 5.5 g; Cholesterol 88 mg; 1675 kJ (400 Cal)

VEGETABLE TAGINE

A high-carbohydrate vegetarian recipe, this tagine provides good quantities of potassium and fibre.

Prep time: 25 minutes
Cooking time: 50 minutes
Serves 6
EASY

1/4 teaspoon saffron threads
100 ml olive oil
2 onions, thinly sliced
3 cloves garlic, crushed
2 thin carrots, cut into 5 mm slices
1 cinnamon stick
2 teaspoons ground cumin
1 teaspoon ground ginger
1/2 teaspoon ground turmeric
1/2 teaspoon cayenne pepper
300 g pumpkin, cut into 2 cm cubes
4 ripe tomatoes, peeled, seeded and quartered
400 g can chickpeas, rinsed and drained
1 litre vegetable stock
1 zucchini, halved lengthways and sliced
1/3 cup (55 g) raisins
1 cup (50 g) chopped fresh coriander leaves
500 g instant couscous
1 tablespoon olive oil
2 teaspoons low-fat margarine
2 tablespoons flaked almonds, toasted

1 Place the saffron threads in a frying pan over low heat. Dry-fry for 1 minute, or until darkened. Remove from the heat.
2 Heat 1/3 cup (80 ml) of the oil in a large flameproof casserole. Add the onion, garlic, carrot, cinnamon, cumin, ginger, turmeric, cayenne and saffron. Cook over medium–low heat, stirring often, for 10 minutes. Add the pumpkin, tomato and chickpeas, and stir to coat. Add half the stock, bring to the boil, then reduce the heat and simmer, covered, for 10 minutes. Stir in the zucchini, raisins and half the coriander. Cover and simmer for 20 minutes.
3 Bring the remaining stock to the boil in a large saucepan. Place the couscous in a heatproof bowl and add the remaining oil and hot stock. Cover and leave for 5 minutes, then fluff the grains with a fork. Stir in the margarine and season.
4 Spoon the couscous onto a large serving platter. Spoon the vegetables and sauce on top and sprinkle with the almonds and the remaining coriander. Serve at once.

NUTRITION PER SERVE
Protein 19.5 g; Fat 20 g; Carbohydrate 86.5 g; Dietary Fibre 7 g; Cholesterol 0 mg; 2525 kJ (605 Cal)

BEEF BOURGUIGNON

This nourishing and comforting meal is perfect for cold winter nights. It is an excellent source of protein, iron, zinc and niacin.

Prep time: 10 minutes
Cooking time: 2 hours
Serves 4–6
EASY

1 kg topside or round steak
plain flour, seasoned with salt and pepper
3 rashers bacon, rind removed
oil, for cooking
12 pickling onions
1 cup (250 ml) red wine
2 cups (500 ml) beef stock
1 teaspoon dried thyme
200 g button mushrooms
2 bay leaves

1 Trim the steak of fat and sinew, and cut it into 2 cm cubes. Lightly toss the beef in the seasoned flour, shaking off the excess.
2 Cut the bacon into 2 cm squares. Heat some oil in a large pan and quickly cook the bacon over medium heat. Remove the bacon from the pan, then add the meat and brown well in batches. Remove and set aside. Add the onions to the pan and cook until golden.
3 Return the bacon and meat to the pan with the remaining ingredients. Bring to the boil, then reduce the heat and simmer, covered, for 1 1/2 hours, or until the meat is very tender, stirring occasionally. Remove the bay leaves to serve. Serve with mashed potato and steamed green beans.

NUTRITION PER SERVE (6)
Protein 40 g; Fat 7 g; Carbohydrate 5 g; Dietary Fibre 1 g; Cholesterol 90 mg; 1150 kJ (275 Cal)

DHAL

This well-known vegetarian dish is based on highly nutritious lentils, combining them with aromatic herbs and spices for a filling meal that provides protein, slow-release starch, fibre, flavonoids and iron. Dhal is a great choice for people with diabetes or high blood cholesterol.

Prep time: 15 minutes
Cooking time: 35 minutes
Serves 4–6
EASY

200 g red lentils
4 cm piece fresh ginger, cut into 3 slices
1/2 teaspoon ground turmeric
1 tablespoon ghee or oil
2 cloves garlic, crushed
1 onion, finely chopped
1/2 teaspoon yellow mustard seeds
pinch of asafoetida, optional
1 teaspoon cumin seeds
1 teaspoon ground coriander
2 green chillies, halved lengthways
2 tablespoons lemon juice
1 tablespoon chopped fresh coriander leaves

1 Place the lentils and 3 cups (750 ml) water in a saucepan, and bring to the boil. Reduce the heat, add the ginger and turmeric, and simmer, covered, for 20 minutes, or until the lentils are tender. Stir occasionally to prevent the lentils sticking to the pan. Remove the ginger and stir in 1/2 teaspoon salt.

2 Heat the ghee in a frying pan, add the garlic, onion and mustard seeds, and cook over medium heat for 5 minutes, or until the onion is golden. Add the asafoetida, cumin seeds, ground coriander and chilli, and cook for 2 minutes.

3 Add the onion mixture to the lentils and stir gently to combine. Add 1/2 cup (125 ml) water, reduce the heat to low and cook for 5 minutes. Stir in the lemon juice and season with salt and pepper. Sprinkle with the coriander.

NUTRITION PER SERVE (6)
Protein 8.5 g; Fat 3.5 g; Carbohydrate 13 g; Dietary Fibre 5 g; Cholesterol 8 mg; 505 kJ (120 Cal)

Chicken and apricot curry (top), and Chilli con carne

CHICKEN AND APRICOT CURRY

The apricots add fibre, beta-carotene and a sweet taste to enrich the flavour of this aromatic curry.

Prep time: 40 minutes + 1 hour soaking
Cooking time: 1 hour 10 minutes
Serves 6–8
EASY

18 dried apricots
1 tablespoon ghee
2 x 1.5 kg chickens, jointed
3 onions, thinly sliced
1 teaspoon grated fresh ginger
3 cloves garlic, crushed
3 large green chillies, seeded and finely chopped
1 teaspoon cumin seeds
1 teaspoon chilli powder
1/2 teaspoon ground turmeric
4 cardamom pods, bruised
4 large tomatoes, peeled and cut into eighths

1 Soak the dried apricots in 1 cup (250 ml) hot water for 1 hour.
2 Melt the ghee in a large saucepan, add the chicken in batches and cook over high heat for 5–6 minutes, or until browned. Remove from the pan. Add the onion and cook, stirring often, for 10 minutes, or until the onion is soft and golden brown.
3 Add the ginger, garlic and green chilli, and cook, stirring, for 2 minutes. Stir in the cumin seeds, chilli powder and ground turmeric, and cook for a further 1 minute.
4 Return the chicken to the pan, add the cardamom, tomato and apricots, with any remaining liquid, and mix well. Simmer, covered, for 35 minutes, or until the chicken is tender.
5 Remove the chicken, cover and keep warm. Bring the liquid to the boil and boil rapidly, uncovered, for 5 minutes, or until it has thickened slightly. To serve, spoon the liquid over the chicken. Serve with steamed rice mixed with raisins, grated carrot and toasted flaked almonds.

NUTRITION PER SERVE (8)
Protein 43 g; Fat 19.5 g; Carbohydrate 11.5 g; Dietary Fibre 3.5 g; Cholesterol 197.5 mg; 1655 kJ (395 Cal)

CHILLI CON CARNE

The kidney beans in this dish add phytochemicals, starch and fibre to a meal rich in protein and iron.

Prep time: 15 minutes
Cooking time: 1 hour 10 minutes
Serves 6
EASY

2 teaspoons olive oil
1 large onion, chopped
1 clove garlic, crushed
1 teaspoon cayenne pepper
2 teaspoons paprika
1 teaspoon dried oregano
2 teaspoons ground cumin
750 g extra lean beef mince
1 1/2 cups (375 ml) beef stock
400 g can diced tomatoes
1/2 cup (125 g) tomato paste
300 g can kidney beans, drained and rinsed
fresh parsley sprigs, to garnish

1 Heat the oil in a saucepan over low heat. Add the onion and cook for 4–5 minutes, or until soft. Stir in the garlic, cayenne pepper, paprika, oregano, cumin and 1/2 teaspoon salt. Increase the heat to medium, add the minced beef and cook for 5–8 minutes, or until just browned.
2 Reduce the heat to low and add the stock, tomato and tomato paste. Cook for 35–45 minutes, stirring frequently.
3 Stir in the kidney beans and simmer for 10 minutes. Serve the chilli con carne on its own in small bowls or over rice. Garnish with a sprig of parsley.

NUTRITION PER SERVE
Protein 30 g; Fat 11 g; Carbohydrate 12 g; Dietary Fibre 4.5 g; Cholesterol 63.5 mg; 1125 kJ (270 Cal)

CHILLI BEANS WITH POLENTA

This vegetarian recipe contains ingredients from four different food groups to provide complete protein. It is also rich in filling fibre and starch, with good amounts of most minerals, niacin, folate and vitamin A.

Prep time: 20 minutes
Cooking time: 45 minutes
Serves 6
EASY

420 g can creamed corn
1 1/2 cups (375 ml) vegetable stock
1/2 cup (75 g) instant polenta
310 g can corn kernels, drained
1/3 cup (40 g) grated low-fat vintage Cheddar
1/4 cup (15 g) chopped fresh coriander leaves
1 tablespoon olive oil
1 red onion, sliced
2 cloves garlic, crushed
1 teaspoon chilli powder
1 teaspoon paprika
1 tablespoon ground cumin
1 teaspoon ground coriander

400 g can kidney beans, rinsed and drained
400 g can borlotti beans, rinsed and drained
800 g can tomatoes
2 tablespoons tomato paste

1 Line a 20 cm round cake tin with plastic wrap. Place the creamed corn and stock in a saucepan, and bring to the boil. Stir in the polenta and corn kernels, and cook over medium heat until it comes away from the side of the pan. Stir in the cheese and 1 tablespoon of the coriander, and place the polenta in the tin. Cool, then cut into wedges.
2 Heat the oil in a large saucepan, add the onion, garlic and spices, and cook until soft. Stir in the beans, tomato and tomato paste. Simmer for 20 minutes. Stir in the remaining coriander leaves. Serve with the polenta wedges.

NUTRITION PER SERVE
Protein 16 g; Fat 7 g; Carbohydrate 43 g; Dietary Fibre 16 g; Cholesterol 5 mg; 1255 kJ (300 Cal)

BEEF STROGANOFF

A reduced-fat version of the traditional favourite, this dish has less fat but all the flavour. It is an excellent source of protein, potassium, iron and zinc.

Prep time: 20 minutes
Cooking time: 25 minutes
Serves 4
EASY

500 g rump steak
cooking oil spray
1 onion, sliced
1/4 teaspoon paprika
250 g button mushrooms, halved
2 tablespoons tomato paste
1/2 cup (125 ml) beef stock
1/2 cup (125 ml) low-fat light evaporated milk
3 teaspoons cornflour
chopped fresh parsley, for serving

1 Remove any excess fat from the steak and slice into thin strips. Cook in batches in a large, lightly greased non-stick frying pan over high heat, until just cooked. Remove from the pan.

2 Lightly spray the pan and cook the onion, paprika and mushrooms over medium heat until the onion has softened. Add the meat, tomato paste, stock and 1/2 cup (125 ml) water. Bring to the boil, then reduce the heat and simmer for 10 minutes.

3 In a small bowl, mix the evaporated milk with the cornflour. Add to the pan and stir until the sauce boils and thickens. Season well and sprinkle with parsley. Delicious over pasta.

NUTRITION PER SERVE
Protein 35 g; Fat 4 g; Carbohydrate 8 g; Dietary Fibre 2.5 g; Cholesterol 85 mg; 900 kJ (215 Cal)

BURMESE PORK CURRY

This dish is a good source of iron, zinc and B vitamins, particularly niacin. The spices add flavour and some minerals, but few calories.

Prep time: 30 minutes
Cooking time: 1 hour
Serves 6
EASY

2 stems lemon grass, white part only, sliced
1 red onion, chopped
1 clove garlic
1 teaspoon grated fresh ginger
2 large dried red chillies
1 teaspoon fenugreek seeds, roasted and ground
1 teaspoon yellow mustard seeds, roasted and ground
2 teaspoons paprika
2 tablespoons Worcestershire sauce
750 g lean boneless shoulder pork, cut into 2.5 cm cubes
2 tablespoons fish sauce
6 new potatoes, peeled and sliced
2 small red onions, diced
2 tablespoons oil
2 tablespoons mango chutney

1 Place the lemon grass, onion, garlic, ginger, chillies, fenugreek seeds, yellow mustard seeds, paprika and Worcestershire sauce in a food processor or blender, and process to a thick paste.
2 Place the pork in a bowl, sprinkle with the fish sauce and 1/4 teaspoon ground black pepper, and toss to coat.
3 Place the potato and onion in another bowl, add 1/4 cup (70 g) of the paste and toss to coat. Add the remaining paste to the pork mixture and mix well.
4 Heat 1 tablespoon oil in a saucepan or wok over medium heat. Add the pork mixture and cook in batches, stirring, for 8 minutes, or until the meat begins to brown. Add more oil as necessary. Remove from the pan. Add the potato and onion, and cook, stirring, for 5 minutes, or until soft and starting to brown.
5 Return the meat to the saucepan and add 3 cups (750 ml) water, 1 cup (250 ml) at a time, stirring after each addition. Stir in the mango chutney, then reduce the heat and simmer for 30 minutes, or until the meat and potatoes are tender.

NUTRITION PER SERVE
Protein 28 g; Fat 11.5 g; Carbohydrate 14.5 g; Dietary Fibre 2 g; Cholesterol 74 mg; 1160 kJ (275 Cal)

MADRAS BEEF CURRY

This popular Indian curry is rich in protein, zinc, niacin, potassium and phosphorus.

Prep time: 20 minutes
Cooking time: 1 hour 45 minutes
Serves 6
EASY

---

1 tablespoon vegetable oil
2 onions, finely chopped
3 cloves garlic, finely chopped
1 tablespoon grated fresh ginger
4 tablespoons madras curry paste
1 kg lean chuck steak, trimmed and cut
    into 3 cm cubes
1/4 cup (60 g) tomato paste
1 cup (250 ml) beef stock
6 new potatoes, halved
1 cup (155 g) frozen peas

1 Preheat the oven to moderate 180°C (350°F/Gas 4). Heat the oil in a large heavy-based 3 litre flameproof casserole dish. Cook the onion over medium heat for 4–5 minutes. Add the garlic and ginger, and cook, stirring, for a further 5 minutes, or until the onion is lightly golden, taking care not to burn it.

2 Add the curry paste and cook, stirring, for 2 minutes, or until fragrant. Increase the heat to high, add the meat and stir constantly for 2–3 minutes, or until the meat is well coated. Add the tomato paste and stock, and stir well.

3 Bake, covered, for 50 minutes, stirring 2–3 times during cooking, and add a little water if necessary. Reduce the oven to warm 160°C (315°F/Gas 2–3). Add the potato and cook for 30 minutes, then add the peas and cook for another 10 minutes, or until the potato is tender. Serve hot with steamed jasmine rice.

NUTRITION PER SERVE
Protein 39.5 g; Fat 13 g; Carbohydrate 15 g; Dietary Fibre 5.5 g; Cholesterol 112 mg; 1410 kJ (335 Cal)

ROGAN JOSH

The exotic blend of spices and herbs in this dish adds some minerals and phytochemicals, while the lamb provides protein, niacin, iron and zinc.

Prep time: 25 minutes
Cooking time: 1 hour 40 minutes
Serves 4–6
EASY

---

1 tablespoon or oil
2 onions, chopped
1/2 cup (125 g) low-fat plain yoghurt
1 teaspoon chilli powder
1 tablespoon ground coriander
2 teaspoons ground cumin
1 teaspoon ground cardamom
1/2 teaspoon ground cloves
1 teaspoon ground turmeric
3 cloves garlic, crushed
1 tablespoon grated fresh ginger
400 g can chopped tomatoes
1 kg boned leg of lamb, trimmed, cubed
1/4 cup (30 g) slivered almonds
1 teaspoon garam masala
chopped fresh coriander leaves, to garnish

1 Heat the oil in a large saucepan, add the onion and cook, stirring, for 5 minutes, or until soft. Stir in the yoghurt, chilli powder, coriander, cumin, cardamom, cloves, turmeric, garlic and ginger. Add the tomato and 1 teaspoon salt, and simmer for 5 minutes.
2 Add the lamb and stir until coated. Cover and cook over low heat, stirring occasionally, for 1–11/2 hours, or until the lamb is tender. Uncover and simmer until the liquid thickens.
3 Meanwhile, dry-fry the almonds over medium heat for 3–4 minutes, shaking the pan gently, until the nuts are golden brown. Remove from the pan at once.
4 Add the garam masala to the curry and mix through well. Sprinkle the slivered almonds and coriander leaves over the top.

NUTRITION PER SERVE (6)
Protein 58.5 g; Fat 22 g; Carbohydrate 7 g; Dietary Fibre 2.5 g; Cholesterol 172.5 mg; 1915 kJ (460 Cal)

PRAWN CURRY

This quickly prepared seafood dish provides niacin and small to moderate amounts of most minerals, including selenium and iodine. Serve the curry with rice for extra carbohydrate, fibre and B vitamins.

Prep time: 25 minutes
Cooking time: 15 minutes
Serves 4–6
EASY

---

50 g butter
1 onion, finely chopped
1 clove garlic, crushed
11/2 tablespoons curry powder
2 tablespoons plain flour
2 cups (500 ml) reduced-fat milk
1 kg raw medium prawns, peeled and deveined
11/2 tablespoons lemon juice
2 teaspoons sherry, optional
1 tablespoon finely chopped fresh parsley

1 Heat the butter in a large saucepan. Add the onion and garlic, and cook for 5 minutes, or until softened. Add the curry powder and cook for 1 minute, then stir in the flour and cook for a further 1 minute.
2 Remove from the heat and stir in the milk until smooth. Return to the heat and stir constantly until the sauce has thickened. Simmer for 2 minutes and then stir in the prawns. Continue to simmer for 5 minutes, or until the prawns are just cooked.
3 Stir in the lemon juice, sherry and parsley, and serve immediately with rice.

NUTRITION PER SERVE (6)
Protein 38 g; Fat 12 g; Carbohydrate 9 g; Dietary Fibre 1.5 g; Cholesterol 280 mg; 1245 kJ (300 Cal)

Rogan Josh (top), and Prawn curry

CASSEROLES AND BAKES

Some of the simplest meals are the ones you pop into the oven and forget about until dinner time. This chapter contains some healthier versions of traditional favourites.

CASSEROLES

A casserole is very similar to a stew, the main difference being that a casserole is cooked in a covered dish in the oven, while a stew is cooked on the stove. Types of casseroles include Asian-style claypot dishes, braised dishes and hotpots. Casseroling can be a healthy method of cooking as the ingredients are slowly cooked in a liquid, which helps retain more vitamins and minerals than frying or boiling.

Casseroles usually contain a number of ingredients, including meat, poultry, seafood, vegetables and herbs, and are a great way to increase the variety of healthy foods you eat. The only fat that is needed in the cooking process is for the initial sautéing and browning.

Healthy casserole tips

■ Use a casserole dish with a non-stick surface or, if you don't have one of these, first sauté the ingredients to brown them in a heavy-based non-stick frying pan, then transfer them to your casserole dish. Use only a light spray of olive or canola oil when sautéing.

■ Make sure the pan is hot before you add the ingredients. This will ensure that the meat browns quickly and evenly, rather than stewing in its own juices.

■ If you are browning vegetables for a casserole and think you may need more oil, add a little water or vegetable stock instead. It will help the vegetables to soften as they cook, without burning.

■ When the casserole is ready, remove it from the oven and leave it for 10 minutes; then, using a metal spoon, carefully skim any fat that may have risen to the surface during cooking.

■ Add soaked dried legumes such as chickpeas, cannellini beans or lentils to your casserole for extra fibre and minerals.

■ Pot roasting is suitable for slowly cooking large cuts of meat until tender. It is suitable for beef topside or bolar blade. First brown the meat over high heat, then add some stock, cover and cook at a low to moderate heat in the oven. An hour before the meat is ready, add some vegetables to the casserole. The vegetables will complement all the delicious meat flavours, and you will have a simple, aromatic and healthy one-pot meal.

■ Casseroles with smaller pieces of meat will usually take between 1 and 2 hours to cook.

■ The oven temperature should be low enough for the casserole to cook at a gentle simmer.

Cuts of meat suitable for casseroling

- beef round
- beef topside
- beef blade
- beef bolar blade
- beef brisket
- beef skirt steak
- beef chuck
- beef spareribs
- beef silverside
- beef mince (for ragouts like bolognese)
- lamb leg
- lamb shoulder
- lamb shanks
- lamb chump chops
- lamb neck chops
- lamb forequarter chops
- veal osso buco
- pork belly
- pork silverside
- pork rump
- pork neck
- pork hock
- pork shoulder
- chicken thighs
- chicken drumsticks
- chicken wings

BAKES

Baking is a great way to cook simple, healthy meals with minimum fuss and effort. The intense application of heat means that only small amounts of fat are needed and this is usually to aid in browning meat and vegetables.

Bakes include roasted joints of meat or poultry and delicious oven-baked vegetables, pies, pizzas and lasagne. Once the initial preparation is done and the dish is in the oven, you can sit back, relax and enjoy the aroma.

Healthy baking tips

- Instead of coating the piece of meat with oil, just give it a light spray with olive oil.
- Lightly season the joint just before it goes into the oven. This will help it develop a crust and a wonderful flavour.
- When baking or roasting meats, sit them on a rack in a baking dish. This will enable the fat to drip off the meat, so there will be less fat in the meal.
- Use filo pastry for pies and tarts. You will need several layers, but only give every third or so layer a light spray with olive oil spray, rather than brushing every layer with butter. This will ensure that the pastry layers stick together, and also aids in browning.
- Use low-fat feta cheese or ricotta in quiches and tarts.
- To reduce the fat in a béchamel sauce for moussaka, use skim milk, low-fat ricotta and low-fat Cheddar cheese.
- Wrap fish fillets in baking paper with seasonings and bake them as a healthy and easy meal. Chop the ingredients finely and place them on the fish fillet or steak, add a squeeze of lemon juice and a little stock, and seal well. Bake for 10–12 minutes, or until the fish is cooked, and serve the wrapped fish on hot plates so it keeps its heat. The fish will steam in its own juices, giving a subtle flavour of the aromatic seasonings you have added, such as:
- spring onion, coriander and ginger
- lemon, anchovy and dill
- tomato, fennel, olives and parsley
- lime, chilli and mint.

Roast chicken (top), and Sweet potato strudel

ROAST CHICKEN

The combination of chicken and vegetables in this favourite family meal provides good amounts of protein, B vitamins, fibre, beta-carotene, folate, iron and zinc.

Prep time: 20 minutes
Cooking time: 1 hour 15 minutes
Serves 4
EASY

1.4 kg chicken
1 lemon, halved
6 cloves garlic, unpeeled
6 fresh thyme sprigs
4 potatoes, chopped
250 g orange sweet potato, chopped
300 g butternut pumpkin, chopped
olive oil spray
2 tablespoons plain flour
1 tablespoon Dijon mustard
1 1/2 cups (375 ml) chicken stock

1 Preheat the oven to moderately hot 200°C (400°F/Gas 6). Season the chicken and place the lemon in the cavity. Place the chicken in a baking dish and arrange the garlic, thyme and vegetables around it.
2 Lightly spray the chicken and vegetables with olive oil, and bake for 1 hour, or until the chicken is tender and the juices run clear. Turn the chicken and vegetables after 30 minutes.
3 Transfer the chicken and vegetables, except the garlic, to separate plates, cover and keep warm.
4 Peel the garlic, return to the pan and mash with a fork. Add the flour and cook over medium heat, stirring, until golden. Remove from the heat and stir in the mustard and stock. Return to the heat and stir until the gravy boils and thickens. Carve the chicken and serve with the gravy, vegetables and green beans.

NUTRITION PER SERVE
Protein 37 g; Fat 9.5 g; Carbohydrate 35 g; Dietary Fibre 6 g; Cholesterol 136 mg; 1614 kJ (385 Cal)

SWEET POTATO STRUDEL

The variety of ingredients in this easy dish delivers good amounts of monounsaturated fat and fibre.

Prep time: 25 minutes
Cooking time: 1 hour 5 minutes
Serves 6
EASY

---

250 g orange sweet potato, cut into 2 cm cubes
2 tablespoons olive oil
3 cloves garlic, unpeeled
250 g English spinach, blanched and excess
    moisture squeezed out, roughly chopped
1/4 cup (40 g) pine nuts, toasted
125 g low-fat feta, crumbled
3 spring onions, including green part, chopped
50 g black olives, pitted and sliced
1/4 cup (15 g) chopped fresh basil
1 tablespoon chopped fresh rosemary
8 sheets filo pastry
2 tablespoons sesame seeds

1 Preheat the oven to moderate 180°C (350°F/Gas 4). Place the sweet potato in a roasting tin and brush lightly with oil. Add the garlic and roast for 30 minutes, or until the sweet potato is soft. Cool slightly.
2 Combine the sweet potato, spinach, pine nuts, feta, spring onion, olives, basil and rosemary. Peel the garlic cloves and roughly chop the flesh, then add to the sweet potato mixture, and season.
3 Cover the pastry with a damp tea towel to prevent it drying out. Lay the pastry out in front of you, in a stack, and brush every second layer with the remaining oil. Spread the filling in the centre of the pastry, covering an area 10 x 30 cm. Fold in the shorter ends of the pastry. Fold the long side closest to you over the filling, then carefully roll up. Place the strudel on a greased baking tray, seam-side down. Brush with any remaining oil and sprinkle with sesame seeds. Bake for 35 minutes, or until crisp and golden. Serve warm.

NUTRITION PER SERVE
Protein 11 g; Fat 15.5 g; Carbohydrate 19 g; Dietary Fibre 3.5 g; Cholesterol 12.5 mg; 1080 kJ (260 Cal)

MOUSSAKA

This reduced-fat version of a popular Mediterranean dish contains good amounts of many nutrients, including B vitamins, folate, vitamin A, fibre, potassium, calcium, iron and zinc. Serve the moussaka with crusty grain bread and salad for a complete meal.

Prep time: 30 minutes + 20 minutes standing
Cooking time: 1 hour 30 minutes
Serves 6
MEDIUM

1 kg eggplants
cooking oil spray
400 g lean lamb mince
2 onions, finely chopped
2 cloves garlic, crushed
400 g can tomatoes
1 tablespoon chopped fresh thyme
1 teaspoon chopped fresh oregano
1 tablespoon tomato paste
1/3 cup (80 ml) dry white wine
1 bay leaf
1 teaspoon sugar

Cheese sauce
1 1/4 cups (315 ml) skim milk
2 tablespoons plain flour
1/4 cup (30 g) grated reduced-fat Cheddar
1 cup (250 g) ricotta
pinch of cayenne pepper
1/4 teaspoon ground nutmeg

1 Cut the eggplant into 1 cm thick slices, place in a colander over a large bowl, layering with a generous sprinkling of salt, and leave to stand for 20 minutes. This is to draw out the bitter juices.
2 Lightly spray a non-stick frying pan with oil and brown the lamb mince, in batches if necessary, over medium-high heat. Remove the meat from the pan.
3 Spray the pan again with oil, add the onion and stir continuously for 2 minutes. Add 1 tablespoon water to the pan to prevent sticking. Add the garlic and cook for about 3 minutes, or until the onion is golden brown.
4 Push the undrained tomatoes through

a sieve, then discard the solids.
5 Return the meat to the pan with the onion. Add the herbs, tomato pulp, tomato paste, wine, bay leaf and sugar. Cover and simmer over low heat for 20 minutes. Preheat a grill.
6 Thoroughly rinse and pat dry the eggplant, place on a grill tray, spray lightly with oil and grill under a hot grill until golden brown. Turn over, spray lightly with oil and grill until golden brown. Arrange half the eggplant slices over the base of a 1.5 litre baking dish. Top with half the meat mixture and then repeat the layers.
7 Preheat the oven to moderate 180°C (350°F/Gas 4). To make the cheese sauce, blend a little of the milk with the flour to form a paste in a small pan. Gradually blend in the remaining milk, stirring constantly over low heat until the milk starts to simmer and thicken. Remove from the heat and stir in the Cheddar, ricotta, cayenne and nutmeg. Pour the sauce over the moussaka and bake for 35–40 minutes, or until the cheese is golden brown and the moussaka is heated through.

NUTRITION PER SERVE
Protein 25 g; Fat 11 g; Carbohydrate 15 g; Dietary Fibre 5 g; Cholesterol 70 mg; 1110 kJ (265 Cal)

NOTE: The moussaka can be frozen for up to 2 months. Thaw it in the fridge, then reheat it in a moderate oven for 30–45 minutes.

VEGETABLE QUICHE

This colourful, reduced-fat quiche provides
vitamin A, B vitamins, potassium and calcium.

Prep time: 45 minutes + 25 minutes refrigeration
Cooking time: 2 hours 30 minutes
Serves 6
EASY

1 large potato
400 g pumpkin
200 g orange sweet potato
2 large parsnips
1 red capsicum
2 onions, cut into wedges
6 cloves garlic, halved
2 teaspoons olive oil
1 1/4 cups (155 g) plain flour
40 g butter
45 g ricotta
1 cup (250 ml) skim milk
3 eggs, lightly beaten
1/4 cup (30 g) grated reduced-fat Cheddar
2 tablespoons chopped fresh basil

1 Preheat the oven to moderate 180°C
(350°F/Gas 4). Lightly spray a 23 cm
loose-based flan tin with oil. Cut the
vegetables into chunks, place in a baking
dish with the onion and garlic, and drizzle
with the oil. Season and bake for 1 hour,
or until tender. Leave to cool.
2 Mix the flour, butter and ricotta in a
food processor, then gradually add up to
3 tablespoons of the milk to form a soft
dough. Turn out onto a lightly floured
surface and gather together into a smooth
ball. Cover and refrigerate for 15 minutes.
3 Roll the pastry out on a lightly floured
surface, then ease it into the tin. Trim
the edge and refrigerate for 10 minutes.
Increase the oven to 200°C (400°F/Gas 6).
Cover the pastry with crumpled baking
paper and fill with baking beads or rice.
Bake for 10 minutes, remove the beads
and paper, then bake for 10 minutes.
4 Place the vegetables in the pastry and
pour in the combined remaining milk, egg,
cheese and basil. Reduce the oven to 180°C
(350°F/Gas 4). Bake for 1 hour 10 minutes,
or until set. Leave in the tin for 5 minutes.

NUTRITION PER SERVE
Protein 14.5 g; Fat 11.5 g; Carbohydrate 40.5 g; Dietary
Fibre 5 g; Cholesterol 126 mg; 1360 kJ (325 Cal)

MEATLOAF

Meatloaf is a great way to encourage children to eat meat and vegetables. It is an excellent source of niacin, vitamin B12, potassium, iron and zinc.

Prep time: 15 minutes
Cooking time: 1 hour 30 minutes
Serves 6
EASY

---

cooking oil spray
2 onions, finely chopped
2 cloves garlic, crushed
1 1/2 cups (120 g) fresh breadcrumbs
60 g pumpkin, coarsely grated
1 carrot, coarsely grated
2 tablespoons chopped fresh parsley
500 g extra-lean beef mince
2 tablespoons Worcestershire sauce
1 teaspoon dried basil
1 tablespoon tomato paste
1 egg, lightly beaten
90 g button mushrooms, thinly sliced

Tomato sauce
400 g can tomatoes
1 tablespoon dry white wine
2 teaspoons soft brown sugar

1 Preheat the oven to moderately hot 200°C (400°F/Gas 6). Lightly spray a non-stick frying pan with oil, heat and cook the onion, stirring, for 2 minutes. Add 1 tablespoon water, then add the garlic and stir for 3 minutes, or until the onion is golden brown. Allow to cool.
2 Use your hands to thoroughly mix together the breadcrumbs, pumpkin, carrot, parsley, mince, Worcestershire sauce, basil, tomato paste and the cooled onion mixture. Mix in the egg and mushrooms. Season. Transfer to a 10 x 18 cm non-stick loaf tin, pressing gently into the tin and smoothing the top.
3 To make the tomato sauce, push the undrained tomatoes through a sieve, discarding the solids. Stir in the wine and sugar. Spoon 3 tablespoons of sauce over the meatloaf and bake for 15 minutes. Spoon another 3 tablespoons of sauce over the meatloaf, reduce the oven to 190°C (375°F/Gas 5) and bake for 1 hour 10 minutes, basting occasionally with sauce. Slice and serve with any remaining sauce.

NUTRITION PER SERVE
Protein 22 g; Fat 7.5 g; Carbohydrate 18.5 g; Dietary Fibre 3 g; Cholesterol 74 mg; 975 kJ (235 Cal)

VEAL CUTLETS IN CHILLI TOMATO SAUCE

Served with a spicy tomato sauce, this veal dish is a perfect choice for winter nights. It provides good-quality protein, B vitamins, folate, potassium, iron and zinc. Serve the cutlets with a carbohydrate-rich food and some vegetables for a balanced meal.

Prep time: 35 minutes
Cooking time: 35 minutes
Serves 4
MEDIUM

―――

5 slices wholemeal bread
3 tablespoons fresh parsley
3 cloves garlic
4 thick veal cutlets, trimmed
1/4 cup (60 ml) skim milk
2 teaspoons olive oil
1 onion, finely chopped
1 tablespoon capers, drained
1 teaspoon canned green peppercorns, chopped
1 teaspoon chopped red chilli
2 tablespoons balsamic vinegar
1 teaspoon soft brown sugar
2 tablespoons tomato paste
440 g can chopped tomatoes

1 Preheat the oven to moderate 180°C (350°F/Gas 4). Place a rack in a small baking dish. Chop the bread, parsley and garlic in a food processor to make fine breadcrumbs.
2 Season the cutlets on both sides with salt and black pepper. Pour the milk into a bowl and put the breadcrumbs on a plate. Dip the veal in the milk, then coat in the crumbs, pressing the crumbs on. Transfer to the rack and bake for 20 minutes.
3 Meanwhile, heat the oil in a small pan over medium heat. Add the onion, capers, peppercorns and chilli, cover and cook for 8 minutes. Stir in the vinegar, sugar and tomato paste, and stir until boiling. Stir in the tomato, reduce the heat and simmer for 15 minutes, then season.
4 Remove the cutlets from the rack and wipe the dish. Place about three-quarters of the tomato sauce in the base and put the cutlets on top. Spoon the remaining sauce over the cutlets and return to the oven. Reduce the oven to slow 150°C (300°F/Gas 2), then bake for another 10 minutes, or until heated through. Sprinkle with extra chopped parsley.

NUTRITION PER SERVE
Protein 24.5 g; Fat 6 g; Carbohydrate 23.5 g; Dietary Fibre 5.5 g; Cholesterol 70 mg; 1035 kJ (250 Cal)

SMOKED SALMON PIZZAS

Topped with cheese and salmon, these reduced-fat pizzas provide calcium, zinc, iodine, some vitamin A and B vitamins.

Prep time: 20 minutes
Cooking time: 15 minutes
Serves 6
EASY

―――

250 g ricotta
6 small oval pitta breads
125 g sliced smoked salmon
1 small red onion, sliced
1 tablespoon baby capers
small fresh dill sprigs, to garnish
1 lemon, cut into thin wedges, to serve

1 Preheat the oven to moderate 180°C (350°F/Gas 4). Put the ricotta in a bowl, season well with salt and cracked pepper, and stir until smooth. Spread the ricotta over the breads, leaving a border.
2 Top each pizza with some smoked salmon slices, then some onion pieces. Scatter baby capers over the top and bake on a baking tray for 15 minutes, or until the bases are slightly crispy around the edges. Garnish with a few dill sprigs and serve with lemon wedges.

NUTRITION PER SERVE
Protein 13 g; Fat 6.5 g; Carbohydrate 24 g; Dietary Fibre 1.5 g; Cholesterol 30 mg; 875 kJ (110 Cal)

Veal cutlets in chilli tomato sauce (top), and Smoked salmon pizzas

CHICKEN WITH BAKED EGGPLANT AND TOMATO

This colourful, hearty meal provides protein, B vitamins and antioxidants.

Prep time: 30 minutes
Cooking time: 1 hour 30 minutes
Serves 4
EASY

---

1 red capsicum
1 eggplant
3 tomatoes, cut into quarters
200 g large button mushrooms, halved
1 onion, cut into thin wedges
cooking oil spray
1¹/2 tablespoons tomato paste
¹/2 cup (125 ml) chicken stock
¹/4 cup (60 ml) white wine
2 lean bacon rashers
4 chicken breast fillets (500 g), trimmed
4 small sprigs fresh rosemary

1 Preheat the oven to moderately hot 200°C (400°F/Gas 6). Cut the capsicum and eggplant into bite-sized pieces and combine with the tomato, mushrooms and onion in a baking dish. Spray with oil and bake for 1 hour, or until starting to brown and soften, stirring once.

2 Pour the combined tomato paste, chicken stock and wine into the dish, and bake for 10 minutes, or until thickened.

3 Meanwhile, discard the fat and rind from the bacon and cut in half. Wrap a strip around each chicken breast and secure it underneath with a toothpick. Poke a sprig of fresh rosemary underneath the bacon. Pan-fry in a non-stick frying pan sprayed with oil, over medium heat, until golden on both sides. Cover and cook for 10–15 minutes, or until the chicken is tender and cooked through. Remove the toothpicks. Serve the chicken on the vegetable mixture, surrounded with the sauce.

NUTRITION PER SERVE
Protein 36 g; Fat 10.5 g; Carbohydrate 8 g; Dietary Fibre 5 g; Cholesterol 95 mg; 1190 kJ (285 Cal)

BAKED FLATHEAD

Flathead is relatively low in calories, yet with its high protein content it makes a filling meal. The combination of fish and olive oil provides monounsaturated fat and essential fatty acids.

Prep time: 15 minutes
Cooking time: 30 minutes
Serves 4
EASY

2 baby fennel bulbs (about 300 g),
　　trimmed and thinly sliced
1 clove garlic, thinly sliced
1 tablespoon chopped fresh dill
1/4 cup (60 ml) olive oil
2 tablespoons lemon juice
1 large flathead (about 1.25 kg), gutted
　　and head removed
small fresh dill sprigs, to garnish
small fresh parsley sprigs, to garnish
lemon wedges, to serve

1 Place the fennel in a bowl with the garlic, dill, oil and lemon juice. Season well with salt and ground black pepper.
2 Preheat the oven to moderate 180°C (350°F/Gas 4). Cut a piece of baking paper 5 cm longer than the fish. Cut a large strip of baking paper wide enough to support the main body of the fish and long enough to wrap around it. Place the strip vertically down the centre of a large baking tray, then place the other piece horizontally over the top, forming a cross. Place the fish in the centre of the baking paper and spoon the fennel mixture into its cavity and over the top. Fold the top and bottom ends of paper over the fish, then fold the sides in about 2 cm, securing with staples. Fold the side ends over the top of the fish and secure with staples. Bake for 30 minutes, or until the flesh flakes easily when tested with a fork.
3 Place the parcel on a warm serving platter and cut a hole in the top. Fold the edges back to expose the fish. Sprinkle with the sprigs of dill and parsley and serve with lemon wedges.

NUTRITION PER SERVE
Protein 40.5 g; Fat 12 g; Carbohydrate 3 g; Dietary Fibre 2.5 g; Cholesterol 107 mg; 1190 kJ (285 Cal)

STUFFED SQUID

This seafood dish provides unsaturated fat, essential fatty acids and vitamins A, B, C and E.

Prep time: 30 minutes
Cooking time: 1 hour 30 minutes
Serves 4
MEDIUM

1/2 cup (100 g) long-grain rice
1 tablespoon olive oil
4 spring onions, chopped
4 cloves garlic, crushed
1/4 cup (40 g) pine nuts
50 g currants
2 tablespoons chopped fresh parsley
2 teaspoons finely grated lemon rind
2 teaspoons lemon juice
1 onion, sliced
1 bird's eye chilli, chopped
2 teaspoons paprika
1/2 cup (125 ml) white wine
2 x 420 g cans crushed tomatoes
1 fresh bay leaf
1/4 cup (7 g) chopped fresh flat-leaf parsley
8 small–medium (450 g) cleaned squid hoods

1 Cook the rice in a large saucepan of boiling water for 12 minutes, stirring occasionally. Drain and cool.

2 Heat 1 teaspoon of the oil in a saucepan. Cook the spring onion and half the garlic over low heat for 1–2 minutes, or until softened. Add the rice, pine nuts, currants, parsley, lemon rind and juice, and season. Remove from the pan and cool.

3 Heat the remaining oil in a heavy-based saucepan. Cook the onion over low heat for 6–8 minutes, or until soft and golden. Add the chilli and remaining garlic, and cook for 1 minute. Add the paprika and cook for 1 minute. Add the wine and cook for 2 minutes, or until reduced by half. Add the tomato and bay leaf, bring to the boil, then reduce the heat and simmer for 30 minutes, stirring occasionally. Stir in the parsley, and season. Discard the bay leaf.

4 Preheat the oven to moderate 180°C (350°F/Gas 4). Spoon the rice into the squid hoods and secure with a toothpick. Place in an ovenproof ceramic dish and pour the sauce on top. Bake for 30 minutes.

NUTRITION PER SERVE
Protein 25 g; Fat 12.5 g; Carbohydrate 38 g; Dietary Fibre 6 g; Cholesterol 224 mg; 1615 kJ (385 Cal)

SHEPHERD'S PIE

This pie is an excellent way to feed children meat and potatoes. It provides plenty of carbohydrate, B vitamins, folate, beta-carotene, potassium, iron and zinc.

Prep time: 40 minutes
Cooking time: 40 minutes
Serves 4
EASY

cooking oil spray
2 onions, thinly sliced
1 large carrot, finely chopped
2 celery sticks, finely chopped
500 g lean lamb mince
2 tablespoons plain flour
2 tablespoons tomato paste
2 tablespoons Worcestershire sauce
1 beef or chicken stock cube
1.25 kg potatoes, chopped
1/2 cup (125 ml) skim milk
1/3 cup (20 g) finely chopped fresh parsley
paprika, to sprinkle

1 Lightly spray a large non-stick frying pan with oil and heat over medium heat. Stir the onion, carrot and celery constantly for 5 minutes, or until the vegetables begin to soften. Add 1 tablespoon water to prevent sticking. Remove from the pan and set aside. Spray the pan with a little more oil, add the lamb mince and cook over high heat until well browned.
2 Add the flour and stir for 2–3 minutes. Add the vegetables with the tomato paste, Worcestershire sauce, stock cube and 2 cups (500 ml) water. Slowly bring to the boil. Reduce the heat, cover and simmer for 20 minutes, stirring occasionally.
3 Meanwhile, steam or microwave the potatoes until tender. Drain and mash until smooth. Add the milk, season with salt and black pepper, then beat well.
4 Stir the parsley through the mince and season. Preheat a grill. Pour the mince into a 1.5 litre baking dish. Spoon the potato over the top, spreading evenly with the back of the spoon. Use a fork to roughen up the potato. Sprinkle with paprika and grill until golden, watching carefully because the potato browns quickly.

NUTRITION PER SERVE
Protein 36.5 g; Fat 9.5 g; Carbohydrate 54.5 g; Dietary Fibre 7.5 g; Cholesterol 87.5 mg; 1895 kJ (450 Cal)

CHICKEN PIES

With less fat than commercial pies, these are rich in beta-carotene, folate, potassium, phosphorus and protein.

Prep time: 50 minutes
Cooking time: 1 hour
Serves 4
DIFFICULT

300 g chicken breast fillet, trimmed of fat
1 bay leaf
2 cups (500 ml) chicken stock
2 large potatoes, chopped
250 g orange sweet potato, chopped
2 celery sticks, chopped
2 carrots, chopped
1 onion, chopped
1 parsnip, chopped
1 clove garlic, crushed
1 tablespoon cornflour
1 cup (250 ml) skim milk
1 cup (155 g) frozen peas, thawed
1 tablespoon chopped fresh chives
1 tablespoon chopped fresh parsley
1^{1}/2 cups (185 g) self-raising flour
20 g butter
^{1}/3 cup (80 ml) milk
1 egg, lightly beaten
^{1}/2 teaspoon sesame seeds

1 Combine the chicken, bay leaf and stock in a large, deep non-stick frying pan and simmer over low heat for 10 minutes, or until the chicken is cooked through. Remove the chicken, set aside and, when cool, cut into small pieces. Add the chopped potato, orange sweet potato, celery and carrot to the pan and simmer, covered, for about 10 minutes, until just tender. Remove the vegetables from the pan with a slotted spoon.

2 Add the onion, parsnip and garlic to the pan and simmer, uncovered, for about 10 minutes, or until very soft. Discard the bay leaf. Purée in the stock mixture in a food processor until smooth.

3 Stir the cornflour into 2 tablespoons of the skim milk until it forms a smooth paste, stir into the puréed mixture with the remaining milk and then return to the pan. Stir over low heat until the mixture boils and thickens. Preheat the oven to moderately hot 200°C (400°F/Gas 6).

4 Combine the puréed mixture with the cooked vegetables, peas, chicken and herbs. Season with salt and pepper. Spoon into four 440 ml ovenproof dishes.

5 To make the pastry, sift the flour into a large bowl, rub in the butter with your fingertips, then make a well in the centre. Combine the milk with ^{1}/3 cup (80 ml) water and add enough to the dry ingredients to make a soft dough. Turn out onto a lightly floured surface and knead until just smooth. Cut the dough into four portions and roll each out so that it is l cm larger than the top of the dish. Brush the edge of the dough with some of the egg and fit it over the top of each dish, pressing the edge firmly to seal.

6 Brush the pastry tops lightly with beaten egg and sprinkle with the sesame seeds. Bake for 30 minutes, or until the tops are golden and the filling is heated through.

NUTRITION PER SERVE
Protein 33 g; Fat 12 g; Carbohydrate 68.5 g; Dietary Fibre 8.5 g; Cholesterol 117.5 mg; 2170 kJ (520 Cal)

VEGETABLE CASSEROLE WITH DUMPLINGS

This casserole is suitable for vegetarians. It is an excellent source of fibre, B vitamins and folate.

Prep time: 30 minutes
Cooking time: 50 minutes
Serves 4
EASY

1 tablespoon olive oil
1 large onion, chopped
2 cloves garlic, crushed
2 teaspoons sweet paprika
1 large potato, chopped
1 large carrot, sliced
400 g can chopped tomatoes
1¹/2 cups (375 ml) vegetable stock
400 g orange sweet potato, cut into
    1.5 cm cubes
150 g broccoli, cut into florets
2 zucchini, thickly sliced
1 cup (125 g) self-raising flour
20 g chilled butter, cut into small cubes
2 teaspoons chopped fresh flat-leaf parsley
1 teaspoon fresh thyme
1 teaspoon chopped fresh rosemary
¹/3 cup (80 ml) milk
2 tablespoons reduced-fat sour cream

1 Heat the oil in a large saucepan and cook the onion over low heat, stirring occasionally, for 5 minutes, or until soft. Add the garlic and paprika, and cook, stirring, for 1 minute.

2 Add the potato, carrot, tomato and stock. Bring to the boil, then reduce the heat and simmer, covered, for 10 minutes. Add the sweet potato, broccoli and zucchini, and simmer for 10 minutes, or until tender. Preheat the oven to moderately hot 200°C (400°F/Gas 6).

3 Sift the flour and a pinch of salt into a bowl. Rub the butter into the flour with your fingertips until it resembles fine breadcrumbs. Stir in the herbs and make a well in the centre. Add the milk and mix with a flat-bladed knife, using a cutting action, until the mixture comes together in beads. Gather the dough and lift onto a lightly floured surface, then divide into 8 portions. Shape each portion into a ball.

4 Add the sour cream to the casserole and transfer to a 2 litre ovenproof dish. Top with the dumplings. Bake for 20 minutes, or until the dumplings are golden and a skewer comes out clean when inserted in the centre.

NUTRITION PER SERVE
Protein 12 g; Fat 13 g; Carbohydrate 51 g; Dietary Fibre 8.5 g; Cholesterol 22 mg; 1560 kJ (375 Cal)

MUSHROOM, RICOTTA AND OLIVE PIZZA

A lower-fat gourmet pizza, this recipe provides good amounts of fibre, B vitamins and folate.

Prep time: 30 minutes + proving
Cooking time: 1 hour
Serves 6
MEDIUM

4 Roma tomatoes, quartered
3/4 teaspoon caster sugar
7 g dry yeast or 15 g fresh yeast
1 3/4 cups (215 g) plain flour
1/2 cup (125 ml) skim milk, warmed
2 teaspoons olive oil
2 cloves garlic, crushed
1 onion, thinly sliced
750 g cap mushrooms, sliced
1 cup (250 g) ricotta
2 tablespoons sliced black olives
small fresh basil leaves

1 Preheat the oven to hot 210°C (415°F/ Gas 6–7). Put the tomato on a baking tray covered with baking paper, sprinkle with salt, cracked black pepper and 1/2 teaspoon sugar, and bake for 20 minutes, or until the edges are starting to darken.

2 Stir the yeast and remaining sugar with 1/4 cup (60 ml) warm water until the yeast dissolves. Cover and leave in a warm place until foamy. Sift the flour into a large bowl and stir in the yeast and warm milk. Mix to a soft dough, then turn onto a lightly floured surface. Knead for 5 minutes, cover and leave in a lightly oiled bowl in a warm place for 40 minutes, or until doubled.

3 Heat the oil in a pan and fry the garlic and onion until soft. Add the mushrooms and stir until they are soft and the liquid has evaporated. Cool.

4 Lightly knead the dough on a lightly floured surface. Roll out to a 36 cm circle and transfer to a lightly greased baking or pizza tray. Spread with the ricotta, leaving a border to turn over the filling. Top with the mushroom mixture, leaving a circle in the centre, and arrange the tomato and olives in the circle. Fold the dough edge over onto the mushroom mixture and dust with flour. Bake for 25 minutes, or until the crust is golden. Garnish with basil.

NUTRITION PER SERVE
Protein 14.5 g; Fat 7 g; Carbohydrate 33.5 g; Dietary Fibre 5.5 g; Cholesterol 20.5 mg; 1085 kJ (260 Cal)

CRUMBED FISH WITH WASABI CREAM

Satisfy a craving for fried fish using this healthier recipe. This meal is high in protein and provides good amounts of B vitamins, folate and minerals.

Prep time: 25 minutes + 15 minutes refrigeration
Cooking time: 20 minutes
Serves 4
EASY

3/4 cup (60 g) fresh breadcrumbs
3/4 cup (25 g) cornflakes
1 sheet nori, torn roughly (see Note)
1/4 teaspoon paprika
4 x 150 g pieces firm white fish fillets
plain flour, for dusting
1 egg white
1 tablespoon skim milk
1 spring onion, thinly sliced

Wasabi cream
1/2 cup (125 g) low-fat plain yoghurt
1 teaspoon wasabi (see Note)
1 tablespoon light mayonnaise
1 teaspoon lime juice

1 Preheat the oven to moderate 180°C (350°F/Gas 4). Combine the breadcrumbs, cornflakes, nori and paprika in a food processor and process until the nori is finely chopped.
2 Dust the fish lightly with flour, dip into the combined egg white and milk, then into the breadcrumb mixture. Press the crumb mixture on firmly, then refrigerate the fish for 15 minutes.
3 Line a baking tray with non-stick baking paper and put the fish on the paper. Bake for 15–20 minutes, or until the fish flakes easily when tested with a fork.
4 To make the wasabi cream, mix the ingredients thoroughly. Serve a spoonful with the fish. Sprinkle with spring onion.

NUTRITION PER SERVE
Protein 36.5 g; Fat 5 g; Carbohydrate 19 g; Dietary Fibre 2 g; Cholesterol 91.5 mg; 1125 kJ (270 Cal)

NOTE: Nori (sheets of paper-thin dried seaweed) and wasabi paste (a pungent paste, also known as Japanese horseradish) are available from Japanese food stores.

SARDINES WITH CHARGRILLED CAPSICUM AND EGGPLANT

The nutritious ingredients of this easy-to-prepare fish meal provide good amounts of protein, and monounsaturated fat.

Prep time: 25 minutes
Cooking time: 35 minutes
Serves 4
EASY

---

2 large red capsicums, quartered and seeded
cooking oil spray
4 finger eggplants, quartered lengthways
16 fresh sardines, butterflied (about 300 g)
1 slice white bread, crusts removed
1/3 cup (10 g) fresh parsley
1 clove garlic, crushed
1 teaspoon grated lemon rind

Dressing
1 tablespoon olive oil
1 tablespoon balsamic vinegar
1/2 teaspoon soft brown sugar
1 clove garlic, crushed
1 tablespoon chopped fresh chives

1 Preheat the oven to moderate 180°C (350°F/Gas 4). Lightly grease a large baking dish with oil. Preheat the grill and line with foil.

2 Grill the capsicum until the skin is blistered and blackened. Cool in a plastic bag or under a damp tea towel, then peel and slice thickly lengthways. Lightly spray the eggplant with oil and grill each side for 3–5 minutes, or until softened.

3 Combine the dressing ingredients in a jar and shake well. Put the capsicum and eggplant in a bowl, pour the dressing over, toss well and set aside.

4 Place the sardines on a baking tray in a single layer, well spaced. Finely chop the bread, parsley, garlic and lemon rind together in a food processor. Sprinkle over each sardine. Bake for 10–15 minutes, until cooked through. Serve the capsicum and eggplant topped with sardines.

NUTRITION PER SERVE
Protein 16 g; Fat 7 g; Carbohydrate 7.5 g; Dietary Fibre 2 g; Cholesterol 40 mg; 665 kJ (160 Cal)

DESSERTS

Desserts can be a constant temptation for those who are trying to eat healthily, but there are many ways of enjoying a sweet treat without sacrificing all of your good intentions.

Many favourite dessert recipes can be modified so that they contain only a fraction of the fat, sugar and kilojoules of the original. By using fresh, seasonal fruits and low-fat products, you can create a delicious treat that will satisfy your taste buds and your nutrient needs.

Traditional favourites

■ Rice pudding is a comforting dessert for a chilly winter evening. Make the custard using skim milk or evaporated skim milk for a lighter alternative to the traditional rich and creamy pudding.

■ Fruit crumbles are an easy and delicious way of using fresh fruit. Try combinations such as apple and raspberry, rhubarb and pear, plum and nectarine, fig and blackberry, and quince and ginger. Or use the same combinations wrapped in layers of filo pastry, and bake until browned for a simple turnover.

■ Use the Lime delicious recipe on page 289, and replace the lime with lemon, orange, blood orange or ruby red grapefruit.

■ Crepes are an easy, healthy dessert option. Serve them with fresh or poached fruit, or simply a dusting of icing sugar and a squeeze of lemon juice. Crepes also freeze well.

■ Poach pears in unsweetened grape and blackcurrant juice, subtly flavoured with cloves and cinnamon. The natural sweetness will enhance the delicate flavour of the pears, and the colour of the juice will give them an interesting purple tinge. Use the poaching liquid as a syrup to pour over the pears, and serve with low-fat vanilla yoghurt.

■ Core green apples or pears, fill with dried fruits and slivered almonds, and bake with apple juice until tender. Serve with the delicious baking syrup.

■ Low-fat ricotta blended with light cream cheese and fresh fruit purée makes a superb cheesecake.

■ Use low-fat yoghurts and fromage frais as the base for a mousse. Add your favourite flavourings and lightly set the mousse with gelatine.

■ Use light fromage frais instead of mascarpone to make a lighter version of tiramisu.

■ Make fruit jelly with fresh fruits set in fruit juice. Use gelatine leaves, softened in a little cold water, then dissolved in boiling water to set the jelly. Try lychees in apple jelly, mandarin segments in orange jelly, poached peaches in lemon and ginger jelly, berries in pear jelly, or poached rhubarb in rhubarb jelly.

■ Individual summer puddings make a spectacular dessert. Line moulds with crustless white bread, and fill with fresh summer berries, moistened with apple  juice, and lightly sweetened. Cover with more bread, and then plastic wrap. Refrigerate overnight with a plate and weight on top. Unmould and serve with whipped vanilla ricotta.

Healthy dessert ideas

■ Soften some low-fat ice cream and stir through some fresh berry, mango or stone fruit purée, finely chopped fresh pineapple and glacé ginger, espresso coffee, fresh passionfruit pulp or chopped dried figs.

■ For a warming winter fruit salad, simmer dried fruits such as apricots, dates and figs in a spiced orange syrup.

■ Grilling caramelises the natural sugars in fruit. Grilled figs and stone fruits such as peaches, apricots and plums are a delicious sweet treat. Serve with whipped vanilla ricotta or light fromage frais.

■ Granita is a light, simple dessert. It consists of a syrup, perhaps fruit, mint or espresso flavoured. As the syrup freezes, it is stirred so that it sets into crystals that release a refreshing burst of flavour.

■ Make a thick skim milk vanilla custard and, when cold, use to fill tartlet shells or small meringue baskets, before topping with fresh seasonal fruit. Drizzle with passionfruit pulp and serve.

■ Low-fat vanilla fromage frais with passionfruit pulp or raspberry purée, served with savoiardi biscuits for dipping is a refreshing summer dessert. Alternatively, layer the biscuits and fromage frais mixture, allow to set in the fridge, and serve sliced with fresh fruit.

■ Make some ice blocks from fresh fruit purées, and keep in the freezer for a refreshing treat on a hot summer day.

■ Freeze chunks of fresh banana, mango, peach, nectarine, orange or whole grapes and serve as a cool sweet.

Accompaniments

■ Whip low-fat ricotta until smooth, sweeten with a little icing sugar and flavour with vanilla essence, and serve it with desserts as an alternative to cream or ice cream.

■ Sweeten low-fat plain yoghurt with a little honey, and serve with fresh figs. As a slightly more exotic alternative, flavour the sweetened honey with rose water or orange flower water, and serve with cinnamon poached quinces.

■ Sorbets or frozen yoghurts are a tasty alternative to full-fat ice creams.

■ Use light cream, gently whipped to soft peaks, instead of full-fat cream.

■ Make a berry purée with ripe strawberries and raspberries. Use as a sauce on ice cream, or to drizzle over your favourite dessert.

Soy desserts

Many soy products are suitable for incorporating into sweet dishes.

■ Silken tofu and low-fat cream cheese will make a delicious cheesecake.

■ Blend or process silken firm tofu, and flavour it with vanilla essence. It will have the same texture as thick cream or yoghurt.

■ Use silken tofu in place of cream in mousses.

■ Serve silken tofu in a hot ginger syrup for a delicious winter dessert.

■ Use fruit-flavoured tofu desserts as a base for mousses, bavarois or panna cotta.

CASSATA

This low-fat ice cream dessert will satisfy sweet cravings with fewer calories than traditional cassata. The fruit and ginger provide some extra vitamins and minerals.

Prep time: 20 minutes + freezing
Cooking time: Nil
Serves 10–12
MEDIUM

---

30 g crystallised ginger, finely chopped
50 g red glacé cherries, roughly chopped or
    sliced
300 g low-fat vanilla ice cream, softened
250 g frozen strawberry fruit dessert, softened
300 g low-fat chocolate ice cream, softened

1 Line a 1.25 litre rectangular tin with plastic wrap, leaving an overhang on the sides.
2 Stir the ginger and glacé cherries into the vanilla ice cream until well combined. Spoon into the prepared tin and smooth down. Freeze for 1 hour, or until firm.
3 Spoon the strawberry fruit dessert over the ice cream mixture, smooth the surface and freeze for another hour.
4 Spoon the chocolate ice cream over the strawberry, smoothing the surface. Cover with plastic wrap, and freeze for at least 3 hours or overnight. To serve, plunge the bottom of the tin into warm water for 10 seconds to loosen and lift out using the plastic wrap. Cut into slices and serve.

NUTRITION PER SERVE (12)
Protein 3 g; Fat 2 g; Carbohydrate 18 g; Dietary Fibre 0.5 g; Cholesterol 5 mg; 375 kJ (90 Cal)

TIRAMISU

You won't miss the fat in this healthier version of the traditional favourite. This recipe is a great source of calcium, phosphorus and potassium.

Prep time: 15 minutes + overnight refrigeration
Cooking time: 5 minutes
Serves 6
EASY

1/4 cup (30 g) custard powder
1 cup (250 ml) skim milk
2 tablespoons caster sugar
2 teaspoons vanilla essence
2 x 130 g tubs low-fat French vanilla
    fromage frais
2 egg whites
1 2/3 cups (410 ml) strong coffee, cooled
2 tablespoons amaretto
250 g savoiardi (sponge finger) biscuits
2 tablespoons unsweetened dark cocoa powder

1 Stir the custard powder in a small pan with 2 tablespoons of the milk until dissolved. Add the remaining milk, sugar and vanilla, and stir over medium heat until the mixture boils and thickens. Remove from the heat. Transfer to a bowl, cover the surface with plastic wrap and leave to cool.
2 Using electric beaters, beat the custard and the fromage frais for 2 minutes. Whip the egg whites until soft peaks form, then fold into the custard mixture.
3 Pour the coffee and amaretto into a dish. Quickly dip the biscuits, one at a time, into the coffee mixture, just enough to cover (don't leave them in the liquid or they will go soggy) and arrange in a single layer over the base of a 2.75 litre dish.
4 Smooth half the custard mixture evenly over the biscuits. Dust half the cocoa over the top and then repeat the layers with the biscuits and cream. Cover and refrigerate overnight, or for at least 6 hours. Dust with the remaining cocoa to serve.

NUTRITION PER SERVE
Protein 5 g; Fat 5.5 g; Carbohydrate 26 g; Dietary Fibre 1 g; Cholesterol 7.5 mg; 755 kJ (180 Cal)

Cassata (top), and Tiramisu

RASPBERRY MOUSSE

This refreshing and nutritious low-fat mousse is a great source of bone-building nutrients.

Prep time: 30 minutes + refrigeration
Cooking time: Nil
Serves 4
EASY

3 teaspoons gelatine
1 cup (250 g) low-fat vanilla yoghurt
2 x 200 g tubs low-fat French vanilla fromage frais
4 egg whites
150 g fresh or frozen, thawed, raspberries, mashed
fresh raspberries and mint leaves, for serving

1 Sprinkle the gelatine in an even layer over 1 tablespoon water in a small bowl and leave to go spongy. Bring a small pan of water to the boil, remove from the heat and place the bowl in the pan. Stir until clear and dissolved.

2 In a large bowl, stir the vanilla yoghurt and fromage frais together, then add the gelatine and mix well.

3 Using electric beaters, beat the egg whites until stiff peaks form, then fold through the yoghurt mixture. Transfer half to a separate bowl and fold the mashed raspberries through.

4 Divide the raspberry mixture into the bases of 4 long glasses or serving bowls. Top with the vanilla mixture. Refrigerate for several hours, or until set. Decorate with fresh raspberries and mint leaves.

NUTRITION PER SERVE
Protein 18 g; Fat 0.5 g; Carbohydrate 21 g; Dietary Fibre 2 g; Cholesterol 8.5 mg; 730 kJ (175 Cal)

PASSIONFRUIT TART

Amaze your guests with this low-fat treat, which provides calcium, potassium and phosphorus.

Prep time: 25 minutes + 30 minutes refrigeration
Cooking time: 1 hour
Serves 8
EASY

3/4 cup (90 g) plain flour
2 tablespoons icing sugar
2 tablespoons custard powder
30 g butter
3 tablespoons light evaporated milk

Filling
1/2 cup (125 g) ricotta
1 teaspoon vanilla essence
1/4 cup (30 g) icing sugar
2 eggs, lightly beaten
1/3 cup (90 g) passionfruit pulp (about
    8 passionfruit)
3/4 cup (185 ml) light evaporated milk

1 Preheat the oven to moderately hot 200°C (400°F/Gas 6). Lightly spray a 22 cm loose-based flan tin with oil spray. Sift the flour, icing sugar and custard powder into a bowl and rub in the butter until the mixture resembles fine breadcrumbs. Add enough evaporated milk to form a soft dough. Bring together on a lightly floured surface until just smooth. Gather into a ball, wrap in plastic and refrigerate for 15 minutes.

2 Roll the pastry out on a floured surface, use it to fit the tin, then refrigerate for 15 minutes. Cover with baking paper and fill with uncooked rice or beans. Bake for 10 minutes, remove the rice or beans and paper, and bake for another 5–8 minutes, or until golden. Allow to cool. Reduce the oven to warm 160°C (315°F/Gas 2–3).

3 Beat the ricotta with the vanilla essence and icing sugar until smooth. Add the eggs, passionfruit pulp and milk, then beat well. Put the tin with the pastry case on a baking tray and gently pour in the mixture. Bake for 40 minutes, or until set. Allow to cool in the tin. Dust lightly with icing sugar just before serving.

NUTRITION PER SERVE
Protein 8 g; Fat 6.5 g; Carbohydrate 21.5 g; Dietary Fibre 3 g; Cholesterol 65.5 mg; 730 kJ (175 Cal)

...ME CARAMEL

...s of traditional crème caramel won't realise ...it this recipe contains much less fat. It is a good ...hoice for those watching their weight.

Prep time: 10 minutes + overnight refrigeration
Cooking time: 45 minutes
Serves 4
MEDIUM

canola oil spray
1/3 cup (90 g) caster sugar
1 1/2 cups (375 ml) skim milk
2 eggs
1 1/2 tablespoons caster sugar, extra
1/2 teaspoon vanilla essence
1 teaspoon maple syrup

1 Preheat the oven to warm 160°C (315°F/Gas 2–3). Lightly spray four 1/2 cup (125 ml) ovenproof ramekins (7.5 cm in diameter) with canola oil. Place the caster sugar and 1 1/2 tablespoons water in a small heavy-based saucepan. Stir over low heat until the sugar is dissolved. Bring to the boil, then reduce the heat and simmer until the syrup turns straw coloured and begins to caramelise. Remove from the heat and divide among the ramekins, coating the bases evenly.

2 Heat the milk in a small saucepan with a pinch of salt over low heat until almost boiling. Place the eggs and extra sugar in a bowl and whisk together for 2 minutes. Stir in the warm milk, vanilla and maple syrup. Strain into a jug and divide evenly among the ramekins.

3 Place the ramekins in a baking dish and add enough boiling water to reach halfway up the sides of the ramekins. Bake for 35 minutes, or until the custards are set. Remove from the baking tray and leave to cool completely. Refrigerate for at least 2 hours, or overnight.

4 To serve, carefully run a knife around the edge of each custard. Invert the ramekins onto serving plates and lift off, giving them a gentle shake if necessary to dislodge the custard.

NUTRITION PER SERVE
Protein 7 g; Fat 2.5 g; Carbohydrate 33 g; Dietary Fibre 0 g; Cholesterol 93 mg; 730 kJ (175 Cal)

LIME DELICIOUS

One serve of this tangy dessert gives you more than a quarter of your daily vitamin C requirement and small to moderate amounts of most other vitamins and minerals.

Prep time: 20 minutes
Cooking time: 40 minutes
Serves 4–6
EASY

30 g butter
1 cup (250 g) sugar
1 tablespoon grated lime rind
2 eggs, separated
1/3 cup (40 g) self-raising flour
150 ml skim milk
1/2 cup (125 ml) lime juice

1 Preheat the oven to moderate 180°C (350°F/Gas 4). Lightly grease a 1 litre ovenproof dish. Beat the butter, sugar and lime rind together until light and creamy. Gradually add the egg yolks, beating well after each addition. Fold in the flour, milk and lime juice alternately.
2 Place the egg whites in a clean, dry bowl and beat until soft peaks form. Gently fold into the butter and sugar mixture, then pour into the prepared dish and bake for 40 minutes, or until golden brown. Serve with low-fat ice cream, if desired.

NUTRITION PER SERVE (6)
Protein 3.5 g; Fat 6 g; Carbohydrate 48 g; Dietary Fibre 0 g; Cholesterol 75 mg; 1070 kJ (255 Cal)

Rhubarb and apple crumble (top), and Fruit jellies

RHUABARB AND APPLE CRUMBLE

This reduced-fat apple crumble satisfies your senses and nutritional needs. The rhubarb adds small amounts of vitamins A and C, calcium and manganese.

Prep time: 15 minutes
Cooking time: 35 minutes
Serves 6
EASY

---

6 Granny Smith apples
1/4 cup (60 g) sugar
250 g trimmed rhubarb, thinly sliced
1 tablespoon cornflour
140 g quick-cooking rolled oats
1 tablespoon soft brown sugar
60 g slivered almonds
2 tablespoons honey
2 egg whites

1 Preheat the oven to moderate 180°C (350°F/Gas 4). Peel, core and chop the apples, and place in a saucepan with the sugar and 3/4 cup (185 ml) water. Cook, covered, over low heat for 6 minutes, or until just tender. Add the rhubarb and cook for a further 2 minutes, or until the apple and rhubarb mixture is soft but not disintegrating.
2 Mix the cornflour with 1 tablespoon cold water, add to the pan and cook for 1 minute, or until thickened. Spoon into six 1 cup (250 ml) ramekins.
3 Place the oats, brown sugar, almonds, honey and egg whites in a bowl and mix until well combined and lumps form. Divide among the ramekins to cover the apple and rhubarb mixture. Bake the crumble for 20–25 minutes, or until the tops are golden brown and crunchy.

NUTRITION PER SERVE:
Protein 7 g; Fat 8 g; Carbohydrate 50 g; Dietary Fibre 6.5 g; Cholesterol 0 mg; 1220 kJ (290 Cal)

FRUIT JELLIES

These home-made fruit jellies are sweetened with natural sugars, and contain no artificial colours or flavours. The berries provide a refreshing blend of fibre, vitamin C, folate and antioxidants.

Prep time: 20 minutes + refrigeration
Cooking time: Nil
Serves 4
EASY

---

4 teaspoons gelatine
2 cups (500 ml) cranberry and raspberry juice
330 g mixed berries, fresh or frozen

1 Sprinkle the gelatine in an even layer onto 1/4 cup (60 ml) of the juice, in a small bowl, and leave to go spongy. Bring a small pan of water to the boil, remove from the heat and place the bowl in the pan. The water should come halfway up the side of the bowl. Stir the gelatine until clear and dissolved. Cool slightly and mix with the rest of the juice.
2 Rinse four 3/4 cup (185 ml) moulds with water (wet moulds make it easier when unmoulding) and pour 2 cm of the juice into each. Refrigerate until set.
3 Meanwhile, if the fruit is frozen, defrost it and add any liquid to the remaining juice. When the bottom layer of jelly has set, divide the fruit among the moulds (reserving a few berries to garnish) and divide the rest of the juice among the moulds, pouring it over the fruit. Refrigerate until set.
4 To turn out the jellies, hold each mould in a hot, damp tea towel and turn out onto a plate. Ease away the edge of the jelly with your finger to break the seal. (If you turn the jellies onto a damp plate you will be able to move them around, otherwise they will stick.) Garnish with the reserved berries.

NUTRITION PER SERVE
Protein 3 g; Fat 0 g; Carbohydrate 25 g; Dietary Fibre 1.5 g; Cholesterol 0 mg; 420 kJ (100 Cal)

STICKY DATE PUDDING

*This reduced-fat version of the traditional
favourite is an ideal winter treat. It is rich in
carbohydrate with some calcium, potassium,
phosphorus and a little iron and vitamin A.*

Prep time: 30 minutes + 15 minutes standing
Cooking time: 1 hour
Serves 6–8
DIFFICULT

___

canola oil spray
1 Earl Grey tea bag
250 g pitted dried dates, finely chopped
1 teaspoon bicarbonate of soda
1/2 cup (95 g) soft brown sugar
2 eggs
1 tablespoon oil
2 cups (250 g) self-raising flour
1 teaspoon vanilla essence
1 cup (250 g) sugar
150 ml light cream, whipped

1 Preheat the oven to moderate 180°C
(350°F/Gas 4). Lightly spray a 20 cm
square cake tin with canola oil. Put the tea
bag in a heatproof bowl with 1 1/2 cups
(375 ml) boiling water. Leave to steep for
1 minute, then remove the teabag.
2 Place the chopped dates in a saucepan,
add the tea and bring to the boil over
high heat. Remove from the heat, add
the bicarbonate of soda and leave for
15 minutes.
3 Place the brown sugar, eggs and oil in
a bowl and beat with electric beaters for
5 minutes, or until thick. Sift the flour
into the sugar mixture and combine with a
metal spoon. Stir in the date mixture and
the vanilla essence. Mix together well.
Pour into the tin and bake for 45 minutes,
or until a skewer inserted in the centre
comes out clean.
4 Meanwhile, place the sugar and 1/2 cup
(125 ml) water in a heavy-based saucepan
and stir over low heat, without boiling,
until the sugar has dissolved. Increase the
heat and bring to the boil. Brush down
the side of the saucepan with a pastry

brush dipped in water to prevent sugar
crystals from forming. Reduce the heat
and simmer for 7–8 minutes, or until the
mixture turns a dark gold colour.
5 Place a tea towel in the sink to stand the
pan on (the hot pan can cause the sink to
buckle if it is not protected). Transfer the
pan to the sink, place a tea towel over your
arm to protect it and pour 1/3 cup (80 ml)
water into the pan. The mixture will
splutter violently. When the spluttering
subsides, return the saucepan to medium
heat and stir with a wooden spoon until
the caramel dissolves and comes to the
boil. Reduce the heat and simmer for
1 minute. Remove from the heat and
leave to cool slightly.
6 Cut the pudding into pieces, place
on serving plates and drizzle the sauce
over the top. Serve with a dollop of the
light cream.

NUTRITION PER SERVE (8):
Protein 6 g; Fat 8.5 g; Carbohydrate 78 g; Dietary Fibre
4 g; Cholesterol 57.5 mg; 1685 kJ (405 Cal)

NOTE: The Earl Grey tea adds a little extra
flavour to the pudding, but is optional.

MANGO PASSIONFRUIT SORBET

You can use any combination of fruit in this recipe, which provides carbohydrate energy, fibre, a refreshing burst of vitamin C and a variety of antioxidants.

Prep time: 20 minutes + 8 hours freezing
Cooking time: 5 minutes
Serves 6
EASY

1 cup (250 g) caster sugar
1/3 cup (90 g) passionfruit pulp
    (about 8 passionfruit)
1/2 large mango, chopped
1 large peach, chopped
2 tablespoons lemon juice
1 egg white

1 Put the sugar in a pan with 1 cup (250 ml) water. Stir over low heat until the sugar has dissolved. Increase the heat, bring to the boil and boil for 1 minute. Transfer to a glass bowl, cool, then refrigerate. Strain the passionfruit pulp, reserving 1 tablespoon of the seeds.

2 Blend the fruit, passionfruit juice and lemon juice in a blender until smooth. With the motor running, add the cold sugar syrup and 150 ml water. Stir in the passionfruit seeds. Freeze in a shallow container, stirring occasionally, for about 5 hours, or until almost set.

3 Break up the icy mixture roughly with a fork or spoon, transfer to a bowl and beat with electric beaters until smooth and fluffy. Beat the egg white in a small bowl until firm peaks form, then fold into the mixture until just combined. Spread into a loaf tin and return to the freezer until firm. Transfer to the refrigerator, to soften, 15 minutes before serving.

NUTRITION PER SERVE
Protein 2 g; Fat 0 g; Carbohydrate 50 g; Dietary Fibre 3 g; Cholesterol 0 mg; 850 kJ (200 Cal)

VARIATION: To make a berry sorbet, use 200 g blackberries or blueberries, 200 g hulled strawberries and 50 g peach flesh. Prepare as above.

CHOCOLATE AND RASPBERRY ICE CREAM SANDWICH

Although this dessert is relatively high in calories, most of them come from carbohydrate, not fat. This dessert is a good source of phosphorus, potassium, calcium and vitamin A.

Prep time: 20 minutes + 2 hours freezing
Cooking time: Nil
Serves 4
EASY

300 g frozen chocolate pound cake
2 tablespoons raspberry liqueur, optional
250 g fresh or thawed raspberries
1 cup (250 g) sugar
1 teaspoon lemon juice
1 litre low-fat vanilla ice cream, softened
icing sugar, to dust

1 Using a sharp knife, cut the pound cake lengthways into 4 thin slices. Using a 6.5 cm plain cutter, cut 8 rounds from the slices of cake. You will need 2 rounds of cake per person. Brush each round with half of the raspberry liqueur if using, then cover and set aside.

2 Line a 20 x 20 cm tin or dish with baking paper, leaving a generous overhang of paper on two opposite sides. Place the raspberries, sugar, lemon juice and remaining liqueur in a blender and blend to a smooth purée. Reserving 1/2 cup (125 ml) of the purée, fold the remainder through the ice cream and pour into the tin. Freeze for 2 hours, or until the ice cream is completely firm.

3 Remove the ice cream from the freezer and use the overhanging baking paper to lift it from the tin. Using a 6.5 cm cutter, cut 4 rounds from the ice cream.

4 To assemble, place four slices of cake on a tray, top each with a round of ice cream and then the remaining slices of cake. Smooth the sides of the ice cream to neaten, if necessary. Return the sandwiches to the freezer for 5 minutes to firm. Dust with icing sugar and serve with the remaining raspberry sauce.

NUTRITION PER SERVE
Protein 6 g; Fat 9.5 g; Carbohydrate 101 g; Dietary Fibre 4.5 g; Cholesterol 51.5 mg; 2155 kJ (515 Cal)

MOCHA CHEESECAKE

This cheesecake is reduced in fat and calories, but not flavour, and also provides calcium.

Prep time: 30 minutes + 4 hours 30 minutes
    refrigeration
Cooking time: Nil
Serves 8
MEDIUM

---

50 g plain sweet biscuits
1/4 cup (30 g) walnuts
30 g butter, melted
1 tablespoon instant coffee
2 teaspoons cocoa powder
1 tablespoon gelatine
250 g low-fat ricotta
1/2 cup (125 g) caster sugar
1 cup (250 ml) reduced-fat evaporated milk,
    well chilled
cocoa powder, extra, for dusting

1 Line the base of a 20 cm springform tin with baking paper. Place the biscuits and walnuts in a food processor, and process until finely crushed. Add the melted butter and pulse until well combined. Press the biscuit and nut mixture into the base of the prepared tin and chill for 30 minutes.
2 Combine the coffee, cocoa, gelatine and 1/2 cup (125 ml) boiling water in a heatproof bowl. Place the bowl in a saucepan of very hot water, and stir until the gelatine has dissolved and the mixture is smooth. Cool slightly.
3 Beat the ricotta and sugar with electric beaters for 2 minutes, or until the sugar has dissolved. Gradually beat in the coffee mixture.
4 Place the evaporated milk in a separate bowl and beat with electric beaters on high speed for 1 minute, or until the mixture is very frothy and holds its shape. Beat in the ricotta mixture until well combined.
5 Pour over the biscuit base. Cover with plastic wrap and refrigerate for 3–4 hours, or until set. To serve, wrap a hot, damp tea towel around the tin for 1 minute, then run a flat-bladed knife around the inside of the tin and remove the collar. Dust with cocoa and serve with raspberries.

NUTRITION PER SERVE:
Protein 9 g; Fat 9.5 g; Carbohydrate 20 g; Dietary Fibre 0.5 g; Cholesterol 26.5 mg; 825 kJ (195 Cal)

STEWED PEAR, APPLE AND RHUBARB WITH CUSTARD

This very low-fat dessert is loaded with potassium, and the rhubarb provides manganese and calcium.

Prep time: 20 minutes
Cooking time: 20 minutes
Serves 4
MEDIUM

---

2 tablespoons blackcurrant syrup
2 large pears, peeled, cored and quartered
1 apple, peeled, cored and quartered
500 g rhubarb, trimmed, cut into 3 cm pieces
2 cups (500 ml) skim milk
1/4 cup (60 g) caster sugar
1 1/2 tablespoons custard powder

1 Place the syrup, pears, apple, and 1/4 cup (60 ml) water in a large saucepan and stir to coat the fruits. Cook, covered, over low heat for 4 minutes, then add the rhubarb. Toss well to combine, then cover and cook for a further 6–7 minutes, or until the fruit is just tender. Remove from the heat, cover and leave to stand.
2 Place the milk and sugar in a saucepan. Bring to the boil, then reduce the heat and simmer for 3 minutes. Mix the custard powder with 1 tablespoon water to a smooth paste. Return the milk to the boil, stir in the custard powder mixture and whisk constantly until the mixture boils and thickens, and can coat the back of a wooden spoon.
3 Place the fruits in serving dishes and drizzle with any liquid from the bottom of the pan. Serve with the warm custard.

NUTRITION PER SERVE
Protein 7 g; Fat 0.5 g; Carbohydrate 51 g; Dietary Fibre 6.5 g; Cholesterol 4 mg; 970 kJ (230 Cal)

Mocha cheesecake (top), and Stewed pear, apple and rhubarb with custard

APPLE PIE

This reduced-fat version of the traditional family favourite is a good source of potassium and fibre, with some vitamin A and phosphorus. Serve the pie with light cream or low-fat yoghurt for a calcium boost.

Prep time: 40 minutes + 30 minutes refrigeration
Cooking time: 1 hour
Serves 8
MEDIUM

canola oil spray
2 cups (250 g) plain flour
125 g reduced-fat dairy spread, chilled and
    chopped
2 tablespoons soft brown sugar
1 1/2 teaspoons ground cinnamon
70 ml chilled water
1 vanilla bean, halved
1.5 kg Granny Smith apples, peeled and sliced
1 tablespoon lemon juice
1/4 cup (60 ml) maple syrup

1 Preheat the oven to moderate 180°C (350°F/Gas 4). Lightly spray a 23 cm pie tin with oil. Sift the flour into a large bowl, then add the dairy spread and rub into the flour with your fingertips until the mixture resembles fine breadcrumbs. Stir in the sugar and 1/2 teaspoon cinnamon. Make a well in the centre and add the chilled water. Mix with a flat-bladed knife, using a cutting action, until the mixture comes together in beads. Gently gather the dough together and lift onto a lightly floured work surface. Press into a ball and flatten slightly into a disc. Wrap in plastic and refrigerate for about 30 minutes.

2 Scrape the seeds from the vanilla bean and place in a saucepan with the pod. Add the apple slices and lemon juice, and just cover with water. Bring to the boil, then reduce the heat and simmer gently for 15 minutes. Remove the vanilla pod and leave the mixture to cool.

3 Roll out two-thirds of the pastry between two sheets of baking paper to 2 mm thick. Invert the pastry into the prepared tin, allowing any excess to hang over the side. Line the pastry shell with a piece of crumpled greaseproof paper, ensuring it covers the base and side. Pour in some baking beads or uncooked rice and bake for 10 minutes. Remove the paper and baking beads.

4 Drain the excess liquid from the apple and discard. Add 2 tablespoons maple syrup and the remaining cinnamon to the apple, gently combine, and spoon the mixture into the pastry shell.

5 Roll the remaining pastry out between two sheets of baking paper to a thickness of 2 mm. Brush the edges of the pastry in the tin with a little water and position the pastry lid over the top of the pie. Trim the pastry, then crimp the edges together to seal. Make two slits in the top of the pie to allow steam to escape. Combine the remaining maple syrup with 2 tablespoons water and brush over the top of the pie (there will be some left over). Bake for 30 minutes, or until the pastry is golden. Leave for 10 minutes before serving with whipped light cream, if desired.

NUTRITION PER SERVE:
Protein 5 g; Fat 6.5 g; Carbohydrate 49 g; Dietary Fibre 4 g; Cholesterol 20.5 mg; 1135 kJ (270 Cal)

NOTES: It is important to make steam holes in the top of the pie, or the filling will boil and create excess liquid, which will result in a soggy pastry base. Vanilla beans are available from good-quality food stores. If they are not available, replace with 1 teaspoon pure vanilla essence.

DRIED APRICOT FOOL

This low-fat fruit dessert is rich in carbohydrate energy, potassium and beta-carotene. It is a good source of fibre and vitamin A, and provides a little iron.

Prep time: 15 minutes
Cooking time: 5 minutes
Serves 4
EASY

30 g finely chopped glacé ginger
175 g dried apricots, chopped
2 egg whites
2 tablespoons caster sugar
1 tablespoon shredded coconut, toasted

1 Place the ginger, apricots and 1/3 cup (80 ml) water in a small saucepan. Cook, covered, over very low heat for 5 minutes, stirring occasionally. Remove from the heat and allow to cool completely.
2 Using electric beaters, beat the egg whites in a clean, dry bowl until soft peaks form. Add the caster sugar and beat for 3 minutes, or until thick and glossy. Quickly and gently fold the cooled apricot mixture into the egg mixture and divide among four chilled serving glasses. Scatter the toasted coconut over the top and serve immediately.

NUTRITION PER SERVE:
Protein 4 g; Fat 1 g; Carbohydrate 33 g; Dietary Fibre 4 g; Cholesterol 0 mg; 630 kJ (150 Cal)

NOTE: The apricots can scorch easily, so cook over low heat. Serve immediately, or the egg white will slowly break down and lose volume.

CREAMED RICE PUDDING

This is a delicious low-fat dessert or breakfast that will fill your body's carbohydrate fuel stores.

Prep time: 10 minutes
Cooking time: 1 hour 10 minutes
Serves 6
MEDIUM

1 vanilla bean, halved
1 cinnamon stick
1/2 cup (100 g) medium-grain rice
2/3 cup (160 g) caster sugar
1.25 litres skim milk
1/3 cup (55 g) sultanas
1 egg
2 egg whites
1 cup (250 ml) light evaporated milk
1/2 teaspoon ground nutmeg
sugar-free jam, to serve

1 Scrape the seeds from the vanilla bean and place in a saucepan with the pod, cinnamon stick, rice, caster sugar and skim milk. Cook over medium heat, stirring frequently, for 50 minutes, or until the rice is cooked. Remove from the heat and take out the vanilla pod and cinnamon stick. Stir in the sultanas. Preheat the oven to warm 170°C (325°F/Gas 3).
2 Place the egg, egg whites and evaporated milk in a bowl and beat until well combined. Stir into the rice mixture.
3 Pour the pudding mixture into a shallow, 2 litre ovenproof dish and sprinkle with the nutmeg. Place the dish in a roasting tin and pour boiling water into the tin to come halfway up the side of the dish. Bake for 20 minutes, or until set. Serve with a spoonful of jam.

NUTRITION PER SERVE:
Protein 15 g; Fat 2 g; Carbohydrate 56 g; Dietary Fibre 1 g; Cholesterol 40.5 mg; 1245 kJ (295 Cal)

Yoghurt and savoiardi parfait (top), and Spiced poached pears

YOGHURT AND SAVOIARDI PARFAIT

This delicate dessert will impress dinner party guests, and is a great source of vitamin C, antioxidants, potassium, calcium and fibre.

Prep time: 20 minutes + 1 hour refrigeration
Cooking time: Nil
Serves 6
EASY

3 cups (750 g) low-fat plain yoghurt
50 g sugar
strained juice from 12 passionfruit
125 g savoiardi (sponge finger) biscuits,
    cut to size
500 g raspberries or strawberries
50 g slivered almonds, toasted

1 Place the yoghurt, sugar and passionfruit juice in a bowl, and mix well. Divide a third of the mixture among six 200 ml parfait glasses.
2 Top the yoghurt mixture with a layer of savoiardi biscuits, then with a layer of the berries.
3 Repeat with another layer of yoghurt, biscuits and berries, and top with a final layer of yoghurt. Garnish with berries and the toasted almonds. Refrigerate for 1 hour before serving.

NUTRITION PER SERVE
Protein 12 g; Fat 6 g; Carbohydrate 32.5 g; Dietary Fibre 4 g; Cholesterol 38 mg; 985 kJ (235 Cal)

SPICED POACHED PEARS

Enjoy the delicate flavours of this low-fat dessert. The pears are easily digested and provide potassium and soluble fibre. Serve them with yoghurt for extra protein, calcium and phosphorus.

Prep time: 10 minutes + 30 minutes standing
Cooking time: 20 minutes
Serves 6
EASY

6 beurre bosc pears
300 ml rosé wine
150 ml good-quality apple or pear juice
4 cloves
1 vanilla bean, halved
1 cinnamon stick
1 tablespoon maple syrup
200 g low-fat vanilla yoghurt

1 Peel, halve and core the pears. Place in a deep frying pan with a lid, and add the wine, fruit juice and cloves. Scrape the seeds out of the vanilla bean and add both the seeds and pod to the pan. Stir in the cinnamon stick and maple syrup. Bring to the boil, then reduce the heat and simmer for 5–7 minutes, or until the pears are tender. Remove from the heat and cover with the lid.
2 Leave the fruit for 30 minutes to allow the flavours to infuse, then remove the pears with a slotted spoon and place in a serving dish. Return the syrup to the heat and boil for 6–8 minutes, or until reduced by half. Strain the syrup over the pears. Serve warm or chilled with the yoghurt.

NUTRITION PER SERVE:
Protein 3 g; Fat 0.5 g; Carbohydrate 32 g; Dietary Fibre 4 g; Cholesterol 2 mg; 690 kJ (165 Cal)

CINNAMON ORANGE MINI PAVLOVAS WITH BERRIES

This citrus-flavoured version of the traditional recipe is topped with berries and light cream for extra vitamins, calcium and antioxidants.

Prep time: 25 minutes + cooling
Cooking time: 45 minutes
Serves 4
EASY

2 egg whites
1/2 cup (125 g) caster sugar
2 teaspoons ground cinnamon
1 teaspoon finely grated orange rind
3 teaspoons cornflour
1 teaspoon white vinegar
150 ml light cream, whipped
fresh berries, to serve

1 Preheat the oven to very slow 140°C (275°F/Gas 1). Line a baking tray with baking paper and mark four 10 cm circles. Turn the baking paper upside down so that the marks don't stain the meringue.

2 Beat the egg whites with electric beaters until soft peaks form. Gradually add the sugar, beating well after each addition. Continue to beat for 4–5 minutes, or until the sugar has dissolved and the meringue is thick and glossy. Gently fold in the cinnamon, orange rind, cornflour and vinegar. Place 2 tablespoons of the mixture into each circle, gently spreading it out to the edges with the back of a spoon. Hollow out each centre to make nest shapes.

3 Bake for 10 minutes, then turn the tray around and bake for 30–35 minutes, or until the pavlovas are pale and crisp. Turn the oven off and leave them to cool completely with the door slightly ajar. The pavlovas may crack slightly on cooling. Spoon a little cream into each pavlova, top with the berries and serve immediately.

NUTRITION PER SERVE:
Protein 4 g; Fat 8 g; Carbohydrate 37 g; Dietary Fibre 1 g; Cholesterol 25 mg; 935 kJ (225 Cal)

LEMON BERRY CHEESECAKE

This tangy, reduced-fat cheesecake provides some calcium, phosphorus, potassium and vitamin C.

Prep time: 25 minutes + overnight refrigeration
Cooking time: Nil
Serves 12
EASY

60 g plain sweet biscuits, finely crushed
30 g butter, melted
300 g ricotta
2 tablespoons caster sugar
2 x 130 g tubs low-fat French vanilla
    fromage frais
2 x 130 g tubs low-fat Lemon Tang
    fromage frais
2 teaspoons finely grated lemon rind
2 tablespoons lemon juice
1 tablespoon gelatine
2 egg whites
250 g strawberries, halved

1 Lightly oil and line the base and side of a 20 cm springform tin with plastic wrap. Combine the biscuits and butter in a bowl and press evenly over the base of the tin. Refrigerate while making the filling.

2 Combine the ricotta and sugar in a food processor until smooth. Add all the fromage frais, the lemon rind and juice, then mix well.

3 Put 1/4 cup (60 ml) water in a small bowl, sprinkle the gelatine in an even layer onto the surface and leave to go spongy. Bring a small pan of water to the boil, remove from the heat and put the gelatine bowl in the pan. The water should come halfway up the side of the bowl. Stir the gelatine until clear and dissolved, then cool slightly. Stir the gelatine mixture into the ricotta mixture, then transfer to a large bowl.

4 Beat the egg whites until soft peaks form, then gently fold into the ricotta mixture. Pour the mixture into the tin and refrigerate for several hours or overnight, until set. Carefully remove from the tin by removing the side of the pan and gently easing the plastic from underneath. Decorate with the halved strawberries.

NUTRITION PER SERVE
Protein 8.5 g; Fat 6 g; Carbohydrate 12 g; Dietary Fibre 1 g; Cholesterol 21.5 mg; 560 kJ (140 Cal)

BAKING

If you can't resist the aroma of a freshly baked cake or loaf of bread, look among this selection of delicious baking recipes for healthier versions of your favourite treats.

Baking your own cakes, pastries or bread is not only a very satisfying experience, it also ensures that you're in control of the ingredients that go into them, so you can make them as healthy as you wish.

Baking is one of the most technical cooking methods. It relies on a series of chemical reactions among the ingredients to cause the food to rise and develop a delicious taste and texture. Although this may sound daunting, if you follow the recipes through step by step, you will achieve the results you are looking for. Once you have become familiar with the process and comfortable with the recipe, you can make slight alterations to flavours to suit your own tastes.

SUGAR

Sugar is an essential ingredient in most baked goods. It increases the shelf-life of cakes and biscuits, adds texture and colour to most baked goods, and also gives yeast the energy it requires for bread to rise. Although moderate amounts of refined sugar won't cause health problems or weight gain, it's better to obtain sweetness from foods that contain natural sugars, so you will also be getting other valuable nutrients. Honey is often used as a substitute for sugar, and while it may contain slightly more nutrients than sugar, it should still be used in moderation.

Tips for using less sugar in baking

- Use fruit purées as a liquid alternative to sugar in cake and biscuit mixtures.
- Use low-fat fruit yoghurts or low-fat vanilla fromage frais to sweeten and moisten cake and biscuit batters.
- When fruit is fully ripe, it will be at its sweetest, and can often be used to totally replace any refined sugar in a recipe.
- Add dried fruits such as sultanas, raisins, currants, apricots or dates, which are naturally very sweet, to cake and biscuit mixtures, and add less sugar.

SALT

Not a lot of salt is used in baking—just a pinch in sweet and savoury products to enhance the flavours. If you are trying to reduce your salt intake, you can leave it out of the recipe altogether without adversely affecting the texture or appearance of the finished baked food. You can also use unsalted butter instead of regular butter for all baking.

FAT

Usually the fat content of baked goods needs to be reduced, in order to make them healthier. Most baked goods will contain fat in some form—usually butter, margarine or oil, but sometimes  cream, sour cream, cream cheese or even chocolate. It is possible to reduce the amount of fat in most bakery recipes to some extent, but not completely, as some fat is needed to achieve the colour, taste and texture you expect from bakery products. Most home-baked breads don't contain fat, but check the labels on bread purchased from the supermarket.

Tips for reducing fat in baking

- Use skim milk in place of full-fat milk.
- Use light or reduced-fat sour cream instead of regular sour cream.
- Instead of using chocolate in a recipe, choose a recipe that uses cocoa powder.
- Use buttermilk in place of milk or sour cream. Buttermilk is a low-fat milk product that has been thickened with a bacterial culture to make it slightly sour.
- Use low-fat cream cheese instead of regular cream cheese in cream cheese icings.
- Use low-fat ricotta instead of butter for making icings.
- Use low-fat natural or fruit yoghurt instead of full-fat yoghurt.
- Substitute a fruit juice for milk.
- Use a fruit purée instead of oil or sour cream. Try apple or pear, or soaked dried apricots.
- Use filo pastry for pies and tarts, brush every third layer with oil, or even with apple juice if you are very concerned about your fat intake.
- Use low-fat margarine in place of regular margarine or butter.

- For a sweet pie crust, use finely crushed low-fat plain biscuits, moisten with a fruit purée and refrigerate or bake until set.
- Be sure to use non-stick baking tins— a light spray of oil and lining with baking paper is all that will be needed to ensure that your cakes or biscuits don't stick.
- Use low-fat evaporated milk in custard fillings for a creamy yet light alternative.
- Use canola oil in recipes requiring vegetable oil—it has a neutral flavour, is a monounsaturated fat, and contains no cholesterol.

SOY

Many people are interested in incorporating soy products into their diet. Soy products are an excellent source of protein, and contain phytochemicals and a range of healthy nutrients.

Soya beans are a good source of fibre, and as most soy products are dairy free they are a good alternative for those who are lactose intolerant.

Tips for using soy products in baking

- Soy milk can generally be substituted for regular milk in most baking, and low-fat soy milk is available.
- Soy butter may be used in baking, but not where melted butter is required.
- Soy margarine is made from soya bean oil, and may be used for cooking. Use this when a recipe calls for melted butter or margarine.
- Soy flour is rich in protein and is gluten free. Because of the lack of gluten, soy flour does not have the same properties as wheat flour, so a direct substitution is not possible. You will need to use a combination of soy flour and wheat flour to get the same texture, particularly for yeast baked goods.

CARROT CAKE

With less fat but all the flavour of regular carrot cake, this version also provides some beta-carotene, fibre and calcium.

Prep time: 20 minutes
Cooking time: 1 hour 15 minutes
Makes 14 slices
EASY

2¹/2 cups (310 g) self-raising flour
1 teaspoon bicarbonate of soda
2 teaspoons ground cinnamon
1 teaspoon mixed spice
¹/2 cup (95 g) soft brown sugar
¹/2 cup (80 g) sultanas
2 eggs, lightly beaten
2 tablespoons vegetable oil
¹/3 cup (80 ml) low-fat milk
140 g apple purée
290 g carrot, coarsely grated

Ricotta topping
125 g ricotta
¹/4 cup (30 g) icing sugar
¹/2 teaspoon grated lime rind

1 Preheat the oven to moderate 180°C (350°F/Gas 4). Lightly grease a 10 x 18 cm loaf tin and cover the base with baking paper. Sift the flour, soda and spices into a large bowl. Stir in the brown sugar and sultanas. Combine the egg, oil, milk and apple purée in a large jug.
2 Stir the egg mixture into the dry ingredients, then stir in the carrot. Spread into the tin and bake for 1¹/4 hours, or until a skewer comes out clean when inserted in the centre of the cake and the cake comes away slightly from the sides of the tin. Leave in the tin for 5 minutes before turning out to cool on a wire rack.
3 To make the topping, beat the ingredients together until smooth. Spread over the cake.

NUTRITION PER SLICE
Protein 4.5 g; Fat 5 g; Carbohydrate 30 g; Dietary Fibre 2 g; Cholesterol 30 mg; 755 kJ (180 Cal)

CHOCOLATE ANGEL FOOD CAKE

This light, airy cake has a chocolate taste, but with relatively little fat and few calories.

Prep time: 20 minutes
Cooking time: 40 minutes
Serves 8
EASY

---

2 teaspoons baking powder
1 cup (125 g) plain flour
1/2 cup (60 g) cocoa powder
1/4 teaspoon mixed spice
12 egg whites
2 teaspoons cream of tartar
1 cup (250 g) caster sugar
1 teaspoon vanilla essence
icing sugar, to dust
250 g fresh or frozen raspberries
1 tablespoon lemon juice
2–4 tablespoons icing sugar, to taste, extra

1 Preheat the oven to warm 160°C (315°F/ Gas 2–3). Sift together the baking powder, flour, cocoa powder and mixed spice three times.

2 Using electric beaters, beat the egg whites in a clean, dry bowl until foamy, add the cream of tartar and continue to beat until soft peaks form. Add half the sugar and beat on high speed for 10 minutes, or until the meringue is very firm and glossy. Fold in the vanilla, flour mixture and remaining sugar, working quickly and gently until combined.

3 Pour into a very clean, ungreased angel food cake tin and bake for 35–40 minutes, or until the cake is firm to the touch and comes away slightly from the sides of the tin. Turn out onto a wire rack to cool completely. Dust with icing sugar.

4 Place the raspberries in a blender or food processor, add the lemon juice and extra icing sugar and blend until smooth. Push through a sieve to remove the seeds and serve with the angel food cake.

NUTRITION PER SERVE:
Protein 9 g; Fat 1.5 g; Carbohydrate 46.5 g; Dietary Fibre 2.5 g; Cholesterol 0 mg; 965 kJ (230 Cal)

CHOCOLATE SWISS ROLL WITH DATE AND ORANGE CREAM

Just like a decadent gateau, this cake has a rich, creamy taste but relatively little fat. It also provides some vitamin A, B vitamins and calcium.

Prep time: 15 minutes
Cooking time: 20 minutes
Serves 8
EASY

1/2 cup (60 g) self-raising flour
1/4 cup (30 g) cocoa powder
3 eggs
1/2 cup (125 g) caster sugar

Date and orange cream
100 g dried dates
1/2 cup (125 ml) orange juice
250 g ricotta
1 tablespoon caster sugar
125 g light cream cheese
2 tablespoons honey
1 teaspoon grated orange rind

1 Preheat the oven to moderate 180°C (350°F/Gas 4). Line a 30 x 25 cm swiss roll tin with baking paper, extending over the two long sides. Sift the flour and cocoa powder together three times. Using electric beaters, beat the eggs in a clean, dry bowl for 4 minutes, or until thick and pale. Gradually add the sugar, beating until the mixture becomes pale yellow and glossy.
2 Using a metal spoon, fold the cocoa, flour and 1 tablespoon hot water into the egg mixture (work quickly and lightly). Pour into the prepared tin, smooth the surface, and bake for 12–15 minutes, or until golden brown and lightly springy.
3 Meanwhile, to make the date and orange cream, chop the dates and place in a small saucepan with the orange juice. Cover and bring to a simmer over very low heat for 4–5 minutes, or until softened. Remove from the pan and leave to cool completely. Place the ricotta in a small mixing bowl and, using a wooden spoon, beat in the sugar. Add the cream cheese, honey and orange rind, and mix together well. Stir in the dates and all of the juice.
4 Place a large sheet of baking paper on a clean tea towel. Turn the cake out onto the paper and leave for 1 minute. Peel the baking paper off the cake and, working quickly and gently, roll the cake up lengthways using the baking paper underneath as a guide. Leave the cake rolled like this until it is completely cool. Unroll the cake, spread evenly with the date cream mixture and re-roll, ensuring that the edge rests underneath the cake. Trim the ends of the cake before serving.

NUTRITION PER SERVE
Protein 9 g; Fat 8.5 g; Carbohydrate 36 g; Dietary Fibre 1.5 g; Cholesterol 90.5 mg; 1045 kJ (250 Cal)

NOTES: It is important to roll up the cake as soon as it is removed from the tin and to allow it to cool while rolled. This will prevent it from cracking when it is re-rolled with the filling inside.

This cake can be made a few hours ahead of time and stored, covered, in the refrigerator.

For something a little special, try adding Grand Marnier to the date and orange cream. Decrease the amount of orange juice by the amount of liqueur that you add. Try mixing strawberries, blueberries or your favourite mixed berries through the ricotta mixture, instead of the dates. Replace the orange juice with your favourite berry or other liqueur to complement the berry flavours.

WHOLEMEAL BANANA BREAD

This banana bread has less fat and more fibre than regular varieties, and provides unsaturated fat, vitamin B6 and potassium. Serve the bread with yoghurt for a calcium boost.

Prep time: 15 minutes
Cooking time: 50 minutes
Serves 4–6
EASY

1/2 cup (95 g) soft brown sugar
1 egg
200 g low-fat vanilla fromage frais or
   whipped yoghurt
2 tablespoons oil
2 ripe bananas, mashed
1/4 cup (40 g) sultanas
1 cup (125 g) self-raising flour
1/4 cup (35 g) wholemeal self-raising flour
1/2 teaspoon bicarbonate of soda
2 tablespoons unprocessed bran
1 teaspoon ground cinnamon
1/2 teaspoon ground nutmeg

1 Preheat the oven to warm 160°C (315°F/Gas 2–3). Cover the base of a 20.5 x 10.5 cm non-stick loaf tin with baking paper.
2 Place the sugar, egg, fromage frais and oil in a large bowl, and whisk until well combined. Fold in the banana and sultanas, then fold in the sifted flours, bicarbonate of soda, bran, cinnamon and nutmeg.
3 Spoon the mixture into the prepared tin and bake for 50 minutes, or until cooked through when tested with a skewer. Serve warm or cold with low-fat yoghurt or fromage frais. Delicious toasted.

NUTRITION PER SERVE (6)
Protein 6.5 g; Fat 7 g; Carbohydrate 49 g; Dietary Fibre 3 g; Cholesterol 1.5 mg; 1190 kJ (285 Cal)

NOTE: You will need 1 cup (240 g) mashed banana. Bananas are a good source of carbohydrate and fibre.

FUDGE BROWNIES

These brownies will prove that reduced-fat foods can be healthy and delicious too. Moist and sweet, they contain carbohydrate and small amounts of most vitamins and minerals.

Prep time: 15 minutes
Cooking time: 30 minutes
Makes 18
EASY

cooking oil spray
1/2 cup (60 g) plain flour
1/2 cup (60 g) self-raising flour
1 teaspoon bicarbonate of soda
3/4 cup (90 g) cocoa powder
2 eggs
1 1/4 cups (310 g) caster sugar
2 teaspoons vanilla essence
2 tablespoons oil
200 g low-fat vanilla fromage frais or
   whipped yoghurt
140 g apple purée
icing sugar, for dusting

1 Preheat the oven to moderate 180°C (350°F/Gas 4). Spray a 30 x 20 cm shallow baking tin with oil and line the base with baking paper.

2 Sift the flours, bicarbonate of soda and cocoa powder into a large bowl. Combine the eggs, sugar, vanilla essence, oil, fromage frais and apple purée. Add to the flour and mix well. Spread into the tin and bake for 30 minutes, or until a skewer comes out clean.

3 The brownie will sink slightly in the centre as it cools. Leave in the tin for 5 minutes before turning onto a wire rack to cool. Dust with icing sugar, cut into pieces and serve.

NUTRITION PER BROWNIE
Protein 3.5 g; Fat 4 g; Carbohydrate 26 g; Dietary Fibre 0.5 g; Cholesterol 21.5 mg; 630 kJ (150 Cal)

APPLE, BLUEBERRY AND BRAN MUFFINS

These fruity muffins are moist and soft, yet relatively low in fat, and also provide fibre, B vitamins and phosphorus.

Prep time: 20 minutes
Cooking time: 20 minutes
Makes 12
EASY

1¼ cups (155 g) self-raising flour
¾ cup (110 g) wholemeal self-raising flour
1 teaspoon ground cinnamon
½ cup (75 g) oat bran
¾ cup (140 g) soft brown sugar
150 g fresh or frozen blueberries
½ cup (135 g) bottled chunky apple sauce
1 egg, lightly beaten
1 cup (250 ml) skim milk
2 egg whites

1 Preheat the oven to moderately hot 200°C (400°F/Gas 6). Sift the flours and cinnamon into a bowl and return the husks to the bowl. Stir in the oat bran, sugar and blueberries.

2 Place the apple sauce, egg, skim milk and egg whites in a jug and mix together well. Pour into the dry ingredients and mix until just combined, but still lumpy. Do not overmix.

3 Spoon the mixture into twelve ½ cup (125 ml) non-stick muffin holes and bake for 20 minutes, or until cooked through. Leave in the tin for 5 minutes before turning out on a wire rack to cool.

NUTRITION PER MUFFIN
Protein 5.5 g; Fat 1.5 g; Carbohydrate 35 g; Dietary Fibre 3 g; Cholesterol 17.5 mg; 720 kJ (170 Cal)

HAM, CORN AND POLENTA MUFFINS

These delicious savoury muffins provide carbohydrate energy, B vitamins and minerals, without too much fat

Prep time: 15 minutes
Cooking time: 20 minutes
Makes 12
EASY

3/4 cup (110 g) polenta
1 tablespoon sugar
1 3/4 cups (215 g) plain flour
1 tablespoon baking powder
2 tablespoons oil
1 egg, lightly beaten
1 1/4 cups (315 ml) skim milk
125 g can creamed corn
4 spring onions, thinly sliced
150 g shaved light ham, chopped
50 g 93% fat-free cheese, grated

1 Preheat the oven to moderately hot 200°C (400°F/Gas 6). Sift the polenta, sugar, flour and baking powder into a bowl. Place the oil, egg and skim milk in a separate bowl, mix together well and pour into the dry ingredients.

2 Add the creamed corn, spring onion, ham and cheese, and stir together with a large metal spoon until just combined. Do not overmix. The mixture should still be lumpy. Spoon the mixture into twelve 1/2 cup (125 ml) non-stick muffin holes and bake for 20 minutes, or until risen and golden brown. Leave in the tin to cool for 5 minutes before turning out onto a wire rack to cool fully.

NUTRITION PER MUFFIN
Protein 8 g; Fat 4.5 g; Carbohydrate 25 g; Dietary Fibre 1.5 g; Cholesterol 25 mg; 730 kJ (175 Cal)

BANANA AND BLUEBERRY TART

A colourful and tasty dessert, this tart delivers carbohydate energy, some B vitamins and minerals. Serve it with yoghurt for extra calcium.

Prep time: 30 minutes
Cooking time: 25 minutes
Serves 6
EASY

cooking oil spray
1 cup (125 g) plain flour
1/2 cup (60 g) self-raising flour
1 teaspoon ground cinnamon
1 teaspoon ground ginger
40 g butter, chopped
1/2 cup (95 g) soft brown sugar
1/2 cup (125 ml) buttermilk
200 g blueberries
2 bananas
2 teaspoons lemon juice
1 tablespoon demerara sugar

1 Preheat the oven to moderately hot 200°C (400°F/Gas 6). Spray a baking tray or pizza tray lightly with oil. Sift the flours and spices into a bowl. Add the butter and sugar and rub in until the mixture resembles breadcrumbs. Make a well and then add enough buttermilk to mix to a soft dough.

2 Roll the dough out on a lightly floured surface to a 23 cm diameter round. Place on the tray and roll the edge to form a lip to hold the fruit in.

3 Spread the blueberries over the dough, keeping within the lip. Slice the bananas, toss them in the lemon juice, then arrange over the top. Sprinkle with the sugar, and bake for 25 minutes, or until the base is browned. Serve immediately.

NUTRITION PER SERVE
Protein 5 g; Fat 6.5 g; Carbohydrate 52 g; Dietary Fibre 2.5 g; Cholesterol 19 mg; 1180 kJ (280 Cal)

SULTANA SCONES

These scones get their sweetness from natural sugars, and are a good source of carbohydrate.

Prep time: 15 minutes
Cooking time: 15 minutes
Makes 12
EASY

2 cups (250 g) self-raising flour
1 teaspoon baking powder
30 g cold butter, cut into small cubes
1/2 cup (80 g) sultanas
1 cup (250 ml) milk
milk, extra, to glaze

1 Preheat the oven to hot 220°C (425°F/Gas 7). Lightly grease a baking tray, or line with baking paper. Sift the flour, baking powder and a pinch of salt into a bowl and add the butter. Rub the butter into the flour with your fingertips, then stir in the sultanas. Make a well in the centre.
2 Add almost all the milk and mix with a flat-bladed knife, using a cutting action, until the dough comes together in clumps. Use the remaining milk if necessary. With floured hands, gently gather the dough together, lift out onto a lightly floured surface and pat into a smooth ball. Do not knead the dough or the scones will be tough.
3 Pat the dough out to a 2 cm thickness. Using a floured 5 cm cutter, cut into rounds. Gather the dough trimmings together and, without handling too much, press out again to a 2 cm thickness and cut out more rounds. Place the scones close together on the baking tray and brush lightly with the extra milk. Bake for 15 minutes, or until risen and golden brown on top. Serve the scones warm or at room temperature.

NUTRITION PER SCONE
Protein 3 g; Fat 3 g; Carbohydrate 21 g; Dietary Fibre 1 g; Cholesterol 9 mg; 520 kJ (125 Cal)

Chocolate-chip cookies (top), and Almond and orange biscotti

CHOCOLATE-CHIP COOKIES

These cookies are lower in fat than regular biscuits, but you still need to eat sensible amounts if you're watching your weight.

Prep time: 10 minutes
Cooking time: 40 minutes
Makes 20
EASY

120 g reduced-fat margarine
1/3 cup (60 g) soft brown sugar
1/3 cup (115 g) honey
2 egg whites
1 teaspoon vanilla extract
1 1/2 cups (150 g) quick-cooking oats
3/4 cup (90 g) plain flour
1/2 teaspoon ground cinnamon
1/2 teaspoon baking powder
1/4 teaspoon mixed spice
1/3 cup (60 g) dark chocolate chips

1 Preheat the oven to moderately hot 190°C (375°F/Gas 5). Line two large baking trays with baking paper.
2 Place the reduced-fat spread, sugar, honey, egg whites and vanilla extract in a bowl and beat with electric beaters until well combined.
3 In a separate bowl, combine the oats, flour, cinnamon, baking powder and mixed spice. Stir the dry ingredients into the wet ingredients, stirring until well mixed. Add the chocolate chips, making sure they are distributed evenly throughout the mixture.
4 Place tablespoons of the mixture on the lined baking sheets and press down with the back of a spoon until the cookies are about 1 cm thick. Allow plenty of room for spreading (you will probably fit about 6 biscuits per tray). Bake for 10–12 minutes, or until crisp at the edges but still a little soft in the centre. Transfer to a wire rack to cool while you cook the remaining biscuits.

NUTRITION PER COOKIE
Protein 1.5 g; Fat 4 g; Carbohydrate 17 g; Dietary Fibre 1 g; Cholesterol 0 mg; 455 kJ (110 Cal)

ALMOND AND ORANGE BISCOTTI

An excellent accompaniment to low-fat puddings, these crisp biscuits provide monounsaturated fat, some niacin and minerals.

Prep time: 20 minutes
Cooking time: 1 hour
Makes 40
EASY

2 eggs
2/3 cup (155 g) firmly packed soft brown sugar
1 cup (125 g) self-raising flour
3/4 cup (90 g) plain flour
125 g almonds
1 tablespoon finely grated orange rind
1/4 teaspoon ground cardamom

1 Preheat the oven to warm 160°C (315°F/Gas 2–3). Line a baking tray with baking paper.
2 Beat the eggs and sugar in a bowl with electric beaters until pale and creamy. Sift the self-raising and plain flours into the bowl, then add the almonds, orange rind and cardamom, and mix to a soft dough.
3 Turn out the dough onto a lightly floured work surface. Divide the mixture into two portions, shaping into two 5 cm x 20 cm loaves.
4 Bake the loaves for 35–40 minutes, or until lightly golden. Transfer to a wire rack to cool. Cut the loaves into 1 cm diagonal slices with a large serrated bread knife. The biscotti will be crumbly on the edges so work slowly and, if possible, try to hold the sides as you cut.
5 Arrange the slices on baking trays in a single layer. Return to the oven for 10 minutes on each side. Don't worry if they don't seem fully dry as they will become crisp on cooling. Cool the biscotti completely before serving. Store in an airtight container for 2–3 weeks.

NUTRITION PER BISCOTTI
Protein 1 g; Fat 2 g; Carbohydrate 5.5 g; Dietary Fibre 0.5 g; Cholesterol 10 mg; 185 kJ (45 Cal)

PUMPKIN BREAD

Delicious served with soups or stews, this bread is a great source of carbohydrate, potassium and beta-carotene.

Prep time: 35 minutes + 2 hours rising
Cooking time: 50 minutes
Makes 1 round loaf
MEDIUM

300 g pumpkin, chopped
7 g sachet dried yeast
1 teaspoon salt
4¹/₂ cups (560 g) white bread flour
1 egg, beaten
pumpkin seeds (pepitas), to decorate

1 Steam or boil the pumpkin for 10 minutes, or until tender. Drain thoroughly, then mash. Grease a 20 cm round cake tin and line the base with baking paper. Place the yeast and ¹/₄ cup (60 ml) warm water in a small bowl and stir well. Leave in a warm, draught-free place for 10 minutes, or until bubbles appear on the surface. The mixture should be frothy and slightly increased in volume. If your yeast doesn't foam it is dead, so you will have to discard it and start again.
2 Sift the salt and 4 cups (500 g) of the flour into a large bowl. Add the pumpkin, yeast mixture and ¹/₄ cup (60 ml) warm water. Mix thoroughly using a wooden spoon, and then your hands, until well combined. The dough will form a rough, slightly sticky ball. Add more liquid if the mixture is too dry—the amount of liquid will depend on the moistness of the pumpkin.
3 Turn the dough out onto a floured surface. Knead for 10 minutes, or until the dough is smooth and elastic. Incorporate enough of the remaining flour to form a smooth dough. Place the dough in a lightly oiled bowl and brush with oil. Cover with plastic wrap or a damp tea towel and leave in a warm place for 1 hour, or until well risen.

4 Punch down the dough, knead for 1 minute, then pull away a golf ball-sized piece of dough. Shape the remaining dough into a smooth round ball and place in the tin. Roll the smaller ball into a rope 35 cm long. Tie into a loose knot and place across the top of the dough, then seal with a little water to hold in place. Cover with plastic wrap or a damp tea towel and leave in a warm place for 1 hour, or until risen to the top of the tin.
5 Preheat the oven to hot 210°C (415°F/Gas 6–7). Beat 2 teaspoons water into the egg and brush over the dough. Sprinkle with the pumpkin seeds and bake for 20 minutes. Reduce the oven to moderate 180°C (350°F/Gas 4), then bake for another 20 minutes, or until cooked. Cover with foil during the last 10 minutes of cooking if the bread is browning too much. Transfer to a wire rack to cool.

NUTRITION PER SERVE (8)
Protein 10 g; Fat 2.5 g; Carbohydrate 53 g; Dietary Fibre 3 g; Cholesterol 25 mg; 1160 kJ (275 Cal)

NOTE: Pumpkin bread is delicious served with butter. It will keep for up to three days in an airtight container, and it also freezes well for up to a month.

PRETZELS

These oven-baked pretzels have less fat than many snack foods, and provide some niacin and fibre.

Prep time: 50 minutes + 1 hour 30 minutes
    rising
Cooking time: 15 minutes
Makes 12
MEDIUM

1 teaspoon dried yeast
1/4 teaspoon sugar
150 ml warm milk
1 1/2 cups (185 g) white bread flour
1/4 teaspoon salt
30 g butter, melted
1 egg yolk, lightly beaten
coarse sea salt, to sprinkle

1 Place the yeast, sugar and milk in a small bowl and stir well. Leave in a warm place for 10 minutes, or until bubbles appear on the surface. The mixture should be frothy and slightly increased in volume. If your yeast doesn't foam it is dead, so you will have to discard it and start again.
2 Place the flour and salt in a large bowl and make a well in the centre. Add the yeast mixture and butter, and mix to a rough dough with a wooden spoon. Turn out onto a floured surface and knead for 10 minutes until smooth and elastic.
3 Place into an oiled bowl, oil the surface of the dough, cover and set aside in a warm place for 1 hour, or until doubled in size.
4 Preheat the oven to moderately hot 190°C (375°F/Gas 5). Line a baking tray with baking paper. Punch down the dough and knead for 2–3 minutes. Divide into 12 pieces. Cover the dough while working. Roll each piece into a long rope 40 cm long. Circle and knot into a pretzel shape. Place well spaced on the tray. Cover with a tea towel. Leave to rise in a warm, draught-free place for 20–30 minutes.
5 Lightly brush the pretzels with the beaten egg yolk and sprinkle with sea salt. Place the pretzels in the oven and spray them twice with water before baking for 12–15 minutes, or until crisp and golden brown. Transfer to a wire rack to cool.

NUTRITION PER PRETZEL
Protein 2.5 g; Fat 3 g; Carbohydrate 12 g; Dietary Fibre 0.5 g; Cholesterol 23 mg; 355 kJ (85 Cal)

SOY AND LINSEED LOAF

This highly nutritious bread contains phytochemicals, carbohydrate and different fibres.

Prep time: 30 minutes + rising
Cooking time: 50 minutes
Makes 1 loaf
MEDIUM

1/2 cup (110 g) pearl barley
7 g sachet dried yeast
1 teaspoon caster sugar
1 teaspoon salt
1 tablespoon linseeds
2 tablespoons soy flour
2 tablespoons gluten flour
1 cup (150 g) wholemeal bread flour
2 1/2 cups (310 g) white bread flour
2 tablespoons olive oil

1 Brush a 26 x 10 cm bread tin with oil. Put the barley in a saucepan with 2 cups (500 ml) water, bring to the boil and boil for 20 minutes, or until softened. Drain.
2 Mix the yeast, sugar and 155 ml warm water in a small bowl. Leave in a warm place for 10 minutes, or until bubbles appear on the surface. The mixture should be frothy and slightly increased in volume.

3 Place the barley, salt, linseeds, soy and gluten flours, wholemeal flour and 2 cups (250 g) of the white flour in a large bowl. Make a well and add the yeast mixture, oil and 155 ml warm water. Mix with a wooden spoon to a soft dough. Turn out onto a floured surface and knead for 10 minutes, or until smooth and elastic. Incorporate enough of the remaining flour until the dough is no longer sticky.
4 Place the dough in an oiled bowl and brush with oil. Cover and leave in a warm place for 45 minutes, or until doubled in size. Punch down and knead for 3 minutes.
5 Pat the dough to a 24 x 20 cm rectangle. Roll up from the long side and place in the tin, seam side down. Cover and set aside in a warm place for 1 hour, or until risen to the top of the tin. Preheat the oven to moderately hot 200°C (400°F/Gas 6).
6 Brush the dough with water and make two slits on top. Bake for 30 minutes, or until golden. Cool on a wire rack.

NUTRITION PER SERVE (10)
Protein 8 g; Fat 5 g; Carbohydrate 41 g; Dietary Fibre 5 g; Cholesterol 0 mg; 1025 kJ (245 Cal)

GLUTEN-FREE BREAD

This bread contains mostly unsaturated fat, and is a good source of carbohydrate and B vitamins.

Prep time: 25 minutes + 1 hour rising
Cooking time: 45 minutes
Makes 1 loaf
MEDIUM

7 g sachet dried yeast
2 teaspoons sugar
2 1/4 cups (400 g) gluten-free plain flour
1/2 teaspoon salt
1/2 cup (50 g) milk powder
1 tablespoon xanthan gum
2 eggs, lightly beaten
1/4 cup (60 ml) oil
1 tablespoon sesame seeds

1 Lightly grease a 22 x 9 x 5.5 cm loaf tin. Place the yeast, sugar and 440 ml warm water in a small bowl and stir well. Leave in a warm place for 10 minutes, or until bubbles appear on the surface. The mixture should be frothy and slightly increased in volume. If the yeast doesn't foam you will have to discard it and start again.
2 Sift the flour, salt, milk powder and xanthan gum into a large bowl. Make a well in the centre and add the yeast mixture, egg and oil. Using a wooden spoon, stir together well until it forms a soft moist mixture. Beat for 1 minute.
3 Spoon the mixture into the loaf tin and smooth the surface with moist hands. Sprinkle the sesame seeds over the top. Cover with lightly greased plastic wrap and leave in a warm place for 1 hour, or until nearly risen to the top of the tin. Preheat the oven to moderately hot 190°C (375°F/Gas 5). Bake the bread for 40–45 minutes, or until it is golden and sounds hollow when tapped. Leave in the tin for 5 minutes before transferring to a wire rack to cool. Allow the bread to cool completely before cutting.

NUTRITION PER SERVE (10)
Protein 5 g; Fat 7.5 g; Carbohydrate 32 g; Dietary Fibre 0.8 g; Cholesterol 40.5 mg; 915 kJ (220 Cal)

CHEESE AND HERB PULL-APART LOAF

Lower in fat than regular garlic bread, this loaf provides carbohydrate, fibre and B vitamins.

Prep time: 25 minutes +
   1 hour 40 minutes rising
Cooking time: 30 minutes
Serves 6–8
MEDIUM

7 g dried yeast
1 teaspoon sugar
4 cups (500 g) plain flour
1 1/2 teaspoons salt
2 tablespoons chopped fresh parsley
2 tablespoons chopped fresh chives
1 tablespoon chopped fresh thyme
1/2 cup (60 g) grated reduced-fat Cheddar
milk, to glaze

1 Combine the yeast, sugar and 1/2 cup (125 ml) of warm water in a small bowl. Cover and set aside in a warm place for 10 minutes, or until frothy.
2 Sift the flour and salt into a bowl. Make a well in the centre and pour in 1 cup (250 ml) warm water and the yeast. Mix to a soft dough. Knead on a lightly floured surface for 10 minutes, or until smooth. Put the dough in an oiled bowl, cover and leave for 1 hour, or until doubled in size.
3 Punch down the dough and knead for 1 minute. Divide in half and shape each half into 10 flat, 6 cm discs. Mix the herbs with the Cheddar and put 2 teaspoons on a disc. Press another disc on top. Repeat with the remaining discs and herb mixture.
4 Grease a 21 x 10.5 x 6.5 cm loaf tin. Stand the filled discs upright in the prepared tin, squashing them together. Cover the tin and set aside in a warm place for 30 minutes, or until well risen. Preheat the oven to hot 210°C (415°F/Gas 6–7). Glaze the bread with milk and bake for 30 minutes, or until brown and crusty.

NUTRITION PER SERVE (8)
Protein 9.5 g; Fat 2 g; Carbohydrate 45.5 g; Dietary Fibre 2.5 g; Cholesterol 4 mg; 1005 kJ (240 Cal)

Gluten-free bread (top), and Cheese and herb pull-apart loaf

CARBOHYDRATE, FIBRE AND FAT COUNTER

The following tables list the carbohydrate, fibre, fat and energy content of commonly consumed foods. The figure next to each food represents the average serving size. For foods that don't have a serving size, we have used a 100 gram amount. In the fibre column, N denotes that the figure has not been calcuated, + that amounts have been detected but not accurately calculated and Tr means that only a trace (less than 0.1 g) has been found.

FOOD	CARB g	FIBRE g	FAT g	ENERGY kcal	ENERGY KJ
ALCOHOL					
Beers					
ale, brown, bottled – small, 275ml	8.3	0	0	82	346
ale, pale, bottled – small, 275ml	5.5	0	0	77	325
ale, strong – small, 275ml	17	0	0	182	756
beer, average, 1 pint, 574ml	13	0	0	182	756
beer, bitter, canned, 440ml	10.3	0	0	143	586
beer, bitter, canned, large, 500ml	11.6	0	0	161	660
beer, bitter, low alcohol, 1 pint, 574ml	12	0	0	75	310
beer, draught, 1 pint, 574ml	13.3	0	0	184	755
beer, keg, 1 pint, 574ml	13.2	0	0	178	741
beer, mild, draught, 1 pint, 574ml	9.3	0	0	145	597
lager, average, canned and draught, 500ml	Tr	0	0	145	605
lager, bottled, large, 500ml	7.5	0	0	146	598
lager, reduced-alcohol, 1 pint, 574ml	8.6	0	0	57.4	235
lager, premium, strong, 500ml	Tr	0	0	295	1220
shandy, canned, large, 500ml	15	0	0	55	240
stout, bottled, small, 275ml	11.4	0	0	100	429
stout, strong, large, 500ml	10.5	0	0	195	817
stout, strong, small, 275ml	5.8	0	0	107	449
Ciders					
cider, dry, 1 pint, 574ml	15	0	0	208	873
cider, sweet, 1 pint, 574ml	24.4	0	0	244	1011
cider, vintage, strong, 1 pint, 574ml	42	0	0	578	2417
Cocktails					
cocktail, Bloody Mary, 165ml	5.5	0.5	0	124	520
cocktail, Daiquiri, 60ml	4	0	0	111	465
cocktail, Tequila Sunrise, 60ml	7	0	0	66	275
Liqueurs					
liqueur, egg-based, 25ml	7	0	1.6	65	273
liqueur, cherry brandy/coffee, 25ml	8.2	0	0	65.5	275
liqueur, cream, 25ml	6	0	4	81	338
liqueur, drambuie, 25ml	6.1	0	0	78.5	330
Spirits					
spirits, average, 40% volume – brandy, gin, rum, vodka, whiskey, 25ml	0	0	0	55	230
spirits, average, 37.5% volume, 25ml	0	0	0	51	214
Wines					
wine, red, small glass, 120ml	0.4	0	0	85	356
wine, rose, 120ml	3.1	0	0	89	367
wine, white, dry, 120ml	0.7	0	0	82	343
wine, white, medium, 120ml	4.3	0	0	94	388

FOOD	CARB g	FIBRE g	FAT g	ENERGY kcal	KJ
wine, white, sweet, 120ml	7.4	0	0	118	493
wine, fortified, port, 50ml	6	0	0	80	327
wine, fortified, sherry, dry, 50ml	0.7	0	0	58	240
wine, fortified, sherry, medium, 50ml	3	0	0	60	252
wine, fortified, sherry, sweet, 50ml	3.5	0	0	68	284
wine, fortified, vermouth, dry, 50ml	1.5	0	0	55	227
wine, fortified, vermouth, sweet, 50ml	7.6	0	0	75	315
champagne, 125ml	1.7	0	0	95	394
APPLE					
chutney, 1 serving, 35g	18	0.6	0	68	288
cooking, stewed with sugar, 4oz, 100g	19	1.8	0	74	314
cooking, stewed without sugar, 4oz, 100g	8	2	0	33	138
eating, raw, unpeeled, 1 average, 5oz, 125g	13	2.2	0	52.5	224
eating, raw, peeled, 1 average, 4oz, 100g	11	0	0	45	190
dried, 1oz, 25g	15	2.4	0	60	254
juice, unsweeted, small glass, 4fl oz, 100ml	10	Tr	0	38	164
juice, concentrated, 1fl oz, 25g	14	Tr	0	57	243
APRICOT					
canned in juice, 6 halves, 120g	9.6	1.2	0	41	176
canned in syrup, 6 halves, 120g	19	1.2	0	76	321
raw, 3, 110g	6.8	2	0	28	119
stewed with sugar, 4oz serving, 100g	18	2	0	72	308
stewed without sugar, 4oz serving, 100g	6	2	0	27	115
dried, 3 whole, 50g	22	4	0	94	401
ready to eat – semi-dried, 4oz, 100g	36	6.3	0	158	674
juice drink, 35% juice, 1 glass, 250ml	20	1	0	18	75
nectar, 50% juice, glass, 250ml	32	0	0	129	540
ARTICHOKE					
globe, boiled, 1 medium, 220g	2.6	1	0	17	70
hearts, canned in brine, drained,					
1 heart, 50g	1	1.5	0	8	35
Jerusalem, peeled, boiled, 1 medium, 100g	10	3.5	0	41	207
ASPARAGUS					
canned, drained, 8 spears, 100g	1.5	2.9	0	24	100
fresh, boiled, 4 spears, 120g	1	1	0	15	63
AUBERGINE (see also EGGPLANT)					
fried in corn oil, 100g	2.8	2.3	32	302	1262
raw, 100g	2.2	2	0.4	15	64
AVOCADO					
medium, 1 raw 100g	1.9	3.4	19.5	190	784
BABY FOOD					
baby rusk, plain, average, 100g	82.8	N	7.9	408	1729
rusk, flavoured, 100g	78.1	N	9	401	1698
rusk, low sugar, 100g	77.8	N	9.7	414	1751
rusk, wholemeal, 100g	76.5	N	10.1	411	1739
cereal, ground muesli, 100g	70	N	8	400	1690
cereal, creamed porridge,100g	58	N	5.5	360	1510
cereal, mixed, powder, 100g	71	N	5	377	1599
cereal, fruit, banana & apple,					
powder, 100g	70	N	3.8	359	1527
cereal, apple & blackberry,					
powder, 100g	77	N	4	365	1552
baby rice, powder, 100g	78	N	3	365	1553
baby rice, mixed, 100g	78	N	2	372	1565

FOOD	CARB g	FIBRE g	FAT g	ENERGY kcal	KJ
dessert, creamed rice, jar, 128g	8	0	0.5	40	155
dessert, fruit, powder, 100g	90	1.3	0.6	383	1635
dessert, caramel custard, 100g	13	N	2.5	82	345
dessert, fruit custard, 100g	17	N	0.5	74	310
dinner, beef, junior, 100g	10	1	0.5	60	240
dinner, chicken & vegetable, 100g	8	1.5	1.5	60	250
dinner, chicken, junior, 100g	9	0.5	1	55	230
dinner, chicken noodle, junior, 100g	9.5	0.5	1	57	240
egg/cheese based meal, canned, 100g	10	1	3.4	82	344
meat based meal, average, canned, 100g	8.6	1.1	3	73	306
dinner, lamb casserole, jar 200g	18	N	2	121	510
dinner, lamb, junior, 100g	7	1	2.5	62	260
dinner, lentil hot-pot, jar, 200g	20	N	0.5	114	480
dinner, fish based, average, canned, 100g	9	0.6	3	76	321
dinner, garden vegetable, jar, 200g	24	N	0.5	124	520
dinner, mixed vegetable, strained, 100g	8.5	N	1	46	195
dinner, pasta & vegetable, jar, 200g	27	N	1	138	580
dinner, pasta based, average, canned, 100g	8.5	0.7	3	71	300
dinner, vegetable based, canned, 100g	10	2	2	67	284
BACON					
bits, 2tsp	0	0	1.5	30	125
fried & 2 fried eggs	0	0	18	215	905
middle rasher, fried, 1 slice, 10g	0	0	3	37	155
middle rasher, trimmed, fried, 1, 10g	0	0	1	23	95
middle rasher, grilled, 1, 10g	0	0	2	32	135
middle rasher, trimmed, grilled, 1, 10g	0	0	1	24	100
BAGEL					
plain, average, 1, 60g	29	+	0.5	137	575
BAKLAVA					
bought, average piece, 100g	40	+	17.5	322	1349
BAMBOO SHOOTS					
canned or bottled, drained, 1 cup, 140g	1.5	2.2	0	11	45
raw, 50g	3	N	0	14.3	60
BANANA					
chips, crystallised, 1oz, approx. 25 chips, 25g	15	0.5	7.8	128	534
dried, 100g	28	3	0	119	500
raw, peeled, 140g	32.5	1	Tr	133	564
BARLEY					
bran, raw, 40g	30	+	1	131	550
cooked, 1 portion, 180g	38	+	1.5	190	800
pearl, cooked, 100g	27.7	+	1	120	510
wholegrain, raw, 100g	64	15	2	301	1282
BEANS & LENTILS					
aduki, cooked, 4oz portion, 100g	22.5	5.5	0.2	123	525
baked, canned in tomato sauce, 100g	15	3.5	0.6	81	345
balor, canned in salted water, 100g	2.8	2.7	0.1	19	83
black-eyed, cooked, 100g	20	3.5	0.7	116	494
black gram, cooked, 100g	13.5	N	0.4	89	379
black kidney, cooked, 100g	24.5	N	0.5	130	545
borlotti, canned, drained, 100g	25	N	0.5	112	470
borlotti, cooked, 100g	28.5	N	0.5	146	612
broad, fresh, cooked, 100g	5.6	5.4	0.8	48	204

FOOD	CARB g	FIBRE g	FAT g	ENERGY kcal	KJ
butter (cannellini), canned, 100g	13	4.6	0.5	77	327
chickpeas, canned, drained,					
100g portion	16	4.1	2.9	115	487
green, fresh, cooked, 100g	3	2.4	0	22	92
green, frozen, cooked, 100g	4.7	4.1	0	25	108
haricot, cooked, 100g	17.2	6.1	0.5	95	406
kidney, red, canned, drained, cooked, 100g	12.2	4.1	0.5	70	380
lentils, canned in tomato sauce, 100g	9.3	1.7	0.2	55	236
lentils, red, split, cooked, 100g	17.5	2	0.4	100	424
lentils, whole, dried, cooked, 100g	17	3.8	0.7	105	446
lima, dried, cooked, 100g	10	5.5	Tr	70	295
mung, cooked, 100g	15.3	10	0.4	91	389
pinto, cooked, 100g	24	N	0.7	137	583
red kidney bean, cooked, 100g	17.4	6.7	0.5	103	440
red kidney beans, in chilli sauce,100g	13.1	3.6	2.6	91	383
runner, fresh, cooked, 100g	2.3	1.9	0.5	18	76
soya, canned, drained, 100g	5.1	6.1	7.3	141	590
soya, canned in tomato sauce, 100g	7	3	3	90	380
soya, dried, cooked, 100g	1.5	6.1	7.5	128	540
three-bean mix, canned, drained, 100g	14	N	0.5	86	360
tofu, soya bean, steamed, 100g	0.7	N	4.2	73	304
BEEF					
steak, lean, grilled, 1 medium, 117g	0	0	10.5	224	940
steak, untrimmed, grilled, 1, 120g	0	0	12.5	250	1040
chuck steak, untrimmed, simmered, 1, 190g	0	0	26	486	2040
corned, canned, 100g	0	0	12.5	217	905
corned, sliced, 100g	0	0	9	150	625
fillet steak, lean, grilled, 1, small, 85g	0	0	7	167	700
fillet steak, untrimmed, grilled, 1 small, 85g	0	0	11	198	830
Beef burgers, grilled, 100g	0.1	0	24.4	326	1355
homemade, 100g	1	0	20	287	1194
takeaway, in bun with salad, 100g	18	N	12.7	238	996
economy, frozen, grilled, 100g	9.7	0.8	19.3	273	1138
heart, simmered, 100g	0	0	5.9	179	752
kidney, simmered, 100g	0	0	6.1	153	641
liver, simmered, 100g	0	0	9.5	198	831
mince, simmered, drained, 170g	0	0	20.5	390	1623
mince, lean, simmered, drained, 170g	0	0	16.5	309	1300
oxtail, simmered, 100g	0	0	13.5	243	1014
pepper steak with cream sauce,					
1 serving, 200g	0	0	35	536	2250
pie, bought, family size, 1 serving, 250g	38.5	+	36.5	560	2355
pie, bought, individual, 250g	45	+	34.5	564	2370
pie, bought, party size, 1, 40g	7.5	+	7.5	111	465
rib steak, lean, grilled, 100g	0	0	5.5	176	740
rissoles, fried, 2, 340g	0	+	30	662	2780
round steak, lean, grilled, 100g	0	0	6	176	740
round steak, untrimmed, grilled, 100g	0	0	9.5	202	850
rump steak, lean, grilled, 175g	0	0	11.5	334	1405
rump steak, untrimmed, grilled, 200g	0	0	33.5	538	2260
silverside, lean, baked, 2 slices, 80g	0	0	3.5	131	550
silverside, untrimmed, baked, 2 slices, 85g	0	0	10	189	795
sirloin steak, lean, grilled, 110g	0	0	9.5	192	806
sirloin steak, untrimmed, grilled, 127g	0	0	24	348	1460

FOOD	CARB g	FIBRE g	FAT g	ENERGY kcal	KJ
skirt steak, lean, simmered, 100g	0	0	5	188	790
skirt steak, untrimmed, simmered, 100g	0	0	6	196	825
steak, lean, grilled, 1 small, 110g	0	0	9	216	910
steak, untrimmed, grilled, 1 small, 130g	0	0	20.5	330	1390
T-bone, lean, grilled, 100g	0	0	5.5	134	565
T-bone, untrimmed, grilled, 100g	0	0	8	164	690
tongue, simmered, 100g	0	0	25	307	1290
topside roast, lean, baked, 2 slices. 80g	0	0	4	124	520
topside roast, untrimmed, baked, 2 slices, 90g	0	0	9	171	720
topside steak, lean, grilled, 1 small, 100g	0	0	5	151	635
topside steak, untrimmed, grilled, 1 small,100g	0	0	6.5	162	680
tripe, simmered, 100g	0	0	3	83	350
BEETROOT					
fresh, peeled, boiled, 2 slices	5	0.4	0	25	105
pickled, 5 slices, 100g	14	1.7	0	64	270
raw, grated, 30g	2.5	0.6	0	12	50
BISCUITS					
assorted creams, 1, 15g	12.5	N	4	75	315
brandy snaps, 1, 10g	6.4	Tr	2	44	183
bourbon, 1, 12.5g	8.5	N	3.2	64	270
chocolate, full coated, 1 small, 25g	17	0.6	7	131	549
chocolate coated, 2, 30g	20	0.9	7.2	148	621
chocolate chip cookies, 1	4.5	N	2	36	150
chocolate shortbreads, 1	5	N	2.5	35	147
choc-chip, 1, 10g	8	N	2	51	215
cookies, 1, 10g	9	N	2.5	62	260
coconut ice, 1	9.5	+	3.5	71	300
cream biscuit, 1, 10g	6.4	N	2	46	194
custard cream, 1, 12.5g	8	N	3	64	270
digestive biscuits, plain, 2, 30g	20	0.7	6.3	141	593
digestive biscuit, chocolate, 1, 15g	10	0.3	3.6	74	311
flapjacks, 1, 25g	15	0.7	6.5	121	552
ginger nuts, 2, 20g	16	0.4	3	91	385
gingernut biscuits, homemade, 1, 20g	13	0.3	3.4	90	377
golden oat, 1, 15g	9.5	0.5	1.5	54	225
jaffa cake, 2	7	N	1	36	153
melting moments, 1, 10g	5.5	0.1	3.6	55	229
oatcakes, homemade, 1, 10g	6.3	0.6	1.8	44.5	187
oatcakes, retail, 1, 10g	6.3	N	1.8	44	185
fruit slice, 1, 15g	8	+	0.5	37	155
sandwich biscuit, 2, 25g	17.3	N	6.5	128	538
semi-sweet, 2, 15g	11.2	0.3	2.5	69	289
semi-sweet, coconut type, 1, 10g	9	0.1	2	56	23
semi-sweet, morning coffee type, 1, 12g	4.5	0.1	1	30	126
semi-sweet, rich tea type, 1, 7.5g	5.6	0.1	1.2	35	145
short-sweet biscuit, 2, 20g	12.4	0.3	4.7	94	393
shortbread, 2 fingers, 35g	22	0.8	9	174	730
shortbread, cream, 1	10.5	0	4.5	87	365
shortbread, scotch finger, 1	12	0.5	4	88	370

FOOD	CARB g	FIBRE g	FAT g	ENERGY kcal	KJ
shortcake, 2, 20g	12	0.3	5	94	393
wafers, filled, 3, 18g	12	N	5.4	96	404
savoury, biscuit, 1	2	N	0.5	14	60
savoury, crackers, cream, 3, 21g	14.3	0.6	3.4	92	390
savoury, crackers, wholemeal, 3, 21g	15	1	2.4	87	366
crispbread, cracotte type, 3, 15g	9.4	0.4	2.3	61	256
crispbread, rye, 3, 24g	17	2.8	0.5	77	328
matzos, 1, 30g	26	1	0.6	115	490
oatcakes, 2, 26g	16.4	1.2	4.8	115	482
water biscuits, 3, 21g	16	0.6	2.6	92	390
BLACKBERRIES					
canned, sweetened, 100g	23	+	0	92	385
fresh, raw, 1/2 punnet, 100g	12.5	3.1	0.5	52	220
frozen, 100g	15.5	+	0.5	64	270
BLACKCURRANT JUICE					
prepared, diluted, 250ml	28	0	0	107	450
BLUEBERRIES					
canned in syrup, drained, 100g	17	+	0	69	290
frozen, 100g	12	+	0.5	51	215
raw, 1/2 punnet, 100g	14	1.8	0.5	56	235
BOYSENBERRIES					
canned in heavy syrup, 100g	22.5	2.6	0	88	370
canned, no added sugar, 100g	4	+	0	27	115
raw, 1/2 punnet, 100g	6	+	0	13	55
BRAN (see **CEREAL**)					
BRANDY BUTTER					
1tbsp, 30g	16	0	8	146	615
BRAWN					
2 slices, 70g	0	0	12	151	635
BREAD					
bagel, plain, average, 1, 60g	29	+	0.5	137	575
breadcrumbs, homemade, 100g	77.5	2.2	1.9	354	1508
breadcrumbs, manufactured, 100g	78.5	N	2.1	354	1505
brown bread, average, 38g	16.8	1.3	0.8	83	352
brown roll, crusty, 48g	24.2	1.7	1.3	122	521
brown roll, soft, 48g	24.9	1.7	1.8	129	547
chapatis, made with fat, 1, 100g	48.3	N	12.8	328	1383
chapatis, made without fat, 1, 100g	43.7	N	1	202	860
corn, 90g	20	+	7	178	750
croissant, 60g	23	1	12.2	216	903
crumpet, wholemeal, toasted, 1, 44g	17	1.5	0.5	84	355
currant bread, 1 slice, 25g	12.7	+	1.9	72	305
focaccia, 1, 50g	30	2	1.5	139	585
focaccia, herb & garlic, 1, 70g	32	2	1.5	170	715
granary, 1 slice, 38g	17.6	1.6	1	89	380
hamburger roll, 85g	41.5	1.3	4.3	224	953
loaf, average, white, 2 slices	35	3.5	2	189	795
loaf, fruit, fruit & spice, 2 slices	34.5	+	2	177	745
loaf, fruit, raisin toast, 2 slices	26	+	1.5	134	565
loaf, fruit, spicy fruit, 2 slices	33.5	+	2	174	730
loaf, gluten/wheat free, 2 slices	12	+	2	64	270
loaf, mixed grain, 2 slices	33.5	+	3.5	196	825
loaf, multi-grains, 2 slices	35	+	2	187	785
loaf, pumpernickel, 2 slices	18	3.7	1	92	385

FOOD	CARB g	FIBRE g	FAT g	ENERGY kcal	ENERGY KJ
loaf, rice bran, 2 slices	2	+	10	69	290
loaf, black rye, 1 slice	42	+	2	214	900
loaf, rye, 2 slices	30	2.2	3	176	740
loaf, soya & linseed, 2 slices	40	++	6	259	1090
malt bread, 1 slice, 35g	19.9	+	0.8	94	399
naan, 1, 160g	80	3	20	538	2264
papadum, fried, 1, 13g	5.1	N	2.2	48	201
pitta, white, 1, 95g	55	2.1	1.1	252	1071
rye bread, 25g	11.4	1.1	0.4	55	233
soda bread, yeast-free, 1, 60g	35	1.2	1.5	178	750
toasted, regular, 1, 45g	19.5	1	0,5	93	390
tortillas made with wheat flour, 1, 30g	15	0.8	2	86	360
wheatgerm bread, l slice, 25g	10.9	0.8	0.8	57	244
white bread, average, 35g	17.3	0.5	0.7	82	357
white bread med. slice, large loaf, 36g	16.8	0.5	0.5	78	333
white bread roll, crusty, 1, 50g	28.8	0.8	1.1	140	596
white bread roll, soft, 1, 45g	23.2	0.7	1.9	121	512
white bread, fried in oil, 45g	21.8	0.7	14.3	226	946
white bread, with added fibre, 1 slice, 38g	17.4	1.1	0.5	81	342
wholemeal bread, average, 38g	15.8	2.2	0.9	82	347
wholemeal roll, 1 average, 48g	23.2	2.8	1.4	116	492
wholemeal, roll, 1 large, 105g	46	6	2.5	250	1050
stick, French (baguette), white, 1, 50g	22.5	0.7	1.5	128	540
stick, French (baguette), wholemeal, 1, 50g	21	+	1.5	119	500
toast, French, 2 slices	20	+	8.5	182	765
BROCCOLI					
raw, 100g	0	2.6	0	24	100
BRUSSEL SPROUTS					
raw, 100g	2	4.1	0	24	100
BUCKWHEAT KERNELS					
boiled, 100g	73	2.1	2.5	334	1400
BULGUR (CRACKED WHEAT)					
cooked, 100g	68.5	+	2.5	319	1340
BUN					
brioche, 1	N	N	16	278	1170
cinnamon, 1, 100g	45	1.5	15	263	1105
chelsea, 78g	43.8	1.3	10.8	285	1203
cream, 1 small, 60g	15.5	0.5	21.5	261	1082
finger, iced, 1, 65g	30	N	5	192	805
fruit, iced, 1, 90g	42	N	7	265	1115
hot cross, 1, 50g	29.3	1	3.5	155	657
BUTTER (see also FAT AND MARGARINE)					
clarified (ghee), 1tbsp	0	0	17	150	630
garlic, 1tbsp	0	0	16.5	145	610
regular, average, 1tbsp	0	0	16.5	145	610
reduced-fat average, 1tbsp	0	0	8	76	320
CABBAGE					
chinese, raw, 40g	0	0.6	0	3	14
chinese, flowering (pak choi), raw, 40g	0	1	0	5	20
mustard (dai gai choi), raw, 75g	0.5	2	0	11	45

FOOD	CARB g	FIBRE g	FAT g	ENERGY kcal	KJ
red, raw, 40g	1	1.2	0	9.5	40
red, cooked, 60g	2	1	0	12	50
rolls, Lebanese, 3 small, 250g	40	+	10	290	1220
savoy, cooked, 60g	1	1.5	0	10	40
savoy, raw, 40g	1	1.5	0	7	30
CAKE					
angel, average slice	40.5	N	0.5	181	760
apricot crumble tea cake, 100g	44	+	15	324	1360
apple, average slice	40	+	10	252	1060
banana cake, 100g	68	+	16	428	1800
banana madeira, 100g	58	+	13.5	367	1540
banana tea loaf, 100g	57	+	12	351	1475
battenburg, 100g	50	N	17.5	370	1551
Bavarian chocolate, 100g	30	N	22.5	332	1395
black forest, 100g	40	N	17	331	1390
bran loaf, large slice, 100g	58.4	4.6	1.6	254	1081
cake mix, sponge, made up, 50g	27	N	8	280	1220
carrot cake, bought, 100g	44	+	23	402	1690
carrot cake, fingers, 100g	64	+	17	420	1770
cheesecake, 100g	30	0.4	20	320	1350
cherry cake, 100g	61.7	1.1	15.8	384	1657
chinese cakes, 100g	51.9	N	21.5	415	1740
chocolate, 100g	55	N	17	391	1645
christmas, 1 piece, 60g	33.5	+	6	193	810
coconut, 100g	51.2	2.5	23.8	434	1815
crispie cakes, 100g	73.1	0.3	18.6	464	1951
date loaf, 1 piece, 55g	27	+	4.5	158	665
date & walnut loaf, 1 piece, 60g	32	+	6	189	795
eclair, chocolate, bought, 70g	22.5	0.5	18	264	1110
flan, fruit, 100g	28.5	0.7	8	187	785
fruit, plain, 1 piece, 50g	271	+	6	165	695
fruit, retail, 1 piece, 70g	39	0.7	7	225	945
fruit cake, iced, 70g	43.9	1.2	8	249	1053
fruit cake, rich, 1 slice, 70g	41.7	1.2	7.7	239	1007
gateau, 1 slice, 85g	36.9	0.3	143	286	1201
gingerbread, 50g	32.4	0.6	6.3	190	800
hazelnut torte, average slice	N	+	30	402	1690
jam fairy, 100g	58.5	N	18	417	1750
jam sponge, 100g	67.5	1.8	2.5	312	1310
lamington, bought, 1, 75g	36	+	9	233	980
lamington, cream-filled, 1, 60g	30	+	7	187	785
lemon rolls, 100g	60.5	N	15	360	1510
madeira, 1 slice, 40g	23.4	0.4	6.8	157	661
madeira, iced, 100g	58	N	14	369	1550
marble, 100g	60	N	13.5	374	1570
mud, 100g	59	N	20	428	1800
rock, 1 medium, 60g	33	0.8	8	221	930
rum baba, average serving	47	N	10	326	1370
sponge cake, average slice, 60g	31.4	0.5	15.8	275	1152
sponge cake, fatless, 1 slice, 58g	30.7	0.5	3.5	171	722
sponge, fairy, 100g	60.5	N	8.5	344	1445
sponge, jam-filled, 1 slice, 60g	38.5	1.1	2.9	181	768

FOOD	CARB g	FIBRE g	FAT g	ENERGY kcal	KJ
sponge with butter icing,					
slice, 60g	31.4	0.4	18.4	294	1228
swiss roll, 1 slice, 35g	22.5	0.5	2.5	114	480
swiss roll, chocolate, individual, 25g	14.5	N	2.8	84	355
CAPERS					
1 tbsp	1	+	0	7	30
CAPSICUM					
green, raw, 100g	2.5	1.6	0	15	65
red, raw, 100g	4	1.6	0	25	105
CAROB					
bar, 1, 45g	18	+	11.5	186	780
coated biscuit 1, 18g	9.5	N	5.5	89	375
powder, 2 tbsp, 40g	15	+	0	59	250
CARROT					
baby, raw, peeled, 50g	3	1.2	0	13	55
canned, 100g	4	1.9	0,	20	85
juice, 125ml	8	+	0	39	165
raw, peeled, boiled, 70g	4	2	0	19	80
CASSAVA					
peeled, boiled, 100g	30.5	1.6	0.5	131	550
CAULIFLOWER					
boiled, 100g	2	1.6	0	19	80
cheese, 200g	11	2	20	269	1130
raw, 50g	1	1	0	9	40
CELERIAC					
fresh, peeled, boiled, 100g	5.5	3.2	0	31	130
fresh, peeled, 120g	5	4.5	0	29	120
CELERY					
chopped, boiled, 63g	1.5	0.7	0	8	35
raw, 2 x 10cm sticks, 40g	1	0.5	0.5	5	20
CEREAL					
bran strands, 40g	18.6	9.8	1.4	104	444
bran with fruit and oats, 45g	34.5	9	1.5	138	580
bran, natural, 12g	7.5	4.5	0.5	33	140
bran, oat, unprocessed, 2 tbsp, 22g	11	3.5	1.5	53	225
bran, rice, 15g	7.5	4	3	70	295
bran, wheat, processed, 45g	31	14	2.5	161	675
bran, wheat, unprocessed,					
2 tbsp, 10g	1	4	0.5	15	65
branflakes, 30g	20.8	3.9	0.6	95	406
chocolate flavoured rice pops, 30g	28.3	0.2	0.3	115	491
cornflakes, 30g	25.8	0.3	0.2	108	461
cornflakes, with nuts, 30g	26.6	0.2	1.2	119	507
crispies, rice based, 30g	27	0.2	0.3	111	472
crunchy oat bran flakes with					
fruit, 45g	31	N	2	160	675
crunchy oat bran flakes, 30g	22.2	3	1.2	107	456
fruit & fibre flakes, 30g	21.6	2.1	1.4	105	444
fruit & nut wheat flakes, 45g	31	3	1.5	157	660
grapenuts, 30g	25.5	+	1	113	475
high-energy multi flakes, 100g	81.7	2	1.7	355	1504
high-energy wheat flakes, 45g	35.5	2	1.5	170	715
high-protein rice flakes, 30g	24.5	0.6	0.3	113	481
honeynut cornflakes, 30g	26.6	0.2	1.2	119	507

FOOD	CARB g	FIBRE g	FAT g	ENERGY kcal	ENERGY KJ
honey wheat puffs, 30g	26.6	0.9	0.6	116	493
instant oats, 36g	24.7	2.6	2.8	134	569
muesli, swiss style, 50g	36.1	3.2	3	182	770
muesli with no added sugar, 50g	33.5	3.8	3.9	183	776
muesli, apricot & almond, 60g	35.5	+	4.5	210	880
muesli, apricot toasted, 30g	20	+	3	121	510
muesli, natural, 60g	39.5	2	2.5	208	875
muesli, oat & honey, 45g	31	+	7	188	790
muesli, traditional, 60g	37	2	4	221	930
muesli flakes, 45g	32	+	1	157	660
multigrain flakes, 30g	21.5	1	3	115	485
nut crunchie clusters, 45g	33.5	+	3.5	177	745
oat bran, crunchy, 45g	30	+	2.5	170	710
oat bran & fruit, 40g	30.5	+	3.5	168	705
oat flakes, 30g	23.5	+	1.5	115	485
porridge oats made with water, 200g	18	1.6	2.2	98	418
porridge, made with whole milk, 200g	27.4	1.6	10.2	232	976
puffed wheat, 20g	13.5	1.1	0.3	64	273
puffed wheat with honey, 30g	25.4	1	0.2	104	445
puffed wheat, sugar coated, 30g	25.4	1	0.2	104	445
rice puffs, 30g	26.9	0.2	0.3	111	472
rice puffs, sugar coated, 30g	28.7	0.1	0.2	114	487
small whole wheat biscuits, 45g	33.3	4.3	0.7	149	635
small whole wheat biscuits with added fruit, 40g	30.2	3.2	0.8	135	573
sugar coated cornflakes, 30g	28.1	0.2	0.2	113	482
sultana bran flakes, 50g	34	5	0.8	150	645
wheat biscuits, 1, 20g	15	1.9	0.5	70	300
wheat flakes, 30g	24	2.6	0.8	108	459
wheat flakes and raisins, 40g	26	4	1.5	140	585
wheat rings, 100g	86.1	N	2.7	372	1581
wheat biscuits, 2, 40g	30	3.8	1	140	600
whole wheat biscuit, 1, 22g	15	2.2	0.7	72	304
CEREAL BAR (see also MUESLI BAR)					
apricot fruity bar, 1 small	18	+	2.5	105	440
low sugar, 1 large	26	+	2.5	136	570
sports, 1	28.5	+	2.5	145	610
CHEESE					
blue brie, 30g	0	0	13.5	126	530
blue castello, 30g	0	0	10	110	465
blue vein, 30g	0	0	9.5	110	465
bocconcini, 20g	0	0	7	76	320
brie, 30g	0	0	8.5	101	425
camembert, 30g	0	0	8	92	385
canola, mild, 30g	0	0	6.5	94	395
cheddar, 30g	0	0	10	122	505
cheddar, low-fat, 30g	0	0	7	99	410
cheddar, processed, 30g	0	0	8	99	415
cheddar, reduced-fat, 30g	0	0	7	98	410
cheddar slices, 20g	1	0	4.5	61	255
cheddar slices, reduced-fat, 20g	1	0	3	48	200
cheddar sticks, 20g	1	0	6	67	280

FOOD	CARB g	FIBRE g	FAT g	ENERGY kcal	KJ
cheshire, 30g	0	0	10	114	480
cottage, 1tbsp	0	0	2	29	120
cottage, with cheese, 1tbsp	0.5	0	0.5	17	70
cottage, low-fat, 1tbsp	0.5	0	0.5	18	75
cottage with pineapple, low-fat, 1tbsp	3	0.5	0	27	115
creamed cottage, 1tbsp	0.5	0	1	24	100
creamed cottage, low-fat, 1tbsp	1	0	0.5	19	80
cream, 30g	1	0	10	101	425
cream, fruit, 30g	0	0	7.5	83	350
cream, light, 30g	1	0	5	48	200
cream, full fat, 30g	0.5	0	10	102	430
double Gloucester, 30g	0	0	10	120	505
edam, 30g	0	0	8	106	445
emmental, 30g	0	0	9	113	475
fetta, 30g	0	0	7	83	350
goat's, 30g	0.5	0	4.5	58	245
gouda, 30g	0	0	9	113	475
hallourni, 30g	0	0	5	73	305
havarti, 30g	0	0	11	120	505
jarisberg, 30g	0	0	9	113	475
jarlsberg lite, 30g	0	0	5	82	346
lancashire, 30g	0	0	9.5	110	465
leicester, 30g	0	0	10	119	500
mozzarella, 30g	0	0	6.5	90	380
mozzarella, reduced-fat, 30g	0	0	5.5	86	360
parmesan, 30g	0	0	9.5	132	555
pizza, grated, 30g	0	0	6.5	93	390
processed, 30g	0	0	7	42	175
quark, 20g	0	0	2.5	26	110
quark, low-fat, 20g	0	0	0.5	15	65
reduced-fat, 20g	0	0	4.5	69	290
ricotta, 20g	0	0	2	30	125
ricotta, reduced-fat, 20g	0.5	0	1.5	25	105
ricotta, smooth, 20g	0	0	2	25	105
sheep's milk, fresh, 30g	0	0	6.5	90	380
soft, 30g	0	0	10	124	520
soya, 30g	0	0	8	93	390
stilton, 30g	0	0	9.5	111	465
swiss, 30g	0	0	9	114	480
wensleydale, 30g	0	0	9.5	112	470
CHERRIES					
canned in syrup, drained, 100g	17	0.6	0	70	295
glace, 6, 30g	20	0.3	0	77	325
raw, weighed with stones, 100g	12	0.7	0.1	53	225
CHEWING GUM					
sugarless, per piece, 10g	0	0	0	4	15
with sugar, per piece, 10g	3	0	0	9.5	40
CHICKEN					
breast, no skin, grilled, 100g	0	0	5	157	660
breast, with skin, grilled, 100g	0	0	12.5	218	915
breast, quarter, no skin, barbecued, 100g	0	0	6	199	835

FOOD	CARB g	FIBRE g	FAT g	ENERGY kcal	KJ
breast, quarter, with skin, rotisseried, 100g	N	0	12.5	214	900
breast, lean, 100g	0	0	1	40	170
chicken pastrami, 1 serving, 30g	N	N	1	40	170
crispy-skinned, 100g	0	0	3	64	270
drumstick, no skin, baked, 2	0	0	9	179	750
drumstick, with skin, baked, 2	0	0	14.5	229	960
drumstick crumbed, 145g	N	0	17	313	1315
fried chicken (see FAST FOOD)					
nuggets, 1, 20g	2.5	0	3.5	57	240
roll, processed, 1 slice, 38g	4.5	N	9.5	158	665
sausage, cooked, skinless, 2	0	0	10	164	690
thigh, no skin, cooked, 2	0	0	6	126	530
thigh, with skin, cooked, 2	0	0	8	145	610
wing, with skin, cooked, 2	0	0	12	179	750
CHICKPEAS					
canned, drained, 186g	29.9	7.6	5.4	214	906
dried, boiled, 180g	32.8	7.7	3.8	218	922
CHICORY GREENS					
raw, 100g	2.8	1	0.6	11	45
CHILLI					
powder, 1 tsp, 5g	Tr	Tr	0	N	N
green, raw, each, 20g	1	N	0	4	15
red, raw, each, 20g	1	0.3	0	6	25
CHIVES					
fresh, 2 tbsp, 40g	Tr	0.8	0	1	5
CHOCOLATE					
after-dinner mint, 1, 6g	11	0	1.5	87	365
block, 100g	55.5	N	32.5	536	2250
coconut, bar, 1, 57g	33.2	+	14.9	270	1129
caramels, 1, 20g	12	0	5.5	99	415
cherry-flavoured centre, 1, 55g	30.5	0	13.5	248	1040
cream, 100g	43	N	46.5	604	2535
cooking, dark, 100g	56	+	31	505	2120
cooking, milk, 100g	61.5	+	28.5	505	2120
coated waffer biscuits, 1, 45g	27	N	11.5	220	945
coated candies, 1 packet, 55g	40	N	10.5	257	1080
coated peanuts, 1 packet, 55g	34	+	13.5	273	1145
coated malt balls, 1 packet, 45g	30	N	9.5	212	890
coated nougat and toffee bar, 1, medium, 65g	43.2	+	12.3	285	1204
coated nougat bar, 1, 25g	13.5	N	9	137	575
coated whipped bar, 1, 26g	16.5	+	4.1	103	435
coated biscuit fruit and nut bar, 1, 55g	27.5	+	16.5	280	1175
coated peanut bar, 1, 60g	36	+	13.5	283	1190
coated biscuit, 1, 55g	35	+	13.8	264	1128
choc bar, 1, 40g	23	+	11.5	204	855
full cream, milk, 1, 54g	32.1	+	16.4	286	1196

FOOD	CARB g	FIBRE g	FAT g	ENERGY kcal	KJ
fruit & nut bar, 100g	54	+	34	540	2270
honeycomb bar, 80g	56	0	163	387	1625
in crisp sugar shells, 1 tube, 37g	27.3	+	6.5	169	711
soft centres, 100g	64.5	0	21.5	469	1970
triangular nougat bar, 1, 50g	28.5	N	15	264	1110
CHUTNEY					
fruit, homemade, 1tbsp	8.5	0.4	0	34	145
mango, 1tbsp	9	0.2	0	30	125
COCOA POWDER					
1tbsp	1.5	1.2	1	21	90
COCONUT					
cream, block,100g	7	+	68.8	669	2760
desiccated, dried, 25g	1.6	3.4	15.5	151	623
oil, 1tbsp	0	0	20	176	740
COFFEE					
for each teaspoon of sugar in					
add ...	5	0	0	19	80
cappuccino, whole milk, 1 cup, 200ml	N	0	5	89	375
cappuccino, skim milk, 1 cup, 200ml	N	0	0	50	210
decaffeinated, black,1 cup, 200ml	0	0	0	0	0
filtered, black, 1 cup, 200ml	Tr	0	0	7	30
ground, 1 cup + 25ml whole milk, 225ml	2.5	0	1	23	95
ground, 1 cup + 25ml skim milk, 225ml	2.5	0	0	18	75
iced, plain, 1 cup, 200ml	1.5	0	7	59	250
iced, with whole milk ice cream & cream, 325 ml	N	0	12	179	750
instant black, 1 cup, 200ml	0	0	0	2	8
instant, 1 cup + 25ml whole milk, 225ml	1.5	0	1	18	75
instant, 1 cup + 25ml skim milk, 225ml	1.5	0	0	13	55
Irish, 1 cup, 200ml	Tr	0	10	189	795
milk, 1tsp coffee + 1 cup whole milk, 200ml	12.5	0	10	173	725
mocha, 1 cup, 200ml	N	0	10	119	500
percolated, black, 1, cup, 200ml	Tr	0	0	0	0
whitener, 1tsp	2	0	1.5	21	90
CORDIAL (see also SOFT DRINKS)					
citrus, 25% juice, prepared, 1 glass, 250ml	17	0	0	65	275
citrus, 60% juice, prepared, 1 glass, 250ml	18	0	0	73	305
citrus, reduced sugar					
lemon, prepared, 1 glass, 250ml	N	0	0	69	290
undiluted, 1tbsp	9	0	0	34	145
CORN					
baby, canned, 6, 100g	2	1.5	0.4	23	96
cob, 1, large, 100g	11.6	1.3	1.4	66	280
creamed, canned, 100g	20	+	1	81	340
kernels, canned, 30g	8	0.4	0.4	37	156
CORN CHIPS (see also SNACK FOOD)					
cheese, 40g	25.5	2	9.5	193	810
flavoured, 40g	20	2	12	198	830
toasted snacks, 40g	21.7	0.4	12.8	208	867
CORNMEAL					
dry, 40g	30	1	0.5	145	610

FOOD	CARB g	FIBRE g	FAT g	ENERGY kcal	KJ
COUSCOUS					
cooked, 100g	23	+	0	112	470
CRABAPPLE					
raw, 60g	12	+	0	45	190
CRACKERS (see also CRISPBREAD)					
cheese flavour, 2	4	+	1	24	100
cream, 2	4.5	0.4	2	40	170
rye, 2	5.5	1.6	1.5	38	160
rice snacks, cheese, 30g	22	+	2	117	490
rice snacks, sesame, 30g	22	+	2	117	490
sesame, 2	3	+	1	20	85
water crackers, 2	4.5	0.4	0.5	25	105
CRANBERRY JUICE					
1 glass, 250ml	36.5	N	0	143	600
CREAM					
aerosol, whipped, 100ml	4	0	30.5	293	1230
clotted, 100ml	2	0	63	586	2413
crème fraîche, 100ml	2.5	0	48	440	1850
double thick, rich, 100ml	3	0	54.5	499	2095
light, 100ml	3.5	0	17.5	189	795
regular, 100ml	3	0	35.5	333	1400
thickened, 100ml	3.5	0	36.5	345	1450
thickened, light, 100ml	6	0	19	211	885
CREAM, SOUR					
extra light, 100ml	7	0	12.5	158	665
light, 100ml	5	0	18	193	810
regular, dairy 100ml	4	0	19	199	835
CREPE					
plain, 20g	7.5	0.5	2.5	65	275
CRISPBREAD					
high fibre, 1, 5g	4	1	0	17	70
bran & malt, 1	3.5	0.5	0	19	80
plain, 1	4.5	0.5	1	27	115
rye, 1, 10g	7.1	1.2	0.2	32	137
fat-free, 1	7	+	0	34	145
original, low fat, 1	5	+	1	32	135
puffed, 1	4	N	0	19	80
wholemeal, 1	5	+	1	29	120
swiss type, 1	16	1.2	0.5	79	330
– with sesame whole rye, 1	15	1.2	1	81	340
– multigrain, 1	9	1.2	1.5	60	250
– wholemeal, 1	9	1	1	58	245
wheatgerm type, original, 1	4	1	0.5	23	95
CROISSANT					
plain, 60g	23	1	12.2	216	903
CROUTONS					
1 serving, 15g	11	1	1	61	255
CRUMPET					
regular, toasted, 40g	17.4	0.8	0.4	80	338
wholemeal, toasted, 45g	17	1.5	0.5	85	355
CUCUMBER					
lebanese, raw, unpeeled, 5 slices, 35g	1	0.5	0	4	15
raw, unpeeled, 5 slices, 45g	3	0.5	0	4	15

FOOD	CARB g	FIBRE g	FAT g	ENERGY kcal	KJ
CUMQUAT (KUMQUAT)					
raw, peeled, 1, 20g	3	0.8	0	12	50
CURRANTS					
dried, 75g	50.9	1.4	0.3	200	854
CURRY PASTE					
curry paste, 1tbsp	1.5	N	2	24	100
curry powder 1tbsp	3	2.8	1.5	30	125
hot curry paste, 1tbsp	1.5	N	2	26	110
Indian, 1tbsp	5	0	9	98	410
tandoori, 1tbsp	2	0	0	49	205
CUSTARD					
baked, egg, 100ml	9	0	4.5	95	400
bread & butter custard, 100ml	15.5	0.5	5.5	132	555
custard & fruit, 100ml	16	+	1.5	86	360
powder, prepared with whole milk, 100ml	12.5	0	4	96	405
powder, prepared with reduced-fat milk 100ml	13.5	0	1.5	82	345
pouring, regular, 100ml	16	0	1.5	88	370
DANISH PASTRY					
almond, 100g	46	2	25	428	1800
apple, 100g	43.5	N	12	298	1250
apricot, 100g	38	N	12	270	1135
blueberry, 100g	40	N	12	286	1200
chocolate, 100g	24	N	19.5	280	1175
continental,100g	37.5	N	17	325	1365
custard, 100g	34.5	N	17	307	1290
pecan, 100g	52	N	20.5	417	1750
DATES					
dried, 6, 50g	28.5	2	0	113	485
fresh, seeded, chopped, 50g	14.5	0.9	0	54	228
DESSERT					
apple pie, bakery, 100g	28	+	8.5	198	830
apple pie, manufatured, 100g	38.5	1.7	12.5	279	1170
apple pie, reduced fat, 100g	32.5	+	7	199	835
apple & blackberry pie, 100g	42.5	+	17	336	1410
apple & rhubarb crumble, 120g	44	2	8	250	1050
apple strudel, 100g	41	+	11	273	1145
apricot pie, 100g	33	+	10	232	975
apricot pie, bought, 100g	38.5	+	14	293	1230
banana split with 3 scoops ice cream	55	1.1	10.5	325	1365
chocolate mocha, 100g	32.5	N	23.5	349	1465
bavarian, chocolate swirl, 100g	30.5	0	19.5	306	1285
blackberry & apple pie, 100g	35	+	10	232	975
chocolate mousse, 100g	28	0	13	232	975
chocolate mousse, dessert, 100g	23	0	9	201	845
chocolate mousse, light, 100g	19	0	4	136	570
Christmas pudding, 1 piece, 50g	29	1	6	167	700
custard tart 1, 135g	41	1.5	17.5	350	1470
junket (blancmange), 100g	48	0	3.5	114	480
lemon meringue pie, 1 piece, 75g	28.5	0.5	12.5	238	1000
pecan pie, 1 piece, 115g	64.5	+	21	450	1890
profiteroles, 1, 55g	N	+	9	130	545
pudding, blackberry sponge, 100g	59.9	+	5	299	1255

FOOD	CARB g	FIBRE g	FAT g	ENERGY kcal	KJ
pudding, bread & butter, 100g	N	0.3	10	299	1255
pudding, chocolate mousse, 100g	32	N	6	209	880
pudding, chocolate sponge, 100g	41.5	+	4	217	910
pudding, creme caramel, 100g	20	N	3	119	500
pudding, lemon sponge, 100g	41	+	3	204	855
pudding, plum, 60g	30	+	4.5	164	690
pudding, rice, banana, canned, 125g	N	+	13	244	1025
pudding, rice, canned, 150g	22.5	0.3	3.75	135	562
pudding, rice, chocolate, canned, 125g	N	+	6.5	209	880
souffle, 100g	10.5	N	14.5	200	840
tiramisu, 100g	N	N	20	328	1380
trifle, bought, 120g	33	0.5	7	209	880
DEVON					
split, 50g	3	+	9	117	490
DIPS					
barbecue, 1tbsp	2.5	0	4.5	51	215
chicken & asparagus, 1tbsp	2	0	3	40	170
chilli, chip & dip type, 1tbsp	1.5	N	0	8	35
chive & onion, 1tbsp	1	0	6.5	65	275
chunky bean, 1tbsp	2.5	+	0	11	45
corn & bacon, 1tbsp	2	+	1	20	85
corn relish, 1tbsp	2	0	3	37	155
cucumber & yoghurt, 1tbsp	0	+	2	26	110
French onion, reduced fat, 1tbsp	1	0	3.5	43	180
French onion, average, 1tbsp	0	0	5	61	255
French onion, low-fat, 1tbsp	3	0	2.5	42	175
gherkin dip, 1tbsp	3	+	4	49	205
herb & garlic, 1tbsp	2	+	4	45	190
hot & spicy, 1tbsp	2	0	3.5	44	185
hummus, 1tbsp	2	0.6	3.5	45	190
taramasalata, 1tbsp	2	+	4	46	195
DOLMADES					
60g	14.5	+	4	101	425
DOUGHNUT					
cinnamon sugar, 1 large, 75g	36.6	+	10.9	252	1061
cream-filled, 1, 70g	21	+	17	251	1055
iced, 1, 80g	38.5	+	19.5	339	1425
DRESSINGS (see also MAYONNAISE)					
caesar, 1tbsp	3	0	7	76	320
caesar, creamy, 1tbsp	2	0	7	70	295
coleslaw, average, 1tbsp	7	0	7	88	370
coleslaw, reduced fat, 1tbsp	5	0	7	82	345
coleslaw, light, 1tbsp	5.5	0	3.5	57	240
French, 1tbsp	2.5	0	4.5	49	205
French, olive oil, 1tbsp	3	0	3.5	43	180
French, low-fat, 1tbsp	3.5	0	0	14	60
Italian, 1tbsp	1.5	0	6	59	250
Italian, light, 1tbsp	2	0	3.5	40	170
Italian, low fat, 1tbsp	3.1	0	0	12	50
lemon pepper, reduced fat, 1tbsp	5	0	2	37	155
potato salad, 1tbsp	2.5	0	7	76	320
thousand island, 1tbsp	3.5	0	7	76	320
thousand island, light, 1tbsp	3.5	0	4	51	215

FOOD	CARB g	FIBRE g	FAT g	ENERGY kcal	KJ
DRINKING POWDER					
barley type milk drink, 1tbsp	6	N	0	31	130
bournvita, 1tbsp	1.5	N	0	24	100
cocoa, 1tbsp	1.5	1.2	1	21	90
diet hot chocolate mix, 1 sachet	7	N	1	44	185
malted milk drink, 1tbsp	8	Tr	0	38	160
milk, 1tbsp	5.5	0	0.5	32	135
milkshake, strawberry, 1tbsp	12	0	0	50	210
Swiss style diet hot chocolate mix, 1 sachet	4	N	0	20	85
DUCK					
roast, no skin, 100g	0	0	9.5	182	765
roast, skin, 100g	0	0	26	307	1290
EGG					
1 small, 45g	0	0	4.5	64	270
1 medium, 55g	0	0	5.5	77	325
1 large, 60g	0	0	6	84	355
boiled 1, 53g	0	0	5.5	80	335
duck, boiled, 1, 65g	Tr	0	9	114	480
eggs benedict, 2 eggs	0	N	52	690	2900
fried, 1, 60g	0	0	8	98	410
fried, 2 x 60g, with 1 lean grilled bacon rasher	Tr	0	19	251	1055
omelette, plain or herb, 2 x 60g eggs	0	0	17	214	900
poached, 1, 60g	0	0	6	76	320
poached, 2 x 60g, with lean grilled bacon rasher	Tr	0	16	236	990
quail, raw, 1, 10g	0	0	1	15	65
replacer, 1tsp	1.5	0	1	31	130
scrambled, 2 x 60g	Tr	0	16	195	820
turkey, raw, 1, 80g	Tr	0	9.5	134	565
white only, 1, 31g	0	0	0	14	60
yolk only, 1	0	0	5	54	225
EGGPLANT (see also AUBERGINE)					
baby, 4, 65g	1.5	1.5	0	11	45
fried in oil, 100g	2.8	2.3	32	302	1262
grilled, 3 slices, 90g	2.5	2	0	18	75
raw, 100g	2.2	2	0.4	15	64
ELDERBERRIES					
raw, 145g	10.5	++	0.5	51	215
ENDIVE					
Belgian, raw, 60g	0	1.2	0	6	25
curly, 80g	0	1.6	0	6	25
FALAFEL					
commercial, 2, 60g	10	+	9	140	590
FAST FOOD (SHOP BOUGHT)					
apple pie, 1, 80g	30.5	1.3	13	239	1005
bacon & cheese chicken fillet burger, 190g	34.5	+	22.2	460	1930
bacon & cheese burger, 1, 213g	52	+	18.3	487	2045
big burger, 1, 345g	55	+	32	646	2715
chips, regular, 117g	33	2.2	20	327	1375
chips, thick cut, 95g	25	2	13	233	980

FOOD	CARB g	FIBRE g	FAT g	ENERGY kcal	KJ
chips, thin, 110g	37.4	2.3	17	308	1291
chicken nuggets, 7, 133g	17.5	+	29.5	411	1725
chicken nuggets, 4, 76g	10	+	17	236	990
chicken fillet burger, 1, 160g	28	+	16.5	282	1185
coleslaw, small tub, 116g	16	+	7	129	540
corn, 1 cobette, 78g	17	1.1	1	89	375
cornish pastie, 1, 155g	48	1.4	31.6	515	2151
fish, battered & deep-fried, 1 fillet, 145g	20	0.6	23	365	1535
fish stick, crab-flavoured, fried, 1, 27g	3.5	0	1.5	38	160
frankfurters, boiled, 2, 100g	3.5	+	20	247	1040
french fries, small, 76g	28.5	1.5	12	226	950
french fries, regular, 114g	42.5	2.3	18	337	1415
french fries, large, 159g	59	3	25	470	1975
fried chicken, coated, 2 pieces, 154g	8.5	+	29	413	1735
grilled chicken burger, 1, 180g	43.5	+	20	484	2035
hamburger, plain, 1, 170g	38	+	17.5	379	1590
hamburger, with bacon, 1, 185g	40.5	+	24	467	1960
hamburger, with cheese, 1, 195g	41.5	+	26	501	2105
hamburger, with egg, 1, 220g	44	+	26	517	2170
hot dog, 1, 100g	18.5	+	15	246	1035
individual cheesecake, 75g	25	0.3	7	175	735
individual chocolate mousse, 75g	17	N	5.5	132	555
mashed potato & gravy, small tub, 120g	12.5	+	2	80	335
nuggets, 6 pieces, 106g	18.5	+	16.5	276	1160
sundae, caramel/chocolate, 1, 141g	36	0	9	240	1010
sundae, strawberry, 1, 141g	36	0	6.5	218	915
thickshake, average, all flavours, 1, 240g	48.5	0	8	299	1255
FAST FOOD (TAKEAWAY)					
apple pie, 1, individual, 100g	56.7	1.7	15.5	369	1554
bacon and egg muffin, 1, 145g	32.5	+	19.5	377	1585
big breakfast, 1, 250g	475	+	31	568	2385
big burger in bun, 1, 205g	40	+	30	562	2360
cheeseburger, 1, 122g	33	+	12.5	300	1260
chicken nuggets, 9 pieces, 171g	26	+	26.5	212	890
cookies, 1 box	47	+	8.5	274	1150
fillet-of-fish, 1, 146g	40	N	16	351	1475
french fries, small	37.4	2.3	17	308	1291
french fries, medium	52	3.2	22.5	414	1740
french fries, large	65	4	30	527	2215
fried chicken, 1, 184g	46	0	20.5	424	1780
hash browns, 1, 54g	15	1.5	7	124	520
hot cakes, with butter & syrup, 1 serving	85	N	15	479	2010
junior burger, 1, 100g	30	N	10	267	1120
pan pizza, cheese, 1 slice, 105g	24.8	1.5	11.8	235	984
pan pizza, hawaiian, 1 slice, 125g	35	2	11	292	1225
pan pizza, premium range, 1 slice, 143g	35.5	2.5	15	339	1425
pan pizza, extra topping, 1 slice, 136g	32	2	16	342	1435
pizza thin crispy base, cheese, 1 slice, 79g	21.5	1.5	9	217	910

FOOD	CARB g	FIBRE g	FAT g	ENERGY kcal	KJ
pizza thin crispy base, hawaiian, 1 slice, 99g	26	2	9.5	242	1015
pizza thin crispy base, premium type, 1 slice, 114g	25.5	2	14	289	1215
pizza thin, crispy base, extra topping, 1 slice, 114g	27	2.5	12.5	286	1200
quarter pounder burger, no cheese, 1, 176g	36	+	19.5	417	1750
sausage & egg muffin, 1, 162g	32	+	22	412	1730
sundae, hot caramel, 1, 175g	56.5	0	8	311	1305
sundae, hot fudge, 1, 175g	50	0	11	319	1340
sundae, strawberry, 1, 171g	47	Tr	6	255	1070
sundae, without topping, 1, 134g	29	0	6	183	770
samosa, meat, commercial, heated, 3, 45g	14	1	9	145	610
sausage roll, 1, 130g	31.5	1.5	23	371	1560
spring roll, deep-fried, 1 large, 175g	48	2	17	398	1670
thickshake, chocolate, regular, 1, 305g	60	+	9.5	360	1510
thickshake, strawberry, large, 1 , 419g	81	0	12.5	480	2015
FAT (see also BUTTER AND FAT)					
cocoa butter, 1tbsp	0	0	20	176	740
dripping, 1tbsp	0	0	20	176	740
lard, 1tbsp	0	0	20	176	740
replacer, 1tbsp	0	0	0	75	315
shortening, 1tbsp	0	0	16	143	600
suet, 1tbsp	Tr	0	17.5	162	680
FENNEL					
raw, 1 bulb, 150g	5	3.6	0	18	75
steamed, 1 bulb, 150g	5.5	3.4	0	16	70
FIGS					
dried, 5, 75g	40	5.6	1.2	40	168
ready to eat, 30g	14	2	0.5	63	267
raw, 1, 40g	4	0.6	0	17	74
stewed, sweetened, 100g	34	3.9	0.8	143	612
FISH (see SEAFOOD)					
FLOUR					
arrowroot, 100g	94	0.1	0.1	355	1515
barley, 100g	74.5	+	1.5	344	1445
besan, chickpea, 100g	49.6	10.7	5.4	313	1328
buckwheat, 100g	76.3	2.1	1.5	364	1522
corn, 100g	92	0.1	0.7	354	1508
maize, 100g	76	+	4	363	1525
millet, 100g	75.4	N	1.7	354	1481
potato, 100g	80	5.7	0.5	329	1380
rice, 100g	80.1	2	0.8	366	1531
rye, wholemeal, 100g	75.9	11.7	2	335	1428
semolina, raw, 100g	77.5	1.2	1.8	350	1489
soya, full-fat, 100g	23.5	11.2	23.5	447	1871
soya, low-fat 100g	28.2	13.5	7.2	352	1488
wheat, white, plain, 100g	77.7	3.1	1.3	341	1450
wheat, white, self-raising, 100g	75.6	3.1	1.2	330	1407
wheat, wholemeal, plain, 100g	63.9	9	2.2	310	1318

FOOD	CARB g	FIBRE g	FAT g	ENERGY kcal	KJ
FRANKFURTER					
canned, drained, cooked, 175g	1.5	N	13	155	650
cocktail, canned. cooked, 1, 30g	0.5	0	5	62	260
cocktail, fresh, cooked, 1, 30g	1	N	6	74	310
fresh, cooked, 1, 75g	2.5	N	15	186	780
FRITTATA					
courgette & spinach, 1 slice, 250g	2	+	38.5	434	1825
Spanish (potato), 1 slice, 250g	13.5	+	27.5	369	1550
FROGS LEGS					
2 fried	0	0	10	178	750
FROMAGE FRAIS					
apricot, honey & vanilla, 130g	20	0	0.5	118	495
orange tangerine, 130g	20	0	0.5	120	505
peach & mango, 130g	14.5	0	5	113	475
strawberry, 130g	15	0	5	115	485
strawberry, light, 130g	18	0	0.5	111	465
vanilla, 130g	15	0	5	115	485
vanilla, light 130g	29	0	6	230	965
petit pot, 60g	10	0	5	87	365
FROZEN DINNERS					
beef goulash, 400g	57	N	10	409	1720
beef hot-pot, 400g	39	N	11	356	1495
beef, healthy eating type, 310g	37	+	8	277	1165
bubble & squeak, 1 serving	8.5	0	2	51	215
chicken carbonara, low fat, 400g	76	N	11.5	424	1780
chicken chasseur, healthy eating type, 310g	34	+	3.5	251	1055
chicken tikka, healthy eating type, 400g	56	N	11	390	1640
curried prawns, 350g	53	N	4.6	299	1255
fettucine carbonara, 375g	49	N	30.8	552	2320
fettucine mediterranean, healthy eating type, 400g	58	N	11	395	1660
fillet of lamb, healthy eating type, 310g	9	+	8	236	990
fish fingers, grilled, 375g	15	0.5	7.5	155	650
French style chicken, low fat variety, 400g	72	N	11.5	486	2040
fried rice, 350g	20	N	7.5	390	1640
Indian style chicken, low fat, 400g	64	N	11	448	1880
roast pork, healthy eating type, 320g	34	N	5.5	277	1165
lamb, low fat, 400g	64	N	10	419	1760
shepherd's pie, 170g	13.5	1.5	8	177	745
Thai style chicken curry, low fat, 400g	64	N	12	438	1840
veal cordon bleu, healthy eating type, 320g	47	N	29	515	2165
FRUIT (see individual fruits)					
FRUIT BAR					
fruit fingers, apricot/strawberry/ tropical, 1, 22g	15	1	0.5	74	310
fruit fingers, raspberry, 1 bar, 15.6g	13	+	0.5	58	245
fruit roll, 1 bar, 37.5g	23	+	2	162	680
FRUIT, DRIED (see individual fruits)					

FOOD	CARB g	FIBRE g	FAT g	ENERGY kcal	KJ
FRUIT SALAD (see also individual fruits)					
canned in pear juice, drained,					
1 bowl, 220g	20.5	3.5	0	92	385
canned in syrup, drained, 1 bowl, 220g	25.5	2.5	0	106	445
fresh, 1 bowl, 140g	19.3	2.1	0.1	77	332
GARLIC					
fresh, 2 peeled cloves, 6g	0.5	+	0	6	25
powder, 1tbsp	7.5	0	0	13	55
puree, 1tbsp, 15g	2.5	N	5	57	236
GELATINE					
1tbsp	0	0	0	42	175
GHERKINS					
drained, 36g	9	0.4	0	38	160
GINGER					
beer, dry, 1 cup, 250ml	22	0	0	82	345
gingerbread biscuit, large, figure					
type, 70g	34.5	1	11.5	249	1045
ground, 1tbsp	4	+	0.5	19	80
raw, peeled, grated, 1tbsp	0.5	N	0	4	15
GNOCCHI					
potato/pumpkin, average serving, 150g	13	N	12	213	895
GOLDEN SYRUP					
1tbsp	21.5	0	0	83	350
GOOSE					
lean, roast, 100g	0	0	23	315	1325
GOOSEBERRIES					
canned, in syrup, 100g	18.5	1.7	0.2	73	310
raw, 100g	3	2.4	0	19	81
GOURD					
bottle, raw, peeled, 75g	0.6	1.9	0	8	35
ridge, raw, peeled, 75g	N	I.5	0	13	55
wax, raw, peeled, 75g	1	1	0	4	15
GRAPEFRUIT					
canned in juice, 125g	19	0.5	0	78	330
juice, sweetened, 1 glass, 200ml	19	0	0	87	365
juice, unsweetened, 1 glass, 200ml	16	0	0	71	300
raw, peeled, 1/2 whole, 110g	5	1	0	27	115
GRAPES					
black, 100g	15	0.7	0	63	265
black, muscatel, 100g	19	0.7	0	78	330
green, 100g	12.5	0.7	0	56	235
green, sultana, 100g	15	0.7	0	61	255
juice, sweetened, 1 glass, 200ml	N	0	1	84	355
juice, unsweetened, 1 glass, 200ml	N	0	1	84	355
GRAVY POWDER					
dry, 1tbsp	8	0	0.5	39	165
prepared, 225g	3	0	0	14	60
GUAVA					
canned in juice, 100g	15.7	3	0	60	258
raw, 1 medium, 100g	5	3.7	0.5	26	112
HAGGIS					
boiled, 100g	19.2	N	21.7	310	1292
HALVA					
30g	14.5	+	5	102	430

FOOD	CARB g	FIBRE g	FAT g	ENERGY kcal	ENERGY KJ
HAM					
& chicken luncheon meat, 2					
slices, 23g	1	N	4	53	225
leg, canned, 2 slices, 35g	0	0	1.5	39	165
leg, fresh, lean, 2 slices, 46g	0	0	1.5	50	210
leg, fresh, untrimmed, 2. slices, 50g	0	0	4	70	295
light, 90% fat-free, 2 slices, 50g	0	0	2.5	36	150
shoulder, 2 slices, 50g	0	0	3	55	230
shoulder, canned, 2 slices, 35g	0	0	2	42	175
steak, grilled, 1, 115g	0	0	9	186	780
HAMBURGER (see FAST FOOD)					
HERBS					
average all varieties, dried, 1tbsp	Tr	N	0	19	80
average all varieties, fresh, chopped,					
1tbsp	Tr	N	0	17	70
HONEY					
1tbsp	22	0	0	84	355
HONEYCOMB 1 piece, 30g	22.2	0	1.5	86	360
HORSERADISH					
cream, 1tbsp	2.5	0.2	2	32	135
fresh, 5g	0.5	0.3	0.5	8	35
HUMMUS					
average serving, 100g	11.6	2.4	12.6	187	781
ICE CREAM BLOCK					
chocolate, 1, 158ml	36.5	0	0	150	630
neopolitan, 100ml	20	0	0	88	370
fruit-flavoured, 100ml	12.5	0	1	67	280
ICE CREAM					
caramel, 1	18	0	6	133	560
chocolate bar type, 1	21	0	19	260	1090
chocolate, 100ml	23	0	11.5	208	875
cone, large, vanilla, 1, 70g	24	0	12.5	220	925
cone, chocolate, 1, 70g	23	0	13.5	226	950
cone, single, plain wafer type, 1, 15g	4	0	0	19	80
cone, sugar, 1, 10g	8.5	0	0.5	40	170
cone, waffle, 1, 18g	3.5	0	0	15	65
cone with 1 small scoop ice cream	8.5	0	3	64	270
cone with 1 small scoop reduced-fat					
ice cream	8.5	0	1.5	54	225
fruits of the forest, 1, 86ml	20	0	6	142	595
lemon, 86ml	18.5	0	6	137	575
mango, 100ml	21	0	8	168	705
raspberry, 1, 90ml	17.5	0	3.5	107	450
soft-serve, 1, 100ml	21.5	0	4.5	137	575
stick, chocolate flavoured, 1, 90ml	19	0	3.5	126	530
stick, vanilla, chocolate coated, 1, 93ml	20.5	0	17.5	248	1040
stick, Belgian chocolate coated					
ice cream 1, 120ml	43	0	27	432	1815
tub, fruit cream, 100ml	10	+	5	94	395
tub, chocolate, 100ml	9.5	0	5.5	92	385
tub, cookies & fudge,100ml	14.5	0	16	215	905
tub, light & creamy vanilla, 100ml	15	0	1.5	77	325
tub, natural vanilla, 100ml	10	0	6	101	425
tub, original vanilla, 100ml	10	0	4.8	89	375

FOOD	CARB g	FIBRE g	FAT g	ENERGY kcal	KJ
tub, original extra creamy vanilla, 100ml	10.5	0	5.5	99	415
tub, strawberries & cream, 100ml	22.5	0	10.5	198	830
tub, double choc, 100ml	21	0	13.5	218	915
tub, vanilla choc-chip, 100ml	N	0	6	106	445
tub, vanilla light, 100ml	12	0	3	83	350
vanilla, 100ml	21	0	10	187	785
viennetta style, chocolate, 100ml	13	0	9	133	559
viennetta style, toffee, 100ml	13	0	10	129	540
viennetta style, vanilla, 100ml	13	0	10	124	520
JAM					
apricot, reduced sugar, 1tbsp	4	+	0	17	70
average, all types, 1tbsp	17	+	0	67	280
berry, 1tbsp	17.5	+	0	68	285
fruits of the forest, reduced sugar,					
1tbsp	4	+	0	17	70
marmalade, orange, 1tbsp	17	+	0	65	275
marmalade, reduced sugar, 1tbsp	4	+	0	17	70
JELLY					
jelly, low-sugar, prepared, 1 bowl, 270ml	0	0	0	24	100
jelly, prepared, 1 bowl, 280ml	45.5	0	0	188	790
JUICE (see individual fruits)					
KALE					
cooked, 65g	3.5	1.5	0.5	18	75
raw, 35g	3.5	1	0	18	75
KIWI FRUIT					
raw, peeled, 1 small, 75g	7.5	1.5	0	36	150
KOHL RABI					
peeled, boiled, 50g	2.5	1	0	18	75
LAMB					
chump chop, lean, grilled, 1, 55g	0	0	4.5	111	465
chump chop, untrimmed, grilled, 1, 65g	0	0	12	182	765
cutlet lean, grilled or baked, 1, 30g	0	0	4	70	295
cutlet, untrimmed, grilled or baked,					
1, 40g	0	0	10.5	131	550
heart, baked, 70g	0	0	5.5	129	540
kidney, simmered, 150g	0	0	6.5	218	915
leg, lean, baked, 2 slices, 80g	0	0	5	158	665
leg, untrimmed, baked, 2 slices, 90g	0	0	10.5	201	845
liver, fried, 40g	0	0	5.5	96	405
loin chop, lean, grilled, 1, 35g	0	0	2.5	62	260
loin chop, untrimmed, grilled, 1, 50g	0	0	15.5	182	765
neck chop, lean, stewed, 1, 40g	0	0	5.5	101	425
neck chop, untrimmed, stewed,					
1, 50g	0	0	14	176	740
shank, lean, cooked, 1, 130g	0	0	4.5	180	755
shank, untrimmed, cooked, 1, 100g	0	0	10.5	223	935
shoulder, lean, baked, 1 slice, 25g	0	0	2	46	195
shoulder, untrimmed, baked,					
1 slice, 30g	0	0	6	87	365
trim, butterfly steak, grilled, 100g	0	0	4.5	125	525
trim, fillet, grilled, 100g	0	0	4	115	485.
trim, roast loin, baked, 100g	0	0	4	119	500
trim, schnitzel steak, grilled, 100g	0	0	3.5	111	465
strips, grilled, 100g	0	0	3.5	114	480

FOOD	CARB g	FIBRE g	FAT g	ENERGY kcal	KJ
LASAGNE (see also PASTA)					
beef, commercial, 400g	62.8	2.8	24	572	2412
bolognaise, 400g	67.5	+	11.5	481	2020
lean beef lasagne, 400g	64	+	8.5	440	1850
LEEK					
sliced, boiled, l serving, 45g	1.2	0.8	0.3	9	39
LEMON					
curd, 1tbsp	10.5	0	3.5	76	320
juice, 100 ml	2.5	0	0	26	110
flavoured-spread, 1tbsp	13	0	1	60	250
raw, whole, 1, 65g	2.1	+	0	12	51
LENTILS					
burger, 1, 70g	15.5	2	1.5	213	895
dhal, 125g	14	2.5	9	177	745
dried, boiled, 200g	35	3.8	0.8	200	848
LETTUCE					
cos, 1 serving, 35g	0.6	0.3	0	6	25
iceberg, 35g	0.6	0.3	0	2	10
average, 35g	0.6	0.3	0	5	21
LIME					
juice, 1tbsp	2	0	0	6	25
raw, peeled, whole, 1, 45g	0.5	+	0	9	40
LINSEEDS (FLAXSEEDS)					
1tbsp	4	+	4	58	245
LIQUORICE					
allsorts, 6, 56g	43	1	1.2	195	821
pieces, 5, 65g	42	1	1	181	759
LIVERWURST					
60g	0.5	+	17.5	198	830
LOGANBERRIES					
raw, 100g	13	2.4	0.5	55	230
LOQUATS					
6 medium, 78g	4	+	0	20	85
LOTUS ROOT					
canned, cooked, 100g	16	+	0	65	275
raw, peeled, 100g	17	+	0	74	310
LYCHEES					
canned in syrup, drained, 100g	17.7	0.5	0	68	290
raw, peeled, 100g	14.3	0.7	0.1	58	248
MACARONI					
cheese, homemade, 1 serving, 150g	20.4	0.8	16.2	267	1115
cheese, bought, 1 serving, 243g	49	1	15.5	405	1700
cheese, traditional, canned, 1 serving, 335g	71	1	21	557	2340
cheese & bacon, 1 serving, 293g	58	1	21	476	2000
cheesy fun shapes, 1 serving, 335g	71	1	21	557	2340
plain, boiled, 1 serving, 100g	18.5	0.9	0.5	86	365
MANDARIN					
canned in juice, drained, 1 serving, 100g	7.7	0.3	0	32	135
peeled, whole, 1, 60g	5	1	0	24	100
MANGO					
canned in syrup, 200g	40.6	1.4	0	144	660
chutney, 1tbsp	8.5	0.5	0	34	145
green, 150g	25	3	0	58	245
ripe, raw, peeled, whole, 1, 150g	21.2	3.9	0.3	86	368

FOOD	CARB g	FIBRE g	FAT g	ENERGY kcal	ENERGY KJ
MARGARINE					
average, 1 portion, 11g	0.1	0	9	81	334
light, salt-reduced, 11g	0	0	4	36	150
lite, 1tsp, 5g	0	0	3	26	110
sunflower spread, 11g	0.1	0	7.3	67	274
dairy blend, extra-soft, 1tsp, 5g	0	0	3	26	110
blended, 1tsp, 5g	0	0	3.5	31	130
butter type, 1tsp, 5g	0	0	4	36	150
high polyunsaturated spread, 1tsp	0	0	4	33	140
olive oil, type, 1tsp, 5g	0	0	4	33	140
sunflower spread, fat-reduced, 1 tsp, 5g	0	0	2.5	21	90
MARROW					
peeled, boiled, 100g	4	0.5	0	19	80
raw, peeled, 100g	3.5	0.5	0	17	70
MARZIPAN					
20g	11	0.6	3.5	80	335
MATZO					
meal, 50g	40	+	0	171	720
plain cracker, 30g	25	1	0.5	118	495
MAYONNAISE					
97% fat free, 1tbsp	9	0	20	45	190
cholesterol free, 1tbsp	7.5	0	3.5	63	265
sunflower type, 1tbsp	7.5	0	7.5	107	450
light, 1tbsp	8	0	7	63	265
olive oil type, 1tbsp	5	0	8.5	97	410
premium type, 1tbsp	7	0	3	58	245
traditional, 1tbsp	3	0	21.5	201	845
reduced calorie, 1tbsp	7	0	3	55	230
MEAT SUBSTITUTES					
micro protein, 100g	2	4.8	3.5	86	360
vegetarian mince, 100g	22	1.4	2.5	304	1280
MELON					
casaba, raw, peeled, 100g	6	0.4	0	32	135
honeydew, raw, peeled, 160g	10.5	0.6	0.5	50	210
rock, raw, peeled, 250g	12	1	0	55	230
water, raw, peeled, 100g	5	0.2	0	23	95
MERINGUE					
25g	22.5	0	0	92	385
MILK					
buttermilk, cultured, dairy, 1 carton, 250ml	4	0	5.5	132	555
calcium enriched, 1 cup, 250ml	12.5	0	2.5	119	500
condensed, sweetened, 1 tin, 250ml	180	0	30	1060	4455
condensed, sweetened, skim, 250ml	199	0	1	901	3785
cultured, reduced-fat, 250ml	12	0	5	134	565
cultured, skim, 250ml	14.5	0	0.5	108	455
evaporated, reduced-fat, canned, 250ml	28.5	0	5.5	241	1015
evaporated, skim, canned, 250ml	28.5	0	1	200	840
evaporated, whole-fat, canned, 250ml	27	0	21.5	373	1565
fat-reduced, protein-increased, 250ml	14	0	3.5	126	530
flavoured, chocolate, 250ml	23	0	9.5	204	855
flavoured, chocolate, reduced-fat, 1 cup, 250ml	21.5	0	4.5	156	655

FOOD	CARB g	FIBRE g	FAT g	ENERGY kcal	KJ
flavoured, malt & honey, 250ml	27	0	2.5	170	715
flavoured, strawberry, 250ml	23	0	9	201	845
flavoured, strawberry, reduced-fat, 250ml	24	0	4	158	665
full-cream, 250ml	12	0	10	167	700
goat's, 1 cup, 250ml	9.5	0	6.5	127	535
lite, 250ml	14.5	0	3.5	133	558
low-fat, high-calcium, 250ml	17	0	0.5	120	505
milkshake, 275ml	47	0	12	349	1465
milkshake, thick, 300ml	60	0	10	355	1490
powder, malted, 1tbsp	5.5	0	0.5	32	135
powdered, full-cream, 1tbsp	3	0	2	39	165
powdered, skim, 1tbsp	4	0	0	29	120
rice, 250ml	N	0	2.5	157	660
sheep's, 250ml	13.5	0	17.5	268	1125
skimmed, 250ml	12.5	0	0.5	88	370
soya, natural, 250ml	18.5	+	7	158	665
soya, low-fat, 250ml	12	N	1.8	91	382
soya, lite, 250ml	15	N	1.5	107	450
soya, flavoured, banana, 250ml	23	+	2	138	580
soya, flavoured, chocolate hazelnut, 250ml	18.5	5	7	158	665
MILLET					
cooked, 174g	41	+	1.5	206	865
MISO (SOYA BEAN PASTE)					
1tbsp	6	+	1	40	170
MIXED PEEL					
100g	59	4.8	1	231	984
MIXED VEGETABLES					
frozen, boiled, 1 serving 100g	6.6	+	0.5	42	180
MOLASSES					
1tbsp	14	0	0	54	225
MUESLI (see CEREAL)					
MUESLI BAR (see also CEREAL BAR)					
apricot & coconut, 1 bar, 31g	19.5	N	7.5	149	625
apricot & fibre, yoghurt-coated bar, 1 bar, 50g	28	+	9.5	202	850
brown rice, macadamia & ginger, 1 bar, 50g	26	+	14	234	985
chewy fruit, 1 bar, 31g	21	1	5	131	550
crunchy fruit, 1 bar, 31g	17.5	1.2	7	146	615
crunchy original, yoghurt, 1 bar, 31g	22	+	4	126	530
fruit, apricot, 1 bar, 32g	22.5	+	4.5	137	575
nut crumble, 1 bar, 31g	20	+	6	143	600
nut & muesli, carob-coated, 1 bar, 50g	28	+	11	218	915
peach & pear, 100% fruit, 1 bar, 25g	15	N	8.6	131	550
yoghurt, apricot, 1 bar, 31g	20.5	+	5.5	138	580
yoghurt tops, fruit salad, 1 bar, 31g	21.5	+	5	136	570
MUFFIN					
1 medium, plain, 60g	29	1.5	8	169	710
1 large, 100g	48	2	13	279	1170
1 extra large, 150g	72	3	19.5	418	1755
blueberry, 1, 150g	56	+	13	352	1480
bran, 1, 190g	67	15	27.5	550	2310
calorie-reduced, 1, 152g	47.5	+	18	370	1555

FOOD	CARB g	FIBRE g	FAT g	ENERGY kcal	KJ
high-fibre, 1, 63g	27.5	+	2	152	640
fruit, 1, 60g	27	+	1.5	151	635
soya & linseed, 1, 67g	N	++	6.5	180	755
spicy fruit topped, 1, 67g	30	+	2	168	705
white, bread type, 1, 67g	28.5	2	1	151	635
wholemeal, bread type, 1, 67g	N	+	2	156	655
low-fat, 1, 152g	57.5	+	2.5	283	1190
mixed berry, 1, 60g	38	+	5	207	870
muffin mix, apple & sultana, prepared, 1, 60g	33	+	7	202	850
muffin mix, blueberry & apricot, prepared, 1, 60g	32	+	6.7	202	850
muffin mix, choc-chip, prepared, 1, 60g	32	N	7	213	895
MULBERRIES					
raw, 100g	4.5	++	0	29	120
MUSHROOMS					
button, raw, 100g	1.5	1.1	0.5	24	100
canned, 100g	1.5	1.3	0.5	15	65
canned in butter sauce, 100g	3.5	1	1	27	115
champignon, canned, 100g	1	1	0	13	55
chinese, dried & rehydrated, 25g	4	N	0	14	60
enoki, raw, 100g	7	N	0.5	35	145
oyster, raw, 100g	6	+	0.5	37	155
shiitake, dried, 4, 15g	11	+	0	44	185
straw, canned, drained, 100g	4.5	+	0.5	32	135
swiss brown, 100g	N	+	0	23	95
MUSTARD					
American, 1tbsp	1	0	0	15	65
English, 1tbsp	1	0	0	15	65
French, 1tbsp	1	0	0	15	65
powder, wholegrain, 1 tsp, 5g	0.5	1	1	18	75
seeded, 1tbsp	1	+	0	15	65
NASHI PEAR					
raw, unpeeled, 1, 130g	9.2	2	0	38	158
NECTARINE					
raw, unpeeled, 1, 75g	6.75	1	0	30	126
NOODLES					
egg, boiled, 1 portion, 100g	13	0.6	0.5	62	264
instand, boiled, 1 portion, 100g	N	+	5	367	1540
rice, boiled, 1 portion, 100g	21.5	0.5	0.5	99	415
rice, fried, 1 portion, 150g	16.8	0.8	17.2	230	964
rice, vermicelli, boiled, 30g	N	+	0.5	110	460
buckwheat, boiled, 100g	21.5	+	0	99	415
quick-cook noodles, all flavours, 1 packet, 85g	54	+	16	390	1640
noodles, rice, dry, 100g	81.5	+	0.1	360	1506
wheat, fried, 80g	50	+	17	374	1570
wheat, steamed, 80g	60	+	2	283	1190
NUTMEAT					
canned, 100g	6	+	8.5	195	820
NUTS					
almond, blanched, 85g	5.8	6.3	47.5	520	2185
almond, chocolate-coated, 75g	49.5	4.5	33.5	517	2170

FOOD	CARB g	FIBRE g	FAT g	ENERGY kcal	KJ
almond, raw, 4	0.5	1.5	8	87	365
almond, raw & unpeeled, 85g	2	2.3	17.5	195	817
almond, smoked, 30g	1.5	N	15	194	815
almond, sugar-coated, 30g	N	N	12	130	545
brazil, raw, 80g	2.5	3.4	54.5	546	2291
cashew, raw, 75g	13.6	2.4	36	430	1805
cashew, roasted, 75g	14	2.4	38	458	1925
chestnut, raw, 72g	26	3	2	122	514
hazelnut, raw, 70g	4.2	4.5	44.4	455	1911
macadamia, salted, 73g	3.5	3.8	56.6	546	2293
mixed, 78g	6	4.7	42	473	1988
mixed nuts & raisins, 100g	31.5	4.5	34	481	2004
peanut, raw, 78g	9.75	4.8	35.9	440	1848
peanut, roasted, 78g	8	5	38.8	459	1930
pecan, raw, 55g	3.2	2.6	38.5	379	1592
pinenut, raw, 1tbsp, 15g	0.6	0.3	10.2	103	433
pistachio, raw, 63g	5	3.8	35	379	1590
walnut, chopped, raw, 55g	1.8	2	38	378	1589
OATMEAL					
40g	29	2.7	3.5	160	674
OIL					
blended, 1tbsp	0	0	20	176	740
cod liver, 1tbsp	0	0	20	176	740
olive oil, 1tbsp	0	0	19	167	703
OKRA					
boiled, 6 pods, 65g	1	2.3	0	13	55
OLIVES					
black, 6 medium, 40g	N	N	7	39	165
green, 6 medium, 50g	Tr	1.5	5.5	56	211
stuffed, 5 olives, 20g	0.5	1.5	1.5	18	75
ONION					
brown, raw, peeled, 1 medium, 100g	4.5	1.4	0	24	100
pickled, drained, 2,36g	4.5	0.4	0	21	90
red, raw, peeled, 1 small, 100g	4.5	1.4	0	25	105
spring, raw, whole, 1, 14g	0.5	0.2	0	3	14
white, raw, peeled, 1 medium, 100g	4.5	1.4	0	26	110
ORANGE					
all varieties, raw, peeled, 120g	10.2	2	0	44	186
juice, freshly squeezed, 100ml	8.1	0.1	0	33	140
juice, commercial, unsweetened, 100ml	8.8	0.1	0	36	153
PANCAKE					
average, homemade, 1, 16 cm, 50g	14	0.5	1	75	315
PAPADUM					
fried, 3 small, 10g	3.9	N	1.7	37	155
grilled or microwaved, 3 small	N	N	0	17	70
PAPAYA (PAWPAW)					
raw, peeled, 100g	8.8	2.2	0	36	153
canned in juice,100g	17	0.7	0	65	275
PARSNIP					
raw, peeled, boiled, 100g	12.9	4.7	1.2	66	278
PASSIONFRUIT					
1 average, 40g	2.5	1.5	0	19	80

FOOD	CARB g	FIBRE g	FAT g	ENERGY kcal	ENERGY KJ
PASTA (see also LASAGNE and SPAGHETTI)					
egg, cooked, 1 serving, 200g	51	2	1	261	1095.
plain, all shapes, cooked,					
1 serving, 180g	44.5	1.8	0.5	213	895
ravioli, cheese & spinach, cooked,					
1 serving, 265g	88	+	16.5	640	2690
ravioli, meat, cooked, 1 serving, 265g	82.5	+	17.5	602	2530
spinach, cooked, 1 serving, 200g	54.5	+	1	258	1085
tomato & herb fettucine, cooked, 200g	39	+	1.5	186	780
tortellini, cheese & spinach, cooked,					
1 serving, 265g	88	+	16.5	640	2690
tortellini, meat, 1 serving	N	N	5	379	1590
wholemeal, cooked, 1 serving, 180g	42	6.3	1.6	203	854
PASTA SAUCE					
carbonara, jar, 1 serving, 125g	21.5	+	6.5	158	665
creamy mushroom, 1 serving, 280g	25	+	0.5	119	500
spicy tomato, 1 serving, 125g	20.5	+	5	140	589
tomato, bottled, 1 serving, 280g	26.5	+	2	134	565
PASTRY					
choux, cooked, 30g	9	0.4	7	108	454
filo, 2 sheets	15	N	0.5	77	325
flaky, average portion, cooked, 50g	23	0.9	20.3	280	1176
hot-water, 50g	27	N	10	213	895
puff, 1 sheet, 170g	63	N	42.3	671	2820
shortcrust, cooked, 100g	54.2	2.2	32.3	521	2174
strudel, 50g	23	N	20	267	1120
suet crust, 50g	27	N	10	213	895
wholemeal, cooked, 100g	44.6	6.3	32.9	499	2080
PATE					
chicken liver, 1tbsp	N	0	2.5	27	112
country, 1tbsp	0.5	0.5	5	59	250
PAVLOVA					
pavlova shell mix, prepared,					
1 serving, 60g	4	0	0	173	725
shell, with cream & passion fruit,					
1 serving	N	+	11	315	1325
PAWPAW					
whole, raw, 100g	7	2	0	30	125
PEACH					
canned in jelly, snack pack	N	N	0	95	400
canned in juice, drained, 140g	12.5	1.2	0	56	235
canned in syrup, 250g	14	2.2	0	61	255
dried, 25g	13	1.8	0	61	255
raw, 1 medium, 140g	9	2	0	44	185
stewed, with sugar, 100g	25.5	2.9	0.5	106	445
stewed, without sugar, 100g	21.5	3	0.5	92	385
PEAR					
canned, snack pack 140g	N	2	0	82	345
canned in pear juice, drained, 250g	25.5	3.5	0	106	445
canned in syrup, drained, 250g	37	2.75	0	148	620
canned in water, drained, 250g	16	3.5	0	64	270
dried, 2, 87g	60.5	7.2	0.5	227	955
juice, canned, 200ml	27.5	0	0	112	470
raw, unpeeled, 185g	18.5	4	0	74	311

FOOD	CARB g	FIBRE g	FAT g	ENERGY kcal	ENERGY KJ
PEAS					
green, cooked, 1 serving, 165g	10.5	7.4	0.5	80	335
peas, raw, 170g	10	8	1	98	410
split, dried, cooked, 1 serving, 180g	12	4.9	1	104	435
sugar snap, 170g	10	2.2	1	98	410
PHEASANT					
raw, meat only, 125g	0	0	4.5	165	695
PIGEON					
breast, lean, roasted, 125g	0	0	14.5	263	1105
PINEAPPLE					
canned in juice, drained, 1 bowl, 250ml	25.5	1.25	0	112	470
canned in syrup, drained, 1 slice, 40g	8	0.3	0	33	140
juice, unsweetened, canned, 250ml	27	0	0	111	465
raw, peeled, 1 slice, 110g	9	1.3	0	42	175
PIE					
meat, average, all types, 1, 190g	34	0.8	26	429	1800
PIZZA (see FAST FOOD)					
PLUM					
canned in syrup, drained, 1 serving, 225g	35	1.8	0.3	132	557
raw, 100g	8.8	1.6	0	36	155
stewed, without sugar, 1 serving, 250g	17	4	0	85	357
POLENTA					
dry, 60g	41	+	1	198	830.
POMEGRANATE					
raw, peeled, 100g	11.8	3.4	0.2	51	218
POPCORN					
caramel-coated, 100g	77.6	N	20	480	2018
plain, commercial, 2 scoops, 16g	8.5	N	4	75	315
PORK					
bacon, breakfast rasher, grilled, 1, 34g	0	0	1.5	48	200
barbecued, Chinese-style, 100g	3.5	N	15	233	980
belly, rasher, untrimmed, grilled, 100g	0	0	22	298	1250
crackling, 30g	0	0	9	142	610
fillet lean, baked, 1, 100g	0	0	5	169	710
forequarter chop, lean, grilled, 1, 95g	0	0	7.5	171	720
forequarter chop, untrimmed, grilled, 1, 100g	0	0	28.5	343	1440
leg roast, lean, 2 slices, 95g	0	0	4	163	685
leg roast with fat, 2 slices, 100g	0	0	26.5	338	1420
leg, lean, grilled, 1, 100g	0	0	3.5	156	655
leg, untrimmed, grilled, 1, 100g	0	0	6	171	720
loin chop, lean, grilled. 1, 100g	0	0	5.5	174	730
loin chop, untrimmed, grilled, 1, 100g	0	0	30	362	1520
medallion steak, lean, grilled, 1 small, 100g	0	0	5.5	187	785
medallion steak, untrimmed, grilled, 1 small, 100g	0	0	22.5	307	1290
mince, 100g	0	0	30	75	315
pie, 1, 180g	46.5	1.8	53.5	763	3205
ribs, spare, 100g	0	0	10	114	480
steak, lean, grilled, 100g	0	0	4.5	161	675
steak untrimmed, grilled, 100g	0	0	17.5	259	1090

FOOD	CARB g	FIBRE g	FAT g	ENERGY kcal	KJ
POTATO					
baked, jacket, no oil, 1 medium, 150g	21.5	2	1	109	460
boiled, peeled, 1 medium, 150g	19.5	1.5	0.5	96	405
boiled, unpeeled, 1 medium, 150g	20	2	0	98	410
chips, oven-cook, frozen, cooked,					
100g	25	2	3	131	550
fries (thin-cut), medium serving	43	1	18	338	1420
oven-fried, 100g	29	6	13	245	1030
hash brown, 1 average, 55g	15	1	12	171	720
mashed with milk & butter,					
1 serving, 120g	N	2.5	1	77	325
mashed with skim milk, 120g	N	2.5	0	71	300
new, peeled, boiled, 3, 165g	21	3	0	103	435
roast, no skin, 150g	26	2.5	4	159	670
roast, with skin, 150g	25	2	4	159	670
steamed, new, peeled, 165g	20	3	0	102	430
wedges, crunchy, 100g	26	4.5	6	165	695
POTATO CRISPS					
(see CORN CHIPS and SNACK FOOD)					
PRICKLY PEAR					
raw, peeled, 86g	7.5	N	0	34	145
PRUNES					
dried, 5, 38g	16.5	2.2	0	70	295
juice, 250ml	44.5	Tr	0	181	760.
stewed, with sugar, 150g	29.5	4.6	0	119	500
stewed, without sugar, 150g	18.5	4.8	0	78	330
PUMPKIN					
peeled, boiled, 85g	6	1	0.5	36	150
pie, 1 slice, 109g	29.5	3	10.5	229	960
roasted in oil with 1/2tbsp oil,					
85g	8	1.5	8	125	525
seeds, dry roasted, 1tbsp	4.5	1	11.5	134	565
PURSLANE					
boiled, 1 cup, 115g	4	N	0	20	85
QUAIL					
roasted, with skin, 180g	0	0	6	180	755
roasted, without skin, 125g	0	0	20	349	1465
QUICHE					
cheese & egg, average homemade,					
slice, 125g	21.5	1	27.5	390	1640
lorraine, average, 100g	18	N	22	293	1230
mushroom, average homemade,					
1 slice, 125g	23	1.5	24.5	352	1480
vegetable, average, 100g	20	N	18	259	1090
QUINCE					
raw, 100g	11	++	0	48	200
stewed, with added sugar, 100g	21	+	0	83	350
RABBIT					
meat only, baked, 100g	0	0	5.5	169	710
RADISH					
red, raw, 3, 45g	1	0.5	0	0.6	2.5
white, raw, peeled, sliced, 90g	2.5	1.5	0.5	15	65
RAISINS					
100g	69.3	2	0.4	272	1159

FOOD	CARB g	FIBRE g	FAT g	ENERGY kcal	ENERGY KJ
RASPBERRIES					
canned in syrup, drained, 100g	22.5	1.5	0	88	374
raw, 65g	3	1.6	0.2	16	71
REDCURRANTS					
raw, 100g	14	3.4	0	56	235
RELISH					
corn, 1tbsp	4.5	0.2	0	20	85
mustard, 1tbsp	4.5	N	0	20	85
tomato, 1tbsp	4.5	0.2	0	19	80
RHUBARB					
raw, 100g	0.8	1.4	0	7	32
stewed with sugar, 125g	14.5	1.5	0	60	252
RICE					
average, cooked, 100g	33.4	0.1	1.1	157	660
basmati, cooked, 1 serving	42	+	0.3	177	742
brown, cooked, 1 serving, 180g	57	1.5	2	270	1135
extra-long grain, cooked, 70g	54.5	0.5	0.5	232	973
fragrant, cooked, 100g	34.6	0.5	0.4	155	651
fried, 190g	56	1.1	16	413	1735
long grain, cooked, 100g	34.6	+	0.4	155	651
white, cooked, 1 serving, 190g	53	0.2	0.5	237	995
wild, cooked, 1 serving, 164g	35	+	N	165	695
RICE CAKES					
corn & buckwheat, 1, 12g	10	+	0	49	205
corn cakes, natural, 2, 10g	9	+	0	36	150
natural brown, 2, 10g	8	+	0.5	14	60
rice & rye, 2, 10g	8	+	0.5	39	165
SAFFRON					
1tbsp	1.5	0	0	6	25
SALADS					
bean salad, commercial, 1 serving, 210g	27	6.3	18	309	1298
coleslaw, commercial, 1 carton, 200g	8.4	2.8	52.8	516	1872
potato salad, 1 carton, 180g	20.5	1.4	47	517	1913
SALAMI					
average, all varieties, 50g	0.5	0	19	214	900
Danish, 4 slices, 20g	0.5	N	8	88	370
pepperoni, 4 slices, 20g	0.5	0	7	80	335
SAUCES					
mayonnaise, 1tbsp	0.1	0	13	118	495
apricot chicken, 1 serving, 118g	15	0	1	69	290
apricot chicken, jar, 1 serving, 115g	16	0	10.5	67	280
barbecue, I tbsp	10	0	0	40	170
beef & black bean, 115g	11	0	1.5	58	245
bolognaise, 160g	3.5	N	14	192	805
butterscotch, 45g	15	0	17	214	900
chilli, 20g	10.5	0	0	9	40
country French chicken, 118g	5	0	11.5	126	530
creamy lemon chicken, 118g	15	0	0.7	69	290
creamy mushroom, 1 serving, 120g	6.5	0	1.5	133	560
golden honey mustard, 118g	12	0	13	170	715
gravy, commercial, 60g	5.5	0	5.5	81	340
gravy, made from powder, prepared, 60g	2.5	0	0	14	60

FOOD	CARB g	FIBRE g	FAT g	ENERGY kcal	ENERGY KJ
herbed chicken & wine, 1 serving, 115g	7.5	0	6.5	14	60
honey & sesame, 1 serving, 120g	23	0	1	108	455
honey, sesame & garlic, 1 serving, 115g	23	0	0.5	85	400
Hungarian goulash, 1 serving, 125g	7.5	0	3.5	105	440
Malaysian satay, 1tbsp	5	+	5	67	280
mild Indian, 1 serving, 115g	8	0	7	93	390
mint homemade, 1 tbsp	0	0	0	9	40
mornay, bought, 1 serving, 120g	5	0	14	161	675
onion, made from powdered mix, prepared, 125g	8.5	0	7	110	460
oyster, 1 tbsp	5	0	0	29	120
packet, average all types, 1 serving, 125g	10	0	20	263	1105
pesto, 1 tbsp	9	+	5	90	380
soya, 1 tbsp	0.5	0	0	9	40
spicy plum, 1 serving, 115g	21	N	0.5	86	360
sweet & sour, 1 serving, 115g	30.5	N	0	120	505
sweet & sour, lite, 1 serving, 115g	20.5	N	0	80	335
sweet Thai chilli, 115g	52.5	N	0.5	204	855
toffee, 1, 20g	15	0	2	80	335
tomato, 1tbsp	5.5	+	0	23	95
white, homemade, 1tbsp	2.5	+	5	27	115
worcestershire, 1tbsp	4	0	0	17	70
SAUSAGE					
beef, fried, homemade, 1, 50g	2	0.3	9	117	490
beef, grilled, homemade, 1, 50g	3	0.3	9	127	535
Bierschinken, 1, 30g	0	0	5	309	1300
black pudding, grilled, 1, 90g	6.5	+	21	281	1180
bratwurst, 100g	0	0	30	362	1520
cabanossi, 1, 30g	0	N	10	109	460
chicken, thin, 2, 50g	0	0	6	89	375
chicken, thin, low-fat, 2, 40g	0	0	3	70	295
chipolates (skinless), 2, 25g	0	0	5	55	230
Italian, cooked, 100g	0	0	30	362	1520
Chinese sausage, 100g	3	0	40	429	1800
low-fat, 1, 50g	0	0	5	75	315
pork, thick, grilled, 2, 150g	9	1	33	425	1785
pork, thin, grilled, 2, 100g	6	0.7	21.5	283	1190
Schinkenwurst, 30g	0	0	15	154	645
vegetarian, 1, 60g	4	1	4	98	410
SCONE					
fruit, 1, 50g	20	+	3	118	495
plain, average, 1, 50g	23	1	5	154	645
SEAFOOD					
baked, 85g	0	0	1	95	400
anchovies, canned in oil, drained, 5, 18g	0	0	1.5	33	140
bass, 100g	0	0	1	93	390
blackfish, 100g	0	0	2	93	390
blue grenadier, 100g	0	0	2	93	390
blue threadfin, 100g	0	0	2	93	390
boarfish, 100g	0	0	2	93	390
bream, steamed, 1 fillet, 149g	0	0	8	206	865
calamari tubes, raw, 100g	0	0	0	69	290

FOOD	CARB g	FIBRE g	FAT g	ENERGY kcal	ENERGY KJ
calamari tubes, fried, 100g	12	N	17.5	276	1160
caviar, black, 1tbsp, 16g	0.5	0	3	40	170
caviar, red, 1tbsp, 16g	0.5	0	3	40	170
clams, 100g	0	N	2	81	340
cockles, raw, 100g	0	0	0	48	200
cod, baked, 100g	0	0	1	76	320
cod, grilled, 100g	0	0	2	95	400
cod, poached, 100g	0	0	2	95	400
cod, smoked, simmered, 1 fillet, 195g	0	0	1.5	89	375
crab, all varieties, 90g	0	0	0.5	54	230
crab, canned in brine, 145g	2	0	1	88	370
eel, 85g	0	0	12.5	190	800
eel, smoked, 100g	10	0	13	167	700
fish ball, boiled, 1, 50g	2	0	0.5	37	155
fish paste, 1tbsp, 20g	2	0	1.5	31	130
fish roe, black, 1tbsp, 20g	0	0	1	18	75
fish roe, red, 1tbsp, 20g	0	0	1.5	30	125
fish, steamed, 1 small fillet, 85g	0	0	2.5	105	440
flake, crumbed & fried, 1 fillet, 165g	10.5	+	8.5	293	1230
flake, steamed, 1 fillet, 150g	0	0	0	187	785
flathead, fried, 1 fillet, 104g	3.5	0	7	183	770
flathead, steamed, 1 fillet, 85g	0	0	1	96	405
flounder, 100g	0	0	1	67	280
garfish, 100g	0	0	2	93	390
gernfish, 1 fillet, 175g	0	0	27	393	1650
groper, 100g	0	0	1	86	360
gumard, 100g	0	0	2	86	390
haddock, smoked, 1 small fillet, 85g	0	0	1	8	35
herring, canned, drained, 125g	10	0	22.5	315	1325
jewfish (mulloway), steamed, 1 fillet, 145g	0	0	4	128	540
kamaboko, 100g	0	0	1	52	220
kingfish, 100g	0	0	3	105	440
leatherjacket, 100g	0	0	2	93	390
lemon sole, 1 small fillet, 85g	0	0	2	79	330
ling, 100g	0	0	2	93	390
lobster, boiled, 165g	0	0	1.5	159	670
lumpfish roe, 10g	0	0	1	12	50
mackerel, 100g	0	0	16	221	930
mullet, steamed, 1 fillet, 74g	0	0	3.5	99	415
mussels, 100g	0	0	2	87	365
mullet, steamed, 1 fillet, 74g	0	0	3.5	99	415
mussels, 100g	0	0	2	87	365
mussels, smoked, canned in oil, drained, 100g	4.5	0	10.5	193	810
ocean perch, 1 fillet, 120g	0	0	2.5	112	470
octopus, 100g	0	0	1	69	290
oysters, raw, 10, 60g	0.5	0	2.5	72	305
oysters, smoked, canned in oil, drained, 10, 60g	0.5	0	7	124	520
parrot fish, 100g	0	0	2	93	390

FOOD	CARB g	FIBRE g	FAT g	ENERGY kcal	KJ
perch, 100g	0	0	1	86	360
pike, 100g	0	0	1	88	370
pilchards, 150g	0	0	3.5	157	660
pilchards, canned in tomato sauce, 225g	2	+	29	430	1805
prawn cutlets, fried, 3, 75g	15	+	12	218	915
prawns, garlic, 100g	2.5	+	7.5	121	510
prawns, king, cooked, 100g	0	0	1	104	435
prawns, school, steamed, 150g	0	0	1.5	114	480
redfish, 100g	0	0	2	93	390
salmon, canned in brine, drained, 100g	0	0	9.5	171	720
salmon, patty mix, 100g	0	0	7.5	202	850
salmon, pink, canned in brine, drained, 100g	0	0	6.5	146	615
salmon, raw, 100g	0	0	12	181	760
salmon, red, canned in brine, drained, 100g	0	0	12	194	815
salmon, roe, 1tbsp, 10g	0	0	1	12	50
salmon, smoked, 50g	0	0	2.5	67	280
sardines, fresh, 100g	0	0	2	67	280
sardines, canned in oil, drained, 100g	0	0	15.5	226	950
sardines, canned in tomato sauce, 100g	1	Tr	13	190	800
scallops, steamed, 160g	1	0	2.5	168	705
scampi, 100g	0	0	2	107	450
scampi, crumbed, fried, 2, 100g	0	1	17.5	314	1320
sea bream, 100g	0	0	5.5	138	580
sea perch, 100g	0	0	1	86	360
sea trout, 100g	0	0	2	93	390
shark, 100g	0	0	1	100	420
snapper, steamed, 100g	0	0	2.5	121	510
sole, 100g	0	0	1	81	340
squid, boiled, steamed, 100g	0	0	1	79	330
squid rings, fried, 125g	8.5	0	12	257	1080
trout, coral, grilled, 100g	0	0	2	93	390
trout, rainbow, steamed, 100g	0	0	6	155	650
trout, smoked, 100g	0	0	5	136	570
tuna, canned in brine/water, drained, 190g	0	0	5	234	985
tuna, canned in oil, drained, 250g	0	0	28	450	1890
tuna, steamed, 100g	0	0	3	119	500
whiting, all varieties, 100g	0	0	1	93	390
SEAWEED					
raw, average all types, 10g	Tr	1.2	0	1	4
SEEDS					
poppy, 1tbsp	2	+	4	46	195
pumpkin, 50g	5	2.6	7	155	650
sesame, 1tbsp	0	0.8	7	76	320
sunflower, 1tbsp	0.5	0.9	8	88	370
SEMOLINA					
cooked, 1 bowl, 245g	15.5	+	0	75	315

FOOD	CARB g	FIBRE g	FAT g	ENERGY kcal	KJ
SHALLOT					
25g	N	0.3	0	6	25
SNACK FOOD (see also CORN CHIPS)					
bacon rings, 1 packet, 25g	N	0	6,5	124	520
burger rings,1 packet, 50g	0	1	13	249	1045
cheese & bacon balls, 1 packet, 50g	N	N	17	265	1115
cheese twists, 1 packet, 50g	30	0.5	13	249	1045
cheese potato puff type,					
1 packet, 50g	30	0.5	15	258	1085
popcorn, microwave, I pack, 100g	4	1	2	32	135
potato crisps, plain, 1 large					
packet, 50g	25	2.6	15	249	1045
potato crisps, 1 large packet, 50g	N	2.6	16	250	1050
potato crisps, lite, 1 packet, 50g	30	3	15	258	1085
potato crisps,					
average all flavours, 50g	N	2.6	18	282	1185
potato twists, plain, 1 packet, 50g	N	1.3	17	258	1085
pork rind, crackling, 1 packet, 30g	N	0.1	8.5	145	610
prawn crackers, 5, 30g	N	0	2	45	190
pretzels-type, 10g	6.5	+	0.5	37	155
sesame seed bar, 1, 45g	20	+	12	167	700
SNAIL					
cooked, 2, 30g	N	0	0.5	29	120
SOFT DRINKS – carbonated					
(see also CORDIAL, SPORTS DRINKS AND WATER)					
cola, 375ml	39	0	0	150	630
diet cola, 375ml	1	0	0	1	5
dry ginger ale, 375ml	28	0	0	124	520
dry ginger ale, diet, 375ml	1	0	0	4	15
orangeade, 275ml	48	0	0	194	815
orangeade, diet, 375ml	1	0	0	2	10
lemonade, 375ml	40	0	0	159	670
lemonade, diet, 375ml	1	0	0	4	15
pineapple & grapefruit flavoured, 375ml	45	0	0	161	675
diet, 375ml	1	0	0	6	25
lemon & lime flavoured, 375ml	40	0	0	179	750
lime flavoured, 375ml	40	0	0	150	630
diet, 375ml	1	0	0	4	15
tonic water, 250ml	0	0	0	82	345
SORBET					
lemon, 50g	7	0	0	62	260
SOUP					
chicken, low calorie, 220ml	8	N	1	50	210
condensed, beef broth, 220ml	12.5	N	2.5	81	340
condensed, creamy chicken,					
220ml	12	N	6	120	505
condensed, creamy chicken &					
corn, 220ml	14.5	N	7	131	550
condensed, creamy chicken &					
mushroom, 220ml	15	N	0	70	295
condensed, creamy chicken &					
vegetable, natural, 215ml	10.5	N	8	139	585
condensed, creamy mushroom,					
1 serving, 215ml	7	N	8	139	585

FOOD	CARB g	FIBRE g	FAT g	ENERGY kcal	ENERGY KJ
condensed, pumpkin, 1 serving, 215ml	13	N	4	96	403
condensed, creamy minestrone, 1 serving, 215ml	15	N	0.5	74	310
condensed, creamy potato & leek, 215ml	12	N	13	180	755
condensed, minestrone, 220ml	15	+	0	70	295
condensed, mushroom, 220ml	13	N	6.5	126	530
condensed, pea & ham, 220ml	15	+	0.5	94	395
condensed, tomato, 1 serving, 220ml	12	+	0.5	57	240
instant, chicken noodle, lite, 1 mug, 200ml	5	N	0.5	29	120
instant, chicken & vegetable, 1 mug, 200ml	14	N	0	60	250
instant, chunky chicken, 1 serving, 1 mug, 250ml,	31	N	3	167	700
instant, creamy cauliflower & cheese, 1 mug, lite, 200ml	9	N	1	45	190
instant, mushroom & chives, 1 mug, lite, 200ml	5.5	N	1.5	38	160
instant, pea & ham supreme, 1 mug, lite, 200ml	9.5	N	1	55	230
instant pumpkin & vegetable, 1 mug, lite, 200ml	9	N	0.5	40	170
minestrone, reduced calorie, 220ml	10	+	0	50	210
tomato, reduced calorie, 220ml	11	1.5	0	50	210
vegetable, reduced calorie, 220ml	9	1.5	0.5	48	200
SPAGHETTI (see also PASTA)					
canned, bolognaise, 130g	12.5	1.3	0.5	68	285
canned, tomato sauce, 130g	16.5	1	1.3	87	365
canned, tomato sauce & cheese, 130g	16.5	+	1	82	345
SPICES					
average all types, 1tsp	0	N	0	9	40
SPINACH					
cooked, 35g	0.3	0.7	0	7	28
frozen, cooked, 35g	0.2	0.7	0	7	28
raw, 35g	0.5	0.7	0	9	37
SPORTS DRINKS					
isotonic type, 500ml	36	0	0	150	630
isotonic type, lite, 500ml	N	0	0	144	605
glucose type, 300ml	58	0	0	151	635
glucose type, lite, 500ml	N	0	0	100	420
SPREADS (see also HONEY and JAM)					
almond spread, 100g	19	+	54	571	2400
cheddar cheese, 1tbsp	0	0	5	60	250
cheddar cheese, light, 1tbsp	1.5	0	3.5	48	200
gherkin, 1tbsp	9.5	+	0	57	240
lemon-flavoured, 1tbsp	13	0	1	59	250
marmalade, orange, 1tbsp	9	0	0	34	145
nut and chocolate, 1tbsp	N	0	6	105	440

FOOD	CARB g	FIBRE g	FAT g	ENERGY kcal	KJ
peanut butter, crunchy, 1tbsp	3.5	1.2	10.5	125	525
peanut butter, crunchy lite, 1tbsp	6	+	7.5	112	470
peanut butter, smooth, 1tbsp	2.6	1	10.5	125	525
peanut butter, smooth lite, 1tbsp	6	+	7.5	112	470
pickles, low-calorie, 1tbsp	N	0	0	8	35
sandwich spread, 1tbsp	6	0.2	2.5	47	195
vegemite, 1tsp	0.5	0	0	8	35
yeast extract, 1tsp	Tr	0	0	8	35
SPRING ONION					
raw, 12g	0.5	0	0	2	10
SPROUTS					
alfalfa seeds, sprouted, raw, 100g	4	+	0.5	29	120
lentils, sprouted, raw, 100g	22	+	0.5	106	445
mung beans, sprouted, raw, 100g	4	1.5	0.5	31	131
radish seeds, sprouted, raw, 100g	3.5	+	2.5	43	180
soya beans, sprouted, raw, 100g	9.5	+	6.5	121	510
wheat seeds, sprouted, raw, 100g	42.5	+	1.5	198	830
SQUASH					
acorn, baked, 70g	9	2.2	0	39	165
butternut, baked, 70g	5	1	0	22	94
STAR FRUIT (CARAMBOLA)					
raw, 100g	7.3	1.3	0	32	136
STOCK CUBES					
all varieties, 1, 5g	1	0	0,5	11	45
STOCK POWDER					
all varieties, 1tbsp	2	0	0.5	19	80
STRAWBERRIES					
canned in syrup, 100g	17	0.7	0	65	279
raw, 100g	6	1.1	0	27	113
STUFFING					
average, small serving, 30g	6.5	0.5	2.5	56	235
SUET MIX					
100g	10	0	90	807	3390
SUGAR					
average, 1tsp	5	0	0	19	80
any type, 1tbsp	17	0	0	64	270
icing, 1tbsp	20	0	0	76	320
SULTANAS					
dried, 1tbsp	13.5	0.5	0	55	230
SUSHI					
Californian roll, 5 pieces	N	N	2	139	585
inari (bean curd pouch with rice), 85g	N	N	2	130	545
nigiri, 30g	N	N	0.5	30	125
SWEDE					
peeled, boiled, 150g	3	1	0	16	69

FOOD	CARB g	FIBRE g	FAT g	ENERGY kcal	KJ
SWEET POTATO					
peeled, boiled, l00g	20.5	2.3	0	84	358
raw, 1, 235g	50	5.6	0	56	237
SWEETS (see also CHOCOLATE)					
boiled, 1	5	0	0	15	65
butterscotch, 1	5.5	0	0	24	100
caramels, 1	4	0	0	24	100
fruit gums, 30g	27	0	0	8	35
fudge, 2 pieces, 35g	28.5	0	4.5	155	650
jaffas, 55g	N	0	18	245	1030
jelly babies, 1	3.5	0	0	15	65
jellybeans, 1	3	0	0	11	45
liquorice allsorts, 100g	77	2	5.2	349	1483
liquorice pieces, 100g	65	1.9	1.4	278	1185
peppermints, 1 packet	N	0	0	84	355
marshmallows, 1 packet, 85g	68	0	0	283	1190
sesame seed bar, 45g	N	+	12	167	700
sherbet lemons, 1	N	0	0	20	85
toffees, 1	3.5	0	0.5	20	85
SWISS CHARD					
raw, 30g	1	N	0	6	25
TACO					
with meat & bean sauce, 1 serving, 180g	N	+	14	231	970
TAHINI					
paste, 1tbsp	0.2	1.6	11.8	121	510
TAMARILLO (TREE TOMATO)					
raw, peeled, 90g	4	+	0	24	100
TANGERINE					
raw, peeled, 100g	8	1.3	0	35	147
TAPIOCA					
cooked, 1 bowl, 265g	18.5	0.3	0	75	315
TEA					
for each teaspoon of sugar in tea, add ...	5	0	0	19	80
black, no sugar, 1 cup, 250 ml	Tr	0	0	Tr	Tr
with whole milk, l cup, 250ml	1	0	1	18	75
with skim milk, 1 cup, 250ml	1.5	0	0	13	55
TINNED FRUITS (see also FRUIT SALAD)					
peach & mango in syrup, 133g	12	1	0	56	235
sliced peaches in syrup, 133g	18	1.2	0	71	300
fruit salad in syrup, 125g	15	1.5	0	59	250
TOFU					
dessert, fruit-flavoured, 100g	12.5	N	1	67	280
firm, 100g	0.7	N	4.2	73	304
fried, 100g	2	N	17.7	261	1086
silken, 100g	3	0	2.5	55	230
tofu burgers, 100g	N	N	9.5	174	730
tofu veggie burgers, 100g	N	N	9.5	174	730
soya burger mix, 30g	26	+	1.3	168	704

FOOD	CARB g	FIBRE g	FAT g	ENERGY kcal	ENERGY KJ
TOMATO					
canned in juice, 250g	7.5	1.7	0.2	40	172
juice, 250g	7.5	1.5	0	35	155
purée, 1tbsp	2	0.6	0	13	55
cherry, 100g	3	1	0.4	18	76
raw, 1 large, 100g	3.1	1	0	17	73
sundried, natural, 5 pieces,					
10g	5.5	+	0.5	26	110
sundried, in oil, drained,					
3 pieces, 10g	2.5	+	1.5	21	90
TOPPING					
caramel, 1tbsp	11	0	0	45	190
chocolate, 1tbsp	12.5	0	0	54	225
strawberry, 1tbsp	9	0	0	39	165
TORTILLA					
corn, 1, 50g	24.5	N	4.5	152	640
wheat flour, 1, 50g	30	1.2	0.5	131	557
TRIFLE					
commercial, made with cream,					
1 serving, 120g	23	0.6	11	199	837
TURKEY					
baked, lean. 120g	0	0	5	186	780
breast, no skin, 80g	0	0	3.5	20	83
breast, with skin, basted, 100g	0	0	8	145	610
1 slice	0	0	4	149	625
cooked meat, 100g	0	0	11.5	167	700
roast, dark meat, 100g	0	0	4	133	560
roast, light meat, 100g	0	0	1.5	133	560
roast, with skin, 100g	0	0	6.5	170	715
salami, 100g	0	0	4	149	625
smoked, 75g	0	0	1	80	335
TURNIP					
peeled, boiled, 240g	4.8	4.5	0	29	121
VEAL					
boneless, unspecified cut, lean,					
1, 190g	0	0	5	282	1185
boneless, unspecified cut, untrimmed,					
1, 200g	0	0	8	319	1340
cutlet crumbed & fried, 1	0	0	5	174	730
forequarter steak lean, 119g	0	0	6	329	1380
forequarter steak, untrimmed, 1,					
200g	0	0	10.5	373	1565
heart, baked, 100g	0	0	6	181	760
kidney, grilled, 100g	0	0	5.51	167	700
leg, lean, baked, 2 slices, 44g	0	0	0.5	54	225
leg, untrimmed, baked, 2 slices, 45g	0	0	0.5	64	270
leg, steak, lean, fried, 1, 85g	0	0	2.5	131	550
leg steak, untrimmed, fried, 1,					
100g	0	0	4	159	670
liver, grilled, 85g	1.5	0	7	159	670
loin chop, lean, baked or grilled,					
1, 50g	0	0	1.5	73	305
loin chop, untrimmed, baked or					
grilled, 1, 55g	0	0	2.5	88	370

FOOD	CARB g	FIBRE g	FAT g	ENERGY kcal	KJ
schnitzel, fried, 1, 85g	8.5	N	23	287	1205
shank, lean, simmered, 1, 80g	0	0	2	117	490
shank, untrimmed, simmered, 1, 90g	0	0	6	160	670
shoulder steak, lean, grilled, 1 small, 50g	0	0	1.5	73	305
shoulder steak, untrimmed, grilled, 1 small, 55g	0	0	2.5	84	355
VEGETABLE JUICE					
average, 250ml	11	0	0.5	51	215
VEGETABLES (see individual vegetables)					
VENISON					
roast, 100g	0	0	5.5	157	660
VINEGAR					
apple cider, 100ml	6	0	0	14	60
unspecified, 100ml	15.5	0	0	21	90
white, 1tbsp	0	0	0	4	15
WAFFLES					
frozen, 1 square, 35g	13.5	1	2.5	88	370
homemade, 1 round, 75g	24.5	2	10.5	218	915
WATER (see also SOFT DRINKS)					
plain mineral, soda, tap, 1 glass, 250g	0	0	0	0	0
bottled, average, all varieties, 1 glass, 250g	0	0	0	0	0
WATER CHESTNUTS					
canned, drained, 40g	3.5	+	0.5	19	80
raw, 5, 50g	12	+	0	49	205
WATERCRESS					
raw, 32g	0.5	0.5	0	6	25
WHEATGERM					
1tbsp	1.5	0.8	0.5	17	70
YAM					
baked or boiled 100g	37.5	1.7	0.4	153	651
YEAST					
dried, bakers, compressed, 1 sachet, 7g	0.5	N	0	8	35
dried, brewers, 1 sachet, 7g	0.5	N	0.5	19	80
YOGHURT					
acidophilus, live, low-fat, 100ml	11	0	0	56	235
acidophilus, plain, 100ml	8	0	3.3	24	100
bio type, acidophilus, low-fat, honey & strawberry, 100ml	13	0	3	100	420
black cherry, with live cultures, 100ml	17	0	4	104	435
drinking, apricot, 250ml	31	N	5	190	800
drinking, 100ml	13	0	1	81	340
drinking, swiss type, vanilla, 250ml	31.5	N	5	184	775
drinking, vitamin-enriched, 250ml	24	N	5	139	585
drinking, fruit, 250ml	31.8	N	5	190	800
frozen, fruit, 100ml	20	0	5	132	555

FOOD	CARB g	FIBRE g	FAT g	ENERGY kcal	KJ
frozen, fruit yoghurt stick, raspberry, strawberry, 85ml	20	0	5	132	555
frozen, low-fat, 100ml	N	0	3	114	480
frozen, low-fat, flavoured, 100ml	22	0	0	83	350
frozen, low-fat, low sugar, 1 cone	N	0	0	45	190
frozen, fat-free, honey, 1 cone	N	0	0	109	460
frozen, reduced-fat honey, 1 cone	N	0	0	90	380
frozen, strawberry, 85ml	N	0	4	127	535
fruit cocktail, diet lite, 100ml	13	0	0.2	92	385
honey, dairy style, 100ml	11.5	0	7	132	555
kiwifruit & mango, diet lite, 100ml	13.6	0	0.2	94	395
lemon, cultured, 100ml	15	0	0	82	345
low-fat, berry, diet lite, 100ml	15	0	1	87	365
low-fat, berry fruits, live, diet lite, 100ml	7	0	0	43	180
low-fat, fruit salad, blueberry, cherry, diet lite, bio type, 100ml	7	0	0	43	180
low-fat, passionfruit, 100ml	16	0	0	89	375
low-fat peach, diet lite, bio type, 100ml	6.5	0	0	42	175
low-fat, peach & mango, diet lite, 100ml	15	0	2	194	815
low-fat, plain. dairy type, 100ml	6	0	0	51	215
low-fat, strawberry, diet lite, bio type, 100ml	6.5	0	0	42	175
low-fat, summer fruits, diet lite, 100ml	16	0	1	93	390
low-fat, vanilla, diet lite, bio type, 100ml	6	0	0	40	170
low-fat, vanilla, fruit & nut, diet lite, 100ml	16	0	1	40	170
plain, bio type, 100ml	5	0	4.5	95	400
plain, dairy type, 100ml	6	0	8	120	505
plain, skim milk natural, 100ml	7	0	0.1	51	215
plain, swiss style, creamy custard, 100ml	1	0	4.5	107	450
plain, traditional, dairy type, 100ml	6.5	0	35	77	325
soft serve, 100ml	16.5	0	0	80	335
soft serve, low-fat, average	N	0	0	80	335
soft serve, natural, 100ml	24	0	2	142	595
soft serve, fat-free, 100ml	4.5	0	0	21	90
strawberry delight, 125ml	20	0	4	136	570
vanilla, cultured, 100ml	19	0	4	114	480
yoghurt, cultured, 65ml	11	0	0	46	195
yoghurt, baby type, banana/ vanilla, 100ml	N	0	4	107	450
yogurt, average, all flavours, 150ml	N	0	5	167	700
YORKSHIRE PUDDING					
small serve, 50g	12.3	0.5	5	104	437
ZUCCHINI					
green, boiled, 90g	1.5	1	0.5	13	55
yellow, boiled, 90g	1	1	0.5	17	70

VITAMIN AND MINERAL COUNTER

The following tables will help you estimate the nutrient content of your diet and thus improve your eating habits by making better food choices. Each table lists the average amount of vitamin or mineral contained in 100 grams of the food. Some are present in larger amounts (milligrams/mg) than others (micrograms/mcg). The tables contain fat-soluble vitamins and other fat-soluble nutrients; water-soluble vitamins and other water-soluble nutrients; as well as the major minerals and trace elements. Good sources of these vitamins and minerals are listed.

VITAMIN A

REFERENCE NUTRIENT INTAKE
Men 700mcg RE/day
Women 600mcg RE/day

FOOD SOURCES	mcg RE per 100 g
Liver, calf, fried	25200
Liver, lamb, fried	19700
Liver, chicken, fried	10500
Pâté, liver	7400
Carrots, raw	1353
Carrots, boiled	1260
Low fat spread	1084
Margarine	905
Butter	887
Sweet potato, baked	855
Red chillies	685
Parsley	673
Double cream	654
Red capsicum (peppers)	640
Spinach, boiled	640
Butternut squash, baked	548
Cream cheese	422
Watercress	420
Mixed frozen vegetables, boiled	420
Spring greens, boiled	378
Hard cheese, average	373
Tomatoes, grilled	307
Mangoes	300
Chicken eggs, whole, cooked or raw	190
Pawpaw (Papaya)	165
Canteloupe melon	165
Greek yoghurt	121
Tomatoes	107
Spring onion	103
Broccoli, boiled	80
Milk, whole	56

VITAMIN D

REFERENCE NUTRIENT INTAKE
No RNI because vitamin D can be made in the skin

FOOD SOURCES	mcg per 100 g
Cod liver oil	210
Kippers, baked	25
Salmon, red, canned in brine	23
Herring, grilled	16
Pilchards, canned in tomato sauce	14
Sardines, grilled	12
Trout, grilled	11
Salmon, grilled	9.6
Smoked mackerel	8
Low fat spread and margarines	8
Egg yolk	4.9
Sardines, canned in brine	4.6
Tuna, canned in brine	4.0
Evaporated milk	4.0
Fortified breakfast cereal	2.7
Scrambled egg with milk	1.9
Eggs, whole	1.8
Butter	0.8

RE Vitamin A comes either as retinol, from animal products, or carotene, from plant foods. Some carotene from foods can be converted into active vitamin A in the body, so the vitamin A content of food is expressed as retinol equivalents (RE).
NE The total niacin content of foods is expressed as niacin equivalents (NE), which is the niacin already in the food plus some of the tryptophan in the food that will be converted into niacin in the body.

VITAMIN E

SAFE INTAKE
Men above 4mg/day
Women above 3mg/day

FOOD SOURCES	mg per 100 g
Wheat germ oil	137
Sunflower oil	49
Safflower oil	41
Sunflower seeds	38
Palm oil	33
Polyunsaturated margarine	33
Hazelnuts	25
Almonds	24
Tomatoes, sun dried	24
Rapeseed oil	22
Wheat germ	22
Mayonnaise	19
Soya oil	16
Peanut oil	15
Pine nuts	14
Salad cream	11
Peanuts, plain	10
Brazil nuts	7.2
Low fat spread	6.3
Peanut butter	5
Bombay mix	4.7
Tomatoes, grilled	4
Walnuts	3.8
Pesto sauce	3.8
Avocado	3.2
Sesame seeds	2.5
Butter	2.0
Spinach	1.7
Salmon, pink, canned in brine	1.5
Eggs, raw, boiled or poached	1.1
Cheese, Parmesan	0.7

VITAMIN B1 (THIAMIN)

REFERENCE NUTRIENT INTAKE
Women 0.8mg/day (Pregnancy
0.9mg/day, Lactation 1.0mg/day)
Men 19–50 1.0mg/day, 51+ 0.9mg/day

FOOD SOURCES	mg per 100 g
Quorn myco-protein	37
Meat extract	9.7
Yeast extract	4.1
Wheat germ	2
Fortified breakfast cereals	1.0–1.8
Sunflower seeds	1.6
Pork fillet, lean, grilled	1.6
Bacon, back, grilled	1.2
Gammon rashers, grilled	1.2
Peanuts, plain	1.1
Malted milk powder	1.0
Tahini	0.9
Wheat bran	0.9
Sesame seeds	0.9
Ham, lean	0.8
Soya flour	0.8
Peas, boiled	0.7
Pine nuts	0.7
Pistachio nuts, roasted and salted	0.7
Cashew nuts	0.7
Liver, chicken and calf, fried	0.6
Wheat germ bread	0.5
Kidney, lamb	0.3
Wholemeal bread	0.3
Pasta, wholemeal, boiled	0.2
Kidney beans, canned	0.2
Red split lentils, boiled	0.2
Rice, brown, boiled	0.1

VITAMIN B2 (RIBOFLAVIN)

REFERENCE NUTRIENT INTAKE
Women 1.1mg/day (Pregnancy
1.4mg/day, Lactation 1.6mg/day)
Men 1.3mg/day

FOOD SOURCES	mg per 100 g
Yeast extract	12
Meat extract	8.5
Liver, lambs, fried	5.7
Kidney, pigs, fried	3.7
Liver, chicken, fried	2.7
Fortified breakfast cereals	1.0–2.2
Malted milk powder	1.3
Pâté, liver	1.2
Almonds	0.8
Wheat germ	0.8
Goats milk soft cheese	0.6
Muesli, Swiss style	0.7
Hard cheese, average	0.4–0.5
Egg, yolk	0.5
Goose or duck, roasted	0.5
Smoked mackerel	0.5
Tomato-based pasta sauce	0.5
Chocolate, milk	0.5
Tempeh	0.5
Eggs, boiled	0.3
Cheese, Brie	0.4
Cheese, Stilton	0.4
Evaporated milk	0.4
Fromage frais, plain	0.4
Wheat bran	0.4
Mushrooms, raw	0.3
Pilchards or sardines canned in tomato sauce	0.3
Ham hock	0.2
Split peas, boiled	0.06
Kale, boiled	0.06
Spinach, boiled	0.05

VITAMIN B3 (NIACIN)

REFERENCE NUTRIENT INTAKE
Women 19–50 13mg NE/day, 51+ 12mg
NE/day (Lactation 15mg NE/day) Men
19–50 17mg NE/day, 51+ 16mg NE/day

FOOD SOURCES	mg per 100 g
Yeast extract	73
Wheat bran	32.6
Liver, lambs, fried	24.8
Tuna, canned in oil	21.1
Fortified breakfast cereals	10–21
Turkey, light meat, roasted	19.7
Peanut butter	19
Calves liver, fried	19.4
Peanuts, plain	19.3
Chicken, light meat, roasted	18.1
Malted milk powder	17.4
Liver, chicken, fried	17.3
Dried yeast	15.5
Nuts, mixed	14.8
Mackerel, smoked	13
Salmon, grilled	12.2
Bacon, back, grilled	11
Sesame seeds	10.4
Salmon, pink, canned in brine	10.3
Tahini	9.2
Sunflower seeds	9.1
Anchovy, canned in oil	8.5
Trout, rainbow, grilled	8.2
Almonds	6.5
Cashews, roasted, salted	6.5
Cheese, Cheddar	6.1
Wholemeal bread	5.9
Eggs, boiled or raw	3.8
Pasta, wholemeal, boiled	2.3
Rice, brown, boiled	1.9
Potatoes, baked	1.1
Milk, whole	0.8

VITAMIN B5 (PANTOTHENIC ACID)

REFERENCE NUTRIENT INTAKE
Intakes of 3 to 7mg/day are
considered adequate

FOOD SOURCES	mg per 100 g
Dried yeast	11
Liver, lambs, fried	8.0
Broad beans, canned	6.7
Liver, chicken, fried	5.9
Egg yolk, raw	4.6
Kidney, lamb, fried	4.6
Liver, calf, fried	4.1
Pork steak, lean, grilled	2.2
Peanuts, plain	2.7
Wheat bran	2.4
Sesame seeds	2.1
Mushrooms, raw	2.0
Salmon, steamed	1.8
Pecan nuts	1.7
Peanut butter	1.7
Soya flour	1.6
Trout, rainbow, grilled	1.6
Chicken breast, grilled, no skin	1.6
Walnuts	1.6
Hazelnuts	1.5
Duck, roast	1.5
Eggs, boiled or poached	1.3
Avocado	1.1
Cashew nuts	1.1
Ham, lean	1.0
Lobster, boiled	1.0
Dried dates	0.8
Dried apricots	0.7
Wholemeal bread	0.6
Cheese, Danish blue	0.5
Yoghurt, whole, plain	0.5
Figs, ready-to-eat	0.5
Almond	0.4
Cheese, hard, average	0.4
Split peas, boiled	0.4
Cottage cheese, plain	0.4
Red split lentil, boiled	0.3

VITAMIN B6 (PYRIDOXINE)

REFERENCE NUTRIENT INTAKE
Women 1.2mg/day
Men 1.4mg/day

FOOD SOURCES	mg per 100 g
Wheat germ	3.3
Fortified breakfast cereals	0.6–2.7
Dried yeast	2.0
Tempeh	1.9
Yeast extract	1.6
Muesli, Swiss-style	1.6
Wheat bran	1.4
Liver, calf, fried	0.9
Salmon, steamed or grilled	0.83
Potato crisps	0.8
Sesame seeds	0.8
Pork fillet, lean, grilled	0.7
Walnuts	0.7
Beef, fillet, lean, grilled	0.61
Chicken breast, grilled, no skin	0.6
Hazelnuts	0.6
Peanuts, plain	0.6
Liver, chicken, fried	0.55
Tuna, canned	0.5
Smoked mackerel	0.5
Red snapper, fried	0.5
Kidney, lamb, fried	0.48
Soya flour	0.46
Haddock, grilled	0.4
Halibut, poached	0.4
Garlic	0.38
Avocado	0.36
Bananas	0.29
Wholemeal bread	0.12

VITAMIN B12 (COBALAMIN)

REFERENCE NUTRIENT INTAKE
Women and men 1.5mcg/day
(Lactation 2.0mcg/day)

FOOD SOURCES	mcg per 100 g
Clams, cooked	99
Liver, lambs, fried	83
Liver, calves, fried	58
Kidney, lamb, fried	54
Cockles, boiled	47
Liver, chicken, fried	45
Winkles, boiled	36
Mussels, boiled	22
Smoked mackerel pâté	18
Oysters, raw	17
Herring, grilled	15
Sardines, canned in oil	15
Kippers, grilled	12
Sardines, grilled	12
Anchovies, canned in oil	11
Kippers, baked	11
Scallops, steamed	9
Prawns, boiled	8
Liver pâté	8
Egg yolk	6.9
Salmon, steamed	6
Tuna canned in oil	5.0

FOLATE or FOLIC ACID

REFERENCE NUTRIENT INTAKE
Women and men 200mcg/day
(Pregnancy 300mcg/day, Lactation
260mcg/day)

FOOD SOURCES	mcg per 100 g
Dried yeast	4000
Liver, chicken, fried	1350
Yeast extract	1150
Meat extract	1050
Soya flour	345
Wheat germ	331
Fortified breakfast cereals	150–330
Liver, lambs, fried	260
Black-eye beans, boiled	210
Sweetcorn, fresh or frozen, boiled	152
Pinto beans, boiled	145
Broccoli, purple sprouting, boiled	140
Egg yolk	130
Brussels sprouts, boiled	110
Peanuts	110
Cheese, Camembert	102
Swiss chard, boiled	100
Liver pâté	99
Sesame seeds	97
Spinach, boiled	90

VITAMIN C (ASCORBIC ACID)

REFERENCE NUTRIENT INTAKE
Women and men 40mg/day
(Pregnancy 50mg/day, Lactation
70mg/day)

FOOD SOURCES	mg per 100 g
Guava	230
Red chilli peppers	225
Blackcurrants	200
Parsley	190
Red capsicum (peppers)	140
Green capsicum (peppers)	120
Spring greens, boiled	77
Strawberries	77
Curly kale, boiled	71
Watercress	62
Cabbage, Savoy	62
Brussels sprouts, boiled	60
Pawpaw (papaya)	60
Kiwi	59
Red cabbage	55
Oranges	54
Orange juice, freshly squeezed	48
Broccoli, boiled	44
Tomatoes, grilled	44
Cauliflower	43
Redcurrants	40
Sweetcorn, fresh or frozen, boiled	39
Orange juice, unsweetened	39
Lime juice	38
Nectarines	37
Mango, ripe	37
Grapefruit	36
Lemon juice	36
Salad, green	36
Raspberries	32
Red cabbage, boiled	32
Sugar snap peas	32
Grapefruit juice, unsweetened	31
Peaches	31
Tomatoes, cherry	28
Cauliflower, boiled	27
Satsumas	27
Melon, Canteloupe-type	26
Spinach	26
Spring onions	26
Gooseberries	26
Mango juice, canned	25
Peas	24
Liver, chicken, fried	23
Sweet potato, baked	23
Passionfruit	23
Cabbage, Chinese	21
Courgette, raw	21
Coleslaw (with mayonnaise)	20

BIOTIN

NO RNI
Intakes between 10 and 200mcg/day
are considered adequate and safe

FOOD SOURCES	mcg per 100 g
Liver, chicken, fried	216
Dried yeast	200
Kidney, pigs, fried	129
Peanuts, roasted, salted	102
Peanut butter	102
Mixed nuts	86
Almonds	64
Plaice, grilled	57
Liver, calf, fried	50
Egg yolk	50
Wheat bran	45
Liver, lambs, fried	33
Wheat germ	25
Soya beans, boiled	25
Eggs, whole	20
Oatmeal	20
Walnuts	19
Muesli, Swiss-style	15
Pâté, liver	14
Cashew nuts, plain	13
Haggis, boiled	12
Pilchards, canned in tomato sauce	11
Brazil nuts	11
Kippers, baked	10
Salmon, pink, canned in brine	9
Salmon, grilled	9
Cheese, Camembert	8
Cheese, hard, average	3
Milk, semi skimmed	2
Yoghurt, wholemilk, fruit	2

CALCIUM

REFERENCE NUTRIENT INTAKE
Women and men 700mg/day
(Lactation 1250mg/day)

FOOD SOURCES	mg per 100 g
Cheese, Parmesan	1200
Cheese, Emmental	970
Cheese, Gruyere	950
Cheese, Edam	770
Cheese, Cheddar, average	720
Tahini	680
Sesame seeds	670
Pesto sauce	560
Cheese, Brie	540
Sardines canned in brine	540
Tofu, soya bean, steamed	510
Malted milk powder	430
Seaweed, nori, dried	430
Salmon, pink, canned, flesh and bone	300
Carob powder	390
Evaporated milk, whole	290
Almonds	240
Figs, ready-to-eat	230
Chocolate, milk	220
Soya flour	210
Parsley	200
Yoghurt, low fat, plain	190
Spinach	170
Watercress	170
Curly Kale, boiled	150
Tortilla chips	150
Greek yoghurt, cows	150
Muffins	140
Hazelnuts	140
Oysters	140
Vanilla ice-cream, dairy	130
Sardines, grilled	130
Egg yolk	130
Winkles, boiled	130
Lemon peel	130
Cocoa powder	130
Tempeh	120
Pineapple, dried	120
Wheat germ bread	120
Milk, skimmed or semi-skimmed	120
Milk, whole, average	115
White bread, average	110
Broccoli, purple sprouting, boiled	110
Prawns, boiled	110
Currant buns	110
Sunflower seeds	110
Cream crackers	110
Scones, wholemeal	110
Cottage cheese, plain	110

MAGNESIUM

REFERENCE NUTRIENT INTAKE
Women 270mg/day (Lactation
320mg/day)
Men 300mg/day

FOOD SOURCES	mg per 100 g
Wheat bran	520
Cocoa powder	520
Seaweed, dried, wakame	470
Brazil nuts	410
Sunflower seeds	390
Tahini	380
Sesame seeds	370
Winkles, boiled	310
Wheat germ	270
Cashew nuts, plain	270
Almonds	270
Pine nuts	270
Soya flour	240
Dried yeast	230
Peanuts	210
Peanut butter	180
Oat and wheat bran	180
Treacle, black	180
Walnuts	160
Yeast extract	160
Hazelnuts	160
Bulgar wheat	140

SODIUM

REFERENCE NUTRIENT INTAKE
Women and men 1600mg/day

FOOD SOURCES	mg per 100 g
Salt	39300
Bicarbonate of soda	38700
Oxo cubes	10300
Soy sauce	7120
Instant gravy granules	6330
Meat extract	4370
Yeast extract	4300
Shrimps, boiled	3840
Miso	3650
Instant soup powder	3440
Bacon, back, grilled	2240
Olives in brine	2000
Ham, gammon, grilled	1930
Salmon, smoked	1880
Salami	1800
Tomato ketchup	1630
Prawns, boiled	1590
Cheese, Feta	1440
Butter	750
Hummus	670
Cheese, Cheddar	670
Digestive biscuits	660

CHLORIDE

REFERENCE NUTRIENT INTAKE
Women and men 2500mg/day

FOOD SOURCES	mg per 100 g
Salt	59900
Oxo cubes	16000
Soy sauce	10640
Yeast extract	6630
Olives in brine	3750
Bacon back, grilled	2780
Prawns, boiled	2550
Cheese, Danish blue	1950
Cheese, Parmesan	1820
Cheese, Edam	1570
Cheese, Camembert	1120
Cheese, Cheddar	1030
Bread, white	820
Oysters	820
Sardines canned in brine	810
Salmon canned in brine	730
Peanuts, roasted and salted	660
Peanut butter	540
Tuna canned in oil	530

PHOSPHORUS

REFERENCE NUTRIENT INTAKE
Women and men 550mg/day
(Lactation 990mg/day)

FOOD SOURCES	mg per 100 g
Dried yeast	1290
Wheat bran	1200
Wheat germ	1050
Processed cheese, smoked	1030
Yeast extract	950
Pumpkin seeds	850
Cheese, Parmesan	810
Cheese spread	790
Tahini	730
Sesame seeds	720
Pine nuts	650
Sunflower seeds	640
Cheese, Gruyere	610
Soya flour	600
Brazil nuts	590
Cheese, Emmental	590
Cashew nuts	560
Almonds	550
Sardines canned in oil	520
Egg yolk	500
Cheese, Cheddar	490

POTASSIUM

REFERENCE NUTRIENT INTAKE
Women and men 3500mg/day

FOOD SOURCES	mg per 100 g
Yeast extract	2100
Dried yeast	2000
Apricots, dried	1880
Treacle, black	1760
Wheat bran	1160
Peaches, dried	1100
Sultanas	1060
Raisins	1020
Figs, dried	970
Wheat germ	950
Pine nuts	780
Almonds	780
Parsley	760
Hazelnuts	730
Sunflower seeds	710
Dates, dried	700
Peanuts	670
Brazil nuts	660
Potatoes, baked with skin	630
Garlic	620
Coriander	540
Red snapper, fried	460

SULPHUR

NO RNI
Most comes from the proteins we eat

FOOD SOURCES	mg per 100 g
Mustard powder	1280
Partridge, roast	400
Peanuts, plain	380
Cod, dried, salted, boiled	370
Peanut butter	360
Veal cutlet, fried	330
Goose, roast	320
Bacon, gammon, lean, fried	310
Pork, loin, lean, grilled	310
Liver, calf, fried	300
Turkey, roast	290
Brazil nuts	290
Kidney, lambs, fried	290
Bacon, lean grilled	290
Kipper, baked	280
Beef steak, lean, grilled	280
Mixed nuts	280
Liver, lambs, fried	270
Duck, roast	270
Chicken, lean, roast	260
Liver, chicken, fried	250

IRON

REFERENCE NUTRIENT INTAKE
Women 18–50 14.8mg/day, 50+
8.7mg/day
Men 8.7mg/day

FOOD SOURCES	mg per 100 g
Cockles, boiled	28
Treacle, black	21.3
Fortified breakfast cereals	2–20
Seaweed, nori, dried	19.6
Wheat bran	19.2
Mussels, canned or bottled	13.0
Liver, calf, fried	12.2
Liver, chicken, fried	11.3
Kidney, lambs, fried	11.2
Liver, lambs, fried	10.9
Tahini	10.6
Cocoa powder	10.5
Sesame seeds	10.4
Winkles, boiled	10.2
Pumpkin seeds	10.4
Wheat germ	8.5
Meat extract	8.1
Clams, canned in brine	8.0
Parsley	7.7
Liver pate	7.4
Mussels, boiled	6.8
Peaches, dried	6.8
Sunflower seeds	6.4
Cashew nuts	6.2
Egg yolk	6.1
Lime pickle	5.8
Oysters	5.7
Pine nuts	5.6
Blackcurrants, canned in juice	5.2
Cous cous	5.0
Bulgar wheat	4.9
Miso	4.2
Apricots, dried	4.1
Oatmeal	4.1
Figs, ready-to-eat	3.9
Raisins	3.8
Lentils, boiled	3.5
Tofu, steamed, fried	3.5
Carob powder	3.2
Hazelnuts	3.2
Digestive biscuits	3.2
Sardines canned in oil	3.1
Almonds	3.0
Soya beans, boiled	3.0
Walnuts	2.9
Prunes	2.9
Sardines canned in tomato sauce	2.9
Wholemeal bred	2.7
Haricot beans, boiled	2.5
Peanut butter	2.5

ZINC

REFERENCE NUTRIENT INTAKE
Women 7mg/day (Lactation 9.5 to
13mg/day)
Men 9.5mg/day

FOOD SOURCES	mg per 100 g
Oysters	59.2
Wheat germ	17.0
Wheat bran	16.2
Liver, calf, fried	15.9
Whelks, boiled	12.1
Beef braising steak, lean, braised	9.5
Yeast, dried	8.0
Quorn myco-protein	7.5
Cocoa powder	6.9
Pumpkin seeds	6.6
Pine nuts	6.5
Liver, lambs, fried	5.9
Cashew nuts	5.9
Crab, canned in brine	5.7
Beef mince, extra lean, stewed	5.8
Corned beef, canned	5.5
Crab, boiled	5.5
Tahini	5.4
Pecan nuts	5.3
Cheese, Parmesan	5.3

COPPER

REFERENCE NUTRIENT INTAKE
Women and men 1.2mg/day
(Lactation 1.5mg/day)

FOOD SOURCES	mg per 100 g
Liver, calf, fried	23.9
Liver, lambs, fried	13.5
Oysters	7.5
Whelks, boiled	6.6
Dried yeast	5.0
Cocoa powder	3.9
Tomato puree	2.9
Sunflower seeds	2.3
Cashew nuts	2.1
Shrimps, boiled	1.9
Crab, boiled	1.8
Brazil nuts	1.8
Winkles, boiled	1.7
Pumpkin seeds	1.6
Sesame seeds	1.5
Tahini	1.5
Lobster, boiled	1.4
Walnuts	1.3
Pine nuts	1.3
Hazelnuts	1.2
Pecan nuts	1.1
Peanuts	1.0

MANGANESE

SAFE INTAKE
Adults more than 1.4mg/day

FOOD SOURCES	mg per 100 g
Wheat germ	12.3
Wheat bran	9.0
Pine nuts	7.9
Seaweed, nori, dried	6.0
Macadamia nuts, salted	5.5
Hazelnuts	4.9
Pecan nuts	4.6
Oatmeal	3.7
Mushrooms, oyster	3.6
Crispbread, rye	3.5
Pineapple, dried	3.4
Walnuts	3.4
Syrup, maple	3.3
Muesli, no added sugar	2.6
Sunflower seeds	2.2
Quorn myco-protein	2.1
Peanuts	2.1
Wholemeal bread	1.9
Peanut butter	1.8
Almonds	1.7
Cashew nuts	1.7
Sesame seeds	1.5

SELENIUM

REFERENCE NUTRIENT INTAKE
Women 60mcg/day (Lactation
75mcg/day)
Men 75mcg/day

FOOD SOURCES	mcg per 100 g
Brazil nuts	1530
Kidney, pig, fried	270
Mixed nuts and raisins	170
Lobster, boiled	130
Tuna, canned in oil	90
Kidney, lamb, fried	88
Lemon sole, steamed	73
Squid	66
Mullet, red, grilled	54
Scallops, steamed	51
Sardines, canned in oil	49
Sunflower seeds	49
Herring, grilled	46
Shrimps, boiled	46
Plaice, grilled	45
Mussels, boiled	43
Kipper, baked	43
Mackerel, canned in brine	42
Wholemeal bread	35
Cod, baked	34
Salmon, grilled	31
Scone, wholemeal, fruit	31

INDEX

ACKNOWLEDGEMENTS

STYLISTS

Kristen Anderson, Janice Baker, Marie-Hélène Clauzon, Jane Collins, Georgina Dolling, Carolyn Fienberg, Mary Harris, Cherise Koch, Sarah de Nardi, Michelle Norianto, Sally Parker, Sophie Ward.

PHOTOGRAPHERS

Jon Bader, Cris Cordeiro, Ben Dearnley, Joe Filshie, Roberto Jean François, Chris Jones, Craig Cranko, Tony Lyon, Andre Martin, Luis Martin, Valerie Martin, Rob Reichenfeld, Brett Stevens, Mil Truscott, Jon Paul Urizar.

HOME ECONOMISTS

Alison Adams, Renee Aiken, Laura Ammons, Anna Beaumont, Kate Brodhurst, Rebecca Clancy, Courtney Dallman, Ross Dobson, Michelle Earl, Justin Finlay, Joanne Glynn, David Herbert, Justine Johnson, Michelle Lawton, Michaela Le Compte, Valli Little, Ben Masters, Tracey Meharg, Beth Mitchell, Evelyn Morris, Kerrie Mullins, Kate Murdoch, Peter Oszko, Briget Palmer, Melissa Papas, Kim Passenger, Anna Phillips, Justine Poole, Wendy Quisumbing, Zoe Radze, Kerrie Ray, Clare Simmonds, Fiona Skinner, Tim Smith, Margot Smithyman, Michelle Thrift, Angela Tregonning, Alison Turner, Maria Villegas.

RECIPE DEVELOPMENT

Alison Adams, Roslyn Anderson, Ruth Armstrong, Julie Ballard, Anna Beaumont, Janene Brooks, Jenie Butler, Jane Charlton, Rebecca Clancy, Judy Clarke, Amanda Cooper, Alex Diblasi, Ross Dobson, Michelle Earl, Stephanie Elias, Jenny Fanshaw, Justin Finlay, Sue Forster-Wright, Joanne Glynn, Jane Griffiths, Lulu Grimes, Fiona Hammond, Vicky Harris, David Herbert, Katy Holder, Malini Jayaganesh, Caroline Jones, Eva Katz, Kathy Knudsen, Jane Lawson, Michelle Lawton, Michaela Le Compte, Valli Little, Barbara Lowery, Nadine McCristal, Tracey Meharg, Kerrie Mullins, Kate Murdoch, Christine Osmond, Peter Oszko, Maria Papadopoulos, Sally Parker, Kim Passenger, Justine Poole, Wendy Quisumbing, Sarah Randell, Kerrie Ray, Jo Richardson, Tracy Rutherford, Claudio Sherbini, Sylvia Sieff, Fiona Skinner, Melita Smilovic, Margot Smithyman, Dimitra Stais, Barbara Sweeney, Angela Tregonning, Alison Turner, Jody Vassallo, Maria Villegas, Lovoni Welch.

INTERNATIONAL GLOSSARY OF INGREDIENTS

capsicum	red or green pepper	snow pea	mangetout
caster sugar	superfine sugar	thick cream	double cream
cream	single cream	tomato paste (Aus.)	tomato purée, double concentrate (UK)
eggplant	aubergine		
golden syrup	light corn syrup	tomato purée (Aus.)	sieved crushed
icing sugar	confectioners' sugar		tomatoes/passata
plain flour	all-purpose flour		(UK)
self-raising flour	self-rising flour	zucchini	courgette

Published by Murdoch Books®
First published in 2001
ISBN 1 90399 214 1
A catalogue record of this book is available from the British Library.
©Text, design, photography and illustrations Murdoch Books® 2001

Managing Editor: Rachel Carter. Editor: Justine Harding. Designer: Wing Ping Tong.
Food Director: Jane Lawson. Food Editor: Vanessa Broadfoot.
Nutritional Text: Dr Susanna Holt.
Picture Librarian: Anne Ferrier.

Publisher: Kay Scarlett.
Production Manager: Liz Fitzgerald.
Creative Director: Marylouise Brammer.
Chief Executive: Mark Smith.

Printed by Tien Wah Press, Singapore.
PRINTED IN SINGAPORE.

Published by:

AUSTRALIA	UK
Murdoch Books® Australia	Murdoch Books® UK
GPO Box 1203	Ferry House, 51–57 Lacy Road
Sydney NSW 1045	London SW15 1PR
Phone: (612) 4352 7000	Phone: (020) 8355 1480
Fax: (612) 4352 7026	Fax: (020) 8355 1499

This book is intended as a source of information and recipes only and this information
should not be interpreted as individual medical advice.
The nutritional information provided for each recipe does not include garnishes or
accompaniments, such as rice, unless they are included in specific quantities in the
ingredients. The values are approximations and can be affected by biological and seasonal
variations in food, the unknown composition of some manufactured foods and uncertainty
in the dietary database. Nutrient data given are derived primarily from the NUTTAB95
database produced by the Australian New Zealand Food Authority.
You may find cooking times vary depending on the oven you are using. For fan-forced ovens,
as a general rule, set the oven temperature to 20°C lower than indicated in the recipe.
We have used 20 ml tablespoon measures. If you are using a 15 ml tablespoon, for most
recipes the difference will not be noticeable. However, for recipes using baking powder,
gelatine, bicarbonate of soda, small amounts of flour and cornflour, add an extra teaspoon
for each tablespoon specified. We have used 60 g (Grade 3) eggs in all recipes.

IMPORTANT: Those who might be at risk from the effects of salmonella food poisoning
(the elderly, pregnant women, young children and those suffering from immune
deficiency diseases) should consult their GP with any concerns about eating raw eggs.